TALKING ANIMALS
AND OTHER PEOPLE

TALKING ANIMALS
AND OTHER PEOPLE

SHAMUS CULHANE

St. Martin's Press
New York

Design by Paolo Pepe

Library of Congress Cataloging in Publication Data

Culhane, Shamus,
Talking animals and other people.

1. Culhane, Shamus.   2. Animators—United States—
Biography.   I. Title.
NC1766.U52C84   1986   741.5'8'0924 [B]   85-25139
ISBN 0-312-78473-2

First Edition

10 9 8 7 6 5 4 3 2 1

This book is dedicated to my wife, Juana,
my cousin, John Culhane,
and my mentors, Don Graham,
Grim Natwick, and Walt Disney.

5761

Contents

Introduction

It is unfortunate that the pioneer producers of animated cartoons did not write autobiographies. We know very little about the personal aspirations and philosophies of Winsor McCay, J. R. Bray, Paul Terry, Raoul Barré, and their peers, except for a few letters and interviews.

I suspect the intrinsic value of interviews. One has a tendency to put on one's best company manners, and even manage to sustain them for several hours of questions and answers.

Grim Natwick, Dick Huemer, and I. Klein, animators in the early days, have all written fascinating articles for trade magazines like *Cartoonist Profiles* and *Funny World* with just enough detail to make the reader wish for more.

In this book I am going to tell about my career as an animator, director, and producer during the period from 1924, when theatrical animation was only eight years old, to 1972, when the Walt Lantz Studio closed its doors. Only Walt Disney Studio survived.

Since it happened in the same time span, I am going to include my experience as a pioneer in television animation, when I borrowed three hundred dollars and ran it up to a gross of over a million dollars a year. This was followed by the usual fate of the entrepreneur, bankruptcy.

Somewhat chastened, but not subdued, I reentered the field of theatrical animation as the head of Paramount's animation studio, so I was in at the death, the doleful period when all the studios closed, one after the other, but Disney Studio.

At the time of this writing I have been in this field for fifty-eight years, never having worked in any other profession for even a day. During this time I have known or worked with almost all the notable people who have made animation history. Because we shared a common love for the art, we often became good friends as well as business associates. I am glad to have the opportunity to honor them in this book.

In the last decade there has been a spate of books and articles about animation. At long last, the younger generation has realized a fact that has been ignored by older writers and students of motion picture history. Like jazz, animation has made an important contribution to American culture.

Even the graybeards have finally recognized that animation is an art form worthy of being exhibited in a museum. In June 1981 New York City's Whitney Museum mounted a show of the work of Disney artists that covered the period between 1932 and 1942, a span of years that has rightly been called The Golden Age of Animation.

It was an enormous show, using the entire second floor of the museum to exhibit thousands of animation drawings, layouts, and background paintings. The show averaged three thousand spectators a day. So, at long last, animation has been given a respectable niche in art history.

Later in 1981 two animators, Ollie Johnston and Frank Thomas, completed a book called *Disney Animation, The Illusion of Life* (Abbeville Press). Johnston and Thomas started their careers in Disney's as youngsters and worked there until they retired, so their story is a saga of the Disney Studio's triumphs and tribulations as seen from the employee's point of view.

John Culhane, my cousin, has had a long and enthusiastic interest in animation and has written many articles for newspapers and magazines about the medium.

In addition we have our young Bernard Berensons, who are writing books about various facets of animation with surprising insight. Many of them are far more expert than I about logistics, and can compile long lists of picture titles and release dates. Others have written scholarly pieces about the possible neurotic tendencies of some of the key figures in the profession, and the sociological meanings that can be extrapolated from the kinds of pictures that were made in the various studios.

I am not going to compete with these efforts. Instead I hope to give the reader details of the daily work in many studios from the point of view of an errand boy right through the hierarchy to the presidency of a studio. I will describe how one studio differed from another and tell some yarns about the colorful people who were responsible for the progression and sometimes the retrogression of animation as an art form. In the doing I will recount some details about my own growth as an artist, and the impact some of these people had on my personality.

I am almost seventy-four years old. I don't feel old, but I do have to shave an elderly gentleman every morning. While he is fairly well preserved, he bears little resemblance to the inner man. That person is the same headstrong, fiesty, opinionated workaholic of my youth.

Unlike wine, I have not mellowed with age, so some of this book is going to be sharply critical, as well as sympathetic to the myriad problems of being an artist in this materialistic society.

If one were to write about personalities in the automobile industry, it would be necessary to explain about the intricacies of production they face. I have much the same problem. At times I will have to veer away from personalities and discuss mechanics. This may be about as welcome as a piece of walnut shell in a fruitcake. Bear with me. I will try to make these detours as short as possible.

Although the first animated cartoons were made about eighty years ago, to this day the general public has only a misguided concept of the role of animators, writers, directors, and the other artists in the field. The impression is so misguided, in fact, that for years the public believed that Walt Disney wrote all the stories and drew the animation for his films. People never questioned this myth although they were also told that Disney had in his employ hundreds of talented artists gathered from the far corners of the earth.

Ironically enough, in this instance truth is stranger than publicity hype. Walt did have hundreds of artists, writers, and technicians. They were the brightest, most creative people he could find. What is amazing is that he was able to take their ideas and funnel them through his own creative abilities. When they emerged they had been tailored to fit his own plans for the development of the animated cartoon.

Disney hardly played a passive role. Walt was particularly active in the story department, with a legendary ability to diagnose a problem and supply the missing ingredient.

The pioneers of animation and early jazz musicians had much in common. Both groups had gone about the humdrum business of earning a daily living, never dreaming that some day their work would attract scholarly analysis and evaluation.

Even now, when I am the subject of a retrospective evening at the prestigious American Film Institute, when my drawings are exhibited at the Whitney Museum, or when I read evaluations of my work as an animator or director by John Culhane, Leonard Maltin, Greg Ford, or Joe Adamson, I feel bewildered. During a lecture on animation I look down at the rapt and enthusiastic faces in the audience, and it is hard for me to realize that animation has become so glamorous.

Basically, I still feel that animation is just my daily work, so it jolts me when some eager young animation buff, working on his Ph.D., asks me for an interview. I catch a look in his eye, a mixture of morbid curiosity and awe, as if he were looking at a real live carrier pigeon, or an ambulatory Great Auk. Believe me, I resist these attempts at fossilization.

Up to the present time I have been able to improve my work on every picture I produce, because I always find something new to be learned. As long as I do that I have no intention of retiring. My ambition is to die of overexertion caused by sharpening a 3B Venus pencil while sitting at my drawing board.

A list of people who have been important in my career, over a span of sixty years, would probably be equal in size to the phone book of Beanpot, Kentucky. Of necessity the following compendium is sharply curtailed.

First I want to thank those people who gave me interesting work: Frank Capra, Walter Lantz, Marvin Grieve, John and Faith Hubley, Burt Hanft, Walt Disney, and Carl Brown.

Then I look over the years to those artists who were most rewarding to work with: Cosmo Anzilotti, Art Babbitt, Zack Schwartz, Ruth Gench, Irwin Wallman, Rod Johnson, the staff of Erredia 70 in Milan, Bill Roberts, Norman Ferguson, Bill Hurtz, Sandy Strother, Pat Matthews, Emery Hawkins, Chuck Jones, Gil Miret, Hal Silvermintz, Cliff Roberts, Al Eugster, Chuck Harriton, Howard Beckerman, Nick Tafuri, Ted Sears, Chris Ishii, Mac Seligman, Bunny Cowan, and the younger people, like Denny Rein, Tom Sito, Frank Ceglia, and Steve Eder.

My special thanks for those who helped me to complete the book: John Culhane for his insightful suggestions; Lou Bunin, Bil Baird, and Paul Julian for their interviews; Victor Laredo for his photography; Art Babbitt for his caricatures and photos; Wendall Mohler of Walt Disney Productions for permission to use Disney's memo to Don Graham; and David R. Smith for his helpful and supportive comments. Special thanks go to Dr. Arthur Kornhaber for helping me to find my agent, Perry Knowlton of Curtis Brown Ltd., and I appreciate Perry's patience in selling my book. Lastly, the people of St. Martin's Press, Tom Dunne, my editor, Margaret Schwarzer, his editorial assistant, Andy Carpenter, art director, and Paolo Pepe, designer, my thanks for making the birth of *Talking Animals and Other People* a rollicking experience.

TALKING ANIMALS
AND OTHER PEOPLE

1

Early Years

Animated motion pictures were not the first use of the principles of animation per se. At the turn of the century, cartoonists were drawing flipbooks for commercial use. The pioneers of the animated cartoon merely translated the basic idea into a new medium.

The timing of the action remains exactly the same in both flipbooks and motion pictures, i.e., the closer a drawing is to the position of the preceding drawing, the slower the action will be. Conversely, the wider the spacing between the drawings, the faster the action.

It doesn't matter if the animated cartoon is as simple in design as *Felix the Cat,* or as ornate and complex as Walt Disney's *Fantasia;* the undeniable fact is they are both generic offspring of the lowly flipbook.

There is some doubt as to whether the first animated cartoon was made by a Frenchman, Émile Cohl, or by James Stuart Blackton, an American cartoonist who made a picture called *The Enchanted Drawing* in 1900. In any event, it is a dubious honor because neither man produced animation of any real artistic significance. A case might be made for Cohl in that he did explore the possibilities of metamorphosis, so he might be considered the first abstractionist.

Winsor McCay can rightly be called the father of the animated cartoon. He could draw with incredible virtuosity, and his comic strip *Little Nemo* contained marvelous draftsmanship. At a time when *Mutt and Jeff, Happy Hooligan, Maggie and Jiggs,* etcetera, offered very crude drawings and even more crude gags to the newspaper-reading public, McCay's flights of fancy resulted in elaborate architectural backgrounds and exotic costumes. He raised the production of comic strips to a fine art.

When he turned his talents to animation, he set a standard that was not equaled until Disney began to improve his own product in the 1930s. McCay's most successful animated cartoon (he made ten) was *Gertie the Trained Dinosaur.*

McCay devised a vaudeville act around the film. My father was very fond of vaudeville and took me frequently, so one day I saw McCay's act. He appeared on the stage in typical animal trainer's costume, complete with jodhpurs and whip. The film was flashed on the screen and, seemingly in response to McCay's orders (supplemented by sharp cracks of the whip), the lumbering Gertie would sit up, roll over, and finally beg for a handout. This was the highlight of the act.

McCay would display a glistening pumpkin, then appear to throw it to Gertie. The synchronization was perfect, because as he threw (and, of course, palmed the pumpkin), a bright orange pumpkin went flying into Gertie's mouth. The film was photographed in black and white, and the pumpkin had been hand-colored exposure by exposure on the film. This gimmick alone made it a very successful vaudeville act.

The reason that McCay's work is so important is that, early on, he grasped the possibility of making his animation appear lifelike. His characters were animated with weight, maintained a constant volume, and moved in perspective.

When it became possible to secure a contract for a series of cartoons for theatrical release, McCay was not interested. He liked to create the whole cartoon himself, with one assistant.

In the rush to cash in on commercial animation, McCay's ability to produce characters with life quality was ignored and the influence of the comic strip took over. All the commercial animators were cartoonists who had worked on strips or comic magazines. Raoul Barré and Charlie Bowers produced *Mutt and Jeff,* and Hearst's International Studio flooded the market with animated cartoon versions of *Happy Hooligan, The Katzenjammer Kids, Krazy Kat,* and the like.

Instead of showing emotions by movement, as McCay had done, these pictures fell back on the symbols that had been created for comic strips. A question mark would appear over a character's head to signify perplexity, drops of sweat in an aureole around the head meant fear, a drawing of a light bulb overhead symbolized the birth of an idea, and "balloons" contained the dialogue. All of this was standard equipment for the comic strip.

Instead of moving the characters in space, they usually stayed in an area parallel to the picture plane, like stand-up comics working in front of a backdrop.

Disregarding McCay's intricate overlapping actions, commercial animators were content with jerky movements which were primitive by comparison. Had these pioneers followed McCay's lead, animated cartoons would have gotten off to a flying start. But they didn't. It is as if McCay had designed the Rolls-Royce, and the others decided to build bullock carts.

While many people think that Walt Disney burst like a meteor on the animation scene and changed the artistic goals of animation overnight, quite the reverse is true.

When the first commercial cartoons were being produced, Disney was working in a series of menial jobs. When still in elementary school he got up at three-thirty in the morning to deliver newspapers, and one summer when he was fifteen, he was a candy-butcher on the Sante Fe Railroad.

Both Walt and his older brother Roy were anxious to enlist during World War I. Roy managed to join the navy in 1917, but Walt was too young. However, when he heard that one had to be only seventeen to become a Red Cross ambulance driver, he falsified his age (with the consent of his mother) and was assigned to a staging area in Connecticut. Walt never saw any action, because the Armistice was signed before he was shipped overseas.

Eventually he was sent to France and added to his meager pay by becoming the unit's official artist. At best his art education was elementary. His father, Elias, had grudgingly allowed Walt to attend Saturday morning classes at the Kansas City Art Institute. Unlike more accomplished artists in World War II who painted portraits of generals, Walt had to be content with earning a few francs here and there by painting camouflage on captured German helmets. As genuine sniper's helmets they were considerably more valuable in the souvenir market, especially with the judicious addition of a bullet hole.

When Walt returned to the United States, he turned down a job with his father. Elias Disney had acquired a small interest in a jelly factory in Chicago. To his vexation his son announced that he was going to become a commercial artist. In spite of his father's disapproval, or perhaps because of it, Walt decided to start his career in Kansas City.

There he met a young artist of Dutch extraction, Ub Iwerks. His name

Winsor McCay standing in front of a drawing from his animation of *Gertie the Dinosaur*, explaining his technique to a party of friends. Circa 1912. *The Museum of Modern Art/Film Stills Archives.*

Humorous Phases of Funny Faces, the first American animated cartoon, drawn by James Stuart Blackton, circa 1900. *Museum of Modern Art/Film Stills Archives.*

Émile Cohl's métier was metamorphosis, as seen in these frames from an early film. Between 1908 and 1918 Cohl drew more than two hundred animated cartoons.

Émile Cohl, the first French animator. His work featured abstractions—line drawings of houses that became huge heads, trees turning into people, etcetera. Cohl made no attempt to imitate live action in his films. *Museum of Modern Art/Film Stills Archives.*

J. Stuart Blackton in 1906. *Museum of Modern Art/Film Stills Archives.*

was really Ubbe Iwwerks, but he had simplified it for commercial purposes. Ub was a much better draftsman than Walt, but he lacked Disney's drive and ambition. Together they formed a small commercial art studio, never dreaming that this association (except for a few years of estrangement) would go on for the rest of their lives.

It was rough going, and very soon Disney left and took a job at the Kansas City Film Ad Company. As the name implies, the company was producing advertisements for local businesses that were shown in motion picture theaters in the area. Very soon Iwerks gave up his studio and joined the company.

Disney and Iwerks were making very crude animated cartoons with figures cut out of paper. They had jointed arms and legs. Understandably, the results were very primitive, but, characteristically, as soon as he had learned the basic technique, Walt decided to make some cartoons on his own.

He borrowed a motion picture camera from his employer and began to experiment with more sophisticated types of animation with the help of Ub Iwerks. The result of this moonlighting was a series of short films about local problems, a kind of neighborhood newsreel.

Disney sold the series to the owner of the Newman Theatre. For this reason the pictures were called Newman Laugh-O-Grams. While the series was successful as a minor box-office attraction, Walt soon found out that in his eagerness to make a sale he had quoted a price that was far too low, so that he and Iwerks were producing the Laugh-O-Grams at cost.

This setback did nothing to diminish Walt's ambition. There was enough of a demand for commercial films in the Kansas City area to enable him to quit his job and set up his own company, Laugh-O-Grams, Inc. But Disney was not satisfied with these occasional jobs. They were cheap and the profits miniscule.

Young Disney was already a very persuasive personality. On the basis of his modest success with his new company, he managed to raise fifteen thousand dollars, and proceeded to make six animated cartoons. They were modernized versions of standard fairy tales, i.e., *Cinderella, Goldilocks, Jack and the Bean-Stalk, Puss-in-Boots, The Four Musicians of Bremen.*

By this time his staff had expanded. In addition to Ub Iwerks, it now included Rudy Ising, Hugh and Walker Harman, and Max Maxwell.

Walt was already displaying his uncanny knack for evaluating latent talents. While all of these new men were completely inexperienced when they were first hired, all went on to have fairly successful careers in the field.

Disney had no trouble in finding a New York distributor for his six fairy tales. However, he soon found that he was the victim of a nefarious system of siphoning off profits, called state's rights. Prints were distributed to various companies that ostensibly rented the films to motion picture theaters in a given area.

There was nothing to prevent the distributors or the theater owner from striking off duplicate prints and pocketing all the profits, which they all did as a matter of routine. Compared to these bandits, Ali Baba's Forty Thieves were like Franciscan monks. So little money trickled back to Disney that he was in danger of going bankrupt.

In one last, desperate effort to save the company Walt produced a film which combined live-action and animation. It was not a new technique. Max Fleischer had already created a series in which he acted with Koko, an animated clown. The audiences were enchanted when Koko popped out of a real inkwell and ran all over Max's drawing board and sometimes Max as well.

Disney's version was directly opposite. His film featured a live little girl named Alice, acting with animated animals against a cartoon background. The picture, called *Alice's Wonderland,* used up the last of Walt's money. He had to lay off the entire staff, give up his room and sleep in Laugh-O-Gram's office.

This whole miserable experience might have sent him, hat in hand, back to the Kansas City Film Ad Company asking for a job. But in spite of the fact that he was only twenty-one years old, he had already developed an indomitable belief in his role as an entrepreneur, so he decided to go to Hollywood.

This decision might have been reinforced by the fact that his brother Roy was in Sawtelle Veteran's Hospital, on the outskirts of Los Angeles, recovering from tuberculosis. During this trying time Roy sent Walt small checks out of his eighty-five-dollar-a-month disability pay. Even with this help Walt was reduced to a steady diet of canned beans.

He managed to raise the fare to Los Angeles and pay off some of his creditors by going house-to-house taking photographs of children, and doing odd jobs as a freelance newsreel cameraman. When he finally did arrive in Los Angeles, Walt had the clothes on his back, forty dollars, and a print of *Alice's Wonderland.* This was not much to show for almost four years of hard work.

After wandering around haphazardly from one studio to the next, looking for any kind of job, Disney decided to revitalize his Laugh-O-Grams. Once again Roy came to his rescue and supplied him with production money. Walt had just finished a sample reel when he received an offer from a New York distributor, Margaret Winkler: Fifteen hundred dollars a reel for a series of *Alice's Wonderland* films.

Walt had been rooming at his Uncle Robert's house, where he had been greeted with open disapproval by the old man. Uncle Robert believed that artists and movie people were a shiftless lot.

Making the sample Laugh-O-Gram had used up most of Roy's slender capital, so there was nothing to do but beard the old curmudgeon. If they were going to accept Winkler's offer, production money would be needed to make the first *Alice.* They wouldn't get a dime from Winkler until the delivery of a finished picture. Would Uncle Robert loan them five hundred dollars?

The idea of lending all that money to a young whippersnapper still wet behind the ears, and a bankrupt at that! Emphatically NO! Winkler's deal almost foundered right there. But Roy stepped in and managed to pry the money loose by promising full payment of the loan as soon as they received the money from the first picture.

Almost single-handed, Walt finished the first picture, and they duly paid back Uncle Robert. Walt went on to write the scripts, draw the animation, direct and shoot the live-action on the next five pictures. Charles Mintz, a film distributor who had married Margaret Winkler, was not pleased with the result. In truth, Walt Disney was not a very good animator.

This motivated the Disneys to send for Ub Iwerks. His animation was so much better that their contract was renewed at the end of the year. Even with the addition of Ub's animation the *Alice* cartoons were never very serious competition for Fleischer's *Koko the Clown,* or Pat Sullivan's *Felix the Cat.*

Walt's concept of the photography of live-action was about on a par with the average box-camera enthusiast, and Iwerks' animation was no match for the sophisticated drawings of Dick Huemer's Koko. In short, there was no indication that this humble beginning was going to grow

Felix the Cat, one of the most popular characters of the silent film era. *Museum of Modern Art/Film Stills Archives. Joe Oriolo Productions.*

The Five Senses as Interpreted by "FELIX"

SEEING	HEARING	SMELLING	TASTING	FEELING

SINGLE REEL NOVELTY
Animated by
PAT SULLIVAN

WORLDS RIGHTS
M. J. WINKLER
220 West 42nd Street, New York

A 1921 advertisement showing an early version of Felix the Cat. Note that Sullivan takes credit for the animation, although by this time he had nothing to do with the production of his films, which were produced by Otto Messmer.

into anything more than an insecure living on the periphery of the movie business.

By 1924 the wave of public enthusiasm about animated cartoons had subsided, chiefly because the pictures were, for the most part, badly done comic strips transplanted into a new medium.

In the East, *Felix the Cat* and *Koko the Clown* had survived the financial vicissitudes which had closed William Randolph Hearst's International Film Service. This ended the film careers of such comic-strip stars as the Katzenjammer Kids, Happy Hooligan, Maggie and Jiggs, and Jerry on the Job. The lone survivor was George Herriman's Krazy Kat.

By some vagary of economics the Kat had been shunted from one studio to the next, and at this point Bill Nolan, a veteran animator, was about to try his hand at interpreting the subtleties of the relationship between Ignatz Mouse, Krazy Kat, and Offissa Pup.

Paul Terry was still grinding out a series of *Aesop's Fables* and *Farmer Al Falfa* cartoons which were merely exercises in banal humor. J. R. Bray's *Heeza Liar* cartoons were to match.

Those were the unprepossessing conditions that prevailed in the animation business when I entered the field.

From the time I was a small child I wanted to be an artist. When I was eleven I had a chance to show that I had an unusual amount of talent. The Wannamaker department store held an annual drawing contest for the schoolchildren of New York City. In 1919 more than six thousand children submitted artwork. My drawing won a silver medal. The next year I submitted two drawings and won a silver and a bronze medal.

When I graduated from elementary school, my parents approved of my decision to enter Boy's High School in Harlem. It was the only high school in New York to have commercial art courses.

Boy's High was essentially a two-year vocational school. It was not exactly a Parisian atelier. Most of the boys were learning car repair, electrical work, plumbing, and related subjects. Out of an enrollment of two thousand boys, only sixty were studying commercial art, and three were learning to do sculpture.

We had a few desultory academic courses every day, and in one of them I met Mike Lantz, one of the potential sculptors. The classes were

Paul Terry, one of the pioneers in animation, sold his first animated film, *Little Herman,* for $1.35 a foot in 1915.

©P.H.T. 1936

FARMER AL FALFA

Farmer Al Falfa was Paul Terry's oldest character. Terry developed him while working for J. R. Bray before World War I. Al Falfa survived the upheavals caused by the use of sound and color in cartoons, innovations that Terry resisted. The Farmer continued to appear in Terry's films until the early 1940s.

very boring, and I used to pass the time drawing caricatures of the teachers.

One day Mike suggested that his brother might like to see some of my cartoons. The next day he came back with the news that his brother liked the sketches very much. I was to come for an interview as soon as I graduated. It seems that his brother ran an animated cartoon studio.

This did not impress me at all. I had visions of painting *Saturday Evening Post* covers or designing Arrow Collar ads for a living. These grandiose plans began to fade as we came to the final weeks of school. The thought of going out into the adult world threw me into a panic. I was not yet sixteen years old. I was grateful when Mike reminded me that his brother expected me to come for an interview.

The day after graduation I packed my bundle of cartoons in a paper bag and went off to see Walter Lantz. He turned out to be a youngster of twenty-four who was in complete charge of Bray Studio and directed all the pictures. In spite of his youth, Walt was one of the best animators in the business.

Lantz was not only a cartoonist, he had studied at the Art Students League and had won many prizes for his draftsmanship. At that time, 1924, he must have been the most highly paid employee in the business. Mike told me that Walt was earning two hundred and fifty dollars a week!

He looked over my drawings and they must have impressed him very much, because in a few minutes I was hired as an errand boy at the magnificent salary of twelve dollars a week.

I never officially met the legendary J. R. Bray. We never had more than a nod-passing-by relationship. He was a sallow, lean man, with a very military bearing. It was hard to believe that he was ever a humorist, yet, before he became involved in animation, Bray was a regular contributor to *Judge, Life,* and *Punch,* the popular comic magazines of the turn of the century. Most of the jokes he illustrated were about birds and animals, which he drew with great skill. They were very realistic in appearance, not really cartoons. He never used this style in his animation.

Bray was the first animator to get a regular theatrical release for his films. He signed a contract with Paramount-Famous Lasky in 1915. The star of his series was a little character called Col. Heeza Liar. Bray had originally created him to illustrate gags in the magazines ten years before.

Heeza Liar had a curious history. In 1913 Teddy Roosevelt led an expedition into the jungles of Brazil. He came back with such hair-raising tales of derring-do that many people accused him of being a latter-day Baron von Munchausen.

The cartoonists had a field day with gags about the former president's adventures. Bray's jokes centered around a caricature of Roosevelt; however, as the years went by Col. Heeza Liar changed so much that he no longer looked remotely like the toothy Teddy. Heeza Liar continued to be so popular that Bray, when he started to animate cartoons, used him as his main character.

The Bray Studio was really two companies. One produced animated cartoons, and the other, called Brayco, made educational slidefilms. J. R. had turned over the management of the cartoon branch to Walter Lantz. Bray never did work in any capacity on the animation. His whole attention was directed to the production of educational slides.

Brayco employed a staff of five or six artists. Most of them worked at retouching photographs, which were later converted into slides. A few slides were drawings. Most of these were drawn by Cy Young, an Oriental, who later became the head of Walt Disney's special effects department.

In an effort to thwart competition, Bray had designed a special projector to show his slidefilms. While this may have looked like a shrewd move at the time, the fact that the projector had to be sold with the slides probably was responsible for the financial difficulties that Bray later encountered.

Bray had employed two men in his animation studio who later became famous. In 1915 Max and Dave Fleischer had come to Bray with an offer to have him distribute a series based on their new character, Koko the Clown. This work was suspended when World War I broke out, and Max joined the army. The association was resumed in 1918, and the Fleischers worked for Bray until 1921, when they started their Out of the Inkwell Studio. By 1924 Koko was a much more popular character than Col. Heeza Liar.

It did not take me long to understand how animated films were made. The animators used a special drawing board. It had a pane of glass, nine-by-twelve inches, inserted into the center of the board. Two metal pegs about a half-inch high were screwed into the wood directly below the glass.

The animator drew on paper which had holes punched near the bottom. These holes fit the pegs on the drawing board, so that the paper was always in registration. After the animator drew his first drawing, he turned on a light under the drawing board. When he started his next drawing he could see the lines of his original drawing underneath, enabling him to gauge just how far he should move the character on this new drawing. The light was strong enough for him to see the action he was drawing through five or six sheets of paper.

Animators drew between fifty and seventy-five drawings a day. There were sixteen exposures to a foot of film, and the picture was projected at the rate of sixty feet a minute, which means that a five-minute cartoon contained about fifteen hundred to two thousand drawings. Animators were paid between a hundred and a hundred and twenty-five dollars a week. This was a fortune in those days, when it not uncommon for an adult male to earn thirty-five dollars a week.

Walt Lantz and Gerry Geronimi were very close friends. They not only wrote the stories, they also did most of the animation. Walter had the light brown hair of the Northern Italian. Gerry, who was about Lantz's age, bore a remarkable resemblance to Edward G. Robinson. However, unlike the actor, Gerry was a rowdy, raucous, bawdy youngster, also of Italian descent. He often spiced up his conversation with juicy expletives and elaborate curses in a Neopolitan dialect. I eventually learned most of them, to Gerry's amusement.

From time to time, Lantz hired newspaper cartoonists who wanted to learn animation. None of them did. Lank Leonard, who later created several comic strips with national distribution, tried to animate for some months before finally giving up. Ving Fuller, a sports cartoonist, also struggled through a few pictures, then went back to the newspaper field.

Dave Hand, who years later became Walt Disney's right-hand man, also worked for a while at the Bray Studio. Hand was one of the pioneers of animation, and a fairly good cartoonist. He had an air of superiority that was foreign to the free and easy atmosphere of the studio. When Gerry's "A fongool!" rattled the windows, Dave's lips tightened in disapproval. He didn't stay long.

My first job was to punch holes in the animation paper, and do the same operation on sheets of transparent acetate for the inkers. These sheets, the same size as the drawing paper, were called "cels," because of the mistaken idea that they were made of celluloid. Actually, cels were made of the same material as motion picture film, nitrate acetate.

Walt Lantz, Dinky Doodle, and Weak-heart, in a J. R. Bray production, circa 1927.

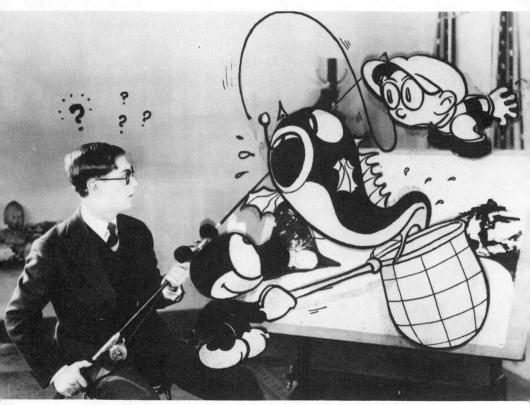

Walt Lantz with Dinky Doodle and his dog Weak-heart, who replaced the character Col. Heeza Liar. Designed by Walt Lantz, they were the featured actors in Bray's films until the studio went bankrupt in 1928.

Nitrate acetate has a nasty habit of spontaneous combustion, and is highly flammable. When it burns, it gives off a gas that can kill almost instantly. Most people paid no attention to the fire hazard, in spite of the No Smoking signs all over the building. Firemen patrolled the buildings in the motion picture area of midtown and gave a summons to any person they caught smoking.

In spite of that, many people smoked. It is a chilling thought that for years inkers and painters worked with ashtrays a few inches from foot-high stacks of cels.

One day I found a roll of film about two inches in diameter in the discard can in the cutting room. I took it home to show my family. When they had all seen it I threw it on a bed of coals in the kitchen stove. The door blew off!

The very earliest cartoons did not use cels, but were all drawn and photographed on paper. If a background was used with the character it had to be laboriously traced on every drawing. Winsor McCay, for example, used an assistant whose sole function was to add the backgrounds on McCay's animation.

In 1915 an animator named Earl Hurd patented a new process whereby the background was drawn and painted on a sheet of watercolor paper. The animated drawings were traced in ink on cels, then very thick paint was applied to the back of the tracings, making them opaque.

When photographing a scene, the cameraman taped down the background and placed the first cel over it. Since the character was opaque and the cell transparent, the figure seemed to be a part of the background. While the cels were changed for every exposure, the background remained until the end of the scene, which of course saved an enormous amount of work.

The camera was a motion picture camera that had been converted to take one exposure at a time. It was fastened overhead to a crude frame made of angle iron. Under the camera was a table equipped with the same kind of pegs the animators and inkers used, so that registration was maintained.

If I wasn't punching paper and cels, I ran errands. Sometimes I was allowed to paint cels. I liked the whole process very much, except for the problems with the paint. In our building we had no heat on weekends. In the winter we would often arrive on Monday morning to find that the cold had caused the paint to separate from the cels. The whole job would have to be done over.

It was worse in the summer. After a very hot night we might come to work to find that the paint on hundreds of cels had melted! Every cel had adhered to the drawing paper underneath. What a mess!

By 1925 Col. Heeza Liar began to show signs of rigor mortis, so Walt Lantz designed two new characters for a series, Dinky Doodle, a nondescript, small boy in a cloth cap and knickers, and Weak-heart, a dog with a bulbous nose and two hooks for ears. He bore little resemblance to a canine. Since he always walked on his hind legs, he might just as well have been called a bear.

Lantz's stories for *Dinky Doodle* were in the style that was current at the time, that is, a heavy emphasis on chases. The only unique feature of the series was that there was always a live-action section in each film. Walt Lantz played the leading role.

In addition to my work as errand boy, painter, and paper puncher, I became the prop boy and erstwhile electrician. Going for props at Eaves Costume Co. was fun, because it was a fascinating place where I could watch actors trying on costumes while I waited for my own order to be filled.

What was decidedly not fun was working as an electrician under beetle-browed Harry Squires, the cameraman. Harry was a saturnine character who had no patience with boys who stumbled over cables or inadvertently kicked the stands for the Klieg lights. I found these monstrous lights very frightening; they hissed and spat sparks. I used to slink around the set expecting the damn things to blow up any second.

The first and only time I worked as an electrician was during an important picture. Walt had managed to hire a celebrity to act with him: Sophie Tucker, billed as The Last of the Red-Hot Mamas. She was a well-known figure in nightclubs.

Harry was on his best behavior when she came on the set, because Sophie was an aggressive, fat lady who didn't look as if she could be trifled with. Even her normal speaking voice had the rasping quality of a grave-digging machine.

Instead of barking at me, Harry turned down the volume to a series of muttered snarls. He led me to a huge switch that was nailed to the back of a flat. "Look, kid," he whispered, "when I yell 'lights!' you yank this son of a bitch down. See that it meshes real good. I don't want any goddamn fuse blown."

With that, he stepped nimbly over a half–dozen cables and started to peer into his camera. Sophie added another dab of lipstick to the half-pound she was already wearing, while I stood looking at that massive switch in an agony of terror.

When Harry yelled for the lights, I was galvanized into action. I grabbed the ten–inch handle and slammed it down. It didn't mesh. Instead, it started hissing and sending off sparks like a Fourth of July sparkler.

Harry came tearing around the flats, reached into the fireworks display, and snapped the handle back to its original position. "What the hell's the matter with you? Just pull the friggin' thing down, y'hear? Straight down!" He stormed off.

The next time he yelled, "Lights!" I didn't fare any better. The switch hit the bottom and bounced back, making an even bigger shower of sparks. Harry barely had time to flip the switch back, and no time to scold me because Sophie had followed right behind him.

"What the hell's this?" she bellowed like the Bull of Bashaan. "Making a poor little kid like that screw around with 'lectricity! The poor little bastard mighta been 'lectrocuted, for Chrissake!" Harry was thoroughly cowed and flipped his own switches for the rest of the day. I went back to running errands and painting cels.

There were other attempts to have me cope with the machine age. For several weeks I was allowed to photograph the animation. The rig had a droning motor that made me drowsy. Then there was the problem of the foot pedal, which controlled the camera shutter. When pressed, it took one exposure. However, if one lingered, it took two or more. I often lingered.

Sometimes I loaded the camera improperly, and the film jammed after a few hours of shooting. This meant that the camera would have to be opened and all the exposed film junked. The rickety, angle iron camera stand was equipped with two Cooper-Hewitt lights, one on each side. I liked them because in their glow everybody had a purple face and green gums. The day that I forgot to turn on one of the lights, and shot happily until it was time for lunch, was my last day as a cameraman.

Next, I was put to work in the darkroom, where we processed hundreds of enlargements from the live-action negatives. The *Dinky Doodle*

The legendary J. R. Bray, then in his nineties, attending Expo '67. *Collection of The Montreal Museum.*

Mike Lantz (left) and Shamus Culhane in 1925 when Mike was just starting his illustrious career as a sculptor.

This still is from a picture made in 1924 or '25, about the time J. R. Bray began to realize that Col. Heeza Liar had outlived his usefulness. Over the years the character had gradually lost his resemblance to Teddy Roosevelt. Walt Lantz was about twenty-five years old here.

series often used a combination of Walt Lantz and an animated character on the screen at the same time.

For example, if Walt was supposed to duel with a cartoon villain, he would first duel with a live person. (Gerry Geronimi usually had this kind of chore.) After the action was photographed, each exposure of the film was enlarged on nine-by-twelve photographic paper, which had been punched like animation paper.

The stack of finished prints was sent to the animator, and over each image of the live actor he drew a cartoon on onionskin paper, making sure that the character was slightly larger than all the areas of the actor's body. When these drawings were duly inked and painted on cels, each combination of a live-action enlargement and cel was shot in the cartoon camera. The final result was Walter Lantz dueling merrily with an animated cartoon.

The darkroom was run by a troll named Dutch Heins. He had the amiability of a bobcat. After I forgot to take the racks of enlargements out of the developer on time, splashed around so much that the darkroom was ankle-deep in water, and almost dropped his prized watch in the hypo, Heins demanded and got another assistant. Dutch was not a patient man. Incidentally, his new assistant was a mild-mannered man named Anton Breuhl, who later became one of the most famous photographers in America.

Walt's brother Mike was finding that making a living as a sculptor was rough going, so he would drop in every few weeks to make a few dollars working as a painter. It was always a time for fun and frolic. Mike had recruited another graduate of Boy's Vocational High, Frank Paiker. He was being trained as an animation cameraman and, unlike me, Frank was doing very well.

We were a trio of Katzenjammer Kids, and the Brayco team was our special target. At least once a day we gave somebody a hotfoot, and drove Cy Young into fits of Oriental hysteria. When we put a piece of Limburger cheese next to the light under his drawing board, the whole studio smelled like a dead cat for a week.

Once we smuggled a piece of squid from a Japanese restaurant into the darkroom. When Dutch Heins returned from lunch and turned on the lights, there was this multitentacled creature sitting on his desk. Dutch almost had a heart attack. To add to our glee, Heins was convinced that Gerry Geronimi was the perpetrator. Gerry was not above such pranks himself. His specialty was inserting pen points into upholstered seats. One time he brought in a specially designed cushion and placed it on a visitor's chair in the office. When the victim sat on it, the cushion let out a thunderous flatulent blast.

Of course we never played these pranks on Walt. He was well aware of all these highjinks, but seemed to accept them as part of the ambience. Finally, we pressed his patience too far.

Paiker and I joined a semiprofessional football team that played on Sundays against similar pick-up teams. Each team put up fifty dollars, winner take all. Frank was the center, and I played left guard. Instead of elaborate offensive systems, we used assault and battery to advance the ball.

One Monday morning, Frank and I came to work after a particularly brutal game (which we lost). Frank had a broken hand in a cast, and I limped in on a cane. He couldn't shoot the camera, and I couldn't run the errands. Walt was fairly calm about the situation until later in the morning when he heard us discussing the fact that we might not heal in time to enter the Golden Gloves boxing competition. Lantz flew into a fine Italian rage and threatened to fire us both if we engaged in any more violent sports. That was the end of our athletic careers.

After my catastrophic attempts to work in various departments, I was given the usual reward for inefficiency, a promotion. I became a full-time painter and even did some inking on simple scenes. Having a great deal of manual dexterity, in a very short time I was the fastest inker and painter in the studio.

In addition, I was learning how to animate. Every lunch hour I wolfed down a box of Fig Newtons and fell to work, painfully learning how to draw Dinky and Weak-heart. Once a week, Walt would go over my drawings and correct them. Finally, he gave me a scene to animate for production. It was a monkey in a barbershop wrestling with a hot towel. When I saw my scene on the screen, I was the happiest animator in New York, and the youngest, sixteen and a half.

Strangely enough, as soon as I had succeeded in putting some animation on the screen, my interest vanished. My ambitions had changed; now I wanted to be a professional musician or a famous painter and etcher. I had been playing the violin ever since I was nine, an hour or more every day, and was beginning to be fairly proficient.

My painting was improving, too. I bought a full-sized easel which competed with the horsehair furniture in the living room. Every weekend I worked until the light failed. With the aid of a book, which detailed the painting methods of Renaissance artists, I was learning how to underpaint, scumble, and glaze. Weeknights I was using another book to teach myself etching.

As soon as I was seventeen I got a job in a parking lot on weekends until I had made seventy-five dollars to buy a small etching press. Now the family would get up in the morning to find vials of nitric acid on the kitchen stove, my etching press still on the table, and the living room floor littered with damp prints, which could not be moved until they had dried. I often worked until dawn and was usually too exhausted to stow away my gear. My family was not pleased to have to live in a makeshift art studio with a confirmed workaholic.

I had no practical reason for wanting to be an animator. Cartoons had lost their novelty, and the entertainment value had sunk so low that I often heard audiences hiss and boo when the main title of an animated cartoon flashed on the screen. It was obvious that very soon animated cartoons were going to be as obsolete as buggy whips. To me this was a temporary job until I found work as a musician, or could establish myself as a serious artist.

The first intimation that all was not well at Bray Studio was the arrival of Mrs. Bray. She was a very forceful woman who announced her intention to save the studio. (J. R. Bray had secluded himself in his office.) With Prussian paranoia, Mrs. Bray decided that the root of the trouble was the sinful waste of the art supplies. It wasn't true, but nobody wanted to argue with this forbidding personality.

There was a large vault in the front office, and Mrs. Bray put all the art supplies in it and mounted guard like a Gorgon. Pens were doled out one nib at a time, and paper was grudgingly yielded up as if each sheet were a five-dollar bill.

In spite of her heroic efforts, the business slid inexorably downhill. There came a time when Bray could not meet the payroll. For three weeks we all worked without pay, a desperate situation for me because we were very poor. Finally, Walt Lantz called me into his room, gave me my three weeks' back salary and a letter of recommendation. His own plans were to leave the animation business and get a job in Hollywood as a gag writer. He did send me a Christmas card the following year, but I didn't see Walt again until 1943.

For a small crew, many of us were destined to do very well. Frank Paiker pursued his career as an animation cameraman, and eventually became head of Hanna-Barbera's camera department. Gerry Geronimi became a successful animator, then a director at Walt Disney's. Walt Lantz and I owned large studios, and the zany Mike Lantz has become a world-famous sculptor.

As for J. R. Bray, he started another animation studio and concentrated on technical animation for government and industry. He lived to be almost a hundred. His small studio is still functioning, making it the oldest animation studio in the country.

J. R. Bray was not the only animated cartoon producer with problems. Walt and Roy Disney were about to be taught a bitter business lesson by their distributor, Charles Mintz. Margaret Winkler had been distributing the Disney *Alice's Wonderland* films, but after she married Mintz, he took over the reins. Another member of the company was Margaret's brother, George Winkler.

They were very successful. In addition to the Disney films they were distributing the even more popular *Felix the Cat*. Recently they had bankrolled a new studio, which was producing the peripatetic *Krazy Kat*.

By this time the Disney crew had turned out fifty-six *Alice* cartoons, which had proven to be lukewarm box-office attractions. In truth, the restrictions of using amateur child actors in combination with animation were weighing heavily on the latent talents of Disney and Iwerks.

When they designed a new character, Oswald the Rabbit, and abandoned the use of live-action, the result was an instant success. The *Oswald* pictures began to receive glowing reviews in the trade papers.

In 1928, after six months of production on the new series, Disney went to New York to negotiate a new contract with Mintz. He had been paying $2,500 a picture, and in view of the popularity of *Oswald*, Walt was going to ask for a raise to $2,750.

Instead of agreeing to Walt's modest request, Mintz curtly turned him down. In the new contract Disney would have to accept a cutback to $1,800! Not only that, Mintz had sent George Winkler to Hollywood to talk to the animators. If the Disneys refused to cooperate they would lose the staff, because with the exception of Ub Iwerks, everybody had agreed to go along with Mintz.

As an added shocker, Mintz pointed out that he owned the copyright to *Oswald the Rabbit* and was ready to work with another producer if Walt proved to be recalcitrant. Walt had to sign up or lose everything.

Instead of meekly submitting, Walt courageously walked out. Before he left he predicted that one day Mintz would find that he was the victim of his own machinations. He was.

Mintz set up a new studio with the four defecting animators, Rudy Ising, Hugh Harman, Walter Harman, and Max Maxwell, and appointed George, his hatchet man, as the producer. The *Oswald* pictures were being released through Universal Pictures. Suddenly, Mintz was informed that Universal was starting its own studio headed by Walter Lantz, and was taking over the production of the *Oswald the Rabbit* cartoons. The four ex-Disney animators and George Winkler were out of jobs. Sic semper tyrannis!

In the interim Walt had wasted no time in mourning his losses. On the train going back to Los Angeles he was already discussing new plans with his wife, Lillian. They were going to make cartoons about a mouse named Mortimer. According to legend, Lillian talked him into using a less pretentious name, Mickey Mouse.

Roy and Walt had saved about $25,000. On that slender capital they would be able to produce three cartoons. As soon as Ub Iwerks had designed a satisfactory character, Mickey Mouse went into production.

Gambling as usual, because the Disney brothers had no distributor, their only hope was that Mickey Mouse would prove to be so entertaining that they would be able to negotiate a good distribution deal. On this pinhead of hope the Disneys built an empire.

The morning after Bray Studio closed down I was in a panic. A normal approach to job-hunting would have involved a visit to all the animation studios in New York, an interview, a discussion about money, and a shrewd choice of the best offer. Instead I went to the nearest studio, Krazy Kat, and gave the producers, Ben Harrison and Manny Gould, a ten-minute exhibition of my skill as an inker.

They were so impressed by my neatness and speed that I was offered thirty-five dollars a week. Ten dollars more than I had been making at Bray's.

I had never met Harrison or Gould before. They were both experienced animators, but this was their first venture as producers. The fact that Charles Mintz was their distributor meant nothing to me. The wheeling and dealing of finance was beyond my understanding.

Mintz made very infrequent visits to the studio. When he did, he made a slow inspection of the premises with Harrison and Gould following one step behind. A grim-faced man, with a pair of cold eyes glittering behind a pince-nez, Mintz never talked to the staff. He looked us over like an admiral surveying a row of stanchions.

Harrison and Gould seemed to be determined never to spend a dime unless it was under duress. Shortly after I was hired, the studio was moved to another building. While the first quarters had been too dark and we worked with the lights on all day, these new rooms were too bright. The sun bounced off the cels most of the day. When we asked for shades, we were brusquely told to put newspapers in the windows. We did, and these makeshift shades yellowed and cracked, then hung in tatters, acquiring a patina of dust, symbols of the penny-pinching management.

Krazy Kat should have been an interesting series. In George Herriman's strip there were several marvelous figures: the love-sick Krazy Kat, Ignatz the Mouse, her love object, and the truculent Offissa Bull Pup. The backgrounds were very imaginative; usually they consisted of buttes, mesas, and sand dunes embellished by weird Joshua trees and cacti.

Herriman's humor was equally offbeat, far ahead of the crude humor of *Mutt and Jeff, Jerry on the Job,* and other popular comic strips of the period. Harrison and Gould chose to ignore these assets. Krazy Kat bore no resemblance to the drawing of Herriman's character; we rarely used Offissa Pup; the romance between Ignatz and Krazy Kat was disregarded, so was the desert atmosphere.

The stories were heavy-handed chases and primitive acting. Every gag was automatically repeated three times, and I am sure that Harrison and Gould would have made it four if they had the nerve. In short, nobody in the animation business had ever had such graphic riches and used them less.

The bosses were both in their thirties, and so were the three animators. They were Art Davis, a much better draftsman than his employers, Al Rose, somewhat less proficient, and Sid Marcus, whose drawings were crude but very funny. Marcus was the best gagman in the studio, but even his contributions were not enough to lift the pictures from the nadir of dreary pedestrianism.

The inkers were all very young, at nineteen I was the oldest. They were Dave Tendlar, who later became a very good animator in Hollywood, Harry Love, who early on veered away from drawing to become a production manager; and Bernie Wolf, who did some fine animation at

Disney's many years later, and now is the producer at Anamedia Productions, a West Coast studio producing television spots.

There was a large turnover of painters because the pay was very small. In spite of the fact that there was good potential talent among the youngsters, unlike Walt Lantz, Harrison and Gould taught us nothing.

In 1928 two western animators, Friz Freleng and Ben Clopton, strolled into the studio. New York clothes looked shabby compared to the sartorial splendor of these two characters. Both wore boldly patterned sport coats, colorful sweaters, and what we used to call "ice-cream" pants.

They were hired immediately, and for a time it looked as if the quality of the pictures would improve. Freleng, especially, was a far better animator than anyone else in the studio. However, they only lasted through a few pictures and went back to the coast.

Shortly after, one of the most famous animators in the business joined our staff. I. Klein had started as an animator in the very early days of animation in Hearst's International Studio, but dropped this career to join the staff of *The New Yorker* magazine, where his drawings were a weekly feature. He was an excellent draftsman, with a wry sense of humor. His gags became very popular, but he made the mistake of taking a sabbatical to go off to Europe to paint.

When he returned, Klein was unable to get back to his old footing at *The New Yorker,* so he wound up at Krazy Kat. The following is part of an article that appeared in *Cartoonist Profiles* in September 1979:

"A very, very quiet place comes to mind when I recollect the studio run by Harrison and Gould. On all previous work occasions, the bullpen always had an undertone of various verbal noises. I was surprised this time by the absolute quietness. It seemed unnatural. It remained that way during the entire time I worked there, which was not too long.

"Later I found out the reason for this disagreeable hush. Someone told me that the *Krazy Kat* series we were grinding out was being made for $900 a picture. So the animation department was obliged to bat out animation footage at breakneck speed. Time only for breathing. No conversation. No horseplay. Yes indeed, that was a very quiet bullpen."

It was so quiet that Klein tiptoed out after a few months, and Krazy Kat Studio lost a great gagman.

One of the most obnoxious features of the studio was the fact that every week or so Harrison would walk down the line of desks and point at various unfortunates. "You, you, and you . . . you bastards are working

A Harrison and Gould version of
Krazy Kat in 1929.

The staff of Krazy Kat in 1929. Front row, left to right: Albert Windley,
cameraman, Al Gould, painter, Al Rose, animator, Manny Gould and Ben
Harrison, producers, Artie Davis, animator, unknown painter. Back row, left to
right: Mike Balukis, painter, unknown painter, Bernie Wolf, painter, Harry Love,
painter, Sid Marcus, animator, Shamus (Jimmie) Culhane, inker, unknown painter,
and Dave Tendlar, inker.

tomorrow night." The next night we were given one dollar apiece for dinner, and it was expected that we work three hours overtime for nothing. One of the two bosses always stayed to police the operation. Since there was no union, the choice was to submit or quit. At that time jobs were not so easy to find, and so nobody wanted to leave; but there was a good deal of smoldering resentment.

The atmosphere was oppressive. We all worked in one big room where Harrison or Gould could keep a beady eye on anybody who got up from his desk and entered into a conversation that wasn't strictly business. I missed the sparring in the hall with Gerry Geronimi, the heated arguments with Dutch Heins over the merits of the Yankees versus the Dodgers; most of all I missed Walt Lantz's benevolent authority.

There were two reasons why I made no move to leave. One, I was too timid. Two, I still thought all this cartoon nonsense was just a stopgap. Every day after work I practiced my violin, and drew far into the night. Some day I was going to make the jump one way or another, music or fine art. In the interim I chafed at the repressive atmosphere.

Another thing that contributed to my sense of alienation was my reading. From the time I was a small child I read voraciously. By the age of ten or eleven, I was reading Conrad, Jack London, Dumas, and stories about exploration. While I was at Krazy Kat I was reading Huxley, Proust, Rostostev on economics in the ancient world, Breasted, the Egyptologist, Herodotus, Livy, and the popular novelists of the day.

In a way it was a lonesome situation. Nobody among my friends had been able to go to college, nor had anybody from Bray or Krazy Kat. Incredible as it may seem in the light of present-day standards, here I was almost twenty-one, and I never had talked to anyone who had gone to college!

I never discussed my experiments in painting and etching with members of the Krazy Kat staff, except for one time when I mentioned to Art Davis that I was thinking of going to the Art Students League. Davis looked at me disapprovingly. "Jesus, I wouldn't do that. You want to keep away from art schools if you want to be a good animator. That art school shit will stiffen you up."

Unfortunately, my education in art history was less eclectic than my reading. My understanding of art stopped at the French Impressionists; anything after that was chaos. Along with my peers and the general public, I firmly believed that all modern artists were either mad or charlatans.

In 1928, I had my first exhibit when I joined the Society for Independent Artists. I submitted a pastel portrait of my dog, and it was accepted. When I went to the opening, there was my very conservative picture of my collie, cheek-by-jowl with huge canvases smeared with splashes of raw color, squiggles, bits of lettering, gunnysacking, and cardboard, all painted in very bad perspective, if any. To me, my artwork was the only sane note in what looked like the product of a lunatic asylum, and I continued to think so for the next seven years.

I was being badly underpaid. The other inkers produced about a hundred cels a day, while I averaged two hundred and sometimes more than three hundred. They were paid thirty dollars a week and I was making thirty-five. When I asked for more money, Harrison told me quite forcibly that thirty-five was the absolute ceiling.

Now the normal reaction to this kind of treatment would be to drop down to the output of the other inkers, but my attitude was more complicated than that. I had far too much kinetic energy to loaf on the job. I had been the best inker at Bray, now I needed to be the best inker in New York. However, while I still turned out a phenomenal number of cels, I embarked on a guerrilla war by coming in late in the morning and ignoring Harrison's peevish complaints about my going out to lunch when I pleased. From a warm, friendly kid, I probably became the most obnoxious employee in the business.

Harrison and Gould made a practice of showing each film to the staff when it was finished. The marvel was that it was on company time. While this was a welcome break in the day's work, the audience reaction was zero. After the screening, we went back to work with no comment.

Like most of the filmmakers during this time, Harrison and Gould had chosen to ignore the use of sound. It was considered by most of the pundits in the business as a transitory gimmick; besides it was inordinately expensive.

Walt Disney and his brother Roy had made another gamble. They had finished a silent version of Mickey Mouse in a film called *Plane Crazy* before Warner Brothers premiered *The Jazz Singer*. This picture, which featured Al Jolson, was so successful that Walt decided to invest some of their precious savings in a sound cartoon.

They completed their second picture, Mickey and Minnie in *Galloping Gaucho,* in silent form and zeroed in on *Steamboat Willie* as their sample of what sound effects and music could do for a cartoon.

After compiling a score for the film, Walt took the picture to New

York. He needed to make a recording of the track and find a distributor before his money ran out. He found that New York was a hotbed of intrigue. While the giants like RCA and Western Electric seemed to control the essential patents for recording motion pictures, there were a host of outlaw sound systems.

One of them was Powers Cinephone, owned by Pat Powers, a distributor. Pat agreed to allow Disney to use his equipment to record *Steamboat Willie.* Walt had a system that would keep the musicians in sync, but they ignored it. After a disastrous first recording, which cost the hard-pressed brothers a thousand dollars, Walt managed to wring from the befuddled musicians a satisfactory track.

Even with the finished picture he was unable to find a distributor. Walt was able to secure a two-week run at the Colony and another at the Roxy. There was a very satisfactory audience reaction in both theaters, but when Walt was approached by distributors and they heard that he refused to sell the films outright, they turned away. However, Walt was not about to repeat his experiences with his fairy tales and the *Alice* cartoons.

Pat Powers was impressed by the audiences' reaction at the Colony and Roxy, and he was desperate for products to use his Cinephone system. He offered to distribute Mickey for ten percent of the gross through state's rights. His eagerness can be measured by the fact that he was willing to allow the Disneys to retain control of the copyright.

By the time Walt had finished scores for his other two cartoons and one new Mickey, *The Barn Dance,* his success was assured. He had the most vociferously acclaimed cartoon character in motion picture history.

All of the youngsters at Krazy Kat were enchanted by the Disney cartoons, but Harrison and Gould steadfastly deprecated the use of sound as a passing fancy.

However, in 1929, a full year after *Steamboat Willie* was released, the two producers sprang a surprise on the staff. With an air of great excitement, Harrison rigged up the projector and called the staff together for a screening.

Krazy Kat with sound was a disaster. The film was the usual insipid story and the gags were to match. The sound track sounded like a tornado in a boiler factory. When the Kat blinked, somebody struck a cowbell. When she walked, her footsteps were accented by a bass drum. It was sheer cacophony!

When the film was over there was a stunned silence, which I broke

A caricature of Grim Natwick by Richard Williams, drawn when Natwick was almost ninety years old. Natwick is famous for creating Betty Boop, the first female star in animated cartoons, and his facile drawings of Snow White. Natwick has recently blossomed as a witty after-dinner speaker.

Group photo of Fifty Year Veterans.

with a sarcastic, "Hah, hah, hah." Understandably, Harrison and Gould were furious.

They did get their revenge (they thought) when it was announced that the studio was being moved to Hollywood. A selected few employees were going to the coast. Naturally, I was not invited. Early in 1930 it was Westward Ho! The Philistines! and I had to look for a new job.

2

Max Fleischer's Studio

In 1930 there were not many places to look for a job. The cost of adding a sound track to a cartoon was now three thousand dollars, and most of the studios were having a hard time adjusting to the new expense. Pat Sullivan refused to add sound to his *Felix the Cat* pictures. His income fell off so rapidly that he had begun to lay off his staff. Paul Terry was doing the same at Fables Studio.

Max Fleischer was the exception. He was now releasing through Paramount and had a staff of more than a hundred artists. Fleischer had been dabbling in sound long before Disney made *Steamboat Willie*. Back in 1924, Max and Dave Fleischer had produced the very first sound cartoon, *Oh Mabel*.

This was a sing-along picture which featured a device that became famous. A ball bounced over the words, enabling the audience to sing together in tempo. But Max was too early, and the picture was ignored as a curiosity, not a commercial breakthrough.

However, now that he had access to Paramount's sound tracks, Max was working at full spate making bouncing-ball films. The Song Car-Tunes were a great source of income because the animation of a bouncing ball over printed titles was much cheaper than animating characters.

The studio was still turning out the Koko the Clown pictures which had made him famous, but Max no longer acted with Koko. He had retired from production to run the business. The result was that the popularity of Koko had begun to wane, and the studio was busily looking for new main characters.

Actually Max's contribution to the popularity of his films was greater than he realized. He probably was one of the most inept businessmen in the field. What he did not appreciate was that his financial success was not due to his business acumen, rather it was the result of his talents as an entertainer.

After a few minutes into my job interview, I felt very much at ease. Max was about forty-five at the time, already carrying a substantial paunch. He was serious, dignified, and scholarly looking, but very friendly. There was something warm and paternal about Max, and I felt that he was really interested in me as a person.

I discovered during our talk that Max had devised a way to take some of the production load off the animators by giving them assistants. Instead of doing all the drawings for a picture, the animator was making the key drawings of an action, leaving the drawings in between for a younger, less-trained artist. These missing drawings were called "inbetweens," so the novice was called an "inbetweener." It would be a marvelous way to learn animation.

I was exhilarated when I found that I was going to get one of these new jobs. The salary, to my surprise, was fifty dollars a week! Max assured me that I was going to get every opportunity to become an animator. What a change from Krazy Kat.

I was awed by the size of the staff. Bray had less than ten people under Walt Lantz's supervision. Krazy Kat's crew was about a dozen. Here were rows upon rows of desks, people were bustling this way and that, and they were smiling. Max ran a happy, relaxed studio.

I knew only three people on the staff: Bernie Wolf, who had been an inker at Krazy Kat; Sid Marcus, who animated at Krazy Kat for a short time; and Al Eugster, recently laid off from his inking job at Felix, and now a novice inbetweener. The rest were all strangers, but they were very friendly when we were introduced.

The Fleischer brothers believed in nepotism. Max was president of the company, Dave was in charge of production, Lou was head of the music department, and Joe was a kind of maintenance man.

Max's business affairs kept him busy in his office, so we rarely saw him in the production areas. Dave spent his whole day working in the story department and going from one animator to the next, feeding them gags. Dave looked like a large teddy bear—rotund rather than fat—with an endearing habit of holding his half-clenched hands against his chest like a puppy begging for a biscuit.

I never saw a man who enjoyed himself more. All day he walked around with a pleased smile on his face, almost euphoric. Unlike Max, who had an excellent vocabulary, Dave's speech was full of grammatical errors and malapropisms, delivered in a strong New York accent.

Dave was a gagman with a flamboyant disregard for story structure and character motivation. His motto was a gag in every foot, and he would cram one into a scene regardless of the fact that it had very little or no connection with the story line—irregardless, even!

Lou Fleischer's music department was in a state of flux. The early bouncing-ball pictures had all been films illustrating old standards like "My Old Kentucky Home," and songs of similar vintage. Paramount's relationship to the studio gave it access to much more modern material, but my impression was that Lou was more comfortable with "Please Go 'Way and Let Me Sleep" than he was with "Minnie the Moocher."

Joe Fleischer, the maintenance man, built desks and drawing boards, put up partitions, and did the necessary wiring. The working area of the studio was very neatly arranged, with the inking and painting department sectioned off from the animators' rooms.

Max had acquired a staff that was the most prestigious in the East. George Stallings, Teddy Sears, Grim Natwick, George Rufle, and Sid Marcus had been animators in the very beginnings of the business. The most famous of all was Dick Huemer, whose animation of Koko the Clown was unsurpassed.

Not only was Dick a great animator, he was also a gourmet and a true bon vivant. Why, he even went to the opera! With the exception of Grim Natwick, who had just come back from Vienna where he had studied painting, the others were more in the tradition of newspaper cartoonists. Their nights were spent in speakeasies, and their main interests seemed to be baseball and boxing. I doubt if any of them had ever been inside an art gallery.

They were all earning from $150 to $200 a week, an enormous salary for those days, and probably spent every cent of it on riotous living.

We inbetweeners were all just barely into our twenties, and most of us still lived at home, dutifully turning over the bulk of our salaries to our parents. It was just beginning to dawn on all of us that there was a flourishing animation business in Hollywood. There had been a small but steady stream of New York animators who went to the coast. Sometimes they sent back snapshots of themselves standing under palm trees. Ben

Sharpsteen had the dubious honor of being the first animator to be attacked by a bear in Yellowstone Park. It all sounded glamorous and exotic.

Every time a new Disney film was released, we youngsters would go en masse to see it, and there would be an excited discussion the next day about the fine quality of the animation. It was rumored that there was an animator with the improbable name of Ubbe Iwerks, the designer of Mickey Mouse, who now was considered the best animator in the business. What the animators thought about this competition was hard to say; as the elite of the staff, they kept pretty much to themselves.

Being an inbetweener was great fun, and the chance to draw all day was very stimulating. I didn't find that the work was beyond my drawing ability, so I came to work every day in a happy, relaxed mood.

One beautiful day in May 1930, I sauntered into the studio to find the place in a turmoil. People were standing around talking excitedly about the catastrophe. Huemer and Sid Marcus had left for the coast, and Stallings and Rufle had moved to Van Beuren's Studio. With only Grim Natwick and Teddy Sears left, the studio couldn't possibly function, not in its present state anyway. It looked as if the Fleischer Studio was going to have to make severe cutbacks in the staff.

Finally, Dave came into the animation department with reassuring smiles. There would be no cutbacks but promotions, instead! Zamora, who was Dick Huemer's inbetweener, was going to finish the animation on *Glow Little Glowworm,* and the rest of us were going to work on a new picture, *Swing, You Sinners,* as trial animators. If we did well, that was going to be our permanent status.

Stunned by this sudden turn of events, Eugster, Cannata, Bowsky, Kneitel, Henning, and I duly picked up our gear and moved into the animation room. I think it was one of the most dramatic moments in animation history. Here we were, a group of neophyte inbetweeners, suddenly faced with the responsibility of saving the studio. Even cocky little George Cannata was subdued.

Ted Sears had made some rough drawings of the different scenes. He had advocated the use of drawings to supplement the typed scripts for a long time, but I believe this was the first time that a concise series of drawings covering *every* shot was ever used to guide the animators. Thus the first storyboard was born to meet this emergency, and it changed the whole method of story presentation ever after.

Unfortunately for us, *Swing, You Sinners* was not an easy picture to animate. There were many crowd shots and a good deal of dialogue. The picture had a prerecorded sound track, and we had to follow music beats which were laid out on exposure sheets.

Exposure sheets were an additional problem for us all. At the other studios, the animators planned their work for two levels of cels, and the action was so simple that it was sufficient to write the number of exposures each drawing would receive in the right-hand corner, under the number of the drawing. Exposure sheets were ruled paper with vertical columns for four cels for each exposure! Down the left side of each sheet, the music department indicated the musical beats and breakdown of the words into single exposures.

For example, the word "swing" might take twelve exposures to sing. "S" might take three exposures, "W" only one, "I" another six, and "NG" two more. We were expected to devise an appropriate mouth for each sound. Nobody was sure about the kind of configuration the mouth should take, not even Sears or Natwick.

Weeks of the most hectic work followed. Sears went around redrawing clumsy layout drawings; Grim, who had designed all the characters, would look at the sweaty drawings and say in his Wisconsin drawl, "Waaal now, this looks pretty goddamn good!" Then he would proceed to sit down and redraw half the animation. Dave would follow close behind and flip the drawings and nod approval.

With the exception of Henning, who was about thirty-five, the rest of us were barely of voting age. It was a hell of a gamble, but we were coaxed, wheedled, and flattered into turning out the picture. Sears and Natwick had very little time to do any animation themselves; they had too much coaching to do.

Dave went around literally patting everybody on the head. In spite of our obvious ineptitude, nobody was impatient or irritated. It was a very gentle introduction to a new and enormously taxing job.

I remember having a great deal of trouble with a cadaverous old man who Grim had designed. He had long hair that streamed to the ground, and when Grim drew him the hair made a design. When I bumbled through the animation, it looked like spaghetti. Finally, under Grim's gentle tuition, I solved the problem.

Max took an incredible gamble, and it paid off. When the cartoon was released, I read a review. It said that in the feature film, Eddie Cantor,

Shamus Culhane was still an ardent Sunday painter at twenty-one. *Collection of Shamus Culhane.*

A character from *Swing, You Sinners*, drawn by Shamus Culhane. 1930.

the banjo–eyed comic, had laid an egg, but on the program was a "jewel of a cartoon, *Swing, You Sinners.*" This was a tribute to Grim, Teddy Sears, and Dave Fleischer.

Every one of us had come through in a pinch. When the picture was finished, we were all given contracts of $100 a week for the first year and $125 for the second. Riches beyond belief.

Looking back over the years, it is obvious that Max and Dave were not caught napping. All the animators who left were on good terms with the Fleischers and must have given sufficient notice of their intention to leave. Wisely, Max had decided not to tell us of the impending ordeal.

The one thing I didn't like was the way screen credit was doled out. Eight of us had animated *Swing, You Sinners,* yet studio policy allowed only two animators to share credit for the picture; so Willard Bowsky and William Henning were given the credit for animation. I have always disliked the idea and I still do. Psychologically, it was unsound, because every person who works on a film wants to see his name on the titles. How this idea of restricting the credits to two animators was ever conceived is lost history, but certainly, ego gratification was not being considered when the system was devised.

Swing, You Sinners is a good case in point. The credits really should have been given to Sears and Natwick. Bowsky was still learning, and Henning never did become a topflight animator, yet they were the ones given screen credit as the animators on the film.

Another problem was credit for direction. David Fleischer had his name on every cartoon as the director, when in reality he was the producer, much to the confusion of latter-day researchers. He never directed an animated cartoon in his life!

The East Coast production procedures were always years behind Disney. In 1929, Walt installed Burt Gillett and Wilfred Jackson as directors. They did no animation. Their function was what is now standard practice: contribute ideas to the story they were going to direct while it was being written; supervise the drawing-up of exposure sheets, layouts, and backgrounds; give work to the animators; call for retakes; work with the musicians; attend the recordings; and approve the final prints.

In comparison, the Fleischer production methods were more complex. Animators never attended recordings. Dave supervised them in their entirety. He also worked with the story department, which consisted of

Joe Stultz, Jack Mercer, and Bill Turner. They could not handle all the work, so as late as 1932 many of the stories were created by so-called "head animators."

They had all the responsibilities of direction except sound track supervision, i.e., they designed characters, wrote timing instructions on the exposure sheets, often drew layouts, and gave out sequences to the animators. Dave's contribution was suggestions to "cuten him up a little" if he didn't agree with the rendition of a new character.

Once the animators had started their work he would come around from time to time to look at the result and suggest more gags. Nobody seems to have noticed that Dave is credited with "directing" between thirty and thirty-eight films year after year, while veteran directors like Jones, Freleng, Hanna and Barbera, and Gillett never averaged more than ten cartoons a year.

Dave Fleischer should have been listed as the producer and dialogue director, yet, because he is listed as the director on the credit titles, he will doubtless go down in history under that misnomer. There is already a book, *The Great Cartoon Directors* by Jeff Lenburg, that includes Dave Fleischer among the eight greatest cartoon directors!

The slapdash system of allocating animation credits in Fleischer Studio will make it impossible for film historians to find out who really directed the pictures.

Bigotry is a very sticky subject these days, and the attitudes of the members of the Fleischer staff of 1930, measured by present-day standards, would be promptly labeled bigoted by anyone viewing the body of the pictures made during that period.

Still, I believe that the charge would not be true. One has to examine the ethnic backgrounds of the crew. Almost every person on the staff had at least one parent who was an immigrant. Practically all the boys spoke a foreign language at home and, I might add, reluctantly.

When I was a child in Yorkville, the only adults I knew who spoke English without difficulty were my parents and my teachers. Even I spoke French at home because my mother came from a French-Canadian family. My father had a brogue because he was raised in a Massachusetts town where the Irish population was an insular, beleaguered minority.

All of the children who I knew had one thing in common: they hated to speak a foreign language because it made them different from Americans. There was a fierce need to conform, and the foreign atmosphere in the home was a source of embarrassment and anxiety.

Still, it was inevitable that this mixed ethnic background would influence us all. Street English was a curious patois, a mixture of Czech, Hungarian, Yiddish, and Italian. There was a kind of rueful acceptance of the fact that some words had more impact in a foreign tongue than they had in English.

There was a derisive quality about our attitude towards the grown-ups. We mocked their attempts to speak English, poked fun at their clothes, and jeered at the Old Country customs which they vainly tried to retain, because they were not American and we yearned to be just that.

When we addressed each other as "Jew boy," "Mick," and "Wop," the terms had the same motivation. Poking fun at somebody's background was not an attempt to be scornful or to make the person feel inferior, but was a continuation of our derisive feelings about the whole ethnic problem. While these terms will make present-day liberals shudder, in those days it was merely good-natured banter, and nobody dreamed of taking offense.

I believe that, with this explanation in mind, it can be seen why one particular scene in *Swing, You Sinners,* where I animated a Jew with a black beard, huge nose, and a derby, was completely acceptable to all the Jews in the studio. As a matter of fact, I recall it was Dave Fleischer's gag! Had he thought up a scene with an Old Country Irishman, I would have drawn him a Hiberian with a plug hat, potato nose, and side whiskers, without thinking twice about it.

I am not defending this attitude as enlightened, but I would not call it xenophobic, because there was no malice involved.

There was only one black in the studio: the porter. But I'm sure that if a black kid had applied for a job in the studio, and had talent, he would have been hired and accepted with no reservations by the whole staff. Later aspects of animation history will bear this out.

When *Swing, You Sinners,* was finished, I was happy to learn that I was going to be teamed up with Rudy Zamora. While we were sweating out work on *Swing, You Sinners,* Rudy was animating a song cartoon that had been abandoned by Dick Huemer. *Glow Little Glowworm* was about half-finished when Huemer left, and in one of Max's desperate moves, he had allowed Zamora to finish the film by himself. The result was incredible; there was no way to tell where Huemer had ended and Zamora had taken up.

Rudy Zamora became the star of the "New Wave" animators. A full-blooded Mexican, he resembled those huge Olmec heads that archaeologists call "baby-faced." However, he made several improvements on the original. A one-inch stub of a cigarette burned in one corner of his mouth, sending up a steady stream of smoke into his left eye, which was usually half-closed. His jet-black hair cascaded down level with the base of his nose. One could glimpse through the strands and see one liquid-brown eye, glinting with mischief. The total effect was of a negative of an English sheep dog. He, along with the rest of us, received a two-year contract.

Zamora had working habits that drove Gilmartin, the production manager, up the pole. He lounged around all day, talking to anybody who would listen. He loved to yarn about his Mexican background, and how his mother nursed Pancho Villa when he was wounded and in hiding. This was fun, but it did hold up production for everyone except Zamora. Late in the afternoon he would sit down and bat out more animation than the rest of us had done toiling and sweating all day, and it was better.

Lacking Zamora's innate expertise, I managed to spend very little time listening to his stories and worked very hard. Ted Sears and Grim Natwick continued to keep a watchful eye over us all, and it was a good thing they did, because it was more than two months before we saw a print of our animation in *Swing, You Sinners*.

As I remember, for our first picture together, Zamora and I animated *Alexander's Ragtime Band,* a bouncing-ball Song Car-Tune. We had a very loose method of working, not unlike playing in a contemporary jazz band. Each animator would take a sequence with a fairly meager story-board, devise his own layouts, camera angles, long shots, close-ups, and his own incidental characters. Aside from that, the animator's ability to think up additional gags was considered just as important as his work as an animator.

Like the jazz musician, the animator took the theme of the script and embellished it to his own taste, never straying so far from the story's theme that his work could not mesh with the other animator's sequence. It might not have meshed very well, but if it did mesh, even approximately, that was good enough.

Rudy and I were delighted to hear that we were going to animate a Song Car-Tune featuring Rudy Vallee. He probably was the first pop singer to give girls the vapors, but his singing style seems to have been universally detested by young males. Those down-drooping eyes, wavy hair, nasal voice, and what seemed to us to be an effete air stirred the macho in us all.

Long before we were officially given the assignment, Zamora and I were hard at work drawing a series of horrendous caricatures of Vallee. Somebody in the Paramount office must have sensed this possibility, because we received a very stern memo: There were to be no offensive gags or drawings in the picture—none!

Somewhat subdued, we redrew our caricatures until they were a watered-down version of the originals and settled down to animate a very innocuous version of *The Maine Stein Song*. As usual, we had to think up a gag, or gags, which were made by animating each word into a figure as soon as the bouncing ball had passed it by. Either we thought of something funny, or Dave would come around to see what was holding up production. Then he would supply his version of a gag.

Because Rudy Vallee was an important star, Dave gave particular attention to this picture. As I mentioned earlier, Dave's vocabulary was not exactly polished. One day, he came around on his usual tour of the animators to find me staring blankly at a pencil tracing of the lettering, "Shout 'til the rafters ring," a line in the bouncing-ball section of the picture.

"Yuh gotta gag?" he asked. I admitted that I hadn't. Dave leaned over and read the line, his lips moving silently. Then he straightened up, looked at the ceiling pensively, and sang, "Shout 'til the rafters ring." Nothing happened. He tried again, "Shout 'til the rafters ring." Then Dave looked at me querulously and asked, "What the hell's a rafter?"

After I told him, Dave shook his head and went away, leaving me to figure out some architectural gag myself. In spite of the restraints, *The Maine Stein Song* was very well received at the box office.

In 1931 the motion picture audiences throughout the country began to become restive as an increasing number of programs contained advertising shorts. Many of them were crudely made films for local merchants, but some of them were pictures that advertised national wares. There was some attempt at including entertainment factors in the scripts, but in general they were a bore, and audiences began to resent the fact that advertising messages were foisted on them when they had paid money to be entertained.

The Oldsmobile company made a deal with Max for a picture that would raise the level of the entertainment value and present the motion picture audience with a more acceptable piece of advertising.

Rudy Zamora and I wrote a script for a Screen Song that featured the old popular song, "In My Merry Oldsmobile." It was no better, and certainly no worse, than the usual bouncing-ball film, with a modicum of advertising.

When it was released, all hell broke loose. It seems that this was the psychological moment for a wave of protest against advertising films, and the resentment focused on this picture. These bouncing-ball cartoons were very popular throughout the country. I think that the audience's reaction was caused by the fact that here was one of their favorite bits of entertainment being subverted to advertising.

The protests were so nationwide that the picture was withdrawn from circulation and, as a result of the bad reaction, advertising films were not used in theaters for many years.

In 1931, despite the depression around us, Max had a very successful year. It was so good that he decided to give a Christmas bonus of five hundred dollars to each animator. In addition he threw a party at the Hotel Wellington that was long remembered by the hotel's staff.

The evening started off with a banquet and an emotional speech by Max. After that, the bootleg whiskey took control, and at one point we had a very drunken football match. I think the ball was a knotted napkin. Max captained one team and Dave the other. We charged at each other, overturning chairs and tables, and ended up in a heap of over a hundred people, all shouting and laughing. When Max found his glasses, he decided it was time to go home, but before leaving he announced that drinks were on the house. The party lasted until five in the morning, and Max was presented with a huge bill from the hotel for breakage. What the hell, it was a great way for us all to start the New Year. Good old Hotel Wellington!

The New Wave animators were like a bunch of puppies who cavorted about in the shadow of Max Fleischer's benevolence. We had no idea of what the future held for us all, and happily we came to work every morning with a kind of mindless joy and full confidence in tomorrow.

There was a timeless quality about our euphoria, as if we would never suffer, never struggle, and all would be well forever. With two jobs, working ninety-six hours a week, my father managed to earn seventy-five dollars. Here I was, working half that time and making one hundred and twenty-five. It was a time of overweening hubris.

One day, to my consternation, I came in to work to find that Zamora had jumped his contract and was headed for Hollywood and the Disney Studio! Very shortly after that, Ted Sears completed his contract and also joined Disney as head of the story department. If this talent drain disturbed Max, he gave no outward sign of it. He merely promoted assistants to animators. Luckily for him, they all managed to survive the promotion, some more successfully than others, of course.

The truth is that what was acceptable to Max was pretty crude stuff. We never did any retakes unless there was a camera error, and I don't remember that anyone ever had to redraw a scene because of poor draftsmanship. The only precaution Max took was to create a new department called "planning."

We all found the exposure sheets a difficult problem of bookkeeping, what with having to keep in mind which combination of cel levels would make a complete drawing. It was easy to make mistakes because it was the style in this studio to break down a figure into as many cel levels as possible. One level might have feet which were not moving, another level a body which was bouncing in a repeated cycle, a third series of drawings of heads, a fourth perhaps mouth movements. The possibilities of error with this kind of fragmentation were endless.

So Max installed two planners: Nellie Sanborn, a prim lady who looked like a librarian, and Alice Morgan, a fat, jolly ex-inker. Their job was in effect to do a dry run on the exposure sheets to see that the notes to the inkers were accurate. They usually weren't, or they were so complicated that Nellie and Alice would rewrite the exposure sheets before the animation was sent to the inking department.

There was a steady stream of scenes coming back to the animators with notes to draw missing elements, a head here, an arm there. Nobody told us why this was being done, and we didn't bother to ask.

There was also the problem of spacing. The good ladies decided that we should never animate a drawing which did not overlap the preceding figure, which of course is arrant nonsense. For very fast action, one must of necessity make drawings in which most of the parts do not overlap at all.

Neither Nelly nor Alice were artists, yet we all submitted meekly to their authority, adding as many extra drawings as they directed with never an argument. I think this docility was because they were both a lot older than we were. There is no doubt that they were responsible for much of the plodding movement that characterizes the Fleischer pictures of the thirties.

While this procedure might have been a necessary stopgap because the fledgling animators were not familiar with the complexities of exposure sheets and timing of action, the long-term effects were that many of the animators who stayed with the Fleischers never learned to properly organize their work. Even decades later they continued to make the same blatant errors that had made it necessary to have a checking department in the first place.

Within a very short time some of the neophyte animators began to exhibit real talent as filmmakers. One was Willard Bowsky. He was about twenty-one at the time, a loudmouthed, opinionated fellow, who had a ready answer for every problem, political, artistic, or ethnic. He was probably the only person in the studio who was openly anti-Semitic. It didn't seem to bother Max or Dave, even when people complained. While they admitted that it was probably true, they had none of the fierce defensiveness about Jewishness that developed later as a result of the rise of the Nazis.

According to the standards of the studio, Willard drew very well and had a great appreciation for contemporary music, so he was given sound tracks like "Minnie the Moocher" and "Stick Out Your Can Here Comes the Garbage Man." He would even go into ecstasies over Cab Calloway records.

With my background of classical music, I thought Calloway sounded like jibberish and avoided those assignments like a plague. While Bowsky really couldn't draw well enough to compete with West Coast films, he did make some of the better jazz cartoons in the studio because he loved the music.

Willard lived at home with his parents and took no part in the usual Saturday night saturnalias. He was what one might call a pre-McCarthy, gung ho, all-American Babbitt, an avid reader of the *New York Mirror,* with social convictions to match. He believed that all the unemployed were just being lazy, and intimated that anybody with ambition could succeed in this country, freely offering himself as a shining example.

Very soon after we had finished *Swing, You Sinners,* Seymour Kneitel exhibited the qualities of leadership that enabled him later to become a head animator. Like most of us, he had no formal art training. However, early on, he endeared himself to the front office by his ability to turn out pictures at an astonishing profit. His approach to a film was always guided by the possibility of reusing material over and over in order to bring down the cost.

Unlike Willard with his abrasive personality, Seymour was genial and outgoing and was well liked by the rest of the staff. When he married Max's only daughter Ruth, most of us were surprised. He had never even mentioned that he was dating her. The marriage made no difference in Seymour's status in the studio: he was never given, nor did he ever ask for, special handling from the management.

Dick Fleischer, Max's son, was then about eleven or twelve years old. His visits to the studio were infrequent. Dick was going to a military academy and was quite a cute child in his smart uniform. He seemed to have no interest in animation; instead, he grew up to become a live-action director. Ironically, one of his best films, Jules Verne's *Twenty Thousand Leagues Under the Sea,* was made for his father's archrival, Walt Disney.

3

Max's Fledgling Animators

One of the things we all argued about, and vociferously, was how to animate mouth action. Willard Bowsky claimed that during dialogue the mouth closed after every word. I went to the library and read books about singing and diction, and I decided that this was wrong. We had many a wrangle about it. Some animators sided with Bowsky, others with me.

While I was partially right, none of us realized that lifelike dialogue is achieved by the movements of the head and hands and, in very forceful speech, by the entire body, with the mouth positions playing a very small part in the general effect.

Fleischer animators continued to ignore this basic principle until about 1938, when the studio began to hire animators from the West Coast.

After Zamora left, I was teamed up with Al Eugster. He was an excellent gagman, but his real penchant was story structure. Before we started to work together, Eugster had animated a bouncing ball about "Gallagher and Shean," a popular song sung by two men who had one of the most successful vaudeville acts of the day.

The picture was a marvel of careful planning. Eugster, a meticulous worker, was expert at drawing objects in perspective, a talent no one else in the studio shared. In one sequence, Gallagher and Shean were high up on the girders of a partially built skyscraper. Just as they would reach the end of a girder and were about to fall, a second girder would swing into the scene, and they walked along that, oblivious of their peril.

There was a succession of these near mishaps, with girders coming in from every direction. The planning of the perspective for each girder was so complicated that Eugster's drawing paper was not big enough to contain the sight lines involved. Al had to paste sheets of paper all over his drawing board. But the complexity of the problem didn't disturb him a bit: he just sat there day after day, completely absorbed and happy, drawing vanishing points. The picture, *Sky Scraping,* especially the girder sequence, was one of the funniest cartoons of the period, so I was very pleased to be working with him.

One of our most successful pictures was *The Herring Murder Case,* which was a spoof on the Edward G. Robinson gangster pictures. In this film, I had a chance to use my knowledge of music. We wanted to use the *Danse macabre,* but the original composition was too long. I created a cutdown version of the piece, and it was recorded very successfully after the animation was completed.

This was contrary to the usual studio practice. Normally, we were given a record of music complete with sound effects. When the track was recorded, nobody had even worked out a rough draft of the story!

Eugster and I would spend hours in the projection room listening to a recording, trying to fit a story to the music. Very often, after we had begun to see a possible story line, we heard some jackass in the effects crew had suddenly blown a horn or clanked a series of sounds on a horseshoe. We would crumple up our notes and throw them into the wastepaper basket that we had set about six feet away. We became experts at tossing balls of paper into that basket.

Since Max was no longer working with Koko, the popularity of the character declined. The trouble was that Koko was a victim of the story department's inability to create personality traits that would have called for some acting. This fault was to a great degree due to Max and Dave's philosophy which seems to have paralleled Mack Sennett's brand of humor: chases, prat falls, and pants falling down.

In 1930, Dick Huemer had created a new character: Bimbo. He seems to have been a dog, rather like Walter Lantz's Weak-heart in that he only vaguely looked like a dog and always walked around on his hind legs. He certainly never was a serious challenge to any Disney character.

One morning, Grim Natwick was given a new assignment: a script for a cartoon called *Dizzy Dishes.* He was to design a girl character, another dog. One clue to her appearance was the fact that she was going to sing a "Boop-Boop-a-Doop" song in the style of Helen Kane, a popular vaudeville singer with cute little curls fringing her face.

Max Fleischer and Betty
Boop.

A model sheet of Koko the Clown, drawn by Shamus Culhane for *The Herring Murder Case,* a 1932 film produced by Fleischer Studio. Written, co-directed, and animated by Al Eugster and Shamus Culhane.

Betty Boop had no name for a while. She was a rather pudgy girl with a black button-nose and poodle ears. Later the ears were changed to long earrings, the black nose eradicated, and, under Grim's skillful guidance, she blossomed into a sexy little woman with a svelte figure. Betty Boop was an instant hit.

Helen Kane promptly sued the Fleischer Studio, claiming that the studio copied her singing style. For a while, it looked as if the Fleischers were going to lose the case. However, under careful cross-examination, Kane had to admit that she, in turn, had copied the boop-boop-a-doop business from an obscure black singer, Baby Esther. Helen Kane lost the case.

With Grim Natwick's talent for animation and his sound knowledge of the female figure, Betty Boop became an alluring little sexpot. Al Eugster, Bernie Wolf, and I were able to make reasonable facsimiles of his conception, but the other animators were not up to the problems of moving her around freely.

While the four of us could draw profiles, the rest of the crew stuck grimly to full faces or, at best, three-quarter views. Very often she would dance and sing with her head in one position, looking very stiff-necked. Foreshortened arms and legs were avoided as well, because of a lack of drawing ability.

Grim gradually accented her sexiness by giving her a provocative cleavage and little bouncing breasts, and we happily followed suit. In one picture, *Bamboo Isle,* I animated a hula dance in which her bare breasts were skimpily covered by a lei. It was probably my best animation of Betty Boop.

Unfortunately, the story department was never sophisticated enough to take full advantage of Betty. Sex was usually depicted as endless attempts on her virginity. She was never given a male counterpart, again because of the flawed concept that action was more important than character motivation.

The obvious progression would have been from a cutie-cute Helen Kane type to a character who had definite ideas about sex, such as Mae West, but that would have required a literary background. Instead, the scripts were like vaudeville skits, sometimes veering dangerously towards burlesque.

There was a definite change among the New Wave animators from naïveté to a more sophisticated social life during 1930. Heretofore, most of the younger animators lived at home and turned over their salaries to their parents. Now, most of them had started to set up bachelor quarters.

The most outstanding feature of the hegira was a brownstone rooming house on Forty-fourth Street, which was completely taken over by Fleischer people. The lone female lodger was Edith Vernick, head of the inbetween department. Every Saturday night, to her vexation, the group gathered for a weekly bout of sex, drinking, and bridge with a bevy of whores from a local bordello. The whores were very good bridge players, in addition to their other attributes, and the games, both horizontal and vertical, usually continued all night.

Monday mornings were always the time for box scores of the previous weekend's exploits—alcoholic, sexual, and bridge playing—with an extra fillip of stories about the seamy side of Harlem. When the boys talked about sex, there was the usual dichotomy of mother and sisters being good, and all other women being fair game. In a bewildering case of misplaced chivalry, a near fistfight ensued when one of the outsiders made a derogatory remark about a particular whore who was a bridge player on a steady basis.

Of course, not all the staff were involved in this dissipation; many of the people were leading more conventional lives. But the chauvinistic approach to sex, as epitomized by the Forty-fourth Street brownstone, would have its effect on the Betty Boop pictures that were being animated during that period.

Nobody can be creative beyond the range of his imagination and his own life's experience. The animators and storymen who worked on the Betty Boop cartoons had the earthy humor of New York street kids. They might never have been able to enjoy the Song of Solomon, but would certainly have whooped at Aristophanes' buffoons who, when frightened, shit in their pants; or would have chuckled over Rabelais' list of bedraggled penises.

Why did Fleischer's storymen never succeed in writing more romantically about Betty Boop? I remember an uncle of mine who used to come to New York several times a year to go to Minsky's Burlesque. He would sit tensely and watch the big breasts wobble, and lean forward excitedly as women with incredibly huge buttocks ground languidly down the runway.

I thought to myself, "If he likes meat that much, why not show him the most beautiful women in show business?" So I took him to Ziegfeld's one year. He sat very quietly as the six-foot Amazons in sequins and peacock tails pirouetted and strutted around the stage. When we came out of the theater, I asked him how he liked the show. "Shit," he growled, "Next time let's go back to Minsky's." I had taken him beyond the range of his fantasies.

When women were thought of in terms like "quiff," "snatch," and "gash," a la Studs Lonigan, there was no possibility of a story being written where Betty Boop used her charms in a light, flirtatious manner. Betty was a "good" girl with a hymen like a boiler plate, and her sex life would never be more than a series of attacks on that virginity by unpleasant characters with heavy hands.

But heavy-handed or not, at least these plots had a certain lusty humor. Diversions from that point of view resulted in maudlin gags that were the height of banality.

There were two intellectual snobs in the animation department: Sid Garber and me. Sid, an indifferent animator, gravitated into my group and very shyly attempted to strike up a relationship with me. He was a thin-faced Jewish boy with no interest in animation except as a way to make a living.

Like me, he was self-educated and winced as I did at the box score discussions each Monday morning. While this was going on, he would furtively look over at me to see if I was reacting to the tawdry details of the bawdy banter with as much distaste as he was feeling. I was.

I left the Catholic Church when, at the age of twelve, I began to read about the Medici and the scandalous behavior of church officials which prompted Martin Luther to rebel. Unfortunately, what I had not discarded were the rigid attitudes of the average, poor Irish Catholic–Victorians of the period. Ironically enough, Garber and I shared with the roisterers of the studio the belief that women were either "good" or "bad."

Garber also maintained an artistic life outside of the studio, which was never discussed with other members of the staff. Once he showed me a letter of commendation from the French government for his illustrations for a new edition of *Candide*. One day he was suddenly rushed to a hospital, and a few days later he died of a brain tumor. Nobody seemed to miss him, except me.

*   *   *

Betty Boop in *Bamboo Isle*. Drawn by Shamus Culhane, 1932, for Fleischer Studio.

Betty Boop in transition from her original role as a dog. In this drawing by Grim Natwick she still has long dog ears.

If different conditions had prevailed in the educational field, Max Fleischer might never have become a famous cartoon producer. Like J. R. Bray, he was convinced that animation was fundamentally more important as an educational tool.

Max had made a four-reel animated film on Einstein's theory of relativity, which was designed for use in schools. After it was finished, in 1923, his attempts to interest the school systems in the film were a failure. As Max ruefully commented, "There were supposed to be only three people in the world who understood Einstein's theory. Now there are four."

Although the sales of the picture were negligible, Fleischer tried again. In association with the Museum of Natural History, he produced a feature-length film on evolution in 1925, the same year as the famous Scopes Monkey Trial. Again, the distribution was a failure.

In 1931, a documentary film about Admiral Byrd's exploration of Antarctica used animated maps which were made at the Fleischer Studios. The picture aroused little interest. That was his last attempt to venture into the educational field.

Not all of Max's attempts to make educational films had been failures. In the beginning of World War I, he had enlisted in the army as a visual aid specialist. He worked at Fort Sill turning out animated training films such as *How to Fire a Machine Gun* and *How to Read an Army Map,* which were probably the first uses of animation in education. The remarkable results of these pictures convinced Max that his intuition was right. Even after the failure of his subsequent educational pictures, he remained convinced that animation should be used in school systems.

In the early months of 1931, the full extent of the Depression had not yet become manifest. When we began to see well-dressed men selling apples in the street, none of us understood the full import. We were all so exuberant about our new jobs and the incredible salaries that it screened us off from what was really happening to the country.

Somewhat later than most of the boys, I decided to live a more independent life. I found an apartment in Greenwich Village and bought a secondhand Aubourn roadster with headlights as big as trap drums. It required a weekly repair bill that would have impoverished a duke, but I didn't care; there was always the next week's salary.

As the Depression got worse, I found myself having to give money to a gaggle of relatives. This, plus the car, started a severe drain on my income. I couldn't believe it, but often, at the end of a week, I was left with only a few dollars in my pocket. One time, I even had to borrow a one-hundred-dollar advance on my salary. Max was shocked at my request and gave me a long lecture on the need to save some of my money. It fell on deaf ears.

When the banks started to fail, it still made no impression on us until the fateful day when the bank that Max used was in trouble. A half-dozen employees got into line with enough checks to clean out the account, and then ran across the street with the money and deposited it in a solvent bank where Max had just opened an account. There was so much money that they had to carry the bills heaped up in their hats.

As the months went by, Grim Natwick continued to help the young animators through the difficult learning process. The trouble was that we would animate a picture and not see our work until it was shown as a finished print. By that time several months had gone by and whatever experiments we had made in the spacing of the drawings or the timings had long since faded from our memories.

Gradually Grim fell into the role of surrogate father. Eugster and I especially spent a good deal of time with him after work. We often had dinner at Pirroles, a French restaurant on Forty-fifth Street where Grim would regale us with stories of his early beginnings as an artist drawing covers for sheet music, and as an animator at Hearst's International Studios.

Al Eugster had some funny stories as well, about working for Pat Sullivan at Felix the Cat. Pat seems to have been the most consistent man in the business—consistent in that he was never sober. He was also making an incredible amount of money from his pictures: they cost less than $3,000 to make, and he was selling them for about $12,000.

Otto Messmer, who must have had the patience of Job, had designed Felix, was running the studio, and took care of Sullivan when he made a visit to New York. Fortunately, these trips were infrequent. Pat and his wife spent most of their time traveling around the world accepting plaudits for Felix and making speeches in which Pat modestly claimed full credit for the production and design of the character.

Because Felix was the most popular animated cartoon of the day, Sullivan got a royal welcome wherever he went, and he spent money to match. However, as often happens, he was very closefisted about salaries he paid the staff, including Otto Messmer.

When Sullivan arrived at the studio, the first thing he would do was toss a bundle of dirty clothes to the nearest person. Even if that person were an animator, he was expected to rush off to the nearest laundry. Any hesitation, fancied or real, and Sullivan would launch into a torrent of drunken abuse and fire the man on the spot. As Pat watched with blurry satisfaction, Otto would solemnly write out a check and the dismissed employee would take the day off. The next day he would appear for work as usual, and Sullivan would remember nothing of the incident because of his alcoholic amnesia.

Pat had always promised Messmer that he would leave him the studio in his will, but when he died there was no will, and the rights to Felix went to an obscure nephew in Australia. Otto never got a dime.

Bernie Wolf joined Eugster, Natwick, and me from time to time. None of us realized that this quartet was going to spend many years working together at different studios. We all shared one specialty: we could animate a female figure. Of course, we youngsters could not compete with Grim, but our animation of Betty Boop was far superior to the other New Wave animators.

The talent drain to the West Coast continued. In early 1932 Grim Natwick left, and Al Eugster soon followed.

Up to this time, it was an accepted routine that a youngster's first job in the business was as an opaquer, then inker, graduating to the inbetween department, and then finally, after many years, becoming an animator. Fleischer Studio in 1931 changed this procedure. Now it was possible to start as an inbetweener, bypassing the other departments.

Gradually the inking and painting was taken over by women who had little or no art training. They did not expect to advance into animation.

Max realized that the inbetween department was probably going to be his only source of future animators, so he enlarged this group in 1931 and put Edith Vernick in charge. The department was adjacent to the animation rooms and well within earshot of the animators' conversations.

Edith, a redheaded Russian, could on occasion exhibit a vocabulary that would have embarrassed a Billingsgate fishwife. At other times she remembered that she was a lady.

New York street English, which was the lingua franca of the Fleischer Studio, made extensive use of the word "fuck." It was at once a descriptive adjective, verb, noun, connective, and just plain noise.

Whenever an argument started among the animators, usually about

Edith Vernick, head of the Fleischer inbetween department. 1940.

Pat Sullivan and his wife in the early 1920s, framed by an early version of Felix.

baseball or boxing, "fuck" was batted back and forth like a shuttlecock. Edith, when she was in her fishwife mood, would pay no attention to the sulphurous banter, but if she remembered that she was a lady, she would let loose a stentorian roar, "Hey you sons of bitches! Cut out saying 'fuck' all the time! You bastards forget we got girls around here?"

It was impossible to omit "fuck" in any normal conversation. It was like the keystone of an arch. So, soon after, the use of the word would be resumed, if perhaps more quietly.

After the departure of Al Eugster, Max changed from teams of animators to larger units supervised by the "head animators." I found myself with a team composed of William Henning, George Cannata, Dave Tendlar, and Bernie Wolf. Two other units were led by Seymour Kneitel and Willard Bowsky.

Willie Henning, unlike the other animators in the New Wave, was a man of thirty-five who had been a captain of machine gunners in World War I. He was a Prussian to the core and was married to a woman who was the daughter of a baron. After the war, he came to New York, and Max rescued him from a job as a car washer. Unlike most Prussians, he was not stiff-necked, at least not around the kids in the studio. While his drawing ability left much to be desired, he managed to do acceptable animation. In spite of the fact that I was many years his junior, he followed my instructions with tact and good humor.

George Cannata was a problem both for me and Gilmartin, the production manager. Barely five feet tall, he was like so many short men: feisty and defensive. Apparently he had been somewhat neglected as a child. According to George, his mother had been Woodrow Wilson's secretary, and it seems she had little time for George during his childhood; at least, that was George's version of his background.

He always wore his hat while working, because newspaper cartoonists did that, and George thought of himself as a very serious cartoonist. He had a snappy drawing style and could easily have created a comic strip except for one problem—George was indolent.

Anyone who was late more than once in a week received a little printed card from Max. There was a space for comments from Max, and another area for the reason for lateness. One time, Max sent George a card and wrote in his space, "Slipping?" George's response was, "No, sleeping."

In early 1932, an Italian artist named Ugo D'Orsi joined my unit. Ugo was a popeyed, excitable fellow, about thirty years old. Unlike Henning, he was not too pleased with the idea of taking orders from a cherubic twenty-three-year-old. While he was a very fine draftsman with a sound academic training, he seemed to bear out Artie Davis' prophecy that "art school will stiffen you up." Ugo's animation was stiff.

Dave Tendlar, who had worked with me at Harrison and Gould's *Krazy Kat*, was an apple-cheeked youngster who peered owlishly at the world through a pair of huge eyeglasses. Even in those early days, he was showing a talent for drawing cartoons and went on to become an important artist at Hanna-Barbera many years later.

Bernie Wolf had become an animator a few months after *Swing, You Sinners,* having moved up to fill the place of one of the veteran animators who had gone west. Bernie had a good feeling for movement, and his ability to draw Betty Boop put him among the few people in the studio who could draw gracefully.

Although being in charge of a unit cut down the amount of time I could do animation myself, I enjoyed the problem of being an executive. I tried to analyze each picture before giving out the work, to see that I allocated the sequences according to the various talents and abilities in my group.

However, this job did take its toll on my creative energy. I stopped playing my violin because I found that I had little time to practice. Finally, I even dropped my habit of painting on weekends. I had set my sights on becoming a success in animation, especially in the job I now held.

As I thought about it, I began to realize the potential of animation for all kinds of artists, not only cartoonists. Some day, fine art would have its place in this medium. The only person I confided in about these theories was Bernie Wolf. He agreed with me that the Fleischer Studio was not the place to air such radical views.

Now that Natwick and Sears had gone, there was nobody in the studio who could teach us anything. I was unhappily aware that much of the animation around me was very poor.

There was a real schism in the animation department. Many of the animators, like Willard Bowsky and Seymour Kneitel, were quite happy with the kind of stories they were given and could not understand the impatience of those animators who chafed at the lack of possibilities. In a kind of blind arrogance, they would admit that Disney animation was different, but they stubbornly refused to concede that it was better.

One lunchtime, I was waiting for the elevator and was joined by Max. We rarely had a chance to talk, and this seemed to me to be an opportunity to air my views. We stood there debating the issue for an hour. I have a letter from Max, which he wrote to me many years later, but I believe it does very clearly state his basic views about animation and the kind of pictures that he believed the public wanted.

These are excerpts from the letter:

> During the span of years from 1914, I have made efforts to retain the "cartoony" effect. That is, I did not welcome the trend of the industry to go "arty." It was, and still is, my opinion that a cartoon should represent, in simple form, the cartoonist's mental expression. In other words the "animated oil painting" has taken the place of the flashiness and delightfulness of the simple cartoon.
>
> In my opinion, the industry must pull back. Pull away from the tendencies toward realism. It must stay in its own backyard of "The Cartoonist's Cartoon." The cartoon must be a portrayal of the expression of the true cartoonist, in simple, unhampered cartoon style. The true cartoon is a great art in its own right. It does not need the assistance or support of "Artiness." In fact, it is actually hampered by it.

It is obvious why our discussion ended in a Mexican standoff, since I was arguing that we needed stories with definite plot and character delineation. Max didn't even see why we needed color!

This long talk made me realize that I was not going to be happy working in the Fleischer Studio. However, I was not sure that I wanted to leave New York. I had a sudden inspiration: the "Thimble Theatre" was a very popular comic strip, especially since Elzie Segar, its creator, had introduced a new character, Popeye the Sailor. I thought that Popeye had great potential as an animated cartoon. Why shouldn't I start my own studio right here in New York? The fact that I had not saved a penny seemed of little consequence. In those primitive days, before the government drowned us in a sea of paper work, one needed a drawing board or two and access to an animation camera, and voilá! A studio was born. At least, that is what I thought.

I went to the syndicate offices and met some very astonished people. They had never thought of the possibility of converting the strip to animation. Hearst had used almost all of his comic-strip characters in animation, but he had closed his International Studios in 1921, and the people at the syndicate office didn't seem to know anything about his foray into the animation business.

It must have taken these graybeards two minutes to realize that I knew absolutely nothing about business, but they were intrigued by the idea, and so it was decided that I would return in a few days, and at that time I would sign a contract.

When I arrived, I came with Bernie Wolf's brother-in-law, who was a lawyer. This gave the boys pause. They thought I would be simpleminded enough to try to deal with them without a lawyer. With obvious uneasiness, they presented him with the contract. He had barely skimmed it when he got up, flushed with anger. "Who the hell do you think you're kidding?" He flung the papers on the desk and stalked out, with me following dutifully after. He told me later that it was a blatant attempt to cheat me out of every penny of profit. I had to take his word, because I never even had a chance to read the contract.

Several weeks later, when I was in Hollywood, I read that Max had just signed a deal to produce Popeye with the syndicate (not with King Features, a deal that came later) and was already starting scripts. Who knows? Had I gone in for my first meeting with an attorney I might have derailed animation history. I never did find out if they had approached Max or vice versa.

Grim Natwick and Al Eugster had not gone to Disney; instead they were hired by Walt's former partner, Ub Iwerks. When Walt signed up with Pat Powers, the old bandit had made several mistakes. First, he allowed Walt to retain ownership of Mickey Mouse, second, he had only signed up for a one-year distributorship. Third, he was sending Walt a few dollars a week, when the Mickey Mouse character had become nationally known within a few months.

Pat was supposed to have been a trolley car conductor in Buffalo in his youth. There is a tradition among trolley conductors that at the end of a run you threw all the money collected up at the ceiling of the trolley. Whatever stuck to the ceiling was turned over to the company. Powers seemed to be acting on the same principle with the Disneys.

Walt made a trip to New York to find out just what was happening to all the money that should have been pouring in. It is interesting to note that he took on the task of these confrontations himself, rather than having Roy handle them.

Pat waited in his offices in the Powers Building like an old battle-scarred boar about to take on a wildly yapping young puppy. He had done this kind of thing so many times before that he was supremely confident of the outcome.

When Disney arrived Powers freely admitted that he had not sent him all the money that should have been forthcoming. In addition he had lured Ub Iwerks away, giving him a contract to start his own studio.

However, Powers really liked the Disney brothers; he had just taken these precautionary steps to cement a new and more businesslike relationship. If Walt would sign a new contract for $2,500 a week, Pat, in a spirit of goodwill, would give Disney the money he was owed and disavow the contract with Iwerks.

When Walt asked for a token gesture while he thought things over, Pat magnanimously wrote out a check for $5,000. Walt promptly cashed it and went back to Hollywood and signed a deal with Columbia. He made no attempt to sue Powers for the rest of his money. It would have involved a long and costly lawsuit.

Still convinced that Ub Iwerks was the real talent behind Mickey Mouse, Powers duly set him up in a small studio in Beverly Hills. Ub created a character called Flip the Frog and went into production with a small staff. Natwick advised me that Disney was not hiring at the time, but Iwerks needed an animator. Unaware of all his machinations, I went to see Powers. To my innocent eyes he seemed to be just a convivial old gaffer. Even hunched over with age he must have been well over six feet tall.

Pat turned on the charm, gave me a few Irish jokes and told me how delighted he was to welcome another son of old Erin into the company. I was dazzled.

Before I quite realized what was happening, the old boy had signed me up to a two-year contract. The salary was $125 a week the first year, $150 the second. Powers urged me to jump my present contract with Max, because Iwerks was desperately in need of another animator. I refused, although my final two months at the studio were going to be interminable.

Betty Boop animation by Lillian Friedman, the first woman animator.

Before I left Fleischer's I found myself in a row in which I became a champion of women's rights. There were two women inbetweeners, Edith Vernick and Lillian Friedman. Lillian, a tiny nineteen-year-old, had the most drawing ability in the whole department.

Most of the animators finished their stint on a scene and sent it on to the inbetween department. The next time they saw it was several months later in a finished print. I was more involved with my work. To my dismay I saw that very often my drawings were butchered by untalented hacks. There was no control over the selection of the inbetweener. The scenes were handed out on a first-come basis.

I decided that I would like to ensure the quality of my work by using Lillian exclusively. When I announced that she was going to work in the animation department where I could watch her more closely, there was an uproar. The animators didn't want any fucking women in their fucking department. My rebuttal was that talent not sex should be the deciding factor. I managed to get Gilmartin, the office manager, on my side by assuring him that this arrangement would enable me to turn out more work.

Neither Max nor Dave took part in these heated discussions. I was furious, but when I saw that I was getting no place with the animators I became crafty. I suggested that all the inbetweeners who were qualified should complete the same test scene. I would let Willard Bowsky, my loudest opponent, pick out the best results from the unsigned work. To his vexation he chose Lillian's, and there was nothing to do but give her the job.

She was so talented that in spite of the studio's chauvinistic environment, Lillian went on to become the first female animator in the business. Women's lib would be hard put to find a better example of sex discrimination in business. Max gave Lillian a contract, dated June 22, 1933, for a starting salary of thirty dollars a week, with a raise of five dollars a week every year for four years! This in contrast to our starting salaries of one hundred a week and one hundred twenty-five the second year.

Lillian worked for Fleischer's until 1939, when she left the business and never returned.

When I said good-bye to Max there was real affection on both sides. While we differed vehemently on some fundamental aspects of the business, I liked him because he was a gentle, paternalistic employer, who had a genuine concern for the happiness of his employees.

The staff gave me the usual drunken farewell party at Pirolles, and a brand-new suitcase. I left convinced that I was going to see some of the boys in Hollywood very soon. Others I knew would never leave the studio. I was right on both counts.

4

Ub Iwerks Studio

Yorkville in 1932 was like a small village, so the night I started packing my car a crowd of curious neighbors gathered around to watch me stow my luggage. Only one other Yorkville kid had ever gone to Hollywood. A little Irisher from Seventy-ninth Street named Jimmy Cagney.

All the other animators had gone to the coast by train, but I was itching to see the country. I'd never gone farther from home than Massachusetts, so I sold my Aubourn dollar-eater for a brand-new Chevy coupé that looked like an oversized roller skate.

It was going to be a long, arduous drive, so I was glad when one of my lifelong friends offered to go along. Adam Kane was my age, a good driver, and fun to be with. Just the kind of person with whom one would want to share such a great adventure.

The crowd gasped its appreciation of the dangers ahead when I fetched out a large canteen and crammed it into the rumble seat. I had read some travel brochures, and they all warned that one must carry water when crossing the Mojave Desert.

Finally, we were off, a little wet-eyed as families and friends waved us godspeed. The roads were good for the first day, but we soon began to encounter some tooth-rattling washboard. At least half of the trip was on dirt roads.

When we stopped for the night we always found a tourist home where dinner, bed, and breakfast cost two dollars. Many a kind old lady watched with approval as we stashed away two or three helpings of her cooking.

One night in Missouri we had to stop in a sleazy cabin, and the snaggletoothed host couldn't supply dinner. That probably was just as well, considering the dirt under his nails. We went to bed hungry. About midnight I suddenly woke up. Some mysterious clicks and thumps made me turn on the light. To my horror there were at least a hundred beetles flying around. They were about three inches long, and my blankets were covered with them.

I let out a yell. Adam woke up, and in two minutes we were dressed and into the car. Bedbugs and roaches were familiar fauna in New York tenements, but beetles, Jesus! We drove all night. By midmorning we were well into Texas.

The sky had lightened to a curious brown. When we asked a filling-station operator if it was going to rain, he spat a stream of tobacco juice. "Rain? Shit! Ain't rained around here for 'bout a year. That there is the fuckin' land blowin' away. All the topsoil from Oklahoma is flying off an' comin' here." We had never heard of the Okies or their problems.

As we drove west we began to see dead steers huddled against the barbed wire fences and shining white rib cages and skulls gleaming in the dried-out grass. Sometimes it looked like a battlefield, clumps of desiccated corpses as far as you could see.

When we got to the Mojave late one night, we found that the old roads, made of railroad ties, were being torn up; so we made the trip bumping over the sand dunes on the right of way. Adam stopped to piss. Suddenly he let out a shriek. When I ran over to see what was wrong, there in the flashlight's circle was a big tarantula. It had emerald-green eyes and was bounding up and down getting ready to jump. We left the spot as fast as we could, Adam's bladder problem forgotten.

Beetles! Spiders! By this time we wouldn't have been surprised if a rattler came slithering out of the luggage. Our spirits were somewhat restored by the sight of our first palm tree, then miles and miles of orange groves. There were signs: A Gross Of Oranges For 25¢. We found out later that tons of oranges were being dumped into the sea to keep the price up!

Downtown Los Angeles was disappointing. It looked like the scruffy area below New York's Times Square. Hollywood was better, but there were whole blocks of vacant stores. Beverly Hills was something else again. This was the ambience that I had dreamed about—beautiful homes, trim green lawns, and flowers of every description. I knew that the spotlights hidden in the palm trees made the streets look like a corny stage set at night, but I loved the whole idea.

Since we arrived on a Saturday afternoon, Iwerks Studio was not open, so we looked around for a temporary apartment. We had no trouble finding a room in a very neat court for twenty-five dollars a month, but we resolved to find a house as soon as possible. After living in tenements, the idea of having a whole house to ourselves was dazzling.

I called my friend Al Eugster, and he announced that the Old Guard from Fleischer's studio was throwing me a bash. He did give me directions, but when we started out that night, we had to stop three times to ask for additional instructions.

Finally, we arrived at Eugster's apartment and got a vociferous welcome. Many of the lads were fairly high already. The drinks were served out of a water cooler, straight grain alcohol with a few drops of juniper berry juice. Eugster poured two water glasses full of this concoction. Neither Adam nor I had ever had more than one small drink in our lives, but we didn't want to look unsophisticated, so we each downed a whole glassful in one draft.

We had been driving all night and were completely exhausted, so that slug of alcohol hit us both like a dose of LSD. Within five minutes I was muzzily trying to greet every newcomer with enthusiasm, but the room was spinning around so fast that I couldn't focus. Then nothing.

I awoke because a bright beam of sunlight was streaming in through the partially open door. The floor was littered with clothes. We seem to have begun shedding them at the threshold. As I turned to look at Adam, my brain fell to the bottom of my skull with a dull thud. I had the mother and father of all hangovers.

When I could focus at all, I could blearily see that Adam, too, was stark naked, and his bedclothes were on the floor. We were both lying on mattresses, which had a particularly hideous pattern of roses as big as cabbages.

During our drunken sleep we must have sweated torrents, because the mattresses were sodden. The moisture acted on the rose pattern like decals: we were ornamented from head to foot with a perfect replica of the mattress covers including the bilious green leaves.

In spite of our suffering, Adam and I started to laugh, but suddenly the sunlight was cut off by the landlady. Watching us with cold anger as we frantically groped for the soggy sheets, she advanced to the beds and announced that the mattresses were ruined. I now owed her forty dollars, which I was to produce forthwith.

I hauled myself out of bed, clutching a wet sheet, fumbled through my coat on the floor, and meekly handed over the money. After a terse reminder that we were not to bring any women into her court, she went off in a tight-arsed walk and slammed the door. Suddenly I realized that, except for some small change, I had given the old harpy all of our money.

Another problem . . . what to do about my physical condition? Adam could recover at his leisure, but I had to appear at Iwerks the next morning clear-eyed and alert. Adam got dressed and found his clothes covered his weird color scheme. He soon staggered back from the market with a large cake of ice and a small bottle of aspirin. That left seventy cents.

I spent the rest of the day with the ice cake balanced in a huge bath towel wrapped around my head like a turban. Adam dispensed aspirin at regular intervals, gamely refusing to take any himself because it was a small bottle.

It wasn't until midnight that we had the energy to get to the shower and wash off the roses. Neither of us could remember who drove or how, because we both had total alcoholic amnesia. With a prodigious effort the soggy mattresses were turned over, and we fell into an exhausted sleep.

Youth is a wonderful thing! When I woke up I found that my hangover was gone, although I was a little pale. As I went out to the car I remembered that we had let the oil level drop because I was going to get an oil change and lube job as soon as we arrived. The dipstick registered only about a quarter inch, so willy-nilly I had to part with fifteen cents for a quart of oil. A bad start for the day!

Iwerks Studio was on the second floor of a neat two-story office building in Beverly Hills. The studio did not occupy the entire floor. I passed a dentist and a real estate office before I came to the door marked "Iwerks Studio." I was early; it was only quarter to eight. Studio hours were eight to five. I found out later that all Hollywood studios started work at that ungodly hour.

I tried the door and to my surprise I found that Ub himself was already seated at his desk. He was a slight man with a pallid complexion, a toothbrush mustache, and dark hair. With his slight frame and fine features he didn't look like the Franz Hals' version of a Dutchman.

Ub had a nice smile, but he rarely used it. Normally he had a very still face, with a carefully controlled absence of expression. Iwerks was laconic to an incredible degree. Where two words would barely suffice, he used one.

A brief handshake, a muttered hello, and I found myself being led down the hall into a small room with four animation desks. He vaguely gestured towards one, placed some layout drawings and a typed script in my hand and, with a scarcely audible, "See you later," left the room.

I barely had time to leaf through the drawings (Flip the Frog driving a stagecoach) when Bela Lugosi entered. His green eyes flicked around the room, noting with obvious disapproval that none of the other animators were at their desks. He submitted to my squeezing a limp hand while he introduced himself. He was not Bela Lugosi at all, but an incredible look-alike named Emile Offeman, Pat Powers' watchdog and erstwhile production manager of Iwerks Studio.

Offeman had a curious accent: it was mostly French, but it had some odd Germanic gutterals. He was an Alsatian and, if the rest of his countrymen were anything like him, the French should have demanded at the Treaty of Versailles that the Germans take back Alsace as a punishment for their war crimes.

His English was terrible, but he did manage to stumble through a few banalities; then Godfrey Bjork came in. Just as he was about to introduce himself, Offeman broke in. "Aha my dear Godfrey, it is that you 'ave trouble with your automobile my dear sir?" Godfrey looked warily at him. "No, I didn't."

Offeman pulled out his watch in a significant gesture, but before he spoke Godfrey showed him his watch. "Exactly eight o'clock, Mr. Offeman." Offeman shook his head. "It is that I 'ave two minutes late, my dear Godfrey." Bjork pushed by him and went to his desk. "Better get it fixed, Mr. Offeman, or we'll be going out two minutes early for lunch." Green eyes blinked as Offeman digested this fact.

Before Offeman could continue this duel of wits, Grim Natwick and Al Eugster came in and, in the general hubbub, Offeman slipped away. Then I met Bjork formally and was given a quick rundown on Emile's origins as visualized by Godfrey. According to Bjork, Offeman was the result of the rape of a clapped-up whore by a syphilitic camel.

Godfrey had good reason to hate Offeman heartily. The poor man was suffering from a slowly deteriorating heart condition, which often confined him to his bed. Emile would call him at home several times a day, ostensibly to find out how he was, but in reality to check to see if Godfrey had possibly gone off to the beach or the movies.

Shamus Culhane
in his early
twenties.

The Iwerks Studio animation staff in early 1930. From left to right: Meryl Gilson, unknown, Godfrey Bjork, Jim Pabian, Ben Clopton, Ub Iwerks.

Whether by accident or design, we were all ex-New Yorkers. In the adjoining room were two more animators, Meryl Gilson and Ben Clopton, along with several assistants, all westerners. Grim Natwick was directing the picture, which had been written by Bugs Hardaway, and Ub had drawn the layouts.

Like a cat, I find it uncomfortable to settle down in strange quarters, so I had difficulty with Iwerks' layouts. The stagecoach I was to animate was drawn very meticulously, but I found Flip the Frog to be a singularly ugly character. Also, I was ravenous. To assuage my hunger I drank a lot of water, which made my tripe gurgle like a bad plumbing job.

At noon, I declined offers to go out to lunch and hurried home to the court. I found that Adam had bought a hand of bananas. I rapidly ate six or seven as I discussed the possibility of getting an advance on my salary. After I described Offeman, Adam agreed with me to drop that approach.

In the afternoon, Iwerks came in to see what I was doing. He was disgusted. The stagecoach wheels were drawn in sloppy Fleischer Studio style, thick and uneven. Ub sat down and drew perfect ovals on several wheels, fixed a few Flip drawings, and left with a very discontented look on his face.

I am singularly inept with rulers, compasses, and the like to this day. That afternoon I struggled manfully with those damn wheels until Grim came to my rescue.

A curious thing happened right after lunch. I was introduced to the western group, and the response was far from cordial. It puzzled me because back in New York every effort was made to make a newcomer feel comfortable.

I found out later that the frigid atmosphere was caused by the fact that the assistants had expected one of their number to be promoted to animator. They were furious when they found out that the job had gone to an outsider, especially a New Yorker!

As the days dragged on, Adam and I existed on bananas and water and a few boxes of crackers. By Friday morning we had not one cent, because I had to buy a gallon of gas for fifteen cents. It was difficult to work because I had dizzy spells. Even a penny apple would have helped.

At long last, five o'clock came and brought Offeman out of his lair with the payroll. Nobody was paid by check in those days, so I raced down the stairs clutching the money in my clammy hand. Adam was waiting on the street, looking pale and wan. Without a word we raced to the diner on the corner.

While our steaks were grilling, we wolfed down a loaf of bread apiece. The waitress was beginning to eye us with suspicion, because hungry people were known to go into a restaurant, eat an enormous meal, and then announce that they were penniless.

Adam and I devoured our steaks and French fries, gulped a malted milk apiece, paid the check, went outside, and promptly threw up in the alley next to the diner. We never had a chance to enjoy the feeling of having a full stomach. A little wiser, we went back to the counter and ordered two bowls of chicken soup and some crackers. This stayed down. The reason I put us through this ordeal instead of borrowing money from Grim or Al can be summed up by an equation: Timidity and grandiosity equal stupidity.

The production methods of Fleischer and Iwerks were similar in that they both used a pool of assistants. Animated scenes were sent to the department, and the first available man completed the work. There might be a three-to-four-week interval between the time the animation was finished and the completion of the cleanups.

After about a month I began to get back finished work from the inbetweeners. During that time I had to redraw some key poses that were mysteriously missing. At first I suspected nothing, but as these incidents became more frequent I began to get suspicious, then I thought I was paranoiac. The climax came when I discovered that a large scene was missing from my desk. I finally found it crammed between the radiator and the wall of our room.

I went home and brooded over this slimy treatment. I couldn't see myself whining about the situation to Iwerks or Offeman. By morning I was in a towering rage. When the studio opened in the morning I stood in the assistants' door and announced that I knew full well what had been happening to my work.

Since I didn't know who the culprit or culprits might be, I was going to take them, one each day, to the roof and beat the shit out of them. Whoever wanted to be first should speak up. There was a stunned silence while I glared from one to the other. Finally somebody said lamely that it must have been a joke, another muttered about "just kidding around." Nobody wanted any action, so I stalked off.

This is the only time I have ever heard of sabotage in our business, ever.

Ub must have heard something about the incident because he stopped me in the hall one day. "How's it going?" I looked grim: "Fine." His eyes twinkled. "I figured you'd work things out." He gave a little nod of approval and walked off.

A few months later, the New York contingent was bolstered by the arrival of Bernie Wolf and Arthur Turkisher, both ex-Fleischer employees. Bernie was now a "seasoned" animator with two years' experience, and Turkisher was replacing Carl Stalling as our music composer. Hiring Wolf meant that Iwerks now had the four best Betty Boop animators, but Ub was oddly indifferent to this possible advantage.

On one picture we did design a feeble version of Betty Boop with the addition of a pointed chin. But Ub redrew the arms and legs into hoselike appendages. She had all the sex appeal of a lawn mower. Why he avoided the use of an alluring girl character Ub never did say. Was it some Victorian hang-up? Nobody knows.

For his small studio Ub had acquired too much machinery. In addition to a fully equipped editing room, he had a recording room with the most advanced console and microphones. The animation camera was the latest model. Powers allowed Iwerks to spend all this money, probably for the reason that it put Ub further in debt.

Disney Studio made the headlines when it was announced that Walt's engineers were creating a new multiplane camera at a cost of $50,000. The purpose of the camera was to enable the cameraman to photograph artwork placed on several layers of glass. The effect would be startling, because the animation would actually move in space. Some areas of a scene would be slightly out of focus, as in real life.

Now that his production was in the hands of capable New Yorkers, Ub withdrew more and more into tinkering with his equipment. When he heard the news about Disney's multiplane camera, Ub vanished altogether. Dorothy Webster, the secretary, would only say that he was working in the cellar and did not wish to be disturbed.

He did appear at lunchtime for the usual horseshoe game, which was played along the right of way of the trains that ran behind the studio building. Oddly enough, in contrast to his usual taciturnity, Ub was as merry as a grig, but he refused to answer even the most oblique questions about his mysterious activities in the cellar.

For several weeks he drove up to the studio every morning with the backseat of his bedraggled coupé chockful of gears and bits of steel

Grim Natwick at Iwerks Studio in 1931. *Collection of Bernie Wolf.*

Bernie Wolf at Iwerks Studio in 1932. *Collection of Bernie Wolf.*

shafting. The cameraman, looking very self-important, would help Ub unload, and they would both vanish into the cellar.

One morning Ub appeared in his office and started to work at his desk as if nothing had happened. It was the cameraman who made the announcement, proudly going from room to room with the news. We now had a brand-new multiplane camera, which Ub had built out of parts from an old Chevy that he had bought for $350! The damn thing worked, too.

We had the usual turnover of inbetweeners. They were not under contract, so there was nothing to stop them from leaving at any time. A good inbetweener was, in his own area, almost as valuable as an experienced animator, because a poor draftsman could bring down the quality of the animator's work.

Iwerks once placed an ad for an inbetweener in a local paper. Shortly after that edition was on the streets, he received an answer to the ad. A hoarse voice said, "Mister, ya got a problem about a snatch or somethin', I'm the best inbetweener in town. I know all the mobs and if ya need, like, some muscle, I got some great boys." He couldn't believe that he was talking to the owner of a legitimate business and finally hung up, convinced that he had almost walked into a police trap.

Offeman's secretary, Dorothy, was a marvel. She was so cool and collected that he never tried his Machiavellian tricks on her. On the other hand, even in the relaxed atmosphere of parties she refused to join in the usual diatribes against Offeman and Powers.

A young animator who had worked for Iwerks used to come around after work to pick Dorothy up. Like the rest of us, he did a lot of job-hopping before he ended up at Warner Brothers. His name was Chuck Jones, and he was not yet launched on a career as one of the greatest directors in the business. At that time he was a rather shy youngster and, like the rest of us, very interested in Disney's films.

In the spring of 1933 the country's banking system was in such serious trouble that President Roosevelt declared a bank holiday. This was a welcome change from Hoover's policy of inactivity, but nobody seemed to know when the banks would reopen, and when they did was the money going to be there? Would the dollar still be worth one hundred cents?

Since we were all completely in the dark, the staff worked as usual, although there was no payroll in the offing. One evening I was working a little late, and as I was leaving, Ub stopped me in the hall. He began to talk about the problem of whether the studio should close until the banks opened, or keep on working. I was flattered that Iwerks should ask me for advice, and we got into a very earnest discussion.

As I mentioned earlier, a railroad ran right behind our building, and several times a day heavy freight trains would run by, making the whole building shake slightly. Ub was just lighting a cigarette when we heard a train rumble.

This time it didn't seem to go by. The rumble grew into a horrendous roar. Iwerks dropped his match and took off down the hall. I stood transfixed at his odd behavior. Just as Ub got to the stairs he looked back and yelled, "EARTHQUAKE!" and vanished.

I looked up stupidly. I was standing under a heavy glass skylight, and I could see the frame buckling as the walls of the building began to sway. I was out on the street in two seconds flat.

It was weird. The telephone poles were bowing to each other like old dowagers. The barber from the shop downstairs was running in the street in little circles, waving his razor. His customer, one side of his face still lathered, was following him around, uttering little yelps of hysteria. I didn't blame them. A bank holiday and an earthquake in the same week are a little too much. Nobody from our business was hurt, but I heard the next morning that several people were packing up and going back to New York.

Just about that time I began to have my own misgivings about Hollywood. It was an intellectual desert. In New York, Arthur Turkisher and I used to go to at least one concert a week at Carnegie Hall; weekends I liked to roam around the museums or visit art galleries.

Here you could go to the museum on Sundays and hear your own footsteps clumping down the halls, because there wasn't another soul in sight. As for Hollywood Bowl, it was a bust. There was no enjoyment in listening to poorly played music while the dew seeped through the seat of your pants.

More important was the fact that I began to see that the Iwerks Studio wasn't going anywhere. For a while Ub had been the most prestigious animator in the business. He had designed and animated the first five Mickey Mouse shorts, then he did the same for the first *Silly Symphonies*. He and Walt had made a great team.

On his own, Ub seemed to be colorless. He lacked showmanship. There was only one writer on the staff, Bugs Hardaway. Hardaway and Iwerks were not a good storywriting team. Instead of trying for sequences that would bring out a definite character in Flip, they were content with "good guys and bad guys" scripts. Anyhow, Flip was just too goddamn ugly, which was the basic mistake. Bugs was about thirty-five at the time. He looked as if he had spent his life walking behind a plow, dodging mule droppings. He had a Kansas drawl and the ungrammatical speech of a person who barely got through a one-room schoolhouse. Bugs did have a native wit and did think of some funny situations. His dialogue wasn't funny because he was uneducated. Often it sounded like written speech, and stilted at that. He was better when the characters were silent.

Iwerks by himself was not a good gagman. Because of his interest in machinery, Ub focused on gags around equipment. One time I was working on a scene of an exaggeratedly long automobile with the hood open. Ub had meticulously drawn the motor in a very realistic style, an eight-cylinder job. He came over and looked at his drawing, took it away from me and added about ten more cylinders, chuckling to himself as he drew, then he walked off smiling. It dawned on me . . . whoever heard of a car with eighteen cylinders? An Iwerks joke!

Ub must have realized that Flip was a flop at the box office, so he cooked up a new character, Willie Whopper. Willie was a fat little boy with freckles and, though Natwick designed him, he was an unappealing personality. He was supposed to be a boy Baron Von Munchausen, but that's a premise that wears thin very quickly.

When Bugs went to Warners, Ub made some radical changes in the structure of the studio. In addition to Willie Whopper, he wanted to do a series of fairy tales, so Grim Natwick headed one unit with Bernie Wolf as his wheelhorse, producing Willie Whoppers, and Al Eugster and I worked as co-directors on the fairy tales. Cal Howard, who had been a storyman at Walt Lantz Studio, was hired to work with Grim.

Our new storyman was Otto Englander, an ex-Disney writer. Otto had not been in this country for very long, yet he spoke impeccable English and four other languages besides. He had been raised in Dalmatia, almost starved as a child during World War I, and had just been married by proxy to a bride who was still in Europe. He was quite a change from Bugs!

Otto proved to be a very nice fellow to work with. He, Eugster, and I began to produce such classic tales as *Jack and the Bean-Stalk, The Little*

In an effort to add more personality to the character of Willie Whopper, Grim Natwick redesigned him in 1933. However, the extra avoirdupois did nothing to make Willie more attractive to the movie audience.

Over Emile Offeman's loud protests, Ub Iwerks took the staff to Beverly Hills Park to make this memorable photo in 1933. In the third row is most of the creative group. Second from the left is Irv Spence, then Steve Bosustow, Dick Bickenbach, Charlie Conners, Art Turkisher (standing), Al Eugster, Shamus Culhane, Ub Iwerks, Grim Natwick, Bernie Wolf, Carl Stalling (standing), and, at the end of the row, Norm Blackburn. In the center in a long skirt is Dorothy Webster, Offeman's secretary. Characteristically, Frank Tashlin is in the background, leaning against the pillar on the left.

Red Hen, and *Puss-in-Boots.* While we were working on the script for *The Little Red Hen,* Otto remembered a milkman, Clarence Nash, who had auditioned on a radio show. He might be just the person for the voice of the hen.

Nash came for an audition and proved to be a very shy man who had come from his milk delivery as soon as he could. He admitted that he had no experience, but his friends had urged him to try to get into the movies. With obvious nervousness he read some lines from the script, and the result was hilarious. Nash sounded just like a hen who could speak English.

If Iwerks had been present we would have hired him on the spot, but Ub wasn't coming to the studio until late afternoon. We urged Nash to come back because we were sure that Iwerks would agree to hire him.

In the late afternoon Nash called in and, very apologetically, he explained that our audition and his enthusiastic reception had given him so much confidence that he had gone to Walt Disney's to look for additional work. Walt heard him and hired him immediately on an exclusive contract. He was sorry, but *The Little Red Hen* would have to be done by somebody else.

By coincidence Nash's first job at Disney's was *The Wise Little Hen,* which was the same basic story as our hen picture. He played a duck named Donald and was a smash. Who knows, if we hadn't been so enthusiastic, Clarence Nash might still be a milkman who amused his friends at parties with his funny voice, instead of being Donald Duck's world-famous voice.

When Englander, Eugster, and I wrote the script for *The Brave Tin Soldier,* it was a faithful version of the original story, so it was the first animated cartoon with a sad ending. The tin soldier and his dancer lover did die and go to heaven. Arthur Turkisher even wrote a heartwringing orchestration of "Taps." It was a real tearjerker, and we all loved it.

Pat Powers did not share our appreciation of dramatics. One day Ub came into our room with a terse telegram from the old curmudgeon. The gist of it was "no more unfunny endings." Ub made no comment, but he had a faint smile lurking around the corners of his mouth. Offeman, that humanoid aberration, came in sputtering that "it is outrageous to 'ave made upset our poor Mistair Power."

Otto, Al, and I were far from chastened. Secure in the fact that we all had contracts, we fired off a telegram that said, in effect, if Powers

Puss-in-Boots, written by Otto Englander and co-directed by Al Eugster and Shamus Culhane, was part of the Comicolor series produced by Iwerks Studio in 1934. Culhane designed the model sheet.

Model sheet for *Jack and the Bean-Stalk,* 1933. Drawn by Grim Natwick, Al Eugster, and Shamus Culhane.

knew anything about the picture business, he would have recognized that we had made a superior cartoon. After we sent it, we showed a copy to Ub. He grinned from ear to ear, but as usual, no comment. Powers never replied.

5

The Unholy Three . . . Offeman, Korda, and Gillett

Iwerks never said anything deprecating about Offeman or Powers, but there was no doubt that he heartily disliked them both. There was no doubt either that Offeman had full managerial control over the staff. He exacted his thirty feet a week from every animator, like a Shylock. Anyone who didn't meet the quota was called into Offeman's office the next Monday morning.

When the luckless animator walked in, Emile would use some silly ploy like, "Ah, come in, my dear fellow. Quickly sit down." If the victim elected to stand, Offeman would go on, "But you must sit. It is necessary because no doubt you are gravely ill!" The astonished animator would explain that he was in perfect health.

Then the Alsatian dragon would pounce. "Well, if you 'ave such good condition, perhaps you can explain to my satisfaction why you 'ave animate only twenty-seven feet last week, hein?" Offeman would brush aside such valid excuses as having to animate a series of mob shots. Green eyes blazing, this poor man's Bela Lugosi would scold for an hour.

Godfrey's heart condition became so bad that he often had to rest at his desk after walking up the flight of stairs. Offeman used to follow him in and wait with visible impatience until the poor man got his breath back. Only after Bjork had feebly picked up his pencil would Emile leave.

At last Godfrey's heart became so bad that he was hospitalized. Offeman had the incredible hardheartedness to send him a drawing board, pencils, and paper, and Bjork was cowed enough to try to work. Finally, we heard that he had died.

Grim had bought a huge house in Westwood, and Eugster, Wolf, and

I often went there for one of Grim's fine dinners. He was an excellent cook and knew a great deal about California wines. We would sit around after dinner, drinking sherry while Grim told us yarns about Wisconsin small-town characters and lumberjacks. I remember one time when he was talking about the Indians who had still gathered near Wisconsin Rapids for their powwows when he was a boy. Grim got up and capered a genuine Indian dance around the living room, complete with yelps and grunts.

This particular night when we sat around after dinner, saddened by Godfrey's tragic death, we began to talk about the fact that the animation business was the only part of the movie industry that remained un-unionized. The good Amontillado sherry sparked our indignation, and we decided to form a union.

The next morning we started to call our friends in various studios and found a surprisingly receptive attitude. The first meeting was held in a restaurant and attracted about twenty animators and assistants. We spent the evening listening to stories about poor working conditions and oppressive management.

By the third meeting we had gathered almost a hundred people. None of us had the faintest idea of the legal steps we would have to take, nor had we ever heard of Roberts' "Rules of Order." Grim acted as an informal chairman.

The growing size of the meetings must have made the producers uneasy, because shortly after the last meeting, Grim received a mysterious phone call. The voice jeered at the whole idea of a cartoonists' union. Grim answered that it was going to be more of a social club, but this was brusquely brushed aside. "Ah!" snarled the voice, "Those guys don't need meetings or social clubs. You know as well as I do that all they want at night is a bottle of booze and a good whore." With that he hung up.

The fourth meeting was set up and, by a coincidence, all the studios except Iwerks called for overtime that night. That was the end of our union efforts. No Disney employee had ever attended.

Arthur Turkisher, our musician, used to go to concerts with me in New York. Although I had long since stopped playing my violin, Turkisher, a fine cellist, still played. He was a zany Hungarian, and we were fast friends. We often went to Hollywood Bowl, wincing in sync at the fact that it was impossible to keep dew-drenched strings in tune.

Layout drawing from *Jack and the Bean-Stalk*, designed by Shamus Culhane. 1934.

Model sheet for *Spite Flight*, 1933. Note that the original Willie Whopper is not fat. Designed by Grim Natwick.

One day Turk came to the studio in great excitement. By some Hungarian grapevine he was told that a group of English financiers were looking for a way to start an animation studio that would rival Disney. Alexander Korda and Jeffrey Duveen were the leaders of the investors.

Korda was a famous Hungarian movie director, and Duveen was the brother of Duveen the art dealer. Why couldn't Natwick, Wolf, Eugster, and the two of us start that studio? I mulled it over for a long time, maybe seven seconds, then I agreed. The others also agreed. Arthur wrote to London outlining our various backgrounds. Back came a letter asking us to prepare for a telephone call from London to discuss the details.

When Duveen called, he arranged for me to fly to New York, then catch a ship to Southampton. I would be in London for two weeks. I asked for a leave of absence from the studio, and in a few days I was at the airport.

The last time I had been even near a plane was when I bought a photograph of himself from Lindbergh for a quarter. He was standing in front of *The Spirit of St. Louis,* making a few bucks before taking off the next morning for Paris.

The first leg of my flight was in a very small plane with a three-bladed propeller. It needed the extra blade to get over the Rockies. We started off across the Mojave, flying so low that I could see blossoms on the yuccas. There were ten passengers, no stewardess, no drinks, no intercom.

We didn't really go over the Rockies. We went in between the peaks, a little like a roller-coaster ride. In my ignorance I thought it was fun. When we arrived at Salt Lake I was awed at the size of the plane that was going to make the big hop to New York, a Ford all-metal tri-motor, with the power of a locomotive and a top speed of seventy miles an hour!

The seats were like old-fashioned barber chairs with adjustable neck rests. We made thirteen stops and covered the route in less than twenty hours, counting time spent in various airports eating dry cheese sandwiches and drinking coffee that had to be boiled rabbit turd.

While I was flying I kept worrying about the problem of my face. At twenty-three I looked a good deal younger. In order to counteract this boyish appearance I had grown a straggling mustache for the trip. The effect was not very reassuring. I looked like a choir boy who had just turned pimp.

We landed in New York without incident, and I spent the next five days on the S.S. *Manhattan* attempting to dodge an old man who was trying to entice me to take a side trip to Paris. The gaffer wanted to give me a free trip through the bordellos of Montmartre—free that is, if he could watch. Eating and dodging kept me busy until we reached Southampton.

After a long ride in the boat train to London, I arrived at the Savoy Hotel at three in the morning with a bad case of time lag. I was dimly aware that the foyer was very luxurious. The hotel also housed some exotic people. As I turned away from the desk to go to my room, I was face to face with a haughty maharaja, complete with turban, a silk costume, and jewelry. Behind him were half a dozen women draped in magnificent saris . . . right out of Arabian Nights!

Jesus! I thought. I wonder what they would say if they knew I was raised in a twenty-five-dollar-a-month tenement. They'd probably throw me out. I staggered after the bellboy who was carrying my cheap suitcase as if it were a dead cat. Even after a five-buck tip he was still showing an insolent eyetooth as he closed the door. Well, one street kid recognizes another. Fuck him. I slept.

The next morning I was awakened by a phone call from Jeffrey Duveen. He gave me a cheery, if adenoidal good morning. He would see me at breakfast. While I shaved, I examined my face, scowling and jutting out my chin. It was no use. I still looked about nineteen years old.

I was just downing my orange juice, which came in what looked like a shot glass, when Duveen arrived. He came right up to my table and introduced himself. I suppose that I looked startled, because he explained that he had come early to the Savoy and had looked in on me sleeping. Christ! My sister always said that when I was sleeping I looked like a Kewpie doll!

I gulped and decided to fire the first shot. "I guess you are surprised to see how young I am." Duveen nodded. "Well, I am just six years younger than Walt Disney." Duveen smiled. A blunt man himself, he liked my directness. From then on, we were very easy and informal.

He supposed that, since this was my first trip, I'd like to do a little sightseeing before we settled down to business. I shook my head. Business first, sightseeing, if any, later. This raised me a couple more points in his esteem.

We went to my room and began juggling some very perplexing figures. I knew what the wages were in the United States, but what were comparable salaries in England? By finding out what shopgirls were paid in London, it was fairly easy to arrive at a suitable wage for inkers and painters.

From there it was possible to compute the salaries for animators and assistants, English animators, that is. Our group would receive the equivalent of Hollywood wages. Duveen's eyebrows went up at the difference, but he was game. It took me three exhausting days to arrive at all the salaries and incidental expenses, like lab work, sound recording, and cutting. A lot of this information was arrived at by long telephone calls, and I often had difficulty with Cockney and other dialects.

Then Duveen generously invited me to a weekend at his country house near Croyden. Promptly at ten the next morning I was picked up by a chauffeur in a gleaming black Daimler and driven through the most beautiful countryside I had ever seen. We whizzed through little villages with thatched-roof cottages, sped down narrow roads enclosed by ten-foot hedges, and always on the wrong side of the road.

Duveen's house looked like a movie set, and the inside was to match. There were about twenty guests, all thin, elegant, and tweedy. Thank God I had a tuxedo, because we did dress for dinner. Before dinner we all assembled in the great hall for cocktails. Everybody was very composed and engaged in skillful chitchat, an art I haven't acquired yet, so I felt like a duck among swans. While I wasn't aware of it, I must have cut a glamorous figure . . . an American moviemaker from Hollywood!

The dining table easily accommodated twenty people. There were ten servants in livery, standing behind us serving the food, and the array of utensils at each plate would have puzzled a brain surgeon.

I was at Duveen's left, and at one point he asked me how long it took to go from New York to Hollywood by train. When I replied that I didn't know because I always went in my car, he asked how many miles it was. When I told him three thousand, Duveen almost fell off his chair. He picked up a spoon and rapped a glass for attention. "Everybody! Listen to this for an adventure. This young man has driven three thousand miles from New York to Hollywood!"

Then they all plied me with questions about the Rockies and the desert. Finally, one very old lady looked at me through her lorgnette. "Tell me, sir, did you have any trouble with the Indians?" I answered that I hadn't and kept a straight face because nobody seemed to think that the question was funny.

Monday, Duveen and I were driven to Shepherd's Bush in what must have been his everyday car, a Rolls-Royce. I was carrying a bulky bundle of papers with my cost breakdown. Alexander Korda was directing a shot with Douglas Fairbanks, and I was surprised to see how small the famous star really was.

Finally, they wrapped up the shot and Fairbanks and Korda came over to be introduced. Fairbanks had a very engaging smile and beautiful teeth, but Korda was looking at me with a beady eye. The other three investors arrived and, to my disappointment, Fairbanks left. I thought he was in on the deal.

Korda took over the meeting as easily as a snake swallows an egg. He went into a pompous and self-satisfied spiel about the important step he had taken in starting the first English animation studio. Korda had signed up the most important cartoonists in the country. He rattled off a list of names that I didn't recognize, except for Bateman.

If the others were as good as Bateman, they were the crème de la crème of English cartoonists. But what we were really going to need as a start was a group of youngsters to learn how to be good assistants for the American group.

Instead of giving him the approval he obviously expected, I told Korda quite bluntly that he had wasted his money. Normally, I would have been reluctant to argue with a total stranger, and a celebrity at that. But Korda looked just like the headwaiter in a Hungarian restaurant on Seventy-ninth Street in Yorkville, so I was not overawed.

Why is it that when a person is outstanding in one field he feels that, *ipso facto,* he is an expert in another. Korda had this failing to a spectacular degree. I was just a pipsqueak kid. Who was I to have the temerity to correct a great director? Nevertheless, I doggedly continued to correct him every time he opened his mouth. Korda was a well of misinformation.

Fortunately he had to go back to the set just before the exchanges became openly insulting. During the next week we had three meetings, each more stormy than the other. Korda wanted to give the Americans three-year contracts at lesser salaries than we were making in Hollywood, and insisted that he would have to be the producer, with all the power and control that went with the job. The errand boy at Iwerks knew more about the technology of animation than did Korda, so I was just as adamant about my being the producer.

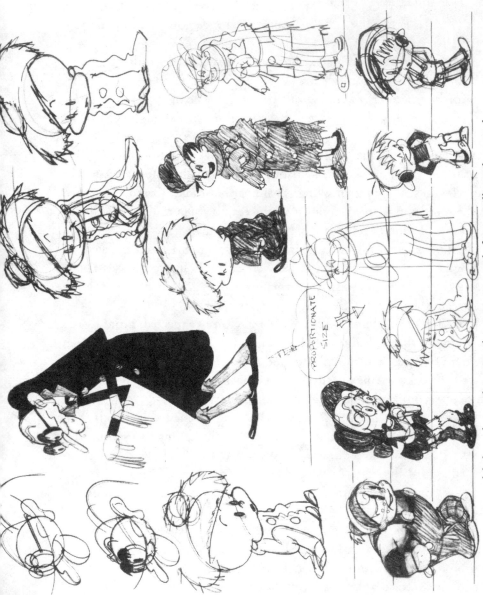

A model sheet designed in 1934 by Grim Natwick for a Willie Whopper short, *Reducing Creme.*

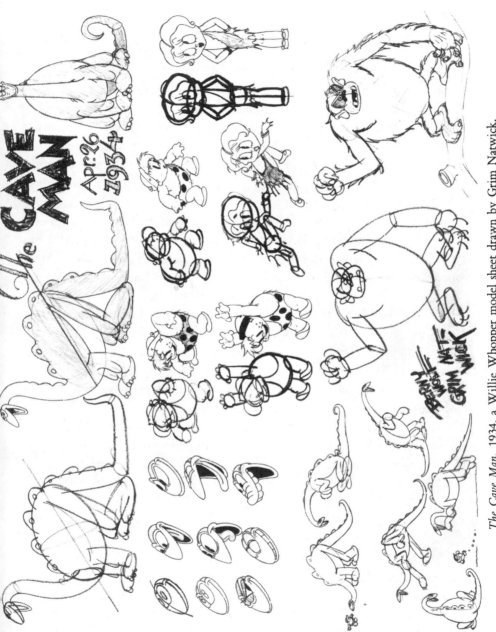

The Cave Man, 1934, a Willie Whopper model sheet drawn by Grim Natwick.

I just kept the image of Korda as a Hungarian headwaiter who was trying to give us a table between the men's room and the cutlery trays. I think the investors did begin to realize that Korda's statements were a mixture of chutzpa and ignorance, because they made no move to back him up, but they didn't side with me either. Finally, I announced that I was leaving for Hollywood in two days, and I rejected every one of Korda's proposals. He refused to back down.

Our parting was less than cordial. Korda stood there glowering as I pointedly omitted shaking hands with him. On the way back to London, Duveen was smiling, then he burst into a guffaw and patted my knee. "Of course, you were perfectly right," he chuckled. "Never thought much of that Korda chap. Too big a head rather." I muttered something about it being a Pyrrhic victory.

Duveen ruefully admitted that our business venture had cost him more than a thousand pounds, but he stoutly maintained that the contest with Korda had been worth it. He bade me a very warm farewell, and invited me to come for a weekend the next time I was in London. I agreed to do that. I did not see England again for another thirty-four years. During the war I wondered if Duveen's beautiful country house survived the bombing. Since it was near Croyden airport, I doubt it.

Back at Iwerks the boys were disappointed but philosophical. I wasn't. I felt that if I had gone there with bags under my eyes and a middle-aged paunch we might have made a deal. In a way it was the Popeye debacle all over again. Maybe I should have grown a beard.

My two-year contract with Iwerks was almost at its end when I heard about a job in New York that seemed almost too good to be true. Burt Gillett, the director of Disney's *The Three Little Pigs,* had left the studio and gone to work as head of the Van Beuren Studio in New York, and was looking for another director.

I wired Gillett asking for the job and in two hours recieved a reply . . . a two-year contract starting at $175 a week, $200 the second year. A few weeks later I was driving back to New York, eager for the familiar sights and sounds of the metropolis. To hell with the palm trees and geraniums!

A few months after I left, Iwerks lost his studio. We all knew it was coming. Iwerks then went through several years of financial hardship. Eventually, Disney rehired him as his technical advisor and inventor. Ub lived out the rest of his life at the studio, and before he died was honored by the movie industry as the greatest inventor and special effects designer in the business.

Fortunately for the animation business, Pat Powers was never able to attract another animator into his web. As for Emile Offeman, he probably went on to a well-paying job with the Spanish Inquisition.

As I drove toward New York I tried to assemble the few facts I knew about Amedeé Van Beuren and Burt Gillett. Van Beuren had grown wealthy working on the fringes of the entertainment business. At one time he had a virtual monopoly on the rental of peep-show machines in penny arcades. When he bought the old Fables Studio, he changed its name to Van Beuren Animation Studio. That was about the only change he made, because he continued to turn out the same kind of low-grade films that characterized Aesop's Fables even before the advent of sound.

Burt Gillett's career went back to Hearst's International Studios, where he was considered to be one of the best animators on the staff. When the studio closed in 1921, Burt drifted around the business and finally went to the coast to animate on Walt Disney's early sound cartoons.

Walt was directing all these pictures, but the pressure of his increasing output made it necessary to siphon off some of his work to other people, so he created a new job. Burt Gillett was the first full-time layout man in the business.

Heretofore, the animators always drew their own layouts, and decided on the size and composition of the characters in their scenes, without much attention to the approach that was being used by the animators who were working on adjoining sequences.

By having one man drawing layouts and positioning characters, the result was a more cohesive approach. Now Walt could see what the whole picture was going to look like before he gave out work to the animators.

By 1929 the complexities of running the studio made it impossible for Disney to direct all the pictures. He took the next step and appointed both Burt Gillett and another animator, Wilfred Jackson, full-time directors.

Each man was given his own room, where he could concentrate on the many problems that sound had created. A great deal of time had to be devoted to the music. Each sequence had to be given a suitable tempo, and this meant long hours of work with a music composer.

Freed from the necessity to help to write stories, draw layouts, design characters, and even animate key scenes, as the rest of the so-called directors were still doing in all the other studios, Jackson and Gillett could focus on the more abstract aspects of filmmaking.

Like the conductor of an orchestra, the director could now supervise writers, character designers, layout men, animators, and background painters, seeing to it that each member of the team was following a definite plan. This meant, for better or worse, that each individual's talents were subordinated to the creative interpretation of the director, a far cry from the hodgepodge approach that all the other studios saw as the function of a director.

Gillett proved to be a brilliant director, and the apogee of his career was probably the most popular short cartoon of all time, *The Three Little Pigs*. The film appeared in 1933, when the Depression was at its worst. The psychological implications of foiling the Wolf at the door struck the public's fancy, so in effect "Who's Afraid of the Big Bad Wolf?" became a kind of marching song for the country.

Several years before, Pat Powers had lured Ub Iwerks away from Disney, because he was sure that he was taking away Walt's right-hand man. Van Beuren had the same idea. He desperately needed to improve the quality of his cartoons. It was either that or close the shop, so he hired Gillett as the epitome of quality.

It looked like a smart move. I had never met Gillett, but the people I knew who had worked with him said that Burt was a genius second only to Walt. I was elated to be given the opportunity to learn from a master. While Eugster and I had directed films that compared favorably with the rest of the field, I knew very well that we had never even approached the finesse and expertise of the Disney directors.

When I walked into Van Beuren Studio I didn't recognize one familiar face. In spite of the fact that Fleischer Studio was right across the street, the two groups did little or no socializing.

Burt Gillett was very cordial, and we had an enthusiastic discussion about my role in the studio and the future success of the company. At the outset of our talk Burt had opened the bottom drawer of his desk, and I saw to my surprise that it was stocked with small liquor bottles and packages of hard candy. I declined the offer of a drink (at ten in the morning!) and settled for a hard candy. So did Burt. We sat with our cheeks bulging and our words somewhat garbled by the candy.

Gillett was a bullet-headed man with a huge neck and a powerful frame. He had a speech pattern that was unusual in that his words would come out with machine-gun rapidity, then there would be a sudden stoppage, not always where one expected a natural pause. Then it would suddenly resume at breakneck speed. He never seemed to finish a thought, but skipped from one subject to the next, as a more compelling thought struck him.

What had started out as a conversation ended up a long, enthusiastic peroration, which made Pericles' speech about the war with Sparta sound like poor stuff. I was mesmerized, and by the end of the discussion Gillett had a devoted follower.

Then we went around the various departments of the studio, and I met the staff. Tom Palmer, a pedantic-looking fellow, was the other director. He had worked on the coast with Gillett, and they were good friends, too good, as it later developed.

I also met my writer, Ray Kelly, and Jim Tyer, another storyman. The music composer was Win Sharples, who had been a musician with big bands and was just getting used to the idea that he was going to stay in one place more than one night.

In terms of East Coast expertise, the animation staff was more than adequate. Two of the animators were inseparable, George Rufle, a huge, easygoing bear of a man, and Frank Amon, a pint-sized fellow who wore a very obvious toupee. It had a part in the middle and he wore it somewhat askew, like a hat cocked at a rakish angle. Rufle and Amon were pioneers who had first worked in the business for Barré, Bowers, and Hearst.

Bill Littlejohn followed the Robin Hood tradition by being well over six feet tall. He was already recognized as one of the top animators in New York. Jack Zander, a youngster who had better than average talent, had been aptly named "The Deacon" by Ray Kelly. Zander was the best deadpan comic in the studio, with a dry-as-dust delivery.

Pete Burness, still in his twenties, was the only well-dressed animator in the studio. Most of the staff could have been mistaken for taxi drivers or stevedores, but Pete had savoir faire as well, and later distinguished himself as a UPA director. George Stallings, another veteran of the early days of animation, completed the staff of animators. There was enough talent in the group to make pictures incomparably better than the lackluster product that the studio had been making. Under Gillett's supervision there was the potential of a really good East Coast studio.

I wasted no time in getting down to work with Ray Kelly. We hit it off immediately. Ray looked like the stereotype of all thin Irishmen, rust-colored hair, a huge nose with ears to match, and a wide mouth with a clutter of horse-sized teeth.

Still under the spell of Gillett's oratory, I was chatting away enthusiastically about the probable success of the studio. I noticed a puzzling lack of response. Kelly was looking at me warily, and his answers were becoming more and more laconic. I soon found out why . . . in the men's room as usual!

About midafternoon I was in there unloading my kidneys, when Gillett came in and stood at the next stall. While he fumbled himself loose he looked around, even peering under the doors of the cubicles to see if anyone was attempting more serious business.

Satisfied that we were alone, Burt leaned over to me in a conspiratorial manner and asked, "What have they been saying about me?" I almost dropped my whatever in surprise. His eyes narrowed. "What are they saying . . . huh . . . huh?" His eyes flashed suspiciously at me because I didn't answer. What should I say? I finally mumbled something about not knowing who or what he was talking about. His face flushed. "I know they're talking about me, and I want a full report every day. I know they won't talk in front of Tom [he meant Tom Palmer], so I want you to get the details."

Sometimes I have a short fuse (no sexual connotation intended) and this was one of the times. I told Gillett very icily that I was hired to direct pictures, not run a gossip column. We must have looked very funny, standing at the urinal glaring at each other, so Gillett stalked out of the john, leaving me wondering just what kind of a mess I had walked into.

When I returned to my office, I gave Ray Kelly a very restrained version of the encounter. When Ray saw that I was seething with anger, he knew I was going to be on the side of the Good Guys, so he gave me a full account of the weird happenings since Gillett had taken charge.

The studio was in a constant state of tumult. People were being hired and fired, seemingly at random. Whole departments were being shifted aimlessly from one area to another. Pictures were being started, then stopped for no apparent reason.

Jim Tyer dropped in, and when he heard the gist of our conversation, he supplied some pithy comments of his own. Win Sharples happened to come in, and I heard stories about music enthusiastically accepted in

Ray Kelly, drawn by
Shamus Culhane,
1935.

Part of the storyboard for *The Merry Kittens,* drawn by Shamus Culhane in 1935.
Ray Kelly and Culhane wrote the script.

the morning and then discarded in the afternoon. Entire sound tracks were being re-done, which meant calling back actors, retyping scripts, redrawing storyboards, even junking finished animation.

What worried the staff was the fact that with all these changes, very few pictures were being produced. Oddly enough, it didn't seem to bother Gillett, and it should have bothered him a great deal, because we had a large staff with an enormous payroll.

That night I tried to digest all this grousing. I decided that it was in the nature of the business for people to resent new modes of working, especially with the obvious need for changes in the staff. While there might be a grain of truth here and there, most of it must have been gross exaggeration, but I could not ignore the implications of my odd encounter with Gillett.

The next day Kelly and I created several story outlines. When we were satisfied that we had good material, we went in to talk them over with Gillett. Burt was in a good mood, rolled out the candy, and listened with great interest to Ray's spiel. After each synopsis Burt would think of additional business and act out the situation with great enthusiasm. What he said made a lot of sense, and I began to relax.

At the end of several hours Gillett announced that all the ideas were good and it was difficult to make a choice. He'd have to think about them overnight. When we got back to the office Ray was beaming and said that I was going to be a good influence on Gillett. I didn't discount the possibility. It had been a hell of a good meeting.

Right after the studio opened the next morning, we sat down with Burt, smiling and confident. Burt did better than that. He was chortling so much that it was hard to strain his words through his candy. He had given the matter a great deal of thought and had come up with an even better idea. Drop those ideas and work on this . . . he got up and started to caper around the room as he told us a new story line. He was obviously making it up as he acted out each character with what seemed to be excessive energy.

At one point he jumped and landed on his arse on the desk. The glass cracked into a dozen pieces, but Burt ignored the incident. Finally, after coming to a panting halt, he assured us that he had just given us a "cracker-jack" story idea.

Kelly and I went back to our haven and gloomily assayed the situation. Neither of us had taken any notes! When we tried to remember what Burt had said, the basic idea didn't seem all that funny. Grimly we fell to work, and in a few days we had what seemed to be a reasonable facsimile of what Burt had done, minus, of course, the calisthenics.

Back we went to Gillett, and this time the air was far from friendly. He hated the story. He hated the *whole* story! When we tried to point out that it was his own brainchild, Burt brushed that aside and waved us out impatiently.

During the next few weeks we struggled all day, and I took to working far into the night, writing new story outlines. We must have come up with a round dozen ideas, all rejected. Finally, when we had one that Burt liked, he announced that this was just the kind of story Tom Palmer was best able to direct, so he gave it to his friend and boon companion, leaving us back on square one. According to Jim Tyer, who had to work with Palmer, he was about as funny as an undertaker's bill, which is probably why Gillett came to his rescue.

Just when Ray and I were in the last stages of mental fatigue, I thought up the idea of a story about three kittens and a wirehaired fox terrier. I worked all night, and the next morning I brought in drawings of a wooden-legged dog and three sickly-sweet kittens. Burt loved them, and this time we did go forward with a picture. In fact we made two, *The Foxy Terrier* and *The Merry Kittens*.

They were cute to the point of being vomitous. Burt had added a half-dozen sticky touches of his own. He was confident that we were following the Disney tradition, but Kelly and I hated the whole saccharin approach.

I noticed that after lunch every day Ray read a prayer book for a few minutes. I put it down as one more eccentricity in a studio full of eccentrics. If he was praying for some kind of order to take place, it didn't work.

Several years later, Kelly left the Disney story department and vanished. Nobody seemed to know where he had gone. When he surfaced again, Ray had become a Jesuit. He must have made a hell of a good priest, because he was one of the most witty and intelligent men I have ever known.

Gillett continued to order new partitions built and departments shifted. From time to time, he would call the staff together to discuss new story ideas. By now his overly enthusiastic capers, as he acted out the roles of his characters, left us all frozen-faced. We knew that whatever he was triumphantly acting would never hit the screen.

As a director I learned absolutely nothing from Gillett, except how to

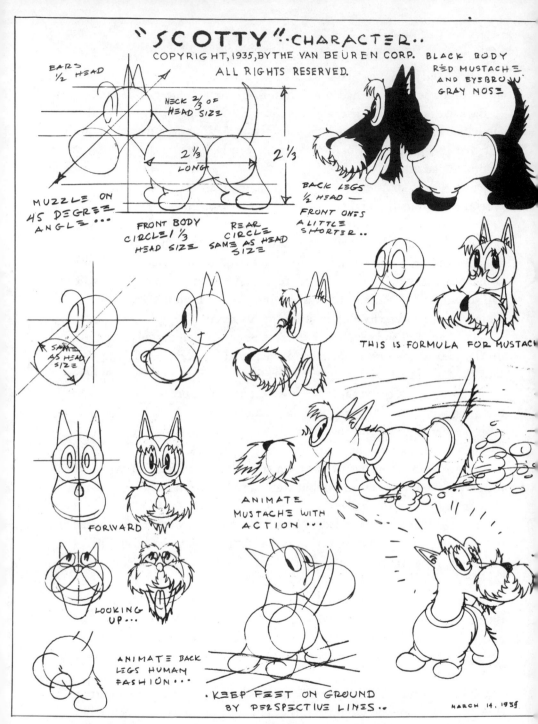

This model sheet designed by Shamus Culhane for *The Merry Kittens* still shows the East Coast traditional approach to figure construction, i.e., circles, which do not in reality comprise the form as indicated. Note the figure on the upper left. Obviously the body is not made up of two circles; it is an oblong larger at one end than the other.

Model sheet for *The Foxy Terrier*. Designed by Shamus Culhane, 1935.

dodge him in the hall. Whatever principles of directing he had used to become such a success he kept to himself. I began to wish that I had stayed in Hollywood.

In the 1930s the only foreign animation any of us had ever seen was George Pal's puppets. He was a Hungarian filmmaker whose stop-motion puppets were entertaining enough to obtain an MGM release.

The pictures did not look foreign, in that Pal never attempted to use ethnic story material or show any Hungarian influence in the design of the puppets or the sets.

When Gillett announced that we were going to see a French animated cartoon, we went into the projection room in a state of excitement. The picture was *Joie de Vivre,* by Hector Hoppin and Anthony Gross. Gillett was fooled by the French title. The cartoon was made by Hoppin, an American, and Gross, an Englishman. We all found the film appallingly crude because it was the first time we had ever seen stylized animation. We had no idea that we were looking at a technique that would become popular ten years later in the work of Chuck Jones at Warner Brothers Studio, and later at UPA. Not only was the drawing style completely unacceptable but the wit was not funny to our unsophisticated minds. Everybody agreed that the picture was a dud and posed no competition to American animation.

We were a typical group of people in the East Coast part of the animation profession. I doubt that more than two or three of us had attempted any fine art, and certainly none of us knew anything about modern art. We were contemptuous of the seemingly crude animation in the *Joie de Vivre* film and we would have been horrified at the suggestion that freaks like Picasso, Braque, and Matisse might some day influence the appearance of animation. We all filed back to work, serene in the knowledge that foreign animators were light years behind us.

That was Gillett's only attempt to educate his staff. We all went to see Disney's newest cartoons as a matter of course, but it never occurred to any of us to ask Burt to talk about the mechanics of making a Disney film. At this time Burt was too formidable. He had long bouts of ill temper, looking at us with brooding eyes, then suddenly he would become so happily frenetic that it was embarrassing to watch.

The winter of 1934–35 was very severe. Often as I trudged through the mush of blackened snow, generously bedecked with orange skins and dog shit, Hollywood, with its sunshine, palm trees, and flowers, seemed like paradise in comparison. We had a studio Xmas party that year. It was the wildest, most drunken brannigan I ever saw. Rotgut whiskey seemed to release all the nervous tension that had been building up for months.

Several more months went by, and the tempo of the hiring and firing picked up. Burt, conscious of the unease of his staff, would call a meeting and assure everybody that he had finally weeded out the malcontents and unfit. A day or two later the tumbrels would start rolling again.

Sharples, Kelly, Zander, and I took to having meetings after work at the Metropole Bar, a few doors away from the studio. Fortified by ten-cent beer and five-cent hard-boiled eggs, we would discuss the situation at great length. What could we do about our Captain Bligh?

Gradually, we began to entertain the idea that Gillett was unbalanced. At first it was more of a joke, but finally, as we reviewed his irrationality, we became convinced that he was insane.

One day in April, Gillett announced very abruptly that Mr. Van Beuren and his accountant were coming in for a full-scale examination of our situation, and the whole staff was going to be gathered to hear the discussion. Van Beuren had never visited us during the months I had worked in the studio. There was a rumor that the old man had suffered a stroke.

The Metropole cabal spent long hours discussing this opportunity to acquaint Van Beuren with some harsh truths. We wondered how Burt was going to explain why the output had dwindled to a pitifully few pictures. We ended up with no plan of action.

When Van Beuren did arrive he was in a wheelchair, trundled by a very cold-faced accountant. Van Beuren was a tiny man, very emaciated and ravaged-looking. Gillett was in a jovial mood and immediately took charge of the meeting.

Beaming with confidence, he started a long, detailed review of the pictures that had been finished, extolling the quality and humor of each subject; then he went on to enumerate the films in production, assuring Van Beuren that they would be even better as the staff reached for higher and higher standards.

He pictured us as a group of dedicated artists who were happily working with the knowledge that we were forging ahead of all the other studios in the business. Poor Van Beuren started to brighten as Burt enlivened his monologue with little quips. Even the frozen face of the accountant began to soften.

Then the incredible happened! Without a pause in his spiel, Gillett began to talk about other pictures in production, pictures we had never heard of! He rattled off a list of films I was supposed to be working on, turning to me for confirmation.

I just stood there with my mouth agape. My mind was in a whirl. Was this the time to unmask the whole charade? Before I could make a decision, Burt finished talking and Van Beuren started a faltering statement. He mentioned the enormous sums that had been poured into the studio with evident pain, but then he went on to say that he was behind Gillett a thousand percent, and Burt was behind us a hundred percent. The irony of the mistake in arithmetic was not lost on the group.

Before any of us could speak up, the accountant had started to wheel the old man towards the elevator, and the opportunity was lost. We drifted back to our desks in silence. What the hell should we do now? Kelly and I had no time to discuss it, because I was called on the intercom to report to Gillett's office.

When I entered, I saw that Burt's happy expression was gone. He sat with his face flushed a bright red, lips compressed. His eyes flashed with barely restrained fury. "Why didn't you back me up?" he grated. "Back up what?" I shot back. "You know damn well what I mean, you should have backed me up."

"If you mean all that shit about the new pictures I was supposed to be working on, I'd never do it." Gillett bunched his muscles in a half-crouch. "Why not?" His lips curled back in a snarl. I began to get frightened, but I stuck to my guns. "Because every goddamn word of it was a lie!"

Gillett's eyes started to roam around his cluttered desk. Right in front of him was a six-inch spindle, which he picked up like a stiletto. "You calling me a liar?" He started to get up. Without answering, I ran out of the room in a panic.

I rushed into my office and, while a startled Kelly watched, plucked up my personal effects, shrugged into my coat, and started to leave. All this time I was giving him a disjointed, almost hysterical account of Gillett's behavior. I expected the madman to fling the door open and come after me with that damn spindle any minute. I told Kelly that Gillett was not only insane, he was dangerous, and I left before he could say a word.

Van Beuren's office was just a few blocks away. When I saw the manager and started to blurt out an account of my confrontation with

Gillett he held out a restraining hand. "Just a minute, I don't want to hear any more. We don't need malcontents like you. Just leave and we'll mail you a check." I walked out baffled.

One has to appreciate the naïveté of the general public in the 1930s. People did glibly rattle off phrases like "inferiority complex," but compared to the current-day acceptance of the possibility of mental illness, we knew nothing. In spite of his irrational behavior, none of us realized just how sick Gillett was. Nobody in the Metropole cabal had ever seen an insane person, which was why we were so reluctant to act.

Poor Burt was obviously a manic depressive, and these days would probably have used some controlling drug like Lithium. As it was, he did become violent a few months later, and was in an institution for many years. The studio collapsed, and Van Beuren died shortly after.

As for me, I set off for Hollywood the next morning with the fervent hope that I would never see New York again. I was well aware that the rest of the business was lagging far behind the Disney Studio. Since Gillett had been unable to give me an education in Disney's methods of filmmaking, I was determined to go to the source.

6

The Disney Novices

I burned up the roads between New York and Hollywood in a high state of euphoria. Here I was at twenty-six a hot-shot director and animator, driving a brand-new Studebaker roadster, and jingling four hundred dollars in my pocket. Not only that, I was on my way to the Mecca of the animation business. In a very short time I'd be working with the most famous artists in the business.

I had heard through the grapevine that Disney was hiring many veteran animators from other studios. I hadn't called Walt before leaving New York because I wanted this, my third trip across country, to be a leisurely sightseeing tour. Not all the sights were reassuring.

The world had been suffering from the Depression for almost six years, and there was no evidence that it was abating. Every small town had its milling crowd of unemployed men in shabby overalls and battered hats. They leaned against scabrous walls or squatted next to the boarded-up windows of vacant stores.

In comparison, I was wealthy. Four hundred dollars may not seem like much money these days, but in 1935 it was a good-sized sum. Gas was twelve cents a gallon, hotels cost three dollars a night, and food was cheap.

In Arizona I had eaten in a respectable-looking restaurant. About half the dining area had been closed down. There was one morose waitress who served me a very good meal, which consisted of pork chops, French fries, salad, and coffee, for a quarter.

I had dawdled for two weeks on the road, enjoying the sights and effectively delaying the thing I dreaded most: the job interview. I spoke with a bad stammer when rattled, and for all my bravado, I was actually quite timid, and interviews were always a torment. It took me some time after I had checked into my hotel to summon the courage to call the studio. When I did, I spoke to Walt's secretary, and after a short pause, she returned to the phone with the message that Walt would see me the next morning, at nine.

Hollywood has been laid out by real estate developers with a blithe disdain for the advantages of the Roman grid. In the two years that I had lived there I never managed to learn my way around Hollywood, perhaps because I have about as much sense of direction as an antelope with his arse on fire. It was quite an achievement that I only lost my way three times before finally arriving at Hyperion Avenue, and the Disney Studio.

Dolores Voght, Disney's secretary, was a very brisk, pleasant woman of about thirty who smiled reassuringly, remembered my appointment, and brought me an ashtray. I appreciated that; I was so tense that I smoked three cigarettes in the fifteen minutes I waited. Finally, the buzzer sounded and Miss Voght indicated that I could go into Walt's office. I jumped up so abruptly that I spilled ashes all over my lap.

Walt's office was far from ostentatious: a few easy chairs, some framed awards on the walls, and a very plain desk. There were none of the usual Hollywood big-shot fripperies, such as the knee-deep carpets, damask drapes, or marble ashtrays as big as bathtubs.

Being an animator makes one acutely aware of the way that people move. I noted that Walt got up from his chair with exceptional grace. Even though I'd seen pictures of him, I think I still expected to find a tough, cigar-smoking tycoon, but here he was, one of the most famous men in the world, yet his manner was friendly and casual. One might even pass him by in a crowd with indifference because there was nothing in his appearance to hint at that steel-trap mind, tremendous energy, or remarkable abilities as a leader. He looked like just a nice, young American man, good-looking, but in a healthy rather than a handsome way. He was unsophisticated and not concerned about it.

We shook hands, and while it must have been obvious from my wet palm that I was nervous, Walt made no attempt to relax me with chitchat. We got right down to business: what had I been doing? I stumbled through a garbled litany of jobs, Bray, Krazy Kat, Max Fleischer, Iwerks, and Van Beuren. I told the tale of my rise from errand boy to director in eight years. Walt listened, puffing a cigarette with his eyes half-closed, and once I finished he became alert.

"You directed *Jack and the Bean-Stalk* at Iwerks?" I explained that Al

Eugster and I had worked as co-directors on that and other pictures. "Who animated the scene where the giant lights his pipe?"

"Why, I did," I gasped in surprise.

"That's what I'd heard," Walt said, laconically. "I liked it."

Now I began to relax. Here's where we would start talking about money. I had been making a salary of $175 a week at Van Beuren's, so there seemed no reason I should get less at Disney's. Maybe, I'd get more, maybe $200. While I hadn't had a chance to talk to them, I knew that Walt had just hired Bernie Wolf, Al Eugster, and Grim Natwick a few weeks before, so I looked forward to a fat salary as well as the chance to work with my old friends.

"Let me give you the situation," Walt began, reaching for another cigarette. "We've just hired three or four fellows from New York, and most of them are bringing a lot of goddamn poor working habits from doing cheap pictures. I've decided to take in more kids right out of school and train them my way. It's a lot easier than trying to retrain somebody who's used to doing crap. In fact, we have a batch of about twenty kids coming in next week. We'll run them through art school and they'll have a good start right off the bat with nothing to unlearn."

He looked sympathetic, but stood up. "Thanks for coming in anyway. Maybe some other time . . ."

Jesus Christ! The interview was over! I couldn't believe it! Desperately, I blurted out, "Listen Walt, I really want to work here. I don't care about the money, I want to learn." Walt shook his head and began to look a little impatient. Then I had a reckless idea. "How about letting me come in with those kids?" Now he was looking at me quizzically. "Those kids are going to get fifty bucks a week," he said. I didn't stop to figure the arithmetic. "I'll take it!" Walt was astounded. "I'll be a son of a bitch," he said, then smiled. "You sure as hell want in." I nodded, speechless. He shrugged, then stuck out his hand, "All right, let's give it a try. Report to the inbetween department on Monday. See George Drake."

On the way back to the hotel, the full import of my rashness was beginning to hit me; I had my wife, my mother, and my mother-in-law to support. It was true that fifty dollars would be ample for two people, but four were going to be a strain. None of them had any skills, so looking for jobs would have been a waste of time. We would just have to make do until I could earn more money.

When I broke the news to them, there were no wild whoops of laughter or back slapping, but one look at my face made them all decide not to bother with any complaining. In a few hours we had found suitable quarters for everybody and I could now look forward to my new job with some equanimity, but not much.

Monday morning I reported for work, and found myself in the middle of a gaggle of excited, chattering youngsters, most of them five or six years younger than I. I must have looked pretty sour and formidable, because nobody talked to me, while they plied each other with questions.

I overheard enough to gather that most of them had been to college, the group being about equally divided between U.S.C. and Stanford. When I remembered that most of my peers in New York went to work as soon as they could get working papers, I became even more sour.

Another aspect of the group that was different was the fact that they all seemed to have had years of art school, some as much as five years. It was enough to make a lesser man drown in self-pity. I didn't drown, but I certainly wallowed.

George Drake, head of the inbetween department, gave us a brief talk about our duties and some details about the work. Disney had refined the whole structure of work allocation. He had set up teams: an animator, his assistant animator, and an inbetweener. They all worked in the same room, so that the animator could constantly supervise the others. That way he was available to answer questions, make corrections, and even explain some facets of his work—how he had solved some particular problem of acting or action.

As the assistant improved he was even allowed to draw simple bits of animation, finally becoming an animator in his own right. At the same time the inbetweener was given the opportunity to learn to become an assistant. Walt had neatly woven a whole training program into the daily work.

Another Disney departure from custom was that the animators only drew very rough drawings, leaving such details as buttons, wrinkles, and other trivia for the other two men.

Novice animators usually had to do their own assistant work, then the scenes were turned over to the inbetween department, where the neophyte inbetweeners struggled under the beady eye of George Drake. Our small group of initiates were the bottom of the barrel, because none of

Otto Englander working on a sequence in *Pinocchio. Collection of Erna Englander.*

Left to right: Otto Englander, Shamus Culhane, and Al Eugster, waiting for lunch in a pensive mood. 1935, shortly after Eugster, Culhane, Wolf, and Natwick joined the Disney staff. *Collection of Bernie Wolf.*

them had ever worked in an animation studio before. I couldn't get lower unless I dug a hole.

Drake ended his talk by warning us that learning how to draw inbetweens was difficult. Not everybody was going to qualify. This part of his speech I brushed aside.

We went on a tour of the studio, and it was a dazzler. In the first place, everything was painted in bright tints of raspberry, light blue, and gleaming white, no institutional greens or bilious browns like the other studios.

Each animation team had its own room with three beautifully designed desks, upholstered chairs, cupboards for storing work in progress, and most amazing of all . . . each room had a moviola. A moviola is a small projector which is designed to run a reel of picture and a sound track separately. Even back in those days they cost more than a thousand dollars.

By contrast the New York studios had desks and chairs that looked as if they had been stolen from the Salvation Army, and everyone worked in large rooms that were separated by nothing more than beaverboard partitions. There was only one moviola in an editing room, and it was for the sole use of the cutter. Animators never saw their work until it was in a finished film, ready for distribution. This meant that everybody had to avoid experiments and only draw actions that they knew were safe. Max Fleischer had brushed aside the idea of making tests of pencil drawings with the remark that any animator worth his salt knew exactly how things moved, so why spend money on tests? The other New York producers shared his opinion; making tests was just a waste of money.

Making pencil tests of the *rough* drawings was another one of Walt's brilliant ideas. Now an animator could sketch a scene, have it inbetweened and photographed, then run it on his moviola. He could then make as many changes as he pleased because, unlike the rest of the business, there was no footage quota of any kind at Disney Studio. When the work had been revised to his satisfaction, the animator would send it to the editor to have it spliced into a reel of pencil tests from the various animators working on the picture.

Walt and the director met each week while the animation was in progress to screen the footage very carefully, not just for technical mistakes or errors in judgment, but for possible additional gags. The story department also sent the writers to these meetings to add their own criticisms and ideas. After this exhaustive process was over, the animator was given a list of changes, and his revised scenes would then be subjected to the same minute scrutiny. Then, when Walt and the director gave the scene its final approval, the drawings would be cleaned up by the assistant and inbetweener, and sent on for inking and painting and color photography.

A picture would remain in a constant state of flux right through the final stages of production. Walt was known to make changes in a film if he wasn't satisfied with the audience reaction at a sneak preview! No wonder Disney had contempt for New York animators. We were totally unprepared to cope with such an avalanche of criticism and changes, technically or emotionally.

Of course, I did not find out all these formidable details during George Drake's guided tour. One of the features of the trip was a pep talk given by an ex-New York animator named Dave Hand. Dave had gone to Disney's several years before and had risen to become the most important executive next to Walt. He had a leonine head like a Roman senator, and he looked very imposing as he stared down at the little band of awestruck neophytes.

The talk was a disappointment, consisting of a banal aggregation of clichés that would have made poor text for even a high school football coach's pre-game speech. At one point, Hand waxed mystical, saying that we would never succeed as animators unless we "got the call." "For Christ's sake," I thought, "what the hell does he think he's preaching? We're not trying out for the priesthood here." Apparently my cynical view was not shared by the kids, who tiptoed out of the room. They had just heard THE WORD. I walked out wondering if Walt had ever heard this pompous spiel. I doubted it.

That afternoon we got down to the serious business of drawing rough inbetweens. Unhampered by previous experience, the youngsters drew well. As for me, unused to drawing roughly, my work was stiff and lacked conviction. I came in for some sharp criticism from George Drake and deservedly so.

The next morning, to my astonishment, I found that we were going to spend the whole day in art school. The instructor was Don Graham, a former teacher at Chouinard's Art Institute. In a recent letter to me Art Babbitt explained how the concept of an art school on the Disney premises came about.

The fabled Nine Old Men of the Walt Disney Studio. From left to right, seated: Wolfgang Reitherman, Les Clark, Ward Kimball, Johnny Lounsbery; standing: Milt Kahl, Marc Davis, Frank Thomas, Eric Larson, and Ollie Johnston. *Copyright © by Walt Disney Productions.*

The art class was started in my home, then in French Village, opposite Hollywood Bowl. We had no instructor.

After our second session, Walt called me in and suggested that it wouldn't look very good if the newspapers reported that a bunch of Disney cartoonists were drawing naked ladies in a private home.

In response to my request for suggestions, he offered the use of the sound stage, and free art materials. "How much do models cost?" he asked. Quickly I mentally doubled the sixty cents an hour paid by art schools then, and added twenty cents for carfare . . . making all the art schools in Los Angeles unhappy.

For many weeks I served as monitor of the class, because I certainly was not equipped to teach. But I could take the roll, and keep the guys and gals in the class from making wisecracks about the models.

Finally, Hardie Gramatky, a budding and vital young animator who had studied at Chouinard's, suggested I try to inveigle Don Graham to instruct the Disney group. This he did, and we all profited enormously in a million ways.

In 1971 we threw a shindig for Don and, on the flyleaf of my copy of his book, *Composition,* he wrote, "To Art, who started me out in the animation business. My great appreciation."

One of the most interesting documents in motion picture history is a memo that Walt Disney sent to Don Graham on December 23, 1935. By the time this memo was written, I had been working at the studio since May and my drawing had been improving almost every night. I was still going to Graham's classes five nights a week. The lectures by various animators and the action analysis classes were converting me from an artistic illiterate to a fairly well-educated artist.

One unusual facet of this document is the fact that Walt seems to have analyzed this particular situation down to the last detail. This was not his usual method of approaching a problem. Very often he would toss it to the people involved and while they struggled for a solution, he would prod and poke them along while maintaining a strict objectivity.

This is the document:

To Don Graham from Walt: Dec. 23, 1935

Right after the holidays, I want to get together with you and work out a very systematic training course for young animators, and also outline a plan of approach for our older animators.

Some of our established animators at the present time are lacking in many things, and I think we should arrange a series of courses to enable these men to learn, and acquire the things they lack.

Naturally the first and most important thing for any animator to know is how to draw. Therefore it will be necessary that we have a good life drawing class. But you must remember Don, that while there are many men who make a good showing in drawing class, and who, from your angle, seem good prospects, these men may lack in some other phase of the business that is very essential to their success as animators.

I have found that men respond more readily to classes dealing with practical problems than to more theoretic treatment. Therefore I think that it would be a good idea to appeal to these men by conducting classes with the practical approach in mind. In other words, try to show in these classes that the men can make immediate practical application of what they are being taught.

The talks by Fergie, Fred Moore, Ham Luske, and Fred Spencer have been enthusiastically received by all those in attendance. Immediately following these talks, I have noticed a great change in animation. Some men have made close to 100 percent improvement in the handling and timing of their work. This strikes me as pointing the way toward the proper method of teaching in the future.

The following occurs to me as a method of procedure: Take the most recent pictures—minutely analyze all the business, action, and results, using the better pieces of animation as examples, going through a picture with these questions in mind:

1. What was the idea to be presented?
2. How was the idea presented?
3. What result was achieved?
4. After seeing the result, what could have been done to the picture from this point on to improve it?

Encourage discussion on the part of the men present; if possible have some of the animators over to talk to them about the problems they were confronted with on the picture, and what the animator himself would do if he had a chance to do the animation over.

I believe these classes could be combined for presentation to all the animators, young and old as well.

It wouldn't be bad if you made up a list of the qualifications of an animator in order of importance. Then all these men could see what it takes to be an animator, and could check on themselves to see how nearly they approach the desired perfection.

The list would start with the animator's ability to draw; then, ability to visualize action, breaking it down into drawings and analyze the movement and the mechanics of the action. From this point, we would come to his ability to caricature action—to take a natural human action and see the exaggerated funny side of it—to anticipate the effect or illusion created in the mind of the person viewing the action. It is important also for the animator to be able to study sensation and to feel the force behind sensation, in order to project that sensation. Along with this, the animator should know what creates laughter—why do things appeal to people as being funny.

In other words a good animator combines all these qualities:

Good draftsmanship
Knowledge of caricature, of action as well as features
Knowledge and appreciation of acting
Ability to think up gags and put over gags
Knowledge of story construction and audience values

Knowledge and understanding of all the mechanical and
detailed routine involved in his work, in order that he
may be able to apply his other abilities without
becoming tied up in a knot by lack of technique along
these lines.

This is all very rough—just a jumble of thoughts—but
what I plan is that we get together after the holidays, as
suggested above, and really get these plans worked out in
detail; then we should strive to see that all the men we are
drilling for animators are given a chance to develop along
the lines outlined.

I am convinced that there is a scientific approach to this
business, and I think we shouldn't give up until we have
found out all we can about how to teach these young
fellows the business.

The first duty of the cartoon is not to picture or
duplicate real action or things as they actually happen, but
to give a caricature of life and action, to picture on the
screen things that have run through the imagination of the
audience, to bring to life dream fantasies and imaginative
fancies that we all have thought of during our lives or
have had pictured to us in various forms during our lives.
Also to caricature things of life as it is today or make
fantasies of things we think of today.

The point must be made clear to the men that our study
of the actual is not so that we may be able to accomplish
the actual, but so that we may have a basis upon which to
go into the fantastic, the unreal, the imaginative—and yet
to let it have a foundation of fact, in order that it may
more richly possess sincerity and contact with the public.

A good many of the men misinterpret the idea of
studying the actual motion. They think it is our purpose to
merely duplicate these things. This misconception should be
cleared up for all. I definitely feel that we cannot do the
fantastic things based on the real unless we first know the
real. This point should be brought out very clearly to all
new men, and even the older men.

Comedy to be appreciated, must have contact with the audience. This we all know, but sometimes forget. By contact, I mean that there must be a familiar, subconscious association. Somewhere, or at some time, the audience has felt, or met with, or seen, or dreamt the situation pictured. A study of the best gags and audience reaction we have had will prove that the action or situation is something based on an imaginative experience or a direct life connection. This is what I mean by direct contact with the audience. When the action or the business loses its contact, it becomes silly or meaningless to the audience.

Therefore, the true interpretation of caricature is an exaggeration of the illusion of the actual; or the sensation of the actual put into action. In our animation we must show not only the actions and reactions of a character, we must picture with the action the feelings of those characters. My experience has shown me that the most hilarious of comedies is always based on things actual, possible, or probable. That idea, behind the things I just mentioned above, can be incorporated in every stage of instruction—from the life drawing clear on through to the planning and staging of the work.

I have often wondered why, in your life drawing class, you don't have your men look at the model and draw a caricature of the model, rather than an actual sketch. But instruct them to draw the caricature in good form, basing it on the actual model. I noticed a little caricature of one of the models in the life class by Ward Kimball, and it struck me that there was an approach to the work that we should give consideration. I don't know why, using this method, you can't give the class all the fundamentals of drawing they need and still combine the work with the development of a sense of caricature.

Would it be a good idea to take a man like Joe Grant and see what could be worked out with him along the lines of giving a talk some night on an approach to caricature, a Harpo caricature—what he sees and what he thinks about when he is trying to make a caricature. It might be advisable to have a talk with Joe on this.

I still think this is a very good idea and constitutes a far better approach for the younger men than giving them too many straight, natural things that direct their minds to the unimaginative end of the business. It is possible that with the comedy you can still teach them the fundamentals of all these actions.

Take for example a walk. Why can't you teach the fundamentals of a straight walk yet combine it with some person that is giving an exaggeration or a comic interpretation of a straight walk. Perhaps for very elementary instruction, it might be best to present straight action; but not to keep giving them straight action as they progress and gain a little experience. Start them going into the comedy angle or caricature angle of the action. For example—a fat person with a big potbelly: What comedy illusion does he give you?

You could at the same time instruct the class regarding the reason why he has to move in a certain way (because of his weight, etc.). Present the walk soliciting discussion on:

What illusion does that person, fat with potbelly, give you as you see him?
What do you think of as you see him walking along?
Does he look like a bowl of jelly?
Does he look like an inflated balloon with arms and legs dangling?
Does he look like a roly-poly?

In other words, analyze the fat person's walk and the reasons for his walking that way. . . . BUT DON'T STOP UNTIL YOU'VE HAD THE GROUP BRING OUT ALL THE COMEDY THAT CAN BE EXPRESSED WITH THAT FAT PERSON'S WALK; also all the character—but drive for the comedy side of the character.

Take a skinny person—somebody that's loose-jointed,

angular, shoulder blades showing—what does he suggest? Does he look hung together with wires like a walking skeleton? Does he look like a marionette flopping around? Does he look like a scarecrow blowing in the wind? What illusion is created by the walk, by the movement, of that skinny loose-jointed person?

In discussing a short person, with short legs, he would naturally have quick movements and seems to move very fast. He would have to take twice as many steps as a taller person, thus making him look as if he were going at a greater speed. What illusion would you get from a person like that? Does he strike you as a little toy wound up and running around on wheels? Does he look like a little Pekinese pup? a dwarf? or midget?

There are a number of things that could be brought up in these discussions to stir the imaginations of the men, so that when they get into actual animation they're not just technicians, but they are actually creative people.

In the study of other problems, is it possible to bring out more the exaggeration of form and action—as in the study of the balance of the body? Can we bring that out even to an exaggerated point? It will probably make it stronger to them—make them realize more the necessity of that balance of the body—and yet point out how they can utilize that to strengthen their business when they get into animation, as in bending. In someone bending over, can we show the exaggeration in that action by showing how the pants pull up in the back to an exaggerated degree that becomes comical? Can we show how the coat stretches across the back and the sleeves pull up and the arms seem to shoot out as from a turtle neck as they shoot out of the sleeves? What can we do to bring these points out stronger to the men?

In lifting, for example—or other actions—we should drive at the fundamentals of animation, and at the same time, incorporate the caricature. When someone is lifting a heavy weight, what do you feel? Do you feel that something is liable to crack any minute and drop down?

Do you feel that because of the pressure he's got, he's going to blow up, that his face is going to turn purple, that his eyes are going to bulge out of their sockets, that the tension in the arm is so terrific that he's going to snap? What sensations do you get from someone rising— different ways of rising? Sitting? When someone is sitting —when he sits down and relaxes, does it look as if all the wind goes out of him? Does he look like a loose bag of nothing? Also in pushing . . . in the extremeness of a push, the line shoots right down from the fingertips clear down to the heel. In pulling—show the stretch, and all that. Bring out the caricature of those various actions, at the same time driving at the fundamentals of them—the actual.

The various expressions of the body are important. The animators go through animation and don't make the positions of the body, hold positions and relaxed positions, express anything. They try to do all the expression with the parts that are moving, whereas the body should enter into it. Without the body entering into the animation, the other things are lost immediately. Examples—an arm hung on to a body it doesn't belong to or an arm working and thinking all by itself. I think something could be worked out to develop this point, even if you got a person up behind a screen, a model perhaps, and threw a light on him. Have the class do nothing but watch the silhouette as the model goes through different poses, noting how the body enters into the expression of the action. Or we could photograph the action to show the men. The study of this would be a big help toward making the men realize the value of getting the story and the business over in their rough drawings that is in the action itself, rather than depending on little trimmings, on the clothes, the facial expressions, and things like that to put over the business.

If the animators get the groundwork right, that is, the action underneath all those trimmings, then what they add is going to be twice as effective. It's a very important point that we must impress upon the new men and the older men.

After we have given the men all the suggestions we can that have to do with expressing ideas through the body, then we can come down to the value of the facial expression—the use of the eyes, eyebrows, the mouth— their relation to one another—how the eyes and the mouth have to work together sometimes for expression—how they may work independently for expression at other times. In other words, then we go into the combined use of expressive features and expressive actions of the body. Then it would be good to take one away from the other and see which is most important.

We should have courses in staging and planning. These courses can be given by our more successful animators.

Also we should try to show how to analyze a scene or a piece of business before starting to work on it. We should try to show men ways of visualizing action in their minds, breaking the action so that the men are prepared in advance to begin animation of the action and know thoroughly what they are going to animate. So many of the men start in now, and have no idea what they're going to do when they start the scene. They know what they're supposed to do, but they can't break it down in a systematic way that will enable them to go knowingly ahead.

Many men do not realize what makes things move— why they move—what the force behind the movement really is. I think a course along that line, accompanied by practical examples of analysis and planning, would be very good. In other words, in most instances, the driving force behind the action is the mood, the personality, the attitude of the character—or all three. Therefore, the mind is the pilot. We think of things before the body does them. We also do things on the spur of the moment by reaction to stimuli that are telegraphed to the mind by the nerves, etc. There are also things carried out by the subconscious mind —reflexes, actions that have become habit through repetition, instincts. In other words, the subconscious mind is an assistant, often times, in carrying out things that may or may not have been taught. Examples of that are sleeping, lighting a cigarette and throwing the match away without any thought, whistling, walking, running, sitting, etc. It's not necessary to think of those actions.

But certain actions we do think about—certain actions we deliberately plan. We plan them very quickly in our mind. The point to bring out there is that when a character knows what he's going to do, he doesn't have to stop before each individual action and think to do it. He has planned in advance in his mind. For example—say the mind thinks, "I'll close the door, lock it, then I'm going to undress and go to bed." Well, you walk over to the door —before the walk is finished, you're reaching for the door —before the door is closed, you reach for the key—before the door is locked, you're turning away—while you're walking away, you're undoing your tie—and before you reach the bureau, you have your tie off. In other words, before you know it, you're undressed—and you've done it with one thought, "I'm going to go to bed."

A lot of valuable points could be brought out to the men in showing them that it is not necessary for them to take a character to one point, complete that action completely, and then turn to the following action as if he had never given it a thought until completing the first action. Anticipation of action is important.

This enters into animation in many ways and we have many serious difficulties coming up because of the men's inability to visualize things in the proper way.

I think a good study of music would be indispensable to the animator—a realization on their part of how primitive music is, how natural it is for people to want to go to music—a study of rhythm, the dance—the various rhythms that enter their lives every day—how rhythmical the body really is—how well balanced the body really is. That, in itself, is music. In other words, it could be music in the body. We dance—we keep time to rhythm without ever being taught—a baby does it—cannibals do it. But fancy dancing or any tricky stuff we have to learn. There are things in life that we do to rhythm that come natural to us. Notice how rhythmic an action like pounding a hammer is! There's a reason for that. You must have that rhythm or you can't carry out the action completely. Also, sawing a board. See how necessary it is to have good rhythm for that. Also walking . . . if you walked without rhythm, where would you get? You'd have to be thinking all the time what to do next. You'd have to set your mind to walking rhythmically, instead of doing it naturally.

Naturally the body is very well balanced. When one hand does something, the other serves to balance it. There are various ways that combine balance in the body— subconscious balance—and yet the animators do not know it. They will do something with one hand—they don't know what to do with the other, so they will do something entirely contrary to what that hand should be doing, because they don't understand the basic concept of balance. This idea of balance of the body ties in with the concept of expression of the body. If there is balance, it adds expression to the things the body is doing. If you don't have that balance of the body, then your expressions are wrong, insincere, unconvincing. These concepts also tie in with overlapping action.

In other words, we could work out all these basic concepts in such a way as to show them all related, interdependent, and having to do with each other, and we could tie them together in various ways, showing different combinations of their application. We will stir up the men's minds more, and they will begin to think of a lot of things that would never occur to them otherwise if the way wasn't pointed out to them.

I'd like also to have a study of dialogue. I want to prepare a course on dialogue—phrasing and rhythm of dialogue, moods and character of dialogue, expressions, gestures, use of the eyes, eyebrows, mouth, head, arms, body, tongue, inhalation and exhalation, and various other aspects that have to do with the successful picturization of dialogue in the cartoon. Let's see if we can't organize something like this and get it going right after the first of the year.

This is certainly one of the most remarkable documents in animation history—probably the most remarkable. One has to remember that the writers and older animators had been trained in the slapstick school of animation, and in 1935 very few members of the crew had anything but the foggiest idea of Walt's determination to produce more complicated animated cartoons.

There is a note of plaintive impatience as he enumerates the faults of the animators, even the veterans. How neatly he sums up the weak spots in their education and recognizes that for the most part they are too old to start learning again unless there is an immediate result.

Obviously, this memo has been dictated. I get a vivid picture of Walt striding up and down his office, stopping to run his fingers through his hair, then resuming his pacing as a new idea takes over, and it is time for another cigarette.

Gene Fleury, who later made some important contributions to production design at Warner Brothers, and Phil Dike, a well-known watercolorist and teacher, were Don's assistants.

Aside from the daylong classes for novices, the school was open five nights a week. Every artist in the studio was required to attend at least one night a week for three hours.

I got off to a bumbling start, because I had never drawn from a model before. To my consternation Graham pointed out a number of drawing tricks I was using. In an effort to avoid repeating them I began to founder, and produced what I thought were terrible drawings, even though Don assured me they were better.

We did quick sketches for about an hour. Next came a series of half-hour poses interspersed with short lectures by Graham. He used terms like, "space and volume," the "picture plane," and "controlled distortion," terms I had never heard before. I was happy to see that no one around me seemed to understand them either.

That night I bolted my dinner and rushed back for three more hours of foundering. The night class consisted of a more heterogeneous group: animators, assistants, background artists, and story sketch men. Looking around, I began to realize that as a self-taught artist I had been a pretty poor teacher.

If anything, my drawing was worse than the mess I had produced during the day. Don Graham seemed to have singled me out for gentle but succinct criticism. To my confusion, he seemed to like the sketches that were to me childish or primitive scrawls. I couldn't recognize these pitiful drawings as my own work.

Some of the drawings I saw around me looked marvelous, but Graham relentlessly took them apart. Not everybody accepted the criticism with good grace. Some even became quite defensive. At one point, Graham mentioned that Rubens used a great deal of distortion in his work. A gray-haired old gent in the class, who had been making some very photographlike drawings, challenged this statement. Don didn't argue, he simply reached into a portfolio of prints and picked out a Rubens drawing. Pointing to the arm of the figure in the drawing, Graham invited his antagonist to assume the same pose. He couldn't do it. There was so much torsion in that drawing that the fellow would have had to dislocate his wrist to match it. I resolved to buy a book of Rubens' work the next day.

The following weeks were a phantasmagoria of painfully scratched out rough inbetweens, and stiff, crude life drawings. Graham predicted that as I divested myself of the drawing tricks I had picked up, I would reach such a point of confusion that I would probably not be able to draw at all. Only then would I really begin to learn to become a good draftsman. I went to the art school every night, eyes red-rimmed with exhaustion, and realized that he was so right: by the end of the month I felt that whatever talent I had when I started was long gone.

In contrast to my frustration, the youngsters I worked with progressed with an air of gay confidence. They seemed to be picking up the idea of drawing rough inbetweens with comparative ease. Unencumbered by drawing habits such as the ones I'd developed from years of drawing cleaned-up figures, these kids had little trouble loosening up, while I still struggled.

Not every New Yorker had trouble making his mark at Disney's. Ted Sears, head of the story department, Dick Huemer, Gerry Geronimi, Norman Ferguson, Art Babbitt, and Bill Tytla, all very important animators in the Disney organization, had never gone through a difficult period of adjustment. They all had from fifteen to twenty years of experience

Ted Sears, head of the Disney story department, was one of the pioneer animators in the business. Walt's respect for his talents was so great that when Sears fell asleep during story conferences, Walt ignored his snores and went on with the discussion. *Copyright © by Walt Disney Productions.*

Norman Ferguson never lost his New York accent or his need to wear a three-piece suit and conservative tie. Despite his sober appearance he had an almost inexhaustible supply of funny poses and expressions for Pluto. Ferguson has been called the Charlie Chaplin of the animation profession. *Copyright © by Walt Disney Productions.*

working with the pioneer producers of the business in New York City. The production supervisor, who was regarded as the most important executive next to Walt, was Dave Hand. He had started as an animator in the very beginnings of eastern animation.

My friends, including Al Eugster and Bernie Wolf, and I were in effect the New Wave of young animators from the Max Fleischer Studio. We averaged about three years of animation, much of it at Fleischer's at a time when there was not one veteran animator left in the studio to teach us the fine points of the craft. None of us had formal art training, and we had collected a number of bad drawing habits in the slapdash approach that was normal in every studio except Disney's.

Wolf, Eugster, and I met for lunch as we had been doing for years. Now instead of blithe and breezy shoptalk, we often sat silently shoveling down our food, each of us wrapped in his own cloud of depression and frustration.

Preston Blair recalls that he was working at Screen Gems at the time and was trying vainly to get into Disney's. After Blair was unable to arrange for an interview with Walt, he switched his efforts to Ben Sharpsteen. Sharpsteen was the director who was usually saddled with newcomers. Preston finally got him on the phone and found Ben in a sour mood.

"Look," he grumbled peevishly, "we don't want any more of you outside animators. Do you want to be a failure like Culhane and Eugster?" Following that short burst, he hung up.

Blair finally managed to get into Disney's several years later and did some outstanding animation. Some of his best work was Mickey's frantic efforts to cope with the army of brooms in "The Sorcerer's Apprentice" and the crocodile dance in "Dance of the Hours," both from the movie *Fantasia*.

After six weeks had passed, Walt called me in for a meeting and gave me a greeting that was less than enthusiastic. He shoved two memos in my direction with no comment. The first was from George Drake:

Subject: Culhane's animation
Results do not compare favorably with that of some of the younger animators, such as Woolie, Towsley, Allen, and Spencer would do. Has accomplished a very amateurish presentation of a scene. Shows lack of analyzation. Not

familiar with our principles of staging, timing, or
anticipation, follow-through, and flow of action. Should
start all over and learn our way.

I reflected that while Drake's grammar was unsound, his evaluation
was quite correct. Then I read the other memo, this one from Don
Graham:

Subject: Culhane's drawing
Coming in cold as a new man, Culhane goes in for
important things. He used his head in solving the problems
submitted. He is rusty and has not drawn for some time.
With brushing up, he will do better than the average
prospect.

Walt tamped out one cigarette and lit another. "I'm kind of disappointed in you, Culhane," he said, thoughtfully, "so I'm not sure what
we should do about it. What do you think?" What did I think? Was this
an invitation to quit gracefully before I got fired? Damned if I would,
so I just shrugged.

"Well, if Graham thinks you have something, I'll go along with him.
We may move you around a little . . . try you out at different things."

That was the end of the meeting. I walked out thinking glumly that
I had come a long way in a month, and it was all downhill. The trouble
was that I was a slob, not that I had started out with the intention of being
a slob, but that was the atmosphere in the other studios. You were paid
to bat out thirty or thirty-five feet a week, some good, some bad, but
the only important thing was that the footage got done. In such a rat race
there were no standards. One day my animation would be good and the
next day poor, but there was never any way to evaluate it until I saw
the completed picture, some two months later.

My competition were those goddamn kids with four and five years of
art school behind them. I was going to have to cram an equivalent
education into a few months, before Walt's patience wore out, and there
was so much to learn!

7

The Don Graham Influence

What I didn't realize at the time was that I had one great advantage: Don Graham. Many art teachers are fairly pedestrian people who fall back on formulas for drawing and painting, and inevitably, they pass these hack tricks on to their pupils in the fond belief that they are teaching. The students think they are learning because they do get a quick result. Actually, they are exchanging their ability to think and feel for a superficial facility.

This may sound like a sweeping generalization, but when I was a youngster making twelve dollars a week as an errand boy, I eked out additional money by posing in art schools at night for a dollar an hour.

I posed in every major school in New York and listened to hours of instruction by various teachers. Although I had no idea that he was an important figure in American art history, Arshile Gorky was the only teacher who impressed me because he was provocative and passionate. The others for the most part fell back on formulas, the human figure is six heads high, etcetera. Even the painters had formulas for palettes which all the students in a class were expected to use.

Don Graham, on the other hand, was probably the greatest art teacher of our time. Unlike the average instructor, he had great talent as a draftsman. His drawings looked like the work of some of the Italian masters in their grace and power. The range of his knowledge was incredible, one minute discussing Cézanne and his point of view, the next showing us a Giotto where he'd tried to make a simulation of animation by painting four angels in poses like inbetweens, all leading up to a key pose.

So it was perfectly possible to learn more in a few months with Don Graham than the youngsters had picked up in years at conventional schools, and I set about to do it. Five nights a week I was hunkered down over a drawing board, trying to use the principles of drawing and composition that Don was propounding. Nobody else in the studio had set himself such a schedule; most of the staff dutifully put in their three hours one night a week.

Not all the classes were held in the studio. About once a month, Don Graham took us all to the Los Angeles Zoo. We were free to wander off and choose some animal or bird that interested us. Don would go from one group to the next, criticizing the drawings. The only restriction we had, and this applied to our drawing in the studio or the zoo, was that we never used shading to indicate a form. We had to work with pure line. We were, after all, concerned with line in our animation to the exclusion of aid from light and shade. A line drawing is the most difficult and austere form of draftsmanship. For most of us, it was a constant struggle to master the subtle changes in a line that would enable us to express a contour.

For Al Eugster, Bernie Wolf, and I, it was an exhilarating experience. Imagine wandering around a zoo, drawing whatever we pleased on company time! The rest of the group, having never worked in a studio before, took it as a matter of course.

I quickly found kindred spirits within the group. Marc Davis liked to work on the anatomy of his subjects. He hoped someday to do a book about the comparative anatomy of animals. Later, he was going to be one of the important artists who created the model sheets of the animals in *Bambi,* and eventually one of the designers of Disneyland.

Another member of the class was Bernard Garbutt. He had been an animal artist long before he came to Disney's. Garbutt drew like nobody I ever met. He used a thin wiry line and never roughed in his drawings. One day I watched him in the studio doing story sketches and I saw that he was drawing without any particular method. He would start on the stomach in one sketch, and begin on the tail on another. Where he began, Garbutt would skate his pencil around the outline and fill in the interior details later. It all seemed to flow from his pencil as if he were tracing something.

When I asked him about this technique and mentioned that it looked as if he was tracing, Garbutt astounded me by saying that in effect that was what he was doing. He was able to project an image of an animal on the page in such perfect detail that he simply converted it into a pencil drawing!

The zoo was a very exciting experience. I could sit for a whole morning watching one duck and fill my notebook with notes as well as drawings. Most of the jottings were about the duck's behavior towards other ducks. In addition, I might make a very detailed series of drawings on the leg action as he swam.

Unlike the classes in the Annex, there were no definite problems to be solved when we were at the zoo. Graham didn't care if we spent the whole morning observing without making a drawing.

My specialty became the big cats. I loved the sleek power in the muscles of the tiger, and there was one mangy-looking lion who was a favorite of mine because he never moved around very much. One of the keepers told me that he was the model for the MGM titles. That might have been true, but he was the sorriest King of Beasts I ever saw.

Many years later, when I was at Warner Brothers, I worked with Chuck Jones on a picture called *Inki and the Mynah Bird,* which featured a decrepit old lion. Before I started to animate him, I pulled out some of these sketches and they were the source of some of my best poses in the picture.

I also started to draw our cat on weekends. However, he began to hide as soon as he saw my sketchbook. For some reason he hated to be stared at. I started to feed a couple of stray cats. Very soon, when feeding time came, I had more than twenty cats running through hedges, scrambling down trees, pushing and jostling each other to get to the food.

The result was that whenever I wanted to draw there were always several cats lurking around the door. I filled dozens of sketchbooks with drawings of kittens gamboling and cats sunning themselves. Don Graham predicted that I was going to be a very good animal animator.

Once a week, we had a session called "Action Analysis." Don would take one of our latest pictures and screen it over and over, sometimes at normal speed and other times at a quarter speed or less. He would discuss the poses and how the characters moved from one position to the other; then he would ask us how we might have improved the animation.

Other times, we would see a live-action comedy, usually starring Charlie Chaplin or Buster Keaton. Again, we would watch the film at

Sketch by Shamus Culhane, 1939. Drawings were rarely rendered in light and shade by animators. Graham expected them to work in pure line.

Characteristic poses of swans in the Los Angeles Zoo, drawn by Shamus Culhane during one of Don Graham's classes. Besides the notes like the foot action in swimming, written comments on behavior were often added to the sketches.

regular speed and then see it frame by frame. The first time I attended one of these sessions I was in for a real eye-opener. Graham showed us one scene of a Charlie Chaplin comedy. Chaplin walked up to a door, took a key out of his pocket, put it in the lock, and walked in.

At regular speed no one noticed anything unusual about the whole action; it looked perfectly normal. Then Don slowed the film down and began to analyze the action. When Chaplin put his hand in his pocket, he didn't just stick it in; he first made a small action with his hand barely in the pocket, drew it out a little, then plunged it in. He then wriggled his fingers, making his pants bulge. When the key was brought out, Chaplin turned it for a split second so that it caught the light, aimed it in a direct line with the lock, then inserted it. As Don went on with his analysis, I realized that what had looked like a simple movement was in reality as stylized as a ballet dance. I began to understand why Charlie Chaplin was considered the greatest pantomimist in the world.

After some time, I realized what a monumental task Don Graham was taking on. In effect, he was single-handedly attacking the traditional concept of animation as simply moving comic strips. Disney's early sound cartoons had been done in that traditional mode, but in 1933, the turn-about began and the studio began to produce characters with lifelike movements, the quality of which improved rapidly in the next three or four years.

There had been no indication that Disney had wanted to break from the limiting moving comic-strip concept before that time. At some point, Walt must have realized how the traditional, simplistic animation of the period made it impossible to produce pictures based on funny acting rather than slapstick. He must have realized, too, that more advanced animation required better taught animators. Walt had always believed in education. Even in the early days of his Hollywood studio Disney had sent some of his employees to Chouinard's night school at his own expense, but never attended classes himself. Walt was such a poor drafts-man that he once ruefully said that he couldn't hold down a job as an inbetweener in his own studio. Nevertheless, as a result of the classes, he must have seen some improvement in his animators, some spark that wasn't there before. That was one important facet of Walt's genius: the ability to evaluate not only what people were presently capable of, but more importantly, to evaluate their potential skills.

Don Graham's hiring was probably the most impressive example of that intuitive ability. Graham had never worked in animation before, yet Walt chose him as the man to lead his studio away from the restrictive, traditional style that existed at the time. Don Graham taught that animation was an art form with myriad possibilities. When he succeeded in pointing the way to a more complex form of movement and acting, he created a schism between the Disney Studio and the rest of the animation field. After Walt, Don Graham has probably made the greatest impact on the philosophy of the medium.

Don taught the animators to explore the possibilities of each character's emotions in a given situation, then add the factors of the character's mental set and his physical characteristics. Only after all these elements were analyzed and evaluated by the animator could he make his contribution. He would call into play his drawing ability, his ability to caricature action, and his ability to predict the possible reaction of the audience to a scene. He was expected to sense when to modify the vigor of his animation if the following scene peaked to a gag. This kind of complex planning was completely foreign to the approach other studios had to animation during the early 1930s.

The switch from slapstick to pantomime, using situations and gags which depicted definite characters, had already occurred in the area of live-action comedy many years before.

Live-action comedies were being exhibited as early as 1914. Under the leadership of Mac Sennett, a definite form of comedy had been created as epitomized by Sennett's famous Keystone Kops. For years this type of humor was enormously popular with the moviegoing public. No matter what their individual styles of comedy had been before, the actors were expected to adhere to Sennett's formula, namely, chases, wrecked cars, pie throwing, explosions, arse kicking, falling off ladders, out of windows, and over cliffs.

The action went by so fast that it was impossible to identify individual actors. Comedians as dissimilar as Charlie Chaplin, Fatty Arbuckle, Wallace Beery, and Harold Lloyd worked within this atmosphere of frenzy as little more than vehicles for kinetic gags.

However, long before Disney had decided to venture into the area of pantomime, Charlie Chaplin's Little Tramp, Harold Lloyd's bespectacled All-American Boy, and Keaton's deadpan acrobatics had overshadowed Sennett's brand of crude humor.

Right through the transition from silent films to sound cartoons none

of the producers of animation paid the slightest attention to these improvements in the quality of live-action comedy. Trapped by the belief
that animated cartoons should be a kind of moving comic strip, all the
producers (including Walt Disney) continued to turn out films that
consisted of a loose story line that supported a group of slapstick gags,
which were often only vaguely related to the plot.

It might be argued that Felix the Cat was a pantomimist. If that is so,
his acting is certainly on a very primitive level, because Felix merely
indicated an emotion by a single pose. Usually that was bolstered by
standard comic-strip symbolism, such as the light bulb overhead indicating an idea, Felix's detached tail becoming a question mark, and so on.

Once Felix's animators had achieved a library of standard poses for
basic emotions, the cat's acting did not improve. The possibility that the
timing *between* poses was an important ingredient never occurred to them.

The most astonishing thing is that Walt Disney took so long to decide
to break the narrow confines of slapstick, because for several decades
Chaplin, Lloyd, and Keaton had demonstrated the superiority of good
pantomime.

The move to acting animation was not made solely by the animators;
it was a dual effort in that the initial thrust had to come from the story
department. Under Walt's guidance, writers began to devise stories and
situations that relied on acting rather than slapstick. The methods taught
by Don Graham were meant to help the animators draw movement that
matched the new approach in the stories.

While it was a tandem effort, it was by no means a smooth transition.
The new mode was initiated by Norman Ferguson working with Pluto;
but often the Pluto sequence might be the only part of the picture that
used subtle pantomime. For me, the first real mesh of story and fine acting
was *The Country Cousin,* made in 1936. Directed by Wilfred Jackson,
with the two main characters animated by Les Clark and Arthur Babbitt,
this film is remarkable for consistent standards of acting from both
animators right through the picture. Although there is a good deal of fast
action, the film never descends into slapstick. It won a deserved Oscar,
but more importantly, it served as the direct forerunner to the dwarfs in
Snow White, a turning point in animation history.

Don Graham's influence spread beyond the Disney Studio, usually by
word of mouth. He talked a great deal to me one evening about the eye
in relationship to film, and advised me to get a book by the Russian

director Pudovkin. I told my friend Frank Tashlin about it, and we both decided to study it. *Film Technique,* by V. I. Pudovkin, deals mainly with the ability to create emotions by the juxtaposition of shots, rather than the use of long-lasting scenes that are merely punctuated by occasional close shots of details. Frank and I were delighted with this concept because we realized that it had great potential in animation. We agreed that there was some use of this idea in Wilfred Jackson's *The Tortoise and the Hare,* made in 1935, but we thought it could have been pushed further.

Most of these discussions between Frank and I took place on the floor. Tashlin was a massive six feet two inches and weighed almost three hundred pounds, consisting more of huge bones than fat. He was so big that he usually couldn't find a chair or settee he could trust, so more often than not, Tashlin would sprawl on the floor for the whole evening. His size was a factor in giving him a very alienated personality. Early in our friendship he told me about it. "You can't imagine what it was like to be six feet tall when I was only twelve. We had these silly goddamn short pants with the black stockings, and I could never get a pair that would fit me. Most of the kids came up to my belly button, and they didn't want me around."

Frank began submitting gags to various magazines while he was still in his teens. After working for a short while at the Van Beuren Studio, he created a fairly successful comic strip called *Van Boring,* which continued in syndication for several years. He used to sign the strip "Tishtash," a pen name he insisted on using years later as a film director.

Tash's often bored and lethargic appearance hid a highly volatile personality. The pictures he went on to write and direct are still some of the most frenetic ever produced. Using Pudovkin's theories of composition and optical retention, Tashlin directed a very successful picture at Warner Brothers entitled *Porky's Romance.* The cutting throughout was very quickly paced, using some shots no more than five or six frames long, but the action was completely understandable. I believe that it was the first time this technique was ever used in an American film, live or animated. In this way Graham's influence spread to Warner Brothers.

What Don was trying to do was create a group of sophisticated filmmakers, educated in the theories of the Old Masters, modern art, acting, and the scientific principles of movement. Disney must have believed wholeheartedly in the same vision, because by 1935, the art school was costing the studio more than $100,000 a year. Remember, this was at a time when the other producers in the business spent not one penny on training!

If Walt had relied solely on the profits from his pictures, such a venture would have been financially impossible. The additional income was available thanks to the business sense of his brother Roy. Roy was responsible for the shrewdest spin-off in the industry. By 1935, he had signed more than three hundred companies to promotional campaigns using the Disney characters. Not only did these companies pay handsomely for this privilege, but the deals they made assured the Disney Studio of an accelerated participation in the profits. The year I started with them, the Disneys were already pulling in a vast income from such diverse products as baked goods, sweatshirts, toys, and the famous Mickey Mouse watches.

If Walt was a genius as a filmmaker, Roy was a genius in the field of finance. Without his business acumen, Walt's grandiose ideas would have been no more than pipe dreams. Any normal businessman would have been hard put to go along with some of Walt's plans since most of these projects had no counterpart in the rest of the business. The brothers were both wandering through unexplored territory, but it was obvious that Roy had full confidence in Walt's instincts and, up to a point, allowed Walt free rein in developing his production methods.

A true "gray eminence" in that his presence was completely unobtrusive, Roy played no part in any of the production meetings, screenings, or any other aspects of the filmmaking process. Nevertheless, while he may have worked behind the scenes, making no effort to share in Walt's fame, it was Roy who had the power to overrule Walt's desire to spend money, and Walt would always accept his brother's dictum. This complement of talents in the Disneys was and is unique in the history of motion pictures.

In some ways, Walt and Roy used the "good guy/bad guy" routine in management. If an employee wanted a raise, the request was directed to Roy, not Walt. While the studio was generous to the elite, the smaller fries' salaries were far from lavish. Milt Schaffer, who worked in the story department, once went to Roy asking for an increase and was met with a frosty reception. Milt was usually a very quiet man, but when Roy asked icily why he was asking for more money, Milt leaned far over Roy's desk and hissed, "Food!"

We generally accepted as fact that Roy was the typical, tightfisted Machiavellian businessman. This opinion was strengthened by the presence of an ominous-looking, four-foot-long row of books entitled *Management vs. Labor,* which occupied the shelf behind his desk. This impressed us, since at the time there was no hint of labor unrest in the studio. Walt, on the other hand, was believed to be a man so dedicated to creativity that he had little or no interest in money. His payment of bonuses for good animation (of which more will be said later), and the immense sums he spent for the education of his staff, seem to bear out the truth in this evaluation of Walt's role.

The management fostered a feeling of isolation between the Disney Studio and the rest of the industry. Most of the younger animators had never worked anywhere else, and it was the nightmare of this group that they might someday get fired and be forced to get a job at one of the "other" studios. This specter was so menacing that many people who were fired left the business altogether. Walt's pursuit of quality was a Juggernaut that claimed many victims.

To a lesser degree, the same attitude could be found among the veterans who had come to Disney's from other studios. Who in his right mind would relinquish the feeling that he was among the elite of the animation field, and willingly go back to dirty surroundings and footage quotas? As it later turned out, many could—and did.

Not all of Walt's experiments in education were successful. A notable failure was the addition to the curriculum of a series of lectures on the fundamentals of humor by one Professor Markoven. He came from the drama department of U.C.L.A. and had a command of the English language on a par with Leo Rosten's character *H*Y*M*A*N *K*A*P*L*A*N*.

Several times a month, we neophytes were ushered into a large room furnished with chairs, a blackboard, and the smiling, confident professor. Somehow this man had persuaded Disney that, with the Markoven system of analysis, humor could be weighed like a loaf of cornbread, mapped out as definitely as the road from Minsk to Pinsk, formulated like a recipe for potato latkes, and canned for the consumer like the best beluga caviar. Where was Rasputin when we needed him?

"Have some chair, have some chair," he would beam as we filed in. "I'm so good to see you." Of course he was "good to see us." Rumor had it that Markoven was getting one hundred twenty-five dollars for each hour lecture. That was a lot of rubles in 1935.

The format of the professor's talks never varied. He would start by discussing one of our newly completed films, and pretty soon the blackboard would be covered by a bewildering crisscross of quasi-scientific equations and diagrams. It looked like skull practice for the football team of a lunatic asylum.

One day when we arrived, Professor Markoven was in a great fettle. He teetered on his toes and looked down happily at the rows of impassive faces. "I am making some very important discovery," he announced triumphantly. "There are three basic kind of humor, *A* and *B!*" (I am quoting verbatim.) Another time, we "had some chair" and waited for Markoven to spout, but this time he had no smile. He was waving a script which had a long sequence about Donald Duck's problems with a plumber's plunger, the suction cup having become attached to his rear. In the script, the plunger was called a "plumber's friend." Obviously, Markoven had not seen the picture because he was looking from the script to the class with Slavic paranoia, "Who is this new character we have, called "plumber's friend"? Happily, Professor Markoven soon faded from animation history.

While hundreds of lusty men and comely women worked at Disney's, the sexual atmosphere there could be described as prim, or even Victorian. The ink and paint department employed women and was located in a separate, restricted area. The rest of the staff were all male, except for the few stenographers who took shorthand notes at every meeting. Romantic attachments were further discouraged by the fact that the lunch hours of the two groups were staggered. As for Walt himself, his everyday conversation was liberally sprinkled with the usual Anglo-Saxon expletives common among men, but I never heard him use any in front of a woman.

Walt made no bones about the fact that an elite corps existed in the studio. A good example of this caste system occurred when he decided to expand his educational program by hiring a movie house one evening a week to run a program of short subjects for the entire staff. Several days before the first screening, a memo appeared on the bulletin board bluntly spelling out the pecking order: directors, animators, layout men, and head storymen were to use the soft seats, everyone else was to sit on the hard seats in the back. These instructions were followed to the letter. The first night of screenings found a row of empty seats in the soft seat area, but none of the lesser folk were so bold as to attempt to occupy them, even after the lights went out.

Walt never included animated cartoons from rival studios, for obvious

Caricature of
Professor Markoven
by Art Babbitt.
*Collection of Art
Babbitt.*

One of the most famous signs in the world topped the main building of the Walt
Disney Studio on Hyperion Avenue. 1935.

reasons. There were many good live-action two-reel films available, because in those halcyon days of block booking, every program included short subjects. Most of the films that Walt chose to include in the programs were nature studies of surprising beauty. One of the few times I saw Walt angry with the staff en masse occurred during the screening of a film on undersea flora and fauna. The narrator was a pompous bore, with a text to match. Suddenly, the camera picked a close-up of a very exotic form. As the narrator droned in a ministerial manner, "Strange flowers bloom beneath the sea . . . " the thing began to open very slowly. At its widest aperture, it stopped moving, giving us a long look at its pink interior, ample time to realize that it looked remarkably like the labia minor of a vagina.

The audience started to snicker, the snicker grew to a giggle, and finally there was a full-fledged roar of Rabelaisian laughter from both sexes in the audience. Walt, according to some people seated near him, was livid. Shortly after, these programs were discontinued.

There was a fairly high rate of attrition going on all the time, which made for fear of failure. Walt's pursuit of perfection created a very tense atmosphere in the studio. At one point I was working in a room with a tobacco-chewing Floridian. His aim at the wastepaper basket was poor, and the wall behind it was gradually acquiring the color of a meerschaum pipe. He was also a nonstop talker, given to describing in detail imaginary trips to different parts of the country. While he worked he exhibited a really remarkable memory for various towns, places to eat, and the condition of the highway. This monologue would continue by the hour.

Whenever I was given something to animate, I had to try to close my ears to this logorrhea. I wondered how he could really be doing good work and continue to chatter. He couldn't. One day Dave Hand burst into the room and started a stream of abuse. Apparently his victim had been slack enough to send a very poor piece of animation into the pencil-test reel. For fifteen minutes Hand gave the hapless animator a dressing down that would have made a drill sergeant at Paris Island sound as if he was giving a benediction. Dave's position as production supervisor allowed him to give his notoriously bad temper free rein. His victim was completely cowed and quit the next day. What was the point of the abuse? Obviously the animator was out of his element. Why not fire him in a civil fashion? Walt's pursuit of perfection seemed to have also supplied a climate for some unhealthy side effects.

Both the inbetween department and Don Graham's life drawing classes were housed in a large, one-story building across the street from the main studio. It was called the Annex, and that was an apt name for it, psychologically as well as topographically. One had a tendency to look wistfully over to the hodgepodge architecture of the studio with the knowledge that there was where the real action was going on. The Annex was a kind of limbo.

One curious feature of the Annex was the fact that the grounds around the building were populated by a small colony of prairie dogs. They crept out of their burrows every morning and kept up a gay chatter, oblivious to the stream of traffic a few yards away. They, and the little owls who shared their burrows, were a reminder that Los Angeles was geologically a part of the California desert. They all vanished when Walt decided to build a volleyball court in that area.

The game was an instant success. Each noon, a crowd of enthusiastic players headed by Jack Kinney, an animator, and his brother Dick, from the story department, would head for the locker rooms that Walt had installed in the Annex. Sides were then chosen up, with many sulphurous comments on the abilities of the candidates, and the games were played in an atmosphere of intense rivalry. Walt had chosen very wisely; the game of volleyball provided a marvelous release of nervous tension, without the possibility of serious physical injury.

Of course, in volleyball the taller players have the advantage of being able to leap high over the net and slam back the ball with such force that it is almost unplayable. However, shorter men like Al Eugster and Nick DeTolly (a former soccer player) were often able to make incredible saves. Sometimes the ball would carom back and forth for minutes with a mounting chorus of yells of delight and triumph.

Ward Kimball was probably the shortest man on the court, but his agility made him an exceptionally good player. He was also a kind of studio pixie, given to practical jokes. Sometimes, at the height of the volley, he would perform very well, then suddenly take the ball that was hit to him and hold it lazily in his hands, drop it to the ground, and walk off with a mischievous grin as the Kinneys and other devotees of the game danced with rage.

One day, Ward sat in his car and waited until the game had reached the height of intensity and then drove right onto the court. This time he got his comeuppance because the enraged group grabbed the fenders of his car and began to bounce it high in the air. They proceeded to bounce the car all the way back to the street, leaving a shaken and subdued Kimball inside, then returned to their game.

Harry Reeves, a veteran in the story department, was a kinky-haired character who usually talked so fast that his words caromed off each other like empty freight cars being shunted in a freight yard. He was essentially a good gagman, but there was one area where he had no sense of humor whatsoever—money. Reeves had decided to make his fortune by buying up stamp collections. The Depression made it possible to snap up some rare bargains, but the terms were always hard cash, leaving Harry inevitably on the lookout for ways to increase his cash position.

The population of the studio was growing so fast that when Harry was told about a rumor that the city was going to appoint a fire warden in Disney's, it sounded very logical. The fact that the salary was going to be forty dollars a month sent him hotfoot to the local firehouse to offer his services. The firemen had already been tipped off to the prank, so when Harry appeared they gravely felt his biceps and advised him that he was a good candidate, but needed a physical fitness program. For several weeks Harry went to the firehouse after work and sweated through push-ups, knee bends, and runs up and down ladders until he was exhausted. Reeves was so convinced that he had the forty-dollar job almost in his grasp that at first he refused to believe it was all just a gag.

In the mid-thirties, nobody in his right mind drank Los Angeles tap water. It was so full of alkali that it looked like milk and tasted like a drugstore mop. Disney installed five-gallon bottles of mountain spring water in every room. The bottles rested on large clay ollas equipped with taps. Art Babbitt once made the mistake of mentioning casually that his doctor had put him on a regimen that included large quantities of water every day. Nobody knows who the prankster was, but someone put several goldfish in Babbitt's spring water. Everyone waited for the inevitable explosion of wrath, for Babbitt could summon up a temper that made the Terrible Tempered Mr. Bang sound like a mewling kitten. We waited for three days because the fish, instead of swimming in plain view in the glass bottle, had decided that the darkness of the clay olla suited them better. Finally, the fish did emerge into the light, and the expected roar from Art Babbitt shook the building. For a long time after, in the interests of Art's personal hygiene, nobody told him that he had shared his drinking water with the fish for three days.

While all this might sound like a daily life of fun and games, these little pranks only slightly alleviated our sense of strain and anxiety because nobody was allowed to ease off from the pursuit of quality for an instant. The old cliché that in Hollywood everybody is only as good as his last picture was a fact of life in Disney's. No matter how prestigious an animator was, he still anxiously waited for Walt's approval every time he went in for a session in the "sweatbox." Sometimes it was not forth-coming.

8

Tooling Up for Snow White

One of Walt Disney's talents was acting. Very often during a story conference he would convulse the group by suddenly creating a bit of funny dialogue and acting it out. Just as suddenly as he had dropped into a character's role, Walt would go back to his normal voice and continue the discussion. He had absolutely no inhibitions about his acting. Indeed there was no need for it, because Disney's acting ability was on a professional level. The public relations people made much of the fact that Walt supplied the voice of Mickey Mouse, but never mentioned Walt's acting, probably because it never appeared directly on the screen; yet it always was a potent force during story discussions.

Perhaps the biggest leap forward in the story department was Walt's insistence on using gags that fit the emotional and psychological structure of a character. Heretofore, in all animation studios this attitude towards story material never came up. A gag was a gag, and if it was a funny idea there was no question about its appropriateness, because there never was a real examination of the emotional attitudes of the characters.

Disney adopted a very strict control over the kinds of humor that were used on his stars. Mickey, Minnie, Donald Duck, Pluto, and Goofy all had very definite character structures. Many funny gags were disallowed because Walt felt that they were not within the limits of a given personality. Such restrictions were almost unheard of in the other studios in the 1930s.

Walt was willing to take ideas from any source. At the beginning of each picture, the writing team would hold a meeting with the entire animation department, even including the inbetweeners. The general structure of the story would be discussed, and gags or sequence ideas were solicited. Disney would pay twenty-five dollars or more for a gag. Sometimes the group submitted some very funny ideas.

Once the picture was completed, there would be a screening for the same group. This time, forms would be passed out and everyone was expected to answer the following questions:

What is your evaluation of this picture? excellent, good, fair, poor.
What is the best sequence?
What is the best gag?
Which had the best animation?
What was unsatisfactory in the picture?
Remarks . . .

All the forms would be collected and read by Walt and the writers. In an effort to get a frank and unbiased criticism, the forms were never signed by the critics. Walt expected these meetings to be taken seriously, so there was always a marked absence of levity or horseplay even though the group met after business hours.

Every time there was a sneak preview, Walt would hold a conference in the foyer of the theater right after the screening. He had a prodigious memory and didn't need to make notes for his analysis of a film. The crew would form a circle around him and listen intently as he shot out a stream of pithy comments. He would cover every aspect of the story, music, animation, backgrounds, right down to the photography and sound effects.

At one such conference, Rudy Zamora, an ex-Fleischer animator who was a newcomer to the studio, was part of the group listening to Walt's litany of complaints, grudging approvals, and plans for retakes. Apparently Rudy was not in tune with the tense feelings of the group because he plucked his one-inch cigarette stub out of his mouth and waved it at Disney. "Excuse me, Walt, could I ask a question?" Disney was startled by the interruption of his thought processes. "What is it, Zamora?" Rudy, looking at him in mock perplexity, said, "Tell me, Walt, what makes these things move?" Lèse-majesté! Despite the fact that he was one of the most promising young animators at the studio, Zamora was fired the next morning.

Another place where levity was frowned upon was the screening room where pencil tests were reviewed. It was nicknamed "the sweatbox." The name was coined in the early days of the Disney Studio, when Walt first initiated the idea of making pencil tests. The director, the animators, and Walt would crowd into the small alcove in the hall and, cheek-by-jowl, sweat copiously from the heat of the projector. Someone understandably dubbed the alcove "the sweatbox" and the name stuck, even after a regular screening room was built with an air conditioning unit. No amount of air conditioning could assuage the emotional strain the animators had to undergo during these screenings—it was a white-knuckle trip all the way—so the term "sweatbox" was still apt.

Walt had a habit of dropping in on every room in the studio during the course of the day. When he came to the storymen, he would usually ask for a quick summation of the work in progress. If he found that a team had worked itself into an impasse, Walt would more often than not come up with the solution on the spot. He was amazingly good at finding out why the work had ground to a halt; whether it was a fault in the basic story line, or a gag that was not quite right for the emotional structure of a character, Walt could usually ferret it out.

His visits to the animators were more perfunctory because he had no interest in looking at drawings per se. He preferred to see pencil tests in the sweatbox. So even if an animator had a long scene on his moviola, Walt usually passed up the opportunity to examine it.

One facet of Disney's many talents was his almost uncanny ability to intuitively ferret out latent abilities in his employees. Very often it was a talent that the person himself was completely unaware of. Walt never hesitated to shunt people from one department to the next until he found the proper niche. Sometimes the results were amazing.

Jim Algar is a good example. He came into the studio with the group of neophytes that I joined, and went through the routine of learning how to draw rough inbetweens. Eventually he was given an opportunity to animate a number of different kinds of animals. He, Milt Kahl, and Eric Larson were assigned to animate all the animals who befriended Snow White.

Several years later, after Algar had shown his ability to direct on *The Sorcerer's Apprentice,* Walt chose him for a position as producer of a series of live-action animal shorts. They were immediately a very successful adjunct to the studio's animated shorts. Algar had found his métier.

At the time there were hundreds of artists at work in the studio, yet somehow Walt must have sensed some particular feeling Algar had for realistic animals and their movements. Normally, when a project that was wholly live-action was being contemplated, it would have seemed like common sense to hire a live-action director, and take advantage of his experience. Instead, Walt played his hunch on Jim Algar, and it certainly paid off.

I have never met anyone else in the business who had anything like Disney's ability to uncover talent. My own case is an almost classic example.

One day I was working alone in a room, wrestling with drawings for a storyboard. I was becoming increasingly frustrated, because I had been with the studio now for more than a year and a half and was still being shunted around from one department to the next. Most mornings when Walt would pop his head in and ask "How's it going?" I would answer almost automatically, "Fine," and he would bob his head in approval and leave. This time, however, when the expected question came I answered "Lousy!" Walt's smile vanished and he came into the room looking very serious. He listened to my complaint, then asked, "What would you like to be doing instead?" I answered somewhat lamely that I wanted to get back into animation. "What kind of animation?" His eyes bore into me like two laser beams. I gulped and mumbled, "I'd like to animate Pluto." He looked at me speculatively for a few seconds, then started for the door. "I'll be in touch," he called back as he left the room.

I had a hell of a nerve, I thought. In asking for a chance to animate Pluto, I was in effect asking to follow in the footsteps of the greatest master of pantomime in the business: Norman Ferguson.

"Fergie" had first started out as an accountant, then became a cameraman at Terrytoons. Eventually he became an animator of no great distinction since the stories were poor. He joined Disney in the early days of sound cartoons. Before Fergie started to animate Pluto, Mickey Mouse was the only star at the studio, Minnie's status being more of a satellite. The acting of both mice, and the characters around them as well, was slapstick—and broad slapstick at that. Fergie's approach to the animation of Pluto resulted in a drastic change in the whole concept of acting because he began to make use of pantomime. He started to slow down the pace of the scenes to the point where audiences could almost watch the thought processes going through Pluto's befuddled head. Then Fergie would put the dog through some wild fast-action and the contrast of the pacing alone was good for a laugh.

Grim Natwick called Norman Ferguson the "Charlie Chaplin of the animation business." I think he was right. Nobody before Fergie had been able to visualize really subtle pantomime. His acting ability gave the writers a chance to write scenes in which Pluto's thinking processes were often the funniest ingredient. The full range of his personality, from greed and curiosity to his sudden shifts from overweening self-esteem to blatant cowardice, made for some of the best material the Disney writers have ever produced.

This created one difficulty: many of the animators in the studio could draw an acceptable Mickey since his character did not call for subtle acting, but aside from Fergie, there were really only two other animators who had the special talent needed to animate Pluto. They were Fred Moore and Bill Roberts.

The basis of pantomime is timing. After many pictures and much experimentation, Ferguson had honed his sense of timing to a fine point. He could bring Pluto to a full stop and then, by merely shifting his eyes, show a whole range of acting. Pluto became the essence of *dog*. Moore and Roberts were fine animators, but Ferguson's talent as a pantomimist bordered on genius.

My request to animate Pluto was not really as mad as it may sound. Before the stock market crash, I had a lucrative sideline making pastel portraits of champion dogs on weekends. I therefore had spent many hours observing dog poses and actions and had also acquired some knowledge of dog psychology (I was only bitten once). Of course, once the stock market blew, even rich folks with fancy dogs were not paying one hundred dollars for fripperies like pastel sketches.

A few hours after Walt left, the intercom buzzed, "Take your belongings and report to Ben Sharpsteen." "Christ, here I go again," I thought. Then it struck me: this must be Walt's doing! I started loping down the hall, laden with my paraphernalia. I didn't care if I was going back to inbetweening, anything was worth a chance to work with Norm Ferguson.

Ben Sharpsteen had directed some of the best Pluto pictures, in my opinion, and he and Ferguson had established a highly successful association. I had animated for Sharpsteen before, during my checkered career in the studio, but the work had usually been on crowd scenes. The disadvantage of animating crowd scenes is that if they're any good nobody notices, and if they aren't you catch hell. Ben's greeting now was less than enthusiastic. It seemed obvious that his previous experiences with me left him feeling there was little to be happy about. I didn't think much of him either; he'd always looked like a cold fish. Whenever we passed in the hall, his acknowledgment of me had been little more than a curt nod, and sometimes even that was omitted.

He outlined my new job in stilted, pedantic tones: I was going to work with Bill Roberts, the other Pluto specialist in his team, not as an assistant but in a special category—I was going to re-animate all of Roberts' corrections and changes, and that was all I was going to do until further notice.

My high spirits took a nose dive. What the hell kind of a job was this? I never heard of such a nitwit assignment, and it was no surprise because there never was a job like that in the Disney Studio before or since. The full implications of the new position didn't dawn on me until later, but not much later.

I had never met Roberts before, and when I entered his room, the prospects were not very reassuring. Bill was a craggy little man who peered at the world over a pair of wire-rimmed eyeglasses, and what he saw he didn't seem to approve of. He smoked a black stubby pipe that smelled as if it had been marinated in bilge water.

The first correction Roberts handed me was a very short scene in *Mother Pluto* in which Pluto crouched down, wriggled his arse, then leaped over a fence. Sharpsteen and Disney had not liked the way he jumped. This looked like a pushover, so I sat down and roughed out the whole action in about fifteen minutes. I brought the work to Roberts, who did not even look up until he'd finished his drawing. He then took my roughs, and without even flipping the paper to see the action, dumped the whole scene into the wastebasket and returned to his animation. I stood there for a minute waiting for some explanation, but soon saw that one wasn't going to be forthcoming. Back I went, and this time it must have taken me all of half an hour to re-animate the scene. Damned if he didn't dump that one in the basket without looking at it, too.

Nine times I did that shot over, finally taking three or four hours on each try. Towards the end of my ordeal, Bill did look at the work. He'd make several laconic comments in a harsh, nasal twang before dropping

Ben Sharpsteen having fun. *Copyright © by Walt Disney Productions.*

it in the basket. Eventually the scene must have seemed acceptable to him, because he ordered me to send it down for a pencil test. Several days later, Bill went for a sweatbox session with Walt and Sharpsteen and I assumed that the scene was approved, because when he returned, he told me gruffly to clean up the drawings. There was no further comment, good, bad, or indifferent.

My first evaluation of Bill's Pluto was that the drawings were crude and the draftsmanship terrible. As the weeks went by, I began to see that he went about his work with a kind of ferocious honesty, the honesty one finds in Van Gogh's drawings of the potato eaters. Roberts was not ashamed to labor over his work. He would grunt, swear, and stop for long periods, looking moodily at his drawing and puffing away at that evil-smelling pipe, then, with a big sigh, he'd rip the drawing off the board, toss it into the wastebasket, and start again.

We both worked with such complete concentration that there was absolute silence for hours on end. Not all of Roberts' retakes were instigated by Sharpsteen or Disney. Bill had a problem with Pluto's legs, and on a long scene he had a tendency to succumb to what Gertrude Stein called "the evidence of the struggle"; the legs would get shorter and shorter as the scene progressed until Pluto looked like a dachshund.

Adding an inch or more to the legs was a complicated job, especially if Pluto was turning around, which meant that I'd have to redraw the whole action on fresh sheets of paper. The work was good practice for me.

For six months I worked for Roberts and during that whole period he never once said I had done a good job. It was either acceptable or I'd have to do it over. At least now he was willing to explain in detail the principle of drawing or animation I had violated. The number of changes I had to make in my work gradually started to dwindle.

I grew to appreciate Roberts' innate honesty as an artist and his thoughtful approach to his work. I found myself absorbing this attitude and taking pride in the fact that every drawing I did was my best possible effort. The old days of my slapdash approach were long gone.

As often as possible, I'd slip into Fergie's room to watch him work. He was a fox-faced Scotsman with a very casual way of working, in contrast to Roberts. He made rough drawings that looked like the map of a freight yard, and turned them out at breakneck speed, yet there was no strain in his posture, no effort reflected in his calm expression. He drew his animation in a way that reflected his background as an accountant. Fergie would go back three pages on his exposure sheets to find a pose he could reuse. One time, in *Moose Hunters,* he made a memorable scene of a moose chewing. He split the scene down the middle of the moose's face to animate the chewing on the left side. He then had his assistant, Johnny Lounsbery, trace the action in reverse. When that was finished, Fergie wrote up the exposure sheet and staggered the sequence of the two chewing actions. The result was a very funny, distorted piece of animation. Only a former accountant could dream up such a complicated use of numbering.

Film goes through a projector at the rate of twenty-four frames a second. For the average person one second is an almost unmeasurable fragment of time, but for a good animator, a twenty-fourth of a second is a solid fact, and he uses it with the accuracy of a violinist who can spear an *E* flat in the fifth position without even thinking about it.

Very few drawings are photographed for one frame; experience has shown that the audience cannot detect when a drawing is shot for two exposures. Since this cuts down on the number of drawings a second to twelve, instead of twenty-four, the savings in time and money are obvious.

However, it is not possible to shoot at three exposures a drawing because the image lingers long enough on the screen to cause a pause in the action, an eighth of a second instead of a twelfth. All these factors of split-second timing become very important in pantomime. The animation of a character like Pluto in the hands of a master animator like Norman Ferguson was honed down to such niceties as whether to sustain a thoughtful look for twenty-two frames or twenty-four. One-twelfth of a second might be the difference between a chuckle from the audience or a belly laugh.

One day during a session in the sweatbox with Ben Sharpsteen, Ferguson rose to leave because his work had been reviewed. However, he paused at the door to watch a new sequence that he had never seen before. When it was finished he casually mentioned that the last drawing of one scene had been shot for three frames instead of two. When it was checked it turned out that Fergie was right. He had been able to detect an error of one twenty-fourth of a second with consummate ease!

During those months I worked with Bill Roberts, I never saw Sharpsteen or Disney because I was never invited to the sweatbox sessions. Thanks to Roberts' vigilance, neither of them ever needed to ask for revisions on my corrections of Bill's animation. Even when Bill allowed me to do a small bit of animation on my own, I never had to make a change. This should have relieved my state of nervous tension, but it didn't. The lack of approval made me feel very insecure.

Although I was barely getting by on seventy-five dollars a week, it never occurred to me to think about quitting. I could have had a job anywhere else in the business at double those wages, but I was determined to make a success at Disney's.

Above all, I appreciated the chance to become an educated artist. Even now, I was going to Don Graham's classes at least two nights a week, and my drawing was improving by leaps and bounds. Graham had a fabulous memory. Although he worked with several hundred pupils a week, he would squat down next to me and mention that I'd had a similar problem with a drawing the week before. Don was extremely articulate and could break down a complex drawing problem into understandable components. Under his tutelage, I began to appreciate the work of Orozco, Cézanne, Picasso, Matisse, and Braque. I even made a cubistic painting one weekend, to the consternation of my family.

One of the most exciting events in our art education was a series of lectures by Jean Charlot. He was a Mexican artist of French ancestry who had painted murals along with Rivera, Orozco, O'Higgins, and Siqueiros during the revolution. This mild-mannered man had often worked on his murals with a revolver strapped to his hip. The lectures were a delightful combination of Gallic wit and erudition. He talked a great deal about composition, and the conscious use of geometry by Renaissance painters.

During one talk he pointed out that it was normal to show several views of the same object in a painting. When this was challenged by one of the more conservative artists in the audience, he answered by saying that we naturally saw everything from two points of view, since we had two eyes. What was unnatural was our acceptance of Italian perspective, since it was based on the theory that the viewer had only one eye!

Charlot's lectures argued for a wider acceptance of the aims of modern art, and he must have been successful because there were many heated discussions in the parking lot after the meetings ended.

Don Graham arranged a similar series of lectures by a famous drafts-man, Rico LeBrun. His animal drawings were very powerful, and they had a strong influence on the animal designs for the movie *Bambi.*

What was most amazing about the lecture series was that Disney had been willing to subsidize the program, even though he himself couldn't tell a Chirico from a Fiat. He went so far as to arrange for Frank Lloyd Wright to lecture to us. Unfortunately, this proved to be a disaster because Wright thought that since he was speaking to a group of cartoon-ists he had to be funny. He wasn't.

During this period, the studio was in a ferment. Disney had decided to use drawings of realistic-looking people for some of the characters in *Snow White and the Seven Dwarfs.* This posed a formidable problem for the animators. Snow White and the Queen would have to be animated to move gracefully and realistically, while the Prince would have to look valiant, regal, and virile. All three would need to have persuasive acting ability. Walt had some reservations about the ability of his animators to bring off such a tour de force unassisted. He decided to hire live actors (including a local dancer, Marge Belcher, in the role of Snow White) to be filmed as a guide for his animators, so in addition to the other work at hand, there was now a daily parade of midgets and dwarfs swarming to the sound stage.

The method that Disney had fallen back on—the tracing of live-action as a backstop for animated drawings—is known as "rotoscoping." In 1915, Max Fleischer and his brother Dave made a picture featuring their character Koko the Clown using this technique. Dave dressed up in a clown suit and was photographed by a motion picture camera. The resulting film was put into a machine that Max had invented, which would project the picture frame by frame, and each exposure was then traced off onto animation paper.

The drawings served as a guide for the animator, who made the necessary modifications to have the tracing conform to a cartoon version of Dave's action. The result was a fairly convincing kind of animation with a lifelike quality that no animator, with the exception of the pioneer Winsor McCay, could have matched in 1915. The method was used with great success by the Fleischer brothers for almost fifteen years, and they took it well beyond the experimental stage during that time. Unfortu-nately, the method piled additional costs on the normal budget for a cartoon production, and when rotoscoping did not prove to be the profitable venture that Max had envisioned, it was abandoned once Koko's popularity waned.

The basic premise of the rotoscope is not sound, because animation is essentially a caricature of real life. The final result is much more related to the formalized movement of ballet than it is to the movement of actors because each movement is choreographed. A good actor does exercise some control over his movements, but usually they are not as choreographed as either ballet or animation. The four exceptions that come to mind are Charlie Chaplin, Douglas Fairbanks, Buster Keaton, and Harry Langdon.

Walt's decision to use rotoscoping was an understandable one; the Disney brothers had put up the studio as collateral for a huge loan from the Bank of America, which had no reputation for being a charity organization. In addition, they had mortgaged their homes and everything else hockable. The picture had to be made within the budget or they were going to be wiped out. The rotoscope was a form of life insurance.

Even with the aid of rotoscoping, the animation of the human characters in *Snow White* was a risky proposition, but the expense of Don Graham's life classes was soon justified. The scenes of Snow White and the Queen were more than adequate, and some of the animation was very beautiful. The action was especially good in those cases where the animator used the rotoscope tracings as a crutch rather than a body cast.

Before production even started on *Snow White*, Walt had anticipated another weakness in his animators' capabilities. *Snow White* was not only going to call for realistic characters, it would need many scenes where there were going to be special effects, such as water, fog, and rain. These effects were going to have to be more convincing than the crude drawings the average animator could produce, so Walt decided to establish a separate department of special effects specialists.

The elaborate and inordinately expensive short subject *The Old Mill* served as a sort of "dry run" to test the possibilities of realistic special effects. Produced in 1937, and directed by Wilfred Jackson, the film was never meant to be a blockbuster of a story. It was instead a showcase for the new department, and the effects they produced for it were far better than anyone had ever animated before. More importantly, the film gave the new specialists the workout they would need before tackling the more difficult *Snow White*.

One of my good friends in the studio was an Oriental named Cy

Young. The relationship started back in 1924 at the Bray Studio where Cy worked on educational films. Most of the work consisted of retouching photographs, but sometimes Cy had to do a spot of animation. He was not a very good character animator, but when he went to work for Disney, Walt, with his eye for oddball talent, put Cy in charge of this new department for special effects.

Under Cy's leadership, the group started to examine the structure and movement of each special effect with the same intensity that the character animators used in studying acting and action. Up to this time, animators throughout the business handled whatever special effects were necessary themselves, along with their character animation. The results were never very convincing, because, when compared to the enjoyment of animating a figure, the special effects were considered to be pretty boring.

For Cy, the opportunity to use his expertise with an airbrush was the height of pleasure. He gathered around him a coterie of people who would never have made it in character animation: Ugo D'Orsi, Josh Meador, and a half-dozen others. They were so dedicated to the problems of animating special effects that it was not unusual for them to go out in a pelting rain to stand over a puddle, watching the way individual rain drops hit the water and created ripples.

Cy drove his group hard. If anybody brought him some animation that was not up to his standards, he would drop it in the wastebasket with some undiplomatic remark like, "Trained dog coo' do bettah."

During the production of *Snow White,* which had an inordinate number of scenes requiring special effects, Cy and his department had to make many retakes on their early work because, as the film progressed, their techniques improved so fast that their initial effects were outdated a few months later.

Cy had his own brand of humor. One weekend, we were up at Lake Arrowhead, and the bracing air had given us a huge appetite. We went into a local restaurant and sat down happily discussing the various dishes we were going to order. After a while, we became irritated at the waitresses, who were walking by as if we were nonexistent.

It finally dawned on me: this place did not want to serve Orientals. I became furious, but Cy remained very composed. Because of my angry insistence, we were served after a long wait. It was a burnt offering in the cause of bigotry; the eggs were charred, the toast was black, and the bacon blacker. While we picked ineffectually through this mess for something edible, the waitress watched with obvious pleasure.

I finally walked over to the cashier to pay the check, and out of the corner of my eye I saw that Cy was still at the table, leaving a tip! When we got outside I said, "For Chrissake, Cy, why did you leave that son of a bitch a tip?" Cy walked a few steps, then looked at me blandly. "Was not much, only penny."

Under Cy Young's leadership, the special effects department became expert at animating every conceivable type of special effect. Whether it was a purling brook, a waterfall, raindrops, fire, lightning, fog, or mist, there was someone in the group who could animate it. Ugo D'Orsi, for example, would work patiently hour after hour rendering single drops of water on cels with oil paint. This was the same D'Orsi whose animation at Fleischer's was considered to be second-rate. Walt always found the right niche for the right man.

For years, the story department had been working with the story sketch men on *Snow White,* and now the animation department began to drop its work on short subjects as team after team of directors and their animators began their work on the feature. There were excited discussions about the problems of animating each character.

The design of the dwarfs had changed radically over the years. They began as a group of characters that looked exactly like illustrations from German storybooks, but they had been refined and redesigned again and again and again. Now they were in the final process of being remodeled by the head animators. No matter how long the designers and story sketch men work on the drawing of a character, animation is the real moment of truth, when unexpected assets and liabilities in the construction of the figure are discovered.

As the months went by, it looked as if Sharpsteen and his group were going to continue producing shorts, because by this time every other unit was working on *Snow White.*

Sharpsteen was one of the few people in the studio whose career spanned the time when commercial animation started, on into the era of the modern sound cartoon. His first job was with Raoul Barré in 1916, and from there he went to Hearst's International, then to a studio founded by John and Paul Terry, and on to Max Fleischer's. His peer group reads like a roll call of animation greats: Walter Lantz, Bill Nolan, Burt Gillett, Bill Tytla, Grim Natwick, and Dave Hand.

Shortly after Walt's amazing entry into sound cartoons, Sharpsteen left Fleischer's and joined the Disney staff as an animator. When Walt decided to allocate some of the direction to others in 1929, Ben was passed over in favor of Wilfred Jackson, Burt Gillett, Ub Iwerks, and Dave Hand. It wasn't until late in 1934 that he was given his first assignment as a director *(Two Gun Mickey).*

He was often saddled with the problem of using ex-New Yorkers like Eugster, Wolf, and me, as well as neophyte Californians like the group I came in with in 1935. Now, in 1937, this quiet, pedantic man's talents were being appreciated. Disney seems to have been drawn more easily to people who exuded confidence, which Sharpsteen did not.

Perce Pearce, another sequence director on *Snow White,* is a good example. Perce came to the studio when I did. The first time I noticed him was when we were all nervously waiting around for George Drake to take us on a tour of the studio. Perce wasn't nervous in the least. He soon gathered a small group of youngsters around him and began to explain to them some aspects of studio production. From what I could overhear, the man had never been in an animation studio in his life, but the kids all listened to him with great awe.

While he was doling out this misinformation, Pearce would interrupt himself at a crucial phrase by producing a kitchen match, lighting it, and resuming his monologue. Just when it was about to burn his fingers, Pearce would apply it to his pipe and take a few puffs before going on, then the pipe would go out and he'd repeat the whole performance.

He was the best gag stealer I ever saw. Every time we went into a gag session on a new picture, I watched him with reluctant admiration. Some youngster would get up and stumble, "Uh . . . ah, how about if Mickey did . . ." and go into a fumbling explanation of his idea. Pearce would wait until he got the full import of the gag, then interrupt the kid before he was finished. With a flourish of his pipe and a seemingly endless supply of matches, Pearce would offer the very same gag, embellished by a flow of adjectives and puffs at his pipe, which always seemed to go out on cue.

His verbal style was somewhere in between the enthusiasm of a salesman of electric health belts, and the pontifical manner of a minister with a rich parish. This, along with the pipe routine, produced a mesmerizing effect. By the time he was finished with his verbalization, the originator of the idea had been forgotten and Pearce had chalked up another gag.

He soon realized that this approach would not cover up his lack of talent in the inbetween department, so he lost no time in vanishing into the story department where his predatory skills could be put to better use. Pearce made it a practice of working with a storyman who was nervous about putting together a good story presentation to Walt. Pearce would step into the breech and make the presentation himself.

Walt would sit openmouthed as the storyboard was explained between flaring kitchen matches and puffs of smoke. Normally, these sessions were a nerve-racking ordeal for writers because Walt would constantly interrupt to probe the validity of a gag or question some point in the story structure. To the annoyance of the other writers, Walt never used these tactics on Pearce. He would sit hypnotized by the pipe routine and the W. C. Fields voice. The result was that Pearce received every sign of Walt's favor, including the chance to work as a sequence director on *Snow White*. From apprentice to director in two years speaks well for nicotine addiction. Too bad Sharpsteen never learned to smoke a pipe.

As for me, I was never envious of people who were working on *Snow White*. My relationship with Bill Roberts was keeping me very happy, because in spite of his forbidding manner, he was essentially a very kind person. As my animation improved, he would willingly take time from his own work to spend as much as a half hour explaining some facet of animation or timing that I needed to know more about.

I gathered from his picturesque vocabulary that Bill had been raised somewhere in the Appalachian Mountains. Bill sounded like Snuffy Smith. He was the only person in the studio who called Mickey Mouse a "varmint."

One day he came back from the sweatbox fuming. He sat for a long time brooding and sucking on that horrible pipe. Finally, he rattled off a list of small changes I was to make, revisions that he obviously considered nit-picking. He went back to his work and after a short time turned to watch me pull out the scenes to be changed from the cupboard. He eyed the growing stack with disapproval. "Jeem," he said, sighing heavily, "If'n you pluck a chicken and come down to the pinfeathers, keep on a-pluckin' an' you jes might start pickin' the meat off'n the bones." With that terse observation, he went back to work.

It was inevitable that a large staff (we had 750 people) would breed factions. There was a group from Northern California that tended to band together, and a large Southern California party that was able to influence the advancement of its members. Oddly enough, the New Yorkers never formed a cabal even though many of the important directors, animators, and writers were easterners.

The men Roberts admired the most were Ferguson, Natwick, Tytla, and Sharpsteen, all former New Yorkers and none of them factional. Sharpsteen, for all his reputation, kept a very low profile, and his lack of aggression might very well have explained the fact that our group was still working on shorts when *Snow White* was going into its final phase.

When Roberts came slouching into the room after a long absence, I knew something important was up because he slumped into his chair and sat for a long time, blowing environment-threatening clouds of smoke. Finally he turned to me and said very casually, "Jeem, I'm agonna work on *Snow White*." I reacted very happily. But then I wasn't so happy when Bill added that I wouldn't be working with him anymore.

For all his gruff manner, Roberts was really a great tease. My dismay was obvious, but instead of telling me what was in store, he casually suggested that I drop in to see Sharpsteen as soon as I finished correcting my work. A few hours later, I was looking at a new storyboard that took up one whole wall of Ben's office.

The picture was called *Hawaiian Holiday* and it had three main themes: One was a musical bit with Mickey and Minnie (with a sub-theme between Donald Duck and a starfish); another was a sequence with Goofy and a surfboard; and the last a section involving Pluto with a crab. The latter looked like a typical Ferguson pantomime job.

In his usual pedantic fashion, Sharpsteen announced that I was going to animate the entire Pluto sequence. From his stiff manner, I could see that Ben felt that he was still saddled with an incompetent, and as I looked at the storyboard, I felt he was right.

My spirits lifted when I found myself in my own room with a brand-new assistant, Nick DeTolly. He was a barrel-chested White Russian refugee who had walked from Moscow to Paris during the revolution. Nick was working there as a caricaturist in a sidewalk cafe when he saw and answered an advertisement Walt had placed in a French magazine. In an effort to find more potential animation talent, Disney had placed ads in dozens of American and European magazines. He expected to find enough competent artists to greatly enlarge the staff. Nick was lucky to be accepted.

Once Don Graham had shown me a waist-high stack of artwork samples which had been sent from all over the world. Graham said that out of five thousand submissions, only thirteen were chosen. To show how difficult it was to survive at the studio, out of the original thirteen only a few managed to become special effects animators. None of them ever became character animators. The remainder were fired or quit.

"Ducky" Nash, the voice of Donald Duck, is now eighty-three years old. He appeared at a recent get-together of old Disney employees. *Collection of Shamus Culhane.*

Pluto drawing from *Hawaiian Holiday.*

When I went into Sharpsteen's room to pick up my first part of the sequence, I was in for a surprise. I had fancied myself to be a competent director, but that was back at Iwerks' and Fleischer's studios where they were producing slapstick, and the director's main problem was to explain the action well enough so that the animator would be sure to turn out thirty feet a week.

Ben went over that storyboard drawing by drawing, showing me where the poses were usable, and the holes in the action where I was going to have to add my own interpretation. It was embarrassing to think that I had ever considered myself a good director. I felt that I had never before faced the problems of direction. The briefing went on for several hours and I left Sharpsteen's room with my head bursting with instructions.

For many years, both at Fleischer's and Disney's, I found that one perplexing aspect of my work was the frightening variance in my ability to draw. One morning I would animate with great enthusiasm and ease, go to lunch, and come back to an afternoon of struggle, often with a very poor result, or I would reverse the procedure and ply the eraser on a series of stiff, insipid drawings for hours, and suddenly there would be a breakthrough and for a few golden hours I felt a compatibility between my mind and my pencil; then the connection would vanish again and I was back to erasing and swearing. Why?

I decided to find out if other animators had the same problem. I discussed it with Grim Natwick, Bill Tytla, Roberts, and Freddy Moore. The most facile animator at Disney's, Fred assured me that he, too, often suffered from this drawing inability. The others admitted that it often happened and offered home remedies like switching from pencil to crayon. The general consensus seemed to be that the best thing was to just keep on drawing and erasing and eventually the block would go away. Even Don Graham had no better solution.

These answers didn't satisfy me. I turned to books on creativity by the eminent psychologists of the day and found myself sunk in a welter of scientific jargon that gave me no solution.

Now I was presented with a Pluto sequence which posed an enormous obstacle to my career. If I failed, the best I could look forward to was a career as a second-rate animator, drawing crowd shots and minor bits of animation, or quitting Disney's and the atmosphere of creativity that I loved.

In spite of my trepidation, my first few scenes in *Hawaiian Holiday* seemed not too difficult. Following a brief encounter with a starfish, Pluto met a cocky crab. After a short scuffle, he was to chase it toward the surf. The crab scuttled along, running sideways, and Pluto would run in the same fashion, at least his front legs would. The rear legs were scrambling over tree trunks and rocks in time to a prerecorded piece of music.

While I was nervous about this scene at first, I managed to rough out the animation without too much trouble. When I ran the pencil test of the crab and Pluto on my moviola, it seemed to synchronize with the music very well, so I sent it in for screening in the sweatbox.

Disaster struck! I was called down to the projection room to find that Sharpsteen was furious. He had run the silent pencil test while waiting for the sound track to come from the editor, and he thought the animation was terrible. On a big screen it did look pretty bad, all jerks and sudden moves.

Ben had a habit of rubbing his forearms with both hands when he was irritable, and this time they were working like pistons on a Mississippi steamboat. He assured me that I would have a huge retake as soon as the track arrived. I left the room dragging my arse.

When I was summoned back to the sweatbox, for the first time I began to think of quitting; it was just too much of a beating. Sharpsteen made no comment as the pencil test and the music started. The animation hit every beat exactly. All the little jerks and hesitations were a perfect interpretation of the music. I didn't have to change a drawing, Sharpsteen admitted grudgingly. Walt, too, approved the sequence with no changes.

These scenes were easy compared to the action that followed. When Pluto decided to think things over, he inadvertantly sat down on the crab. In its struggle to escape, the crab started to drag Pluto's rear end with him. When the dog stood up to see what was behind him, the action swung his tail high over his head so that he couldn't see that the crab was now attached to it. Pluto started to walk away and the action caused the crab to slap against his rump with every step. He continued into a series of contortions trying to see what it was that was annoying him, but in each new position the crab was still out of his view.

Finally there was a confrontation; the sequence ended with the crab stalking over, honking Pluto's nose, and making an exit, leaving behind a bewildered dog. All this pantomime was typical of Ferguson's animation, but I had never attempted anything so difficult in my life.

Instead of grabbing a piece of paper and starting on drawing number one, I found myself sitting around looking out of the window and thinking about the sequence in a kind of daydream. While the storyboard gave Pluto many funny poses, the crab was given no specific character. After a while an amusing idea came to me: what would Edward G. Robinson do if he were a crab?

With that premise, I tore into the animation at top speed, not even stopping to number the drawings. Each drawing was so rough that it was just a tangled mass of lines, a form of graphic shorthand. I only drew what was essential to my concept of the important action, which meant that some drawings were only an eye or a tail with the crab hanging on, others were the whole dog drawn with no details whatsoever.

By the end of the day, I had several hundred drawings, and by the end of the week there was a stack of six or seven hundred sketches and the complete sequence was roughed out. For the next two months, I drew over these scribbles, trying always to retain the strength and vitality of the originals in the more complete drawings. I was now working very slowly, paying strict attention to the proper proportions of the two characters, but still keeping the drawings loose and rough.

When the first few scenes were shown in the sweatbox, Walt and the writers immediately saw that I had created a very funny character in the crab. He was now much more than a mere foil, so each time they saw more animation, they would think up small additions to the scenes. The sequence expanded, one foot here, three there.

By the end of a few weeks, what with renumbered drawings, added animation, and revised exposure sheets, I was a nervous wreck. Otto Englander came in from the story department to congratulate me and found me in a petulant mood. "Look at these goddamn messed-up exposure sheets!" I fumed. Otto looked at me in amazement, "Are you nuts? You're a big success!" I was just too tired to appreciate it.

Al Eugster, an ex–New York animator and my good friend, had done a marvelous job on his first real chance at doing an important sequence by animating the Mickey, Minnie, and Donald scenes. Woolie Reitherman and Frenchy De Trémaudan had knocked off the hilarious sequence of Goofy and the surfboard. In the 1938 International Film Festival in Venice, *Hawaiian Holiday* won an award as the best short of the year. Animation buffs consider it to be one of the classic Disney short subjects.

More important to me than the success of the picture was the fact that I had evolved a different way of working. By sketching at top speed, I didn't have time to think about the individual drawings. Instead, I was drawing emotionally and tapping my unconscious. Sometimes the characters seemed to be acting on their own. Actions came so spontaneously that I was often unaware that they were about to happen.

When this process was over, I had gone back and approached my work intellectually, using my knowledge of drawing to analyze what I had barely indicated in the heat of creativity. At this point, it was proper to draw slowly, stopping to erase and correct with deliberation.

Now I understood why Norman Ferguson was able to constantly improve Pluto's acting, and why, in every picture, Fergie was able to create some new facet of Pluto's character. Later, when I read the writings of Samuel Johnson, Pablo Picasso, and Joan Miró, I found that they all had written about the separation of the emotional and the intellectual functions during creativity.

Over the years, I have expounded this theory to students of animation and not many of them have accepted it. Too often animators draw with a pencil in one hand and an eraser in the other, in the mistaken belief that they are exercising strict control over their work. To me, the headlong plunge into the unconscious is an exhilarating method of drawing, like riding bareback on a wild horse. I leave the saddle and bridle to the more timid. As Nikos Kazantzakis said, "The intellect should be the servant, not the master."

During this period, I had my salary raised to one hundred dollars a week. When the picture was finished, I received a bonus of several thousand dollars. The bonus system was another of Disney's ideas. While the base pay for animators was just about the same as the rest of the industry, under the bonus system, if you did very good work, it was possible to make a very high salary.

Walt looked over each finished picture, scene by scene, and decided the bonus rate for each shot. He paid twelve dollars a foot for the best animation, and then it would scale down to eight, then four dollars. If a scene was just passable, or if it was a crowd shot, there was no bonus at all.

Under the aegis of the bonus system, I went from rags to riches on the basis of one picture. For the rest of my time at Disney's, I never earned less than twelve dollars a foot as a bonus on my animation.

Bill Roberts was very pleased with my success. The old curmudgeon admitted that all the time he had been chewing me out, he'd been sending very favorable reports to Walt. We got into a discussion about the fact that my interpretation of Pluto was somewhere in between his drawing style and Fergie's. None of us drew a streamlined Pluto, like Fred Moore.

Fergie's Pluto, all sharp angles with a skinny nose, and Roberts' Pluto, with its bunched up body and big snout, were a far cry from Moore's highly polished version of Pluto. We agreed that Fred was a great animator, but we both felt that he pushed his love for designing too far. He reminded me of Renoir who sometimes, in his paintings of women, got so involved in his paint quality that the figure lost its structure and looked as if it were made of pink rubber.

Another highly polished design came about in the evolution of Donald Duck from a long-billed, gangly duck, to a bird with a truncated bill and a body design so beautifully controlled that Donald looked as if he had been turned out on a lathe. Somehow in the process Roberts and I thought that he had lost some of his fiesty look.

"Jeem," Roberts said peevishly, "someday people like Fergie, you, and me are a-gonna be out. We won't be able to make those cutie-cute characters. They'll jus' ruin them all, Donald Duck, and Pluto, even Goofy." I agreed.

The most successful redesigning that Fred Moore did was in changing Mickey Mouse. In the early days animators used half-dollars and quarters to draw Mickey's head and body. It was almost impossible to get any life quality out of such a rigid construction. Moore gave Mickey a pear-shaped body, which could squash and stretch, and more important, he gave Mickey two eyes. Heretofore, Mickey's pupils floated around on a big expanse of white. There was no way to draw subtle expressions with such a face.

Oddly enough, although the studio's reputation was built on Mickey Mouse, and he was an internationally known character, he never went very far as an actor. In the early sound cartoons Mickey was a fairly violent character at times, but as the story department grew more sophisticated, and stars like Pluto and Goofy emerged, Mickey subsided into a kind of master of ceremonies. He never rose beyond this concept. As a mouse his acting ability was bland compared to the mice in *The Country Cousin,* for example.

As for Minnie, she was almost reduced to being a prop. In *Hawaiian Holiday* she did a hula-hula and was about as sexy and alluring as a Westchester matron taking her first dancing lesson.

All this is in sharp contrast to the strong delineation of Pluto, Goofy, and a dozen other characters in the shorts and features.

There is a nonsensical urge in this country: the need to make comparisons. Was Muhammad Ali a better fighter than Rocky Marciano? Was Willie Mays a better center fielder than Mickey Mantle? It has been taken to the point of complete absurdity, even using computers to try to prove the unprovable. I am not going to join in this nonsense by trying to select the best animator at Disney's during the making of *Snow White*.

I do have to note that certainly one of the outstanding animators was Bill Tytla. This fiery, inarticulate man, whose massive black mustachios made him look like a Cossack, did some of the best dwarf animation in *Snow White*.

One characteristic of his work was that even seemingly passive poses in his drawings suggested an inner turmoil. In addition, Tytla had a complete mastery of space. His handling of crowds on the screen was a good example of this forte. In the sequence where Grumpy is washed by the other six dwarfs, the scenes are full of violent action, yet there is no time when the composition is not under perfect control. The struggle produces one interesting pattern after another, instead of just becoming a meaningless mass of writhing bodies.

His instinctive feeling for the smallest action gave his animation the ring of truth. When Doc took off his glasses to make a forceful point in his dialogue, Tytla did not have him pluck the eyeglasses off with both hands, rather, the dwarf did what many people do under stress: one hand released the frame from one ear, then Doc turned his head and pulled himself impatiently away from the constriction of the glasses. A small action, but indicative of Tytla's ability to totally submerge himself in the emotions of the character he was drawing.

Bill was a person who had passionate opinions about his role as an artist. While he appreciated the standards of quality in the studio, he had a great contempt for the political jockeying for power among the various factions. Secure in his own strivings for perfection in his animation, he had only ridicule for some of the gung ho, banal interpretations of Disney's efforts to improve the standards of his staff. He was too sophisticated to be affected by exhortations that sometimes bordered on the old college try. If he had been subjected to Dave Hand's welcoming speech, Tytla would probably have dissolved into loud laughter.

Every scene he animated was a painful, intense, emotional experience. When he talked about animation, he could only bring forth broken, inarticulate sentences, punctuated by "you see," a phrase that he used as a kind of stepping-stone to the next fragmented idea. What I could piece together from our discussions about animation made me realize that Tytla, Roberts, Natwick, and Ferguson had a great deal in common. They all approached animation with an intense honesty. To them, drawing was a complete submersion of self.

Arthur Babbitt has said that Tytla read Boleslavsky's *Acting: The First Six Lessons,* a book that stresses six principles: concentration, memory of emotion, dramatic action, characterization, observation, and rhythm. While we had several discussions about creativity, Tytla never mentioned Boleslavsky. If he had, I certainly would have been eager to read the book. At that time, I had never heard of it.

Tytla's assistant was Bill Shull, who was the direct antithesis of Bill in personality. Where Tytla was volatile and passionate, Shull was a cool, calm, and amused observer of the scene. He had a mordant wit, the kind the English relish. Sometimes Tytla would sputter and fume for ten minutes about some aspect of the studio, or world politics, waving both hands to emphasize a point, and then Shull would add a comment, a spare dozen words, every one of them dripping with acid, but delivered with a complete deadpan.

Assistants like Bill Shull who worked with the great animators had a tremendous advantage in that, as they matured, they were given bits of animation to do themselves. Their work had to be comparable in quality to the work of their mentors. The result was that when they became full-fledged animators themselves, they never went through an awkward stage.

John Lounsbery, Fergie's assistant for many years, and Marc Davis, who worked with Grim Natwick on *Snow White,* both started off doing superb animation as soon as they were off on their own. Lounsbery and Davis wound up as members of the fabled group of star animators at Disney's, dubbed the "Nine Old Men."

Arthur Babbitt and Bill Tytla were great friends. They made a curious contrast both in physiques and lifestyles. Tytla had the powerful but truncated figure of a typical Slavic peasant, while Babbitt was whippet-lean. Tytla tended to brood and treated the political machinations of the various factions in the studio with great contempt, but tended to keep these feelings to himself. Babbitt, on the other hand, was very outspoken about his views of the studio management, world politics, the new state sales tax, or whatever. Armed with an extraordinarily good vocabulary, he would present his ideas in a succinct, logical manner. He was a formidable opponent on any subject. This was in sharp contrast to Tytla's often incoherent remarks puntuated by the inevitable "You see . . ." Often, you didn't.

They shared a large house, but the decor of the living room seems to have been Babbitt's choice rather than Tytla's. Art had a great fondness for classical music and had a large library of records with the best sound equipment available at the time. The living room had comfortable chairs and a settee, as well as a number of large cushions for those who liked to recline on the floor in Greenwich Village fashion. This arrangement seemed not to be very enticing to Tytla. One night, while a group of us were sitting around enjoying the music, Tytla walked in and surveyed the figures sprawled on the floor with a faint smile. "Looks like a Turkish whorehouse," he said and strode off to his bedroom with a muttered "G'night" trailing after him.

Recently, I chanced on a book by Joseph Meeker, *The Comedy of Survival,* in which he postulated the theory that there are two kinds of heroes: the comic and the tragic. The tragic hero is a person who is willing to risk everything for a goal he knows is right. He is unswerving in defense of moral principles and does not hesitate to take on powers greater than himself. The comic hero's goal is survival the best way he can. Life is an end in itself rather than a struggle between right and wrong. I can't imagine better definitions of the lifestyles of Babbitt and Tytla.

In addition to Babbitt's fine animation, such as his sympathetic rendering of the characters in *The Country Cousin,* he was the acknowledged expert at animating Goofy. In my opinion, his success with this jovial, brain-damaged oaf was achieved by a cold, objective examination of a personality that was the direct antithesis of Babbitt's intellectuality. It was as if, in his distaste for stupidity, Art strove to exhibit Goofy's ridiculous antics, parading them before the audience in order to confirm his negative feelings about him. This is in sharp contrast to Woolie Reitherman's happy-go-lucky, dim-witted Goofy in *Hawaiian Holiday,* who enjoys himself to the fullest and invites the audience to share in his small victories.

Babbitt animated the Queen in *Snow White* and pushed the dramatic

Wilfred Jackson by Art Babbitt. Jackson was responsible for the idea of animating to a fixed set of musical beats, making it possible to write a musical score after a picture was finished. In addition, he is regarded as one of the all-time great directors.

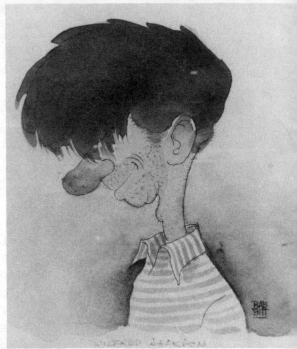

Art Babbitt and Bill Tytla in 1934. Soon after this photo was taken, Tytla stopped playing polo due to a cracked pelvis suffered when a pony rolled onto him during a match. *Collection of Art Babbitt.*

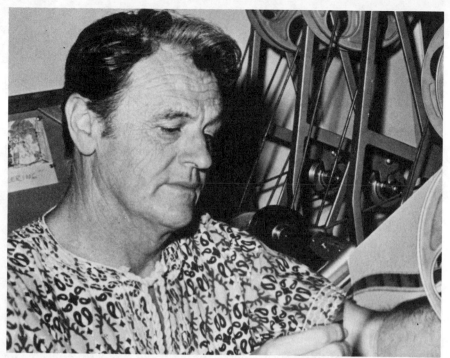

Wolfgang (Woolie) Reitherman's physical energy was unmatched in the animation business. He was solely responsible for the direction of four feature films—*The Sword in the Stone, The Jungle Book, The Aristocats,* and *Robin Hood*—a feat unequaled by any other American animation director. *Copyright* © *by Walt Disney Productions.*

Caricature of Bill Tytla by Shamus Culhane, 1936.

impact of her personality into a realm of acting that established him as one of the truly great animators of all time. Nobody could have animated her character in such an inspired manner unless he was able to call up tremendous feelings about her evil personality. There are depths of passion in Art Babbitt that are usually masked effectively by a facade of cold logic.

A few years before, while he was still working for Max Fleischer, Grim Natwick had created the first female star in animation: Betty Boop. With this expertise, Grim chafed under the restrictions of the rotoscope tracings. The one area where he ignored the tracing altogether was in the drawing of Snow White's hands. The other animators followed the live-action hands fairly closely with the usual lack of vitality that is found in a tracing. Natwick's hands, however, stressed a definite design. One can easily pick out his animation of Snow White (he drew more than eighty scenes), because of the beautiful action of her hands. Sometimes his innate feeling for design cropped up in shots where he ignored the live-action altogether.

There is one scene where Snow White runs down the stairs. For an instant, her voluminous dress swirls in a lovely, intricate pattern. When Disney saw the scene in the sweatbox, he exclaimed, "There, goddamn it! That's the kind of stuff I want!" Nobody who knew that Grim had ignored the rotoscope completely had the nerve to tell Walt.

I had several talks with Fergie about his approach to animation. While I was animating my crab and Pluto sequence, he was drawing the Wicked Witch in *Snow White*. As usual, his work turned out to be some of the best acting in the picture. I had hoped to glean from him a few ideas about creativity, but Fergie just sat there, chewing gum and drawing those hieroglyphics of his, the pencil skating over the paper with no hesitation.

It seemed to vaguely trouble him to discuss theories. It was as if he had never thought in abstract terms about animation and didn't want to start now. His answers to my hesitant questions were laconic and somewhat impatient, so finally I stopped asking him questions about his work habits.

Anyone who thinks that making a good drawing is some kind of an intellectual effort should have been able to watch some of these great animators at work, as I have. The amount of physical effort was sometimes enormous. I remember Bill Roberts hunched over his drawing board, pipe clenched in bared teeth, making little grunts as he hacked at a Pluto drawing, or Bill Tytla, with his huge black eyebrows drawn down into a sharp *V*, fierce mustache half hiding an agonized mouth. What is he drawing? A pensive Doc addressing the other dwarfs. There was also Grim Natwick, his massive shoulders hunched, his eyes narrowed to slits, his mouth snarling with one tooth showing, looking like a fullback getting ready to receive the ball. He is working on a mass of lines which Marc Davis or Les Novros will translate into a lithe, happy Snow White singing to a bird.

It may seem strange until one remembers that at the highest point of sexual consummation, the expressions of the partners are often what we label agonized or ferocious. Creativity and sex are experiences that seem to be parallel, even to that vague feeling of depression when the experience is over.

Snow White and Pinocchio

Just as I was putting the finishing touches to my animation on *Hawaiian Holiday,* I ran into Walt in the hall. "Hi there, Culhane," he said casually, "you're going to work with Ben Sharpsteen on *Snow White.*" I stood there, mouth agape. "Jesus Christ! Thanks Ben . . . I mean Walt!" Walt walked away laughing at my happy confusion.

Sharpsteen went over my sequence with me and it was a ball buster. The dwarfs marched home from the mine singing the "Heigh-Ho" song. They ducked under branches, went over fallen tree trunks, and there was a shot of them marching in perspective, throwing huge shadows on the face of a cliff. I was glad I had received lessons in the perspective of shadows in Don Graham's class.

The major gag was that Dopey was going to hop and skip throughout the sequence in an effort to get in step with the other dwarfs. This wasn't particularly difficult. The real problem was that I would have to control the other six dwarfs (all with different patterns of walking) in such a way as to avoid crowding together or falling behind and leaving spaces.

The answer was to make elaborate plans for every step for each dwarf before I made a drawing. Every scene was a problem of perspective, so there was no possibility of animating with my high-speed technique. This was going to need careful drawing of each dwarf, with his feet falling exactly where the perspective plans decreed.

It took me almost six months of backbreaking work to finish the sequence, but it went through the sweatbox without my having to change a drawing. One day, Bill Roberts came in to see the pencil test on my moviola. When he was finished, he turned to look at me over his wire eyeglasses. "Jeem," he said quietly, "I couldn't have done that." The sequence has been praised by many people, but I value this craggy old character's remark the most. (The Walt Disney Studio's contribution to the screening of excerpts from American Film Classics at Expo '67 was my "Heigh-Ho" sequence. The drawings and the sequence were a part of the Disney Show at the Whitney Museum in 1981.)

Because many of the scenes were drawn on paper thirty-six inches long, we were given a special set of shelves to store the drawings in while Nick was cleaning them up. The unit was long enough, but it lacked sufficient depth, so that stacks of animation paper protruded an inch or more over the edge of the shelving.

Nick DeTolly was a chain smoker, and he was also very untidy. Behind his drawing board was an accumulation of discarded drawings, and at his elbow there was always an ashtray filled to overflowing with cigarette butts. One day as I worked I heard a scrabbling sound from Nick's direction. When I looked up, there he was beating out a fire with his bare hands. A lighted cigarette had fallen out of the ashtray, rolled behind his drawing board, and ignited the crumpled pile of old drawings. Flames began to leap from one shelf to the next, facilitated by the fact that the drawings protruded. My whole goddamn sequence was on fire in seconds!

Before I could help, Nick had grabbed a towel and smothered the flames. The miracle was that none of the drawings was damaged, although in some cases the fire had burned to within a quarter of an inch of the figures. Walt issued a very stern warning about careless smoking, and Nick nursed a pair of slightly burned hands.

As *Snow White*'s production neared the deadline, it was obvious to us all that it was going to be a near thing. The possibility of a Bank of America takeover created a feeling of tension in the studio that almost made the air crackle. When we were asked to work Saturday afternoons without pay, we all did so very willingly. Many of us worked Sundays as well. I never heard a single person grouse about working for nothing.

Two entire sequences were abandoned even though they were completely animated. One was a bed-building sequence. Snow White was much too big to sleep in one of the dwarf's beds, and since she was going to live with them, the dwarfs decided to build her an elaborate bed. Ward Kimball and Dick Lundy did much of the animation, and my friend Al Eugster spent weeks on the sequence, only to see it all end up on the cutting room floor.

The other sequence that had to be junked was a very funny one. Snow White had prepared some soup. As the dwarfs sat down to eat, Grumpy curled one arm protectively around his bowl and began to slurp his soup very noisily. Snow White was horrified at his bad table manners, but with his nose in the bowl, Grumpy paid no attention to her reaction. When one of the other dwarfs tugged at his sleeve, Grumpy, in what should have been one of the best bits of acting in the picture, swung around fiercely with his soup spoon overhead, ready to repel all intruders.

The official reason for dropping the two sequences was that they slowed down the picture. That might have been true in the case of the bed-building sequence, but I can't see how the lusty humor in the soup sequence would have done anything but contribute to the story. Probably time and lack of money were important elements, if not chief factors, in arriving at this decision.

The soup sequence was finished at a later date, and was used in the Disney TV show. The bed-building sequence was never completed.

One horrendous piece of animation had to be left in *Snow White* because there was no way to omit it. Some of the scenes of the Prince (when he reappeared in the closing minutes of the picture) were apparently the victims of the frenzied rush to finish the film on time. I would guess that the tracings of the live-action were not accurate, and the animator had followed the tracings very closely. The Prince trembled and shook as if he were in an advanced state of palsy! Under normal conditions, no animator in his right mind would have sent his first rough to the sweatbox looking like that.

It must have been a heartbreaking decision for Walt. The fact that the palsied Prince went into the picture uncorrected is an indication of the dangerous financial condition of the studio at that time, and the breakneck speed of production as the release date drew nearer and nearer.

Suddenly, near the end of the picture, the tension in the studio was too much. To relieve it, there was a spontaneous avalanche of pornographic drawings from all over the studio. Drawings of Snow White being gang raped by the dwarfs, and mass orgies among the dwarfs themselves. Even the old witch was involved.

Some of the drawings were about comic sexual aberrations that Krafft-Ebing would never have dreamed of. This mania went on for about a week, and as suddenly as it started the whole thing stopped. It must have

A drawing by Shamus Culhane for the sequence of the dwarfs marching home from the mine singing "Heigh-ho, Heigh-ho." This animation was shown as the Disney contribution to Expo '67, a part of the exhibit called Great American Film Classics. It was also a part of the Whitney Museum's show of Disney films, drawings, and backgrounds, The Golden Age of Animation. *Snow White and the Seven Dwarfs*, 1938. *Copyright © by Walt Disney Productions.*

been a form of hysteria brought on by fatigue and the relentless schedule. As far as I know, Walt never heard about it.

If ostentatious vulgarity had not already existed, the movie moguls would have hired somebody to invent it. How else could they have built the Roxy and the Paramount theaters in New York, and the Carthay Circle and Grauman's Chinese Theater in Hollywood?

Who knows what dreams of luxury disturbed the sleep of children, huddled on the tops of tiled stoves in Russian shtetls at the turn of the century, perhaps dreams of the Byzantine grandeur of the czar's court. Now, years later, these phantasmagorical images had been transformed into reality by these same sleepers.

The movie audiences loved these gaudy palaces of entertainment. They tiptoed through the ankle-deep crimson carpets, awed by the rows of paintings in the lobby (the work of each nonentity surrounded by a frame that would have honored a Rembrandt), and submitted meekly to the crisp orders of ushers dressed in uniforms that had all the ornate trappings of Hungarian hussars and more.

Inside, they watched greedily as the vast silken curtain rose with a sensuous susurrus like the nightgown of a king's mistress, and saw nothing incongruous in the fact that this movement, with its intense sexual connotations, ended by revealing nothing more than an austere white rectangle.

Settling back in their plush seats, they could forget the unpaid rent, the rumblings of impending war in Europe, and an uninspired sex life, to pursue their fantasies in stories where the good guys always won, the heroine never was seduced (although it was a close call), and justice always triumphed. Lenin was wrong about religion; in 1937, motion pictures were the opium of the people.

Weeks before the opening of *Snow White,* the publicity department of Disney Studio had done a superb job. The newspapers were full of articles about *Snow White* and Walt Disney. The readers were given awesome statistics about the number of drawings per minute and other bits of impressive trivia. Following the usual policy of the studio, Walt was eulogized as the creator of *Snow White,* with no mention of any individuals on his staff.

Snow White was slated to open at the Carthay Circle on December 21, 1937. This was the accolade, the sign that animated cartoons had at last entered the big time. Hollywood opening nights were as formalized as Australian bushmen circumcision rites. One had to be driven to the theater and dropped off, since Bronco Nagurski in his prime could not have bulled his way through the squirming, shoving mass of fans that butted against the police barriers lining both sides of the entrance.

A friend volunteered to act as chauffeur and neatly stopped the car, with a flourish, in front of the red carpet that ran to the curb. My wife was wearing a new green evening gown, which showed off her superb figure to perfection; and my tuxedo, in spite of six years of disuse, smelt only faintly of mothballs. I thought we made a handsome couple.

As we started toward the theater, the crowd surged against the barriers to see who we were. There was a continuous roar from the mob, but as we started through this gauntlet of frenzied humanity, one voice could be heard through the din, "Who's that?" Another voice answered in disgust, "Aaaah, that's nobody!"

We found that most of the Disney employees had seats in the back of the theater. The front seats were occupied by an assembly of the most prestigious stars in Hollywood, as well as the top executives from every major studio. Walt must have been gratified at this turnout of Hollywood's elite.

All of us were keyed up, greeting each other with strained smiles or jerky headbobs of recognition, then after the picture started, we all relaxed. It was the most receptive, enthusiastic audience I have ever seen. Every song, every gag, every good piece of acting worked on those people like a bow on a fiddle. There was almost continuous laughter and applause until Frank Thomas' sequence, where the sorrowing dwarfs gather around Snow White's bier. The house fell silent, gripped by the emotional impact of the acting. It was the first time grief had been so dramatically depicted in an animated cartoon.

As the picture faded there was a thunderous ovation, which continued long after the houselights flashed on. We all left the theater with the happy knowledge that we had worked on one of the greatest films in the history of motion pictures. None of us will ever forget that night. As we waited for our car, I thought with satisfaction, "Screw those sons of bitches in the crowd. I am somebody. I have worked on a picture that's going to be around long after these bastards are dead."

Film critics all over the world almost unanimously agreed that *Snow White* was a masterpiece. Jean Charlot, in 1939, wrote a book, *Art from the Mayans to Disney*, in which he said, "We have already seen the seven dwarfs, emerging from their cave into the sunset, shed their flat Gothic livery for the contrasting light and shade of the High Renaissance!" The popularity of Walt Disney Studio reached its apogee with *Snow White*. Although there were some notable efforts later, this height of approval seems never to have been regained.

Disney critics and admirers have battled over the years, often in terms that seem directly contradictory. His detractors claim that he was ruthless, cruel, manipulative, tyrannical, a poorly educated man given to vulgar, banal, simplistic interpretations of life. His followers point to his creative ability as a storyman, his sympathy and patience in encouraging latent talent, his willingness to spend hundreds of thousands of dollars to educate his staff, the worldwide enjoyment of his pictures, and the fact that he brought together what was probably the greatest assemblage of talent since Peter Paul Rubens' picture factory.

In many ways, all of these charges and countercharges may have some basis in fact. In a man of Disney's stature, his faults as well as his virtues are magnified, and there is no way that any of them can be diminished or ignored because they comprise the whole of a very complex genius.

Plato dreamed of the ideal philosopher-king. I think of Walt Disney as the ideal philosopher-capitalist, a towering figure in this shoddy machine age. At a time when cars by the thousands have to be sent back to the factories because of faulty work; when companies knowingly endanger lives by concealing dangerous faults in airplane design; when drug companies, stopped by our government from selling pharmaceutical products with lethal side effects, promptly sell them in other countries where the laws are lax; when planned obsolescence is a way of life, Disney's vision of excellence, demanding that his workers do their best possible work at all times, shines out like a beacon through this murk.

Think about the result if other captains of industry had his philosophy. What a beneficial effect it would make on the millions of people who drudge in dull jobs, turning out inferior goods because of company policy. Disney showed the way to a humanistic approach to capitalism, and it came to its full flower in the production of *Snow White*. I am grateful to have been a part of that era because it has enhanced the quality of my life ever since.

The fact that this wonderful period only lasted for a comparatively short time is of little importance. What is important is that it ever happened at all.

Snow White was a milestone in the animation field, but it was also the gravestone of a happy time.

The first sign of trouble came when the trade papers started to headline the astonishing grosses that *Snow White* was piling up. In the United Kingdom alone, the exhibitors were reported to have paid Disney two million dollars. A crisp memo from Roy Disney was put up on the bulletin board, advising the staff to pay no attention to these figures. That was a tactical error, because we all knew that, in this area at least, trade papers are fairly accurate.

A vague feeling of uneasiness began to permeate the studio. Rumors began to circulate that there were not going to be any bonuses for work done on *Snow White*. A counter-rumor started that the first rumor was deliberately false, and was started by the management so that when the bonuses were finally given, they were going to be very small, but the staff would be conditioned to accept them as better than nothing.

Some of these cynical and hostile feelings might have been dissipated by better communication between management and the staff. If, for example, the Disney brothers had made known a definite date for the disbursement of bonuses, and had issued a scale that showed exactly what one could expect for various types of work, the rumors would never have started. Unfortunately, this was not done.

Lacking any overall information, there was more confusion and hostility once the bonuses were finally handed out. There were rumors that a small group of favored animators had been given a good deal more than the others, and that some directors had also been more rewarded than others. Lack of definite proof did nothing to quiet the open dissatisfaction; in fact, it intensified it.

My own bonus was just about equal to the sum I would have collected if I had continued to work on shorts. I was not discontented because I felt that, compared to some of the other animators, I had made a very modest contribution to the picture. In addition, I was too happy with my status as a Pluto specialist to pay much attention to my income.

The Disney brothers had made no secret of their financial straits and their perilous relationship with the Bank of America. Why did they not follow the same policy now, and, if they had abandoned the structure of the bonus system, admit it?

The management was faced with three problems that were going to cost millions of dollars. First, they had to pay off the loans that were outstanding. Second, they needed funds for the production of *Pinocchio* and subsequent feature films, as well as the shorts that were going to be sandwiched in between. Third, they needed to build a new studio.

In the light of the conditions that already existed, these three were all reasonable and necessary expenditures. Obviously, the bank loan had to be paid as soon as possible. No business could exist for very long if it continued to make desperate gambles as the Disney brothers did on *Snow White*. The ideal condition for a studio would be to produce all its pictures without resorting to bank loans.

The problem of studio space was acute. With the inbetween department in an annex across the street, there was an inevitable loss of time going from the main building to the Annex, not to mention dodging the traffic. The writers were working in makeshift quarters on the side street where Disney had rented several bungalows. The sound stage was now too small because Walt was already thinking of producing live-action features in addition to the cartoons.

Not only were these goals reasonable, they were imperative, and the facts were obvious to everybody. They were never kept secret. What was unknown was why there was a hidden scale (if one existed) for the bonus payments? Compared to the enormous amount of money needed for all these plans, the bonus must have been a drop in the bucket. Walt had been more than generous with the bonuses on the short subjects, and my case was a good example. Whether or not I was contented at the time, the fact is that what I had done on *Snow White* was infinitely more profitable to the studio than my Pluto animation.

If the amount I received was any example of what others earned on the picture, it constituted a change in the basic policy. It may well be that Roy took Walt to a high place and showed him a vista of stocks and profits so huge that Walt could do anything he wanted, no matter how grandiose. Bigger equates better, the fatal American syndrome.

While the Disney staff was, in some respects, almost completely isolated from the rest of the business, we were all very much aware of the fact that an animation union had finally been formed. The Screen Cartoonists Guild was organizing all the other studios on the West Coast. In answer to this maneuver, the Disney Studio began to conduct a series of seminars about unionism, or rather against industry-wide unionism. This was, again, another fatal error.

If Walt had talked to the various groups about his reasons for opposing unions, it might have carried some weight, but he turned the job over to the company lawyer, Gunther Lessing, a man who was a stranger to most of us. He was a very smooth man, too smooth, who obviously knew nothing about us or the people "on the outside," as he put it.

He painted the other workers in the business as lazy, incompetent, untalented people. How they survived should be no concern of ours because we were the elite. Therefore, why not form a company union and let them shift for themselves? We found his evaluation of the rest of the business insulting. Many of the most important artists in our studio came from "the outside." We knew that the crass, moneymaking policies of most studios were subverting the talents of many gifted artists in the industry. The only way that working conditions could possibly improve was through a union.

Had the seminars been presented before the bonus fiasco, the arguments Lessing presented might have fallen on more receptive ears. As it was, many of the employees left the meetings with an awakened interest in the possibility of an industry-wide union.

Since the guild was absorbed in lining up membership in smaller studios, no move was made to recruit anybody from Disney's. Because of this lack of emergency, the seminars dwindled and finally stopped. The vague plans for a company union only came to fruition many months later. We all went on with the business of producing shorts, while the writers were polishing the final stages of the story of *Pinocchio*.

During the latter days of *Snow White,* I began to be troubled by vague pains in my right arm. Very rapidly the pain grew in intensity and spread over my upper torso. It was diagnosed as neuritis, and I was given pain-killers which seemed to have little effect. Twelve years as a member of a track team had given me a very strong constitution, but months of agonizing pain and sleepless nights began to take their toll.

My high-speed drawing technique could only be maintained by grueling effort, but I stubbornly continued to use it. I looked forward to my work on *Pinocchio* with understandable anxiety, because suddenly the tremendous reservoir of energy that had allowed me to put in ten and twelve hours of daily work whenever I needed to was gone.

While we were impatiently waiting to start on *Pinocchio* I worked on *Society Dog-Show,* which Bill Roberts directed. I believe that my Pluto animation was much improved over my work on *Hawaiian Holiday.* At one point, I remembered a little piece of Chaplin acting, where he was attempting to curry favor with a girl and he hunched his shoulders up, crossed his hands in his lap and smiled a very artificially shy smile. I did the same with Pluto when he was trying to flirt with a little female dog. Again, the scene was the result of working at high speed on very rough drawings. There was no indication of this kind of acting on the storyboard or in Bill Roberts' direction.

It was another one of those spontaneous bits of acting which comes with no preconceived idea. I liked this particular bit of animation because it was independent of Fergie's approach to Pluto. A new facet of the dog's character was found. It was only after I had roughed out the action that I realized it had stemmed from a Chaplin scene in the action analysis class.

To be a good animator, like any other actor (or any other artist, for that matter), it is necessary to be a constant observer of, for example: the peculiar walk of a duck; the way a sandpiper runs; how people eat, gesticulate, walk, run; how a tired horse slogs along; the reaction of a cat when it is frightened, and so on. Bits and pieces of information are gathered all day long and stored in a memory bank. Year after year the bank acquires more and more information. Of course, this is the difference between a great animator like Ferguson, who, in picture after picture, created new ways to show Pluto's emotions, and an average animator who has no such store of observations, no large memory bank to cull from.

The difference between looking and seeing is no mere exercise in semantics. Laymen look at the world around them; artists *see* it, then interpret it. André Malraux has said that everybody sees the world in his own personal way. An artist is someone whose vision of the world is unique to the extent that other people are more interested in his version, his interpretation of the environment, than their own. Malraux's observation holds good in the history of animation.

By this time, the public has been exposed to the work of perhaps two hundred animators since the process of animation was invented, yet the work of very few of these artists will be remembered. Tytla, Ferguson, Natwick, Moore, Clark, McCay, Babbitt, Tashlin, and perhaps a half-dozen others have been responsible for the progress of animation as an art. They were great because each one of them brought to the screen a compelling sense of individuality.

Even when the people around them were turning out animation that was substandard, it never influenced these men's work. Ferguson came from Terrytoons, as did Babbitt and Tytla, Tashlin worked at Van

Preliminary sketches for *Mother Pluto*, drawn by Shamus Culhane. 1936.
Copyright © *by Walt Disney Productions.*

A love-smitten Pluto
in *Society Dog-Show*,
drawn by Shamus
Culhane. *Copyright*
© *by Walt Disney
Productions.*

Beuren and Screen Gems. Natwick animated for Hearst's International and Fleischer's.

The question might be raised, "Why did these animators, working in studios that turned out films of low artistic quality, not succeed in raising the standards of these studios?" Sometimes they did, but the result was always ephemeral. When Grim Natwick created Betty Boop, she appeared in banal stories. Tashlin raised the quality of Screen Gems' product as long as he was there, but when he left, management had learned no lesson in producing better films. Dave Fleischer was hired to replace him and the studio fell back to its more natural torpor.

It was only when these great artists, the innovators, came together at Disney's, a place where everyone, in every department, was allowed to do the best possible work according to his individual talents, only then did their animation come to full flower. The reason is that animation, at least up to the present time, is a group effort. A staff of inept artists, writers, and directors can pull down the work of even the most talented animator so that his scenes are barely distinguishable from the work of the less talented.

When *Pinocchio* was put into animation, Walt appointed Ben Sharpsteen and Ham Luske as supervising directors. Norman Ferguson became our sequence director. His responsibility was to supervise the work of the other animators in the unit after they had received their assignments from Sharpsteen. This involved not only making sure that the drawing of the characters was accurate, but he was expected to give advice about acting and movement. Besides all this work, he managed to turn out animation with his own team headed by John Lounsbery.

Fergie was the fastest animator in the studio. A footage average of ten feet a week was not unusual for most animators. Norman turned out about eighteen feet a week, and it was always top-quality work. He never seemed to run out of ideas for new ways of expressing emotion in his animation.

We had not worked together on *Snow White*. While I was laboring through my marching dwarfs, Fergie was doing a monumental job on the Wicked Witch. Now I looked forward to a chance to work closely with him with great excitement.

I shared two interesting sequences with Fergie. They both centered on J. Worthington Foulfellow the Fox and Gideon the Cat. The first sequence was their first sighting of Pinocchio, and the second was at the inn where the Fox and the Cat are gleefully enjoying the fact that they have sold Pinocchio to Stromboli, gleeful until they encounter the sinister Coachman.

For about two weeks, I made sketches of the Fox, sometimes spending days drawing the hands alone. The hands were going to be important because they would express the Fox's false air of elegance. In effect, his hands were going to overact. For another week I drew the Cat, who was going to have to look absolutely brainless but very willing to obey the Fox. Usually the results of the Cat's efforts were devastating, a case of energetic stupidity. The comedy was going to be in his eager hyperactivity as he fouled up everything.

I needed to be very familiar with the proportions of the characters so that my first high-speed drawing would not be hampered by an inability to draw the proportions accurately.

Ferguson and I began to animate the first scenes of the Fox and the Cat at about the same time. I was uneasy about my drawings, but couldn't focus on any specific problem. I didn't say anything to Fergie because I presumed it was my usual insecurity. When we submitted our first rough animation on a few scenes to Sharpsteen and Disney, it was obvious that the trouble was in the design of the Fox. He had a very long muzzle, and when he turned his head, his nose seemed to sweep across half the screen.

Ben and Walt very wisely decided to junk all the work, and Fergie redesigned the Fox with a more truncated muzzle and a more compact head. Another week of sketching this new head followed. The new design gave the Fox's face better acting possibilities and these had to be explored before we could start to animate again.

Not only was I using my high-speed technique, but I was also discovering that I was becoming more concerned with the underlying geometry of each pose. Fergie was very pleased with this, and showed me instances where I could push it further. He had been using this method himself all this time, but had been too inarticulate to explain it. Now, with some concrete examples, he could talk.

Most of the time I was drawing with my arm in a sling, but that didn't stop me from getting a new sweep and power in my roughs. Our first sequence went through the sweatbox smoothly and with very few changes. The changes that were asked for were mostly additions to the acting rather than corrections.

With this accent on geometry, I felt that I was breaking new ground for myself, and Fergie was very approving. I was still using the speed-drawing method, but the underlying search was for geometrical possibilities, the idea Fergie had never been able to explain.

My assistant Nick DeTolly had been shunted to another unit, and I was given two assistants to work with me on *Pinocchio*. One, Norman Tate, had not been at the studio for very long, but was an excellent draftsman and a very methodical worker. This was an asset for me because I had a tendency to make mistakes on my exposure sheets. The other assistant was Bill Hurtz, who as a teenager had had the advantage of studying with Don Graham while Don was still teaching at Chouinard's. Tate, Hurtz, and I worked very well together. I had the satisfaction of seeing that my rough drawings were losing none of their virility when they were cleaned up by either man.

I socialized with both of them, the Tates occasionally and Bill and Mary Hurtz more often. Mary also worked at Disney's as a shorthand machine operator, taking notes of sweatbox discussions and Don Graham's lectures. Bill and I were enthusiastic Sunday painters. After working together all week and spending most of our weekends together as well, we became very close friends. This association, many years later, resulted in a decision that had a great impact on our lives.

When I animated the Fox and the Cat at the inn, we used a new technical development. The Fox was to sing a song, "Hi Diddle Dee Dee, an Actor's Life for Me." I animated the sequence on the usual twelve-inch drawing paper, but before it was inked, the scene was photographically reduced to a much smaller size, resulting in a longer shot. If the scene had been animated at this size originally, it would have been difficult to draw the small figures without getting bogged down into more constricted action. The reduction was another of Walt's good ideas.

There was something ironic about the fact that I was animating this lusty, stein-swinging Fox, and then finding myself unable to bring my arm up to put my coat on. I had become a semi-invalid, unable to walk a whole block without experiencing pain that was so devastating I would have to rest on the curb until it passed. I had learned to drive and park my car with one hand.

Mysteriously enough, I had absolutely no pain in the mornings. It was

The Fox in the Red Lobster Inn, drawn by Shamus Culhane. From *Pinocchio. Copyright* © *by Walt Disney Productions.*

A drawing by Shamus Culhane from a scene in *Pinocchio. Copyright* © *by Walt Disney Productions.*

only by midafternoon, as the temperature dropped, that the pain would come on with a rush. Finally, my doctor made a blunt pronouncement: Obviously, the change in the barometric pressure kicked off my neuritis. I would have to live in another part of the country where the temperature did not drop twenty degrees or more in a few hours. If I did not move away, he predicted that I would die of exhaustion within six months.

Reluctantly I went to talk to Walt about the situation. "Christ," he said authoritatively, "Those goddamn doctors don't know what the hell it's all about. What you need is some good exercise. Tell you what, you go over to the Hollywood Athletic Club and work out with the wrestling coach a couple of times a week. Tell them to put it on my bill." He dismissed me with a pat on the back and the assurance that I was going to be fine.

Damned if I didn't think so, too. I wrestled, as best I could for two weeks, and then spent the next week in bed. My doctor said I was being a fool, leave California before there were complications. I went back to Walt again.

"All right, maybe exercise isn't the right idea. I'll send you to my doctor. He'll fix you up because this guy's a real genius. Tell him to send me the bill."

The new doctor was really far-out. The first thing he did was try to make me stop smoking by hypnosis. I wasn't a candidate for hypnosis, so that didn't work. He was certainly knowledgeable, because he next tried feeding me carotene, a crude form of vitamin A. None of the other doctors had even mentioned the possibility of a vitamin deficiency.

While these treatments were going on, I started the most difficult part of my work: the meeting of the Fox, the Cat, and the Coachman. I could see a way of handling the action so that the massive bulk of the Coachman with its minimal action contrasted with the flamboyant poses of the Fox. The Cat, in the interim, sat there blowing smoke rings and eating them like doughnuts. His action was very toned down, with no sudden moves that might have conflicted with the extravagant gestures of the Fox.

When, in a shot animated by Fergie, the Coachman suddenly leaned over and said, "I takes them to Pleasure Island," the two pseudo-villains in my following shot slammed back against the wall, paralyzed by fright. It was the culmination of the three kinds of action. I thought that this sequence was the best animation I had done at Disney Studio, and Fergie agreed.

Some exploratory poses for a scene in which the Fox is badly frightened by the sinister Coachman. The pinpoint pupils used in these drawings are based on the fact that adrenaline released into the bloodstream in response to fear causes the pupils to contract. Drawn by Shamus Culhane for the 1940 *Pinocchio. Copyright © by Walt Disney Productions.*

The evil Coachman divulges his plans to kidnap boys and take them to Pleasure Island. Drawing by Shamus Culhane, for *Pinocchio. Copyright © by Walt Disney Productions.*

* * *

The Disneys had another brother, Ray, who was an insurance agent. Since just about everyone in the studio had a car, Ray was able to build up a very lucrative business. The symbol of his newfound prosperity was his penchant for smoking long, expensive cigars with unconscious ostentation. Another characteristic was his almost furtive manner. Even when he said, "Good morning," it was as if he were fomenting a conspiracy.

Walt was once viewing some of my scenes of the Fox and Cat at the inn, where both characters were smoking cigars with great pretentiousness. The screening was interrupted by Ray Disney, who opened the door just wide enough to poke his head in. Through the gloom we could see Ray's eyes swivel from one side of the room to the other without moving his head. Then with one puff of his cigar he was gone.

Walt burst out laughing. "That's the goddamn Fox!" He was right. It was an extraordinary little bit of pantomine. I didn't mention that I had been studying Ray's manipulation of his cigar whenever he came into my room.

The ink and paint department was off limits to most of the males in the studio. However, Ray was allowed to visit there in order to service his clients. One rule that could not be ignored was the No Smoking sign at the entrance. Ray would dutifully pluck his expensive Havana out of his mouth and place it carefully on the nearest window ledge before he went in.

When Ray emerged he would pick up his cigar with a flourish and stride off jauntily to the next building. One day when he came out and reached for his cigar, he made a take like Donald Duck. There on the ledge was a six-foot assembly of the most battered, chewed-on cigar butts imaginable—dozens of them.

Ray whirled around to see if anyone was watching. The courtyard was empty. He swung back to the cigar butts. Somewhere in that welter of cheap stogies was his precious Havana. With a forlorn shrug he walked off disconsolately. Ray never again came to the ink and paint department smoking a cigar.

As for the prankster, it must have taken him months to make such a collection, because very few people in the studio smoked cigars.

From time to time, we were seeing rough animation from other sequences of the picture. Unlike *Snow White*, *Pinocchio*'s pace seemed uneven, and various bits of animation looked padded. A few cynics intimated that this was because some of the directors and animators were trying to expand their work in order to get bigger bonuses. I firmly believe that there was no truth in this accusation. What is important is that it was even made at all. A remark like that would have been unthinkable during the production of *Snow White*. It is evidence of the fact that the manner in which the *Snow White* bonuses were given out still rankled.

When Walt realized that *Pinocchio* was faltering, he called for a series of meetings between groups of animators and the story department. During the first meeting I attended, Walt pointed out that the picture was too loose; what it needed was another character to pull it together, and there didn't seem to be a person in the original book that could act as a catalyst. Out of these meetings, the character of Jiminy Cricket was created and at once the whole story tightened up.

Happily for our unit, Sharpsteen was handling his direction with his usual crisp style and we had no dead footage to edit.

The story department was tooling up other films while *Pinocchio* was in production. With his habit of getting the best man possible for the job, Walt was holding meetings with Leopold Stokowski about the score for *Fantasia*. He soon became a familiar sight in the studio, his cranelike figure swooping through the halls followed by Disney and a retinue of writers and story sketch men, all struggling to keep pace.

Stokowski had to be the biggest poseur since Richard Wagner. One afternoon, while Stokowski and Disney were involved in a story confernece, the refreshment cart was wheeled in. Walt turned to Stokowski and inquired politely, "Care for a Coke?" Stokey looked blank, "Ah, Coke? What is that?" Disney explained that it was a soft drink. When he was handed a paper cup of the most advertised liquid on earth, Stokowski looked at it as if it was a Chateau Margaux of suspicious vintage. He took a cautious sip, rolled it around in his mouth in approved wine taster's style, and swallowed. "Quite good," he murmured, "really quite good."

As my work on the Coachman sequence drew to a close, my illness increased to the point where I was at work one day and absent the next. Even the normally easygoing Ferguson was growing impatient. Finally, after one pain-wracked night, it was too much. I made an appointment to see Walt. When I told him that I intended to wire the Fleischer Studio for a job, he got up and started to pace around the room. "Look Culhane, for Chrissake you have a great future here. I never saw anybody improve so damn fast. Come on, don't be a goddamn fool." I sat silent, looking at the floor.

"Listen, I have big plans for you. You're going to animate that dog, what's its name . . . Nana, in *Peter Pan*. She's going to be all yours." When I sat, silent and miserable, he went to his desk and started looking through some papers. The interview was over.

I sent a telegram to Max, asking for a job. Witlessly, I rather hoped he'd turn me down, but two hours later I received an answer of acceptance: a two-year contract.

Adam didn't leave paradise more reluctantly than I left Disney Studio. Here I had struggled to rid myself of my bad habits, spent countless nights in Don Graham's classes, and now that success was within my grasp, I had to leave.

A few days later, I went around to say good-bye to a few people. There was a lump in my throat as big as a baseball. Painfully, I climbed the stairs to Walt's office and told Dolores that I'd like to see Walt to tell him good-bye. Her eyes were full of sympathy, but she shook her head. "I can't do it," she said gently. When I stared at her uncomprehendingly, she added, "Walt said he didn't want to see you."

10

Fleischer Studio in Miami

n 1932, when I left Max Fleischer Studio to go to the coast, there was no sign of labor unrest. In fact, it was generally agreed that Fleischer's was the best animation studio in New York as far as wage scales were concerned. While there were no paid vacations or sick leave, and the work week was forty-five hours, those were the conditions that prevailed in every studio in New York. Unlike the other studios, Fleischer's paid for overtime. Discipline was very loose, and Max allowed all sorts of horseplay and practical jokes among his employees.

There was a fierce loyalty to Max among the animators. When it was necessary to meet a deadline, it was quite common for the animators involved to work around the clock, sometimes as long as two days and nights without rest. The other animators brought them coffee and sandwiches which they ate while they worked. Instead of resenting the ordeal, there was a feeling of pride and accomplishment. They had done it for Max.

It came as a shock to those of us who had worked in Fleischer Studio to hear that a group of almost a hundred inkers, painters, and inbetweeners had joined an organization known as the Commercial Artists and Designers Union (CADU) and had gone on strike. Max had refused to negotiate with the representatives of the dissidents.

In a recent talk with me (1981), Nick Tafuri, a veteran Fleischer animator, recalls some of the details of the fracas:

> After you guys left, Natwick, Eugster, Wolf, and all, it
> gave us a chance to move up. I was an inbetweener

making a big twenty-eight dollars a week. So I got a
contract as an animator starting at sixty-five dollars,
and in three years I got up to ninety-five dollars. Most
of the inkers were working for around eighteen
dollars.

When you were there, Max used to come around
sometimes, but after a while he stopped altogether, so he
never talked to the staff. He did go bowling once a week
with some of the boys, and I was invited once or twice. I
found out that they didn't really get together to bowl.
Usually it was only executives like Sam Buchwald,
Seymour Knietel, Izzy Sparber, and Frank Paiker. All they
did was talk business, so I quit going.

What were they going to tell Max? That they were
having trouble with the staff? They kept telling him that
everything was fine, so when the strike came, it was a big
shock to Max. He felt the kids had turned against him, and
he was sore as hell.

Everybody joined the strike except the animators and
assistants. You could look down and see about a hundred
pickets milling around 1600 Broadway, waving signs.
Things got rough. One time while we watched, we saw
Dave Fleischer, Sparber, and Paiker try to go through the
middle of the picket line instead of using the entrance
where the cops were. All of a sudden they just disappeared
under a lot of picket signs. Paiker lost a tooth.

When Max hired a bunch of private detectives, the
strikers came up with a goon squad from the
Longshoremen's Union. Our bodyguards escorted us to the
subway every night and met us there in the morning. It
got too risky to go out to lunch, so Max had food sent up
every day. None of us did any work except Seymour.
After all, he was Max's son-in-law. The rest of us shot
crap all day.

When the strike was settled, practically all the inkers,
painters and inbetweeners joined the union, but the
animators and assistants didn't. The place was really split
up.

The most startling aspect of this mess was the huge drop in salaries in the various departments. In 1928 even the parsimonious owners of Krazy Kat would spend thirty-five dollars a week for an inker. In 1930 neophyte animators started at Fleischer's at one hundred dollars a week, yet in 1933, with the animation business booming, a Fleischer animator's starting salary was sixty-five dollars, and inkers were getting eighteen dollars. Why?

Edith Vernick, who had been head of the inbetween department during that period, thinks that this came about when the Fleischers made a deal with Paramount. She believes that the brothers were each put on a salary of seven hundred dollars a week, but that Paramount had control of the stock, which in turn gave them control of the policies of management. This might account for the studio's hard-nosed attitude during the strike, as well as the dramatic drop in wages. It is doubtful if the Fleischers had enough money of their own to stave off the strikers for six long months.

The picture of mild-mannered Max Fleischer hiring thugs and private detectives of his own volition just doesn't gel. Neither does the idea of the strikers, of their own accord, seeking out a goon squad from the longshoremen's union. Much more likely is the possibility that the real antagonists—Paramount and the Commercial Artists and Designers—chose the methods of combat.

After all, the major producers later countered the growing unrest in the motion picture business by hiring two of Al Capone's henchmen, Bioff and Brown, to put down the unions; and certainly unions that are concerned with winning victories strictly by legal means did not organize goon squads.

In the tumultuous era of labor-management relations in the nineteen twenties and thirties, Fleischer Studio was a bastion of Victorian management. At the turn of the century an employer had been a dictator by sheer force of custom, but, if he was a benevolent dictator, he won approval not only from his peers but from his employees as well. Max Fleischer followed these precepts because he was still a Victorian, and to a great extent so was the staff. Both were essentially anachronisms.

The strike was an attack on Max's ego. It threatened his self-esteem and violated his beliefs in the traditional roles of management and labor. Nick Tafuri was right: Max's "kids" were betraying him, and his reaction was one of outraged fatherhood.

For the employees, the cuts in basic pay were not only a financial problem, they also signified an abandonment of Max's rôle as the protective father-image. The strike was a manifestation of dislocated emotional attitudes on both sides.

When the strike was finally settled on October 13, 1937, the strikers had won most of their demands. CADU was accepted as the bargaining agent for 62 percent of the employees, and the inkers, painters, and inbetweeners managed to gain a few more dollars, but not as much as they had demanded.

It proved to be a temporary victory because, following the axiom, "If you can't lick 'em, leave 'em," Paramount loaned the Fleischers three hundred thousand dollars to build a new studio in Miami.

The purposes of this move at first glance seemed reasonable. Following the smashing success of *Snow White,* Paramount wanted the Fleischers to begin work immediately on an animated feature. The staff would have to be enlarged to approximately seven hundred people, with a corresponding increase in floor space. Rents in midtown Manhattan were too expensive for the project, and Miami was offering a huge tax break.

A look at the disadvantages made these arguments very feeble. There were plenty of empty factories in Queens, the Bronx, and Staten Island that could have been acquired for less than $300,000. As far as motion picture facilities were concerned, Miami might just as well have been in Tibet. Every foot of film would have to be shipped to New York laboratories for development; any breakdown of equipment would have to be serviced from the East; there were few experienced sound engineers in Florida, no actors, no labor pool of experienced artists. In the face of all these problems, the move to Miami was mad.

Mad or not, ground was broken in March 1938, and the staff moved into the new studio six months later. The new plant was an impressive structure with enough space to house seven hundred artists. It had ample and well-kept grounds, a large parking lot, and a commissary. There was even an air conditioning unit (a rarity in those days), which kept the studio a breezy seventy degrees.

Every week the lawn was cut by a chain gang from the county jail. It was an all-black crew. Stripped to the waist and heavily muscled, they moved languidly about their tasks. An obese white cracker guard sat in the shade, a huge cud of tobacco bulging out one cheek and a double-barreled shotgun cradled against his belly. In the beginning, several kindhearted northerners had made the mistake of offering bottles of cold Coca-Cola to the sweating blacks, but the fat guard had promptly leveled the shotgun and warned them off—a grim reminder that they were now in the Deep South.

Ironically enough, since Max could not very well start the feature from scratch, he had to invite the union inkers, painters, and inbetweeners to join the hegira. The terms were conciliatory: paid transportation, a week's sojourn in a hotel while looking for homes. The studio would pay the fare back to New York for anyone who wished to leave within one year. Most of the unionists elected to accept the offer, and the union as an entity was dissolved.

Additions to the higher echelons of creativity, the animators, storymen, layout and background artists, were lured from Hollywood by the offer of more money than the West Coast studios were paying. Fleischer succeeded in attracting some very talented people. Veterans like Grim Natwick, Al Eugster, Bill Nolan, and Ben Clopton beefed up the animation department. Tedd Pierce, Cal Howard, and Dan Gordon, all West Coast writers, were better educated in their craft than the New York contingent.

In a way Max bought a pig in a poke. Among the hundred people who arrived from Hollywood there were many who had applied for employment and falsified the extent of their experience. Inbetweeners had boldly claimed to be animators, and animators of little talent had been hired on the basis of mythical jobs in prestigious studios on the coast. These carpetbaggers played havoc with the early beginnings of production, and fed the xenophobic attitudes of the New Yorkers.

The Hollywood group took to the tropical environment with ease. The climate was not much different from the weather in Southern California. On the other hand, most of the New Yorkers were acutely homesick within a few months. They longed for Ebbets Field and the comfortable sight of the debris-strewn sidewalks of Coney Island.

Most of all they loathed the insects. There were spiders whose span was the diameter of teacups, and flying roaches. Mosquitos descended on Miami in clouds when the wind blew off the Everglades. Everyone soon learned to shake out shoes in the morning because scorpions had a nasty habit of using them for catnaps.

One day Cal Howard traumatized the hapless easterners by walking into the studio leading a huge land crab on a leash. As one New Yorker remarked ruefully, "If I had of known what Miami was like I would of stood in bed."

Max still needed additional hundreds of people for the inbetween, inking, and painting departments. He turned to the only source in town, Miami Art School. The instructors there tried valiantly to fill the breach. They scoured the town for anyone who had even cherished the ambition to paint moonlight scenes on black velvet, or burn pictures on coconut shells for the tourist trade. The recruits were given a few hasty hours of instruction, then turned loose on regular production.

The results were about as uneven as one would expect. Some people managed to learn and within a few months were turning out acceptable work. Others never acquired enough skill and pulled the quality of the inbetweening, inking, and painting below the standards that could be expected of a Fleischer cartoon.

The original story for *Gulliver's Travels* was written in New York and, complete with storyboards and character sketches, shipped to Miami. When Pierce, Howard, and Gordon arrived they threw out the whole concept on the grounds that the story was too slapstick, and the continuity was clumsy. They set to work on a revision, and soon even the most loyal Fleischerite had to admit that the Hollywood writers had created a better story.

The production methods used on *Gulliver* were a curious amalgam of Hollywood and Fleischer procedures. Unlike Disney's, where every animator of proven ability had his own moviola, Max had one machine for the whole staff.

Reluctantly, Max had agreed to make pencil tests, but they were used more to check the scenes for technical errors than as a means to further improve the animation or enhance the story.

As in the old days in New York, Nelly Sanborn and Alice Morgan checked the animation before it was pencil-tested, adding inbetweens here and there to "smoothen out" the action. The Fleischers saw nothing incongruous in the fact that these dear little old ladies were now, in effect, editing the work of outstanding veterans like Natwick and Eugster.

There were eleven sequence directors, each one operating in a vacuum, as if a feature picture were just eleven shorts strung together. The lack of finesse in drawing the characters made the model sheets seem like throwbacks to the early 1930s. Princess Glory looked as if she had been copied from the cover of a box of cheap candy, and Gabby's strained,

One of the most successful sequences in the Fleischer Studio's *Gulliver's Travels* (1937) was when the Lilliputians swarmed all over Gulliver's body and tied him up with an ingenious use of nets, ropes, and derricks. *Paramount Pictures. Museum of Modern Art/Film Stills Archives.*

Even the addition of veteran screen writers like Cal Howard, Dan Gordon, and Tedd Pierce to the Fleischer staff could not rescue the studio from its heavy-handed approach to romance. Here Princess Glory and Prince David in *Gulliver's Travels* act out a typically banal scene. 1939, Fleischer Studio. *Paramount Pictures. Museum of Modern Art/Film Stills Archives.*

puffy figure appeared to be in the terminal and explosive stages of constipation.

Dave Fleischer always directed the dialogue tracks for the shorts, so he assumed these duties on *Gulliver*. Dan Gordon and Cal Howard usually sat in on the recording sessions, and, in one instance at least, it was a good thing that they were there.

Dave was having a good deal of trouble with an actor, although he was doing a very simple line: "I'm king around here." Dave was having him repeat it over and over and shaking his head in dissatisfaction after every attempt. Finally, Gordon asked Fleischer what seemed to be the trouble. Dave fumed that the actor wasn't pronouncing "king" properly.

Now, there is one feature of the New York dialect that is possibly unique in the country. New Yorkers, and especially people from Brooklyn, use a very hard G, so hard, in fact, that it lingers in the air like a bash on a tympany. For example, "Long Island" is rendered "Longgisland." It took quite a bit of persuasion on the part of Gordon and Howard to convince Dave that "I'm king garound here," might be the acceptable pronunciation in Brooklyn Heights, but was not quite *de rigueur* in the rest of the United States.

By the time I rolled up to the best hotel in Miami my impression was that, for a famous resort town, it looked downright shabby. The clerk at the desk, as I found out later, was at one time a millionaire on paper during the boom-and-bust days. After I had signed in, he swung the register around and looked at my scribble with some distaste.

"One of them Hollywood fellers, hey? Gonna work in that there pitcher studio?" When I admitted it, he leaned over the counter and grew confidential. "You Hollywood folks is all right, but them New Yorkers, when they first come here, bust into the lobby like a passel of hound dogs, barkin' an' yelpin'. Seems like they never been in a hotel before. They didn't even know you was supposed to tip the bellhop.

"First night one of them comes over to me an' asks what time he has to be home. I swear to Christ! Morning clerk tells me that some feller stops on his way out an' apologizes 'cause he didn't have time to make his bed, he's late for work. Jesus! You wouldn't believe it!" I believed it.

The next morning when I arrived at the studio, I was very impressed.

It was a very modern-looking plant, and I swung into a parking spot with the feeling that this might not be a bad move after all. For the next few hours I went from one room to the other, meeting my old friends. They all looked very well. When you are in the late twenties the ravages of time are not very apparent, even after seven years.

The exception was Max. He had gotten fatter, and his hair was gray. While he greeted me warmly, as we sat down to talk his face lapsed into a very morose expression.

Max had seen *Snow White,* but he dismissed it as "too arty." He was sure that the audience throughout the world would recognize *Gulliver* as a *real* cartoon. He brightened up as he mentioned the fine work of Natwick and Eugster. It was good to have his boys come back. He got up from his chair with visible effort and invited me to have lunch with him.

The commissary was putting out some very appetizing food. As I stood on line, waiting to heap my tray, I looked over the array of white chairs and tables. I noticed that the Hollywood people were eating together, and the Fleischer people seemed to have staked out an area for themselves.

When I went to Max's table there was the Palace Guard: Bowsky, Sparber, Paiker, Buchwald, and Kneitel. Max sat at the head, looking like an old, wounded lion, with Bowsky at his elbow. Between copious mouthfuls, Bowsky kept up a running fire of comment as he glared at one section of the commissary. "Look at them, Max, eating your good food!" Of course, he was talking about the strikers who, even after this long time, were still shunned by the Loyalists. The fact that they had paid for the lunch did not seem to be a factor.

The monologue was sheer glucose. "Don't worry, Max, we still love you." Max seemed to lap it up, but Kneitel shot me an embarrassed glance when the going got really sticky. Buchwald was looking at Bowsky with open disgust, but the rest of the table beamed approval at Bowsky's snow job. This cheap-jack Iago never stopped until the last napkin was tossed on the table.

I excused myself and went over to a group of inkers and painters whom I had not seen during my morning tour.

After a warm welcome it was time to go back to work. As I sauntered toward the animation wing, Bowsky intercepted me. "Look, Jimmie, you don't know what the score is around here, and I wouldn't like to see you get into trouble. Some people you just don't talk to, get what I mean?"

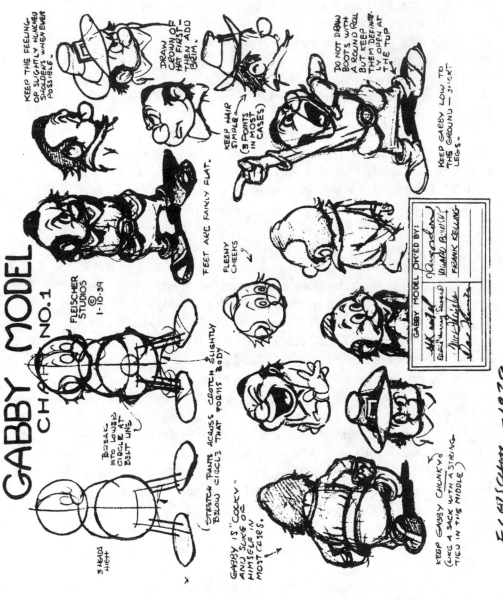

In spite of the fact that Gabby's nerve-scraping voice and ear-bending logorrhea were singled out by many critics as a major fault in *Gulliver's Travels*, after the feature was released the Fleischer Studio made six shorts in 1940–41 that featured Gabby. Since no effort was made to improve his voice or delivery, the films were not successful, and the character was abandoned. *Gulliver's Travels*, 1939, Fleischer Studio. *Paramount Pictures.*

After the release of *Gulliver's Travels*, Snitch was featured in a short called *Sneak Snoop and Snitch* in *Triple Trouble* made in 1941. The film was not successful enough to warrant further use of the characters. *Gulliver's Travels*, 1939, Fleischer Studio. *Paramount Pictures.*

I understood him very well . . . let's keep the feud going so that Max will appreciate how loyal we are, and show his gratitude in a nice fat pay hike. In a few pungent phrases I turned down Willard's advice. However, he and a few others managed to keep picking at the scab that covered Max's wounded self-esteem. The result was that Max never forgave the strikers.

Because it was a winter resort and nothing more, Miami had been hard hit by the Depression. One of the first things I had seen was a picket line outside a butcher shop. The pickets carried signs like, "We want the American way of life! A sixty-hour week!" The same day I arrived, the taxi drivers went on strike for a guaranteed dollar a day!

For fifty dollars one could hire an adult male for a month, and maids were normally paid fifty cents a day. Yet when I went to a local movie house to see *The Grapes of Wrath,* the audience roared with laughter at the plight of the Okies. America is a crazy country, and Florida in those days seems to have been in need of a frontal lobotomy!

When I had found a suitable house (forty dollars a month completely furnished), I decided to have a barbecue for my close friends. At the butcher shop the man eyed me tentatively. "Ten pounds of the best steak? Look, I got filet mignon, but it's thirty-five cents a pound!" When I slapped the bills and change on the counter, the butcher couldn't believe it.

I had hired a black maid, at five dollars a week. When I had the barbecue she was given a few dollars more. Around ten o'clock I decided that her services were no longer wanted, so I bade her goodnight. She looked at me in terror. "I got to have my note!" I looked at her stupidly. "What note?"

She wrung her hands. "I got to have my note, otherwise I gets picked up." Finally, I managed to get the information out of her. She needed a note saying I had detained her past the curfew for blacks, otherwise she was in danger of being picked up by the police and sent to the county jail! That was America in 1939!

Despite the multitudinous problems, by the time I arrived in Miami, *Gulliver* was into the final stages of animation, which was unfortunate for me. I was given some animation on the last sequence. Most of the scenes consisted of dozens of Lilliputians waving to Gulliver as he sailed off. They were singing a dreary song, "Come back again." I began to feel that I was back at Disney's doing crowd shots for Ben Sharpsteen.

I had an assistant, Benny Solomon, a voluble Brooklynite who puffed all day at luscious Havana cigars in a transport of happiness. He confided to me, "Back home I cunta have afforded this kinda butts."

One day, after drudging through another crowd of overstuffed midgets, I sighed wearily, "Benny, isn't this crowd stuff a fucking bore?" Benny looked up in surprise. "Huh? Bored? What's to be bored? I never think about it!!" I guess Benny had the right idea.

December 22, 1939, *Gulliver's Travels* opened in a local theater with as much fanfare as could be mustered in a resort town like Miami. A few portly Paramount executives from New York, in tuxedos, mingled with the shirt-sleeved studio employees. Unlike the apprehension of the Disney staff on the opening night of *Snow White,* the Fleischer people strolled into the theater with an air of great confidence and self-satisfaction.

For my part, I had my doubts. I had seen my own animation only in pencil test and, due to the lack of quality in the cleanups, the results were not reassuring. For Max and Dave and all my friends in the studio, I was hoping for a solid success. A lot of time, effort, and money had gone into *Gulliver.* Maybe the whole future of the studio was on the line.

I found the picture not as bad as I had expected. There were some interesting situations. Gulliver being tied up by the natives, King Little's Lindy Hop with Gulliver's fingers, and some scenes of the spies were very good entertainment.

However, the film had many flaws. The Fleischer Studio's inability to handle romantic sex was never more apparent. The songs were typical of Tin Pan Alley banalities. A special effects department was lacking, and the studio fell down badly in that area. Most of the dialogue was stilted, and often the lines seemed to be read rather than spoken spontaneously. Gabby's shrill chatter was irritating rather than funny.

In spite of these problems, *Gulliver's Travels,* for the most part, had the lusty vigor that the Fleischer animators always managed to achieve. The one thing I found dismaying was the fact that Grim Natwick's animation of Princess Glory had been butchered by crude cleanups. The final result bore no resemblance to his exquisite drawings of Snow White.

The atmosphere of the studio the next morning was pretty much what I had expected. Willard Bowsky led the Old Guard Fleischerites in a vociferous bout of self-congratulations. According to Willard and a few

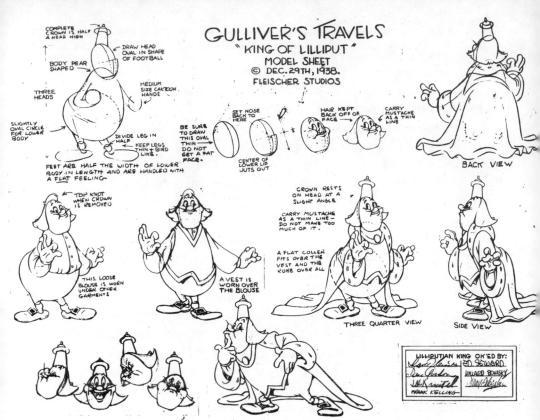

This model sheet is another example of the Fleischer Studio's lack of knowledge of the contemporary principles of animation draftsmanship. The figure of the king in the center row has instructions that "the crown rests on the head at a slight angle." No such restrictive instructions would be given a Disney animator. Some years before, the artists at Disney Studio had found that hats and clothing could be drawn in such a manner as to reinforce the mood of a character. For example, the third head in the bottom row would have been improved if the crown had been cocked forward over one eye. By remaining perched on the back of the head, it contributes nothing to the king's angry mood. *Gulliver's Travels,* 1939, Fleischer Studio. *Paramount Pictures.*

Opposite page: The Fleischer Studio's basic lack of draftsmanship is nowhere more apparent than in this model sheet. The notes about the construction of Snoop, which appear on the upper left-hand side, derive from the early days of animation when characters were drawn using dimes and quarters for their construction. In this case the directions must have been added *after* the drawings were completed. The figure at the lower left-hand side shows that in reality the fundamental shape of the body is a long oval. The dotted lines indicating a circle are obviously no use in drawing the character, in fact, they would be confusing. *Gulliver's Travels,* 1939, Fleischer Studio. *Paramount Pictures.*

A model sheet of the King of Lilliput, drawn by Shamus Culhane for *Gulliver's Travels.* Produced by Fleischer Studio in 1940.

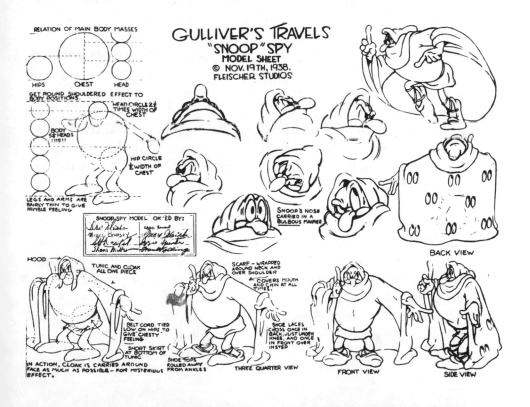

others, *Gulliver* was a much better picture than *Snow White*. The Hollywood contingent was more conservative, but most of them felt that all the faults were not that serious and the picture should be well received by the public.

Further developments seemed to bear out the latter evaluation. The majority of the critics gave *Gulliver* good reviews, usually with the reservation that the quality of the film was far below the expertise in *Snow White*.

At the end of *Gulliver*'s first day at the Paramount Theater in New York the film had broken the attendance record by playing to almost 14,000 people. Similar records were broken throughout the country.

This good news led Paramount to demand another feature cartoon from the Fleischers. Cal Howard, Dan Gordon, and Tedd Pierce began to brew up some ideas. One proposal was to make a feature about Mount Olympus and the Gods.

They approached Dave Fleischer with the concept, and there was much discussion about Zeus, Athena, Apollo, and the other Gods. Dave's reaction was a little subdued. He would never have qualified as a theologian because, after the meeting, one of the Fleischer veterans asked him what that Mount Olympus shit was all about. "Oh," said Dave airily, "It's all in the Old Testament."

When I arrived at Fleischer's I had made it a policy to make no mention of the conditions that drove me to leave Disney's. The doctor's prognosis was accurate: I had no more pains, but even so, I felt fragile and seemed to tire very easily.

After a few months in Miami, I realized that my annual checkup by a dentist was long overdue. I never had any cavities, so I had been fairly casual about dentists most of my life. After probing for cavities and not finding any, the dentist announced that he was going to take X-rays as a final check.

I protested that I had been going to a dentist in Hollywood for years, and he didn't believe in X-rays because I have very sound teeth. This fellow stubbornly took the X-rays anyhow, and went off to his darkroom. A few minutes later he burst through the door waving a damp negative under my nose and sputtering excitedly.

"You have a tremendous abscess! It's eating away your jawbone. I mean it's dangerous . . . you're being poisoned!"

I looked at the little square of film with its ominous dip in the bone under one tooth. Of course, this explained the source of my mysterious neuritis. I remembered that the first doctor I saw about my pains had told me to have my teeth checked—not "have your teeth X-rayed," just *checked*. This bit of sloppy semantics had cost me my career at Disney's.

There was no such thing as root-canal work in those days. I had to lose a perfectly good tooth. Within a few weeks my health was restored, and I could look forward to almost two years of work in a studio where I would never be able to make full use of my talents. I was depressed for weeks, but it never occurred to me to break my contract. Victorian tradition demanded that I fulfill it to the letter.

While our next feature was being mulled over, the studio went back to producing shorts. I was given a group to direct, consisting of my friend Al Eugster, Bob Wickersham (who was another ex-Disney animator), Rube Grossman, Nick Tafuri, John Walworth, Hal Seeger, and Abner Kneitel, a cousin of Seymour. Except for Eugster and Wickersham, none of them had ever worked in another studio, so I intended to give them some of the education in acting theory and animation that they would have received in Disney's. Nick Tafuri was very pleased at the prospect. As he put it succinctly, "I need to know something about that space and volume shit."

My first move was to direct a program of life drawing on Saturdays in my garage. It took some doing to wring from the people at the Miami Art School the name and address of the only professional model in town. They were convinced at first that I was a white slaver.

Jackie, our model, appeared a little startled at the idea of posing in a garage, but soon she settled down.

She was a young girl with a huge pair of breasts, capped by the largest aureoles I have ever seen. The whole group of animators and assistants began to draw, and I began to teach. They were all as ignorant of the principles of drawing as I had been when I first went to Disney's.

We stopped at noon, and everybody went off happily except for Nick. He stayed behind and looked at me mournfully. "Hey boss, this is the first time I ever drew from a live model, so how come we have to draw one with funny-lookin' tits?"

When the news that I was conducting an art class began to circulate around the studio, animators from other groups wanted to join. I turned them down. It was enough work to concentrate on my own crew.

At Max's request, however, I did give a series of lectures to the other animation units on acting and the basic principles of animation, such things as the various ways to bring a character to a smooth stop, paying attention to the need for proper anticipatory poses before a fast action, etcetera.

Most of the Fleischer veterans used these principles at times, but it was always instinctive rather than knowledgeable. I used examples from old shorts to illustrate my points and, as is often the case with zealots, I was completely insensitive to the fact that these animators were not used to criticism.

In a dozen two-hour lectures I doubt that they really learned very much. Instead, there were a lot of hurt feelings, and, as one aggrieved animator put it, "All that Disney shit has turned Culhane into a real Hollywood wise guy." This wasn't the attitude in my unit. The lads sopped up information and tried very hard to apply the precepts I was teaching.

Our layout man was a real find. Shane Miller was a young man whose only experience in the business was with Max. Shane had a great talent for staging a scene, because he was sensitive to the dramatic possibilities of light and shade and enjoyed creating oddball camera angles. While working with me on storyboards Miller would often have good ideas about the acting as well as the staging.

In a West Coast studio he might easily have gone on to directing. This was impossible at Fleischer's because it was not the tradition to promote head animators (as they continued to call directors) from the ranks of the layout men.

Our first picture, *A Kick in Time,* was a tearjerker about two mules, Hunky and Spunky. They had been designed by Myron Waldman in 1938, and his picture had been nominated for an Academy Award. In our film, Spunky was kidnapped from his mother, Hunky, and sold to a tough hombre. Bolstered by some good acting bits by Eugster, the picture had a little more depth than the usual Fleischer product.

What I really wanted to do were some pictures featuring Wimpy, a neurotic character in the "Popeye" comic strip who had an insatiable hunger for hamburgers. While Wimpy was very popular in the comic strip, the Fleischers had never really exploited him in animation.

I knew we could get some good material for Wimpy because he was a character who, like Pluto, could be used to show thinking processes.

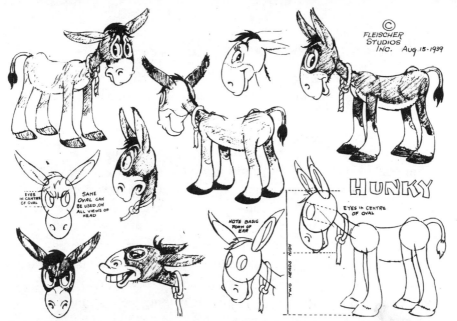

Myron Waldman designed the characters and directed *Hunky and Spunky*, a film that is notable because it was one of three pictures produced by Fleischer Studio that was nominated for an Academy Award.

Although this model sheet exhibits the usual Fleischer inability to draw a figure unless it is firmly planted on both legs and therefore static, this film, *Popeye Meets William Tell*, had better animation than the average Fleischer short. Animated by Al Eugster, Nick Tafuri, and Bob Wickersham, with layouts by Shane Miller, it was directed by Shamus Culhane.

The story department was reluctant to write such a script, so I went to Max. He turned me down because, as he said, "Wimpy is not an action character." I offered to write a script myself, but Max refused. Wimpy was "too psychological."

It was frustrating because we had a good crew. Eugster and Wickersham could have done a marvelous job on Wimpy where the characterization needed some good pantomime, and Tafuri was becoming very expert at fast action. Our group—what with the art class and some long lectures from me—was trying for much better quality than the rest of the studio. We were developing a very strong esprit de corps.

Max was allowing us to make pencil tests on these shorts, contrary to his production methods in New York. In spite of some resistance, Hollywood customs and attitudes about picture making were beginning to have an impact on the Fleischer veterans.

Not that they were completely won over. One frustrating exchange in the cutting room was a case in point. I was at the moviola looking intently at some experimental timing in a scene. A Fleischer vet walked in and looked over my shoulder.

"Hey, that don't look right," he exclaimed.

"I know, it was an experiment."

"But it's no good."

"I realize that. It was an experiment."

"But it came out wrong!"

"I know that. It was an experiment."

We could have gone on all afternoon. He simply could not understand that it was useful to range beyond a "safe" piece of timing, doing something that might not be usable, so he walked off, shaking his head, no doubt remembering Max's statement when he initially rejected the idea of making pencil tests: "If an animator doesn't know exactly what he's doing, he's no animator."

Our next film, *Popeye Meets William Tell,* was a good example of my efforts to take a typical lusty Fleischer Popeye script and superimpose some Hollywood finesse in acting and cutting. The result was something like putting a lace sunbonnet on a wild boar.

One thing that puzzled me was the method of producing the sound tracks for the Popeye series. Jack Mercer, who did the voice of Popeye, was a man with a marvelous sense of humor. During the final recording session, when the sound effects, dialogue, and music were being mixed,

Jack would stand at a mike and ad-lib muttered remarks by Popeye. These wisecracks were often the funniest bits of dialogue in the picture.

The question is, why do them at this late date when they had no possibility of being incorporated into the animation? On the other hand, maybe they were better that way. A kind of stream-of-consciousness process. Whatever the reason, they were spontaneous bits of humor which enhanced Popeye's role in every picture.

Just before Christmas 1940, Sam Buchwald, the accountant, called me into his office and complained about the fact that my group was falling behind schedule. His solution for this was going to be an exchange of some of my personnel for faster animators.

I was appalled. I had been training my group, with art lessons and talks about acting, for months. Now these efforts toward quality animation were going to be ruined by the exchange for some Fleischer veterans who wouldn't have the faintest idea of our goals.

I made a deal with Sam. We would catch up on our schedule by New Year's, or I would agree to the dispersal of our group. Buchwald was very sympathetic but firm. "Jimmie," he said sadly, "the day of the rosy dollar is over."

I went back to my room and laid it on the line. Somehow we had to finish our film by New Year's. The boys responded with great enthusiasm. Nobody wanted to be transferred to another group, so we worked furiously day and night. When the usual Christmas party started, we were still too far behind to give ourselves a holiday. While the rest of the studio resounded with drunken screams and laughter, we all sat there churning out the footage. Occasionally some raucous drunk would open the door, but the sight of rows of silent forms bent over the drawing boards would bring him up short. The door would be closed, very carefully, as if he had intruded on a church service.

No one got up until it was time to go home. The party was long since over, but nobody complained. We did finish the picture on time and stayed as an intact unit for the next feature, *Mr. Bug Goes to Town.*

In February 1940, *Pinocchio* appeared in the local theater, and of course most of the people in Fleischer's went to see it. I went with a group of friends in a state of happy anticipation. None of my animation had gone past the pencil test stage at the time I left Disney's, and of course I was anxious to see the finished result.

When the picture started, and the credit titles appeared, I saw in the

A model sheet of Popeye drawn by Shamus Culhane for *Popeye Meets William Tell*. Fleischer Studio, 1940, directed by Shamus Culhane.

Popeye, drawn by Shamus Culhane for *Popeye Meets William Tell*. A 1940 production of Fleischer Studio, directed by Shamus Culhane.

list of animators that my ex-assistant Norman Tate had made the grade after I left. To my consternation, my name was missing. It was almost a physical shock, like getting a karate kick in the crotch.

Screen credit is so important, especially on a picture of this stature. *Pinocchio* was sure to be rated as one of the most important films in animation history. I had literally risked my life to remain at Disney's as long as it was possible. For months I had recklessly attacked my drawings with my arm in a sling, knowing that every vigorous movement I made as I worked was going to cost me hours of pain later.

What the hell did Walt want? Perhaps if I had collapsed and died at the drawing board, I would have been buried on the front lawn with my head pillowed by a box of pencils and my favorite eraser. What possible motivation could have caused Walt to be so vengeful? He never had a more loyal employee, yet my contribution to *Pinocchio* had been sunk without a trace. I sat through the rest of the picture, shaking with rage and frustration.

It was a very impressive picture, in many ways better than *Snow White*.

The use of the multiplane camera in the opening long shot of the village was worth the price of admission. Cy Young and his crew of special effects experts had animated the waves and spray around Monstro the Whale with a quality of believability that they never could have achieved in *Snow White*.

To me, the best animation in the picture was Bill Tytla's interpretation of Stromboli, the abductor of Pinocchio. No matter how expert in drawing and animation the native California animators were, I doubt if they could have been able to conceive the dynamic force of Stromboli as he harangues Pinocchio and his audience. The swift changes from one grimace to the next, the shrugs, wild gesticulations, the tortured positions of his mouth as he struggles to express himself in English, could only have been drawn with such authenticity by someone who was familiar with foreigners.

Tytla, the son of Ukranian immigrants, was raised in New York City, where one can walk down the streets of Little Italy and see fifty Strombolis in an hour. In my opinion Tytla never did a better piece of dialogue animation in his life.

The drama and tension of Snow White's flight through the forest and the pursuit of the witch by the dwarfs and the animals, while terrifying in themselves, were not on par with the nightmarish quality of Monstro the Whale's savage fury, the menacing bulk of the evil Coachman, or the spine-shivering atmosphere of Pleasure Island.

Pinocchio posed some very difficult problems for the layout department, particularly in the difference in size between the whale and the other characters. The use of interesting camera angles very deftly solved the scale problem and did it so well that there was not one scene in which the vast bulk of the whale was in doubt, even when the shot was a closeup of his baleful eye.

Pinocchio himself was animated so well that one had the feeling that he was a stiff-jointed puppet who could at any moment lose his precarious coordination. Using Jiminy Cricket as a catalyst had successfully smoothed out the kinks in the original story. Taken as a whole, I believe that the film is better than *Snow White* in every department except for the songs.

As for my own animation, while the scenes where the Fox and the Cat spy Pinocchio and the "Actor's Life for Me" song were somewhat better than any of my previous work, the sequence in the inn with the Coachman was a big jump forward. The emphasis on geometry in the drawing made for good strong poses. This is probably the best animation I have ever done, which made the omission of my name from the credits all the more bitter.

It was many weeks before I could think about *Pinocchio* without experiencing a wave of anguish.

When production on *Mr. Bug* was begun, our unit was given the responsibility for the opening sequence, which involved all of the insect characters. As any filmmaker knows, if the opening of a picture does not succeed in capturing the full attention and empathy of the audience, there is very little chance that the following development of the story is going to fare much better, even if that material is superior to the faltering efforts in the start.

Acting on that assumption, I spent long hours discussing the dramatic and comic possibilities of each character with my unit. In the interim, the rest of the staff had plunged into their work and began to turn out footage with the usual Fleischer disregard for the complexities of first-class animation. We soon fell far behind the other units.

Sam Buchwald would call me into his office and point to the flow chart and its telltale gap in our footage figures. He didn't want to hear about the problems of setting each character's acting style in relation to the others, or the fact that many scenes had five or six characters working, which was not true of the later sequences in the picture.

Of course we were both wrong. A director is supposed to work within a budget, restrictive or not, because that money is what is available for the picture. From the commercial point of view, I was at fault.

On the other hand, management is supposed to know enough about the difficulties of filmmaking to do much more than divide the budget into equal amounts for all the footage in the picture. This mechanical approach presupposes that every foot of the film is equally difficult or easy to animate and every sequence is of equal importance in the story. So Buchwald was wrong, too.

I really posed a dilemma. Prickly, stubborn, and arrogant, I opposed Sam's pleading for a little more cooperation with the timeworn phrase, "I'm doing the best I can," always the last refuge of a dissident.

Nick Tafuri recently reminisced about that stormy period:

> One day Sam called me into his office and said, "What the hell is going on in the back room [our unit's]? We can't get any work out of you guys. What is Culhane doing? We sent him a good, fast animator to help with the footage, and pretty soon he's dragging his ass like the rest of you!"
>
> When I tried to tell him that we had a lot of characters to deal with, he didn't want to listen. "Come on," he says, and we go off to the moviola room. He says to the cutter, "Gimme that Dave Tendlar reel." While the guy is putting the reel on Sam says, "Dave's group has already done three hundred feet, and all Culhane's got so far is one hundred."
>
> So we start looking at the Tendlar reel and I almost bust. The whole thing is nothing but shots of sidewalks and buildings; one shot was a crack in the pavement with Hoppity's head bobbing along. Out of the whole reel there was maybe fifty feet of character animation, the rest of it was all camera work. What the hell am I goin' to say? Sam just didn't know the difference, so I just walked out without saying anything.
>
> Then I went to Tendlar and I asked him what was the

idea? Dave says that he just wanted to get the easy stuff on
the reel first. Of course, we could have done that too. The
trouble was that we had no scenes where the camera just
pans along a background. Every shot was a ball breaker.
Without knowing it, Tendlar made our unit look bad.
Sam was just goin' by the numbers.

Being the studio accountant and production manager, Sam was justified in "going by the numbers," but there should have been someone
in the organization, Dave Fleischer presumably, to interpret these numbers in the light of the physical work and the technical problems involved.
The studio never operated with such complex principles. Given a sequence with crowd shots, an animator was expected to slam out those
scenes with scant regard for quality, because his footage quota was
threatened, and footage was the prime factor above all others, so even
Dave would have not been much use in the role of a modifier of "the
numbers."

There were so many employees of Fleischer Studio who had come
from Hollywood that there was always a brisk interchange of news from
one coast to the other. We knew all about the formation of a company
union in Disney's, and the successful unionization of the other West Coast
studios almost as soon as these events occurred.

While Walt Disney had an extraordinary ability to detect latent talent,
he also had a weakness in that he was easily impressed by charismatic
personalities and awed by sophistication, often to his detriment. From the
beginning of the studio's labor problems Gunther Lessing, the studio
lawyer, seems to have been given carte blanche as Disney's counselor and
representative.

A more unwise choice could not have been made. During the preliminary seminars about unionism, Lessing's approach was too slick, too facile,
and too arrogant. When some employee had the temerity to get up and
ask a question, Lessing, while listening, would roll his eyes up toward
heaven, in the age-old gesture of weary patience with blatant stupidity.
It was a bit of acting that probably was supposed to indicate Lessing's
superiority over the lumpen proletariat he had to deal with.

It had just the opposite effect. While Lessing did succeed in organizing
a company union, there were elements of hostility within the group that
he had fostered by his deprecating manner.

Company unions are formed with a definite purpose in mind, namely, to make palatable to the membership the wishes of management. Usually these aims are camouflaged by allowing the employees to set up a constitution and by-laws and holding employer-employee discussions. It seems to work in some countries, but here, in many cases, it's a little like allowing the hens to stipulate that the fox may not enter the hen-coop unless he is wearing a tie and comes equipped with a clean knife and fork.

Whatever Lessing envisioned about the passive character of the company union, he had a rude awakening. Art Babbitt became one of the leading figures in the group and began to urge the membership to take a more belligerent stance on some of the more obvious issues. When he realized that many of the people involved had no intention of opposing management on any level, Babbitt, in a gesture of defiance, joined the Screen Cartoonists Guild. Other people followed suit.

Babbitt further acerbated the situation by demanding that a raise be given to his assistant. His salary, fifty dollars a week, was an obvious case of underpayment. Disney's response to the challenge was predictable. It was a case of one tragic hero confronting another, with the usual loss of objectivity or even common sense. Declaring that Babbitt was too involved with union activity, Disney fired him. The next day, May 29, 1941, three hundred picketing strikers swarmed around the gates. Three of them were youngsters who would later make a great impact on the business: Dave Hilberman, John Hubley, and Zack Schwartz. Possibly the biggest blow to Walt's ego was the loss of Bill Tytla. While not a striker himself, he refused to cross the picket line.

After a few weeks the lines of demarcation were firmly drawn. The strikers and those who remained in the studio seemed to have locked horns. Nobody left to join the pickets, and none of the strikers rejoined the workers inside. I was an unwitting catalyst. Norman Tate, my ex-assistant, had been very dubious about the merits of the strike, so he had not joined the dissidents. However, he was very troubled about his role in the quarrel and wrote to me, asking for my advice.

I sent Norman a letter in which I expressed the feeling that Walt did not really understand the working conditions of the business. It was not that he was a villain; he just could not see that there was a need for an industry-wide organization. Yet, was I not a good example of the fact that people were often forced to find employment in one area or another due to circumstances other than financial gain? There was no way for the business to become stabilized without having all the employees in one union.

Motivated by my letter, Norman left the studio and joined the strikers. Not only that, but the union made flyers of the letter, and handed out copies to the employees as they filed out after work. The result was that a surprising number of workers who, like Tate, had been hesitant about joining the strike, now did so.

I had no intention of becoming a propagandist, but I was acutely aware that all the other artists in the animation industry were in effect being cheated of their right to explore their natural talents to the fullest. I envisioned a time when all the studios in the business would be run like Disney's. I thought that it would only be a matter of time until every studio in the country would be under the umbrella of one union, with the working conditions of Disney Studio as a model.

A naïve zealot, I reckoned without taking into consideration the apathy of the many animators and other creative people who, having never tasted the heady brew of working without footage quotas, placed no value on these ideal conditions.

Eventually the union did win its goals, and the employees at Disney's joined the guild. Even so, for a long time the Disney group filed into union meetings and sat down in a compact, isolated group, a significant manifestation of the fact that the Disney artists still considered themselves separate from the rest of the industry.

As our work progressed I began to see that *Mr. Bug* had many of the faults of *Gulliver*. Hoagy Carmichael and Frank Loesser wrote songs and lyrics that were not up to their usual standards of quality. The story and storyboards had been rushed out under increasing pressure from Paramount. While they made a good first draft, the story structure was never fully explored, and the characters, especially Hoppity, were simplistic. As usual the love interest was the Fleischer stereotyped banality between a gauche Hoppity and an insipid Honey, heavy-handed and dull.

Fleischerites always defended their work by stoutly maintaining that if they had more time the quality of their work would rival, or be better than, Disney's. They never could accept the fact that time wasn't the factor; it was education. Disney's artists and writers were working with principles of their craft which had been arrived at by intensive study.

Fleischer people were operating from instinct and a scornful rejection of the idea that principles of writing and animation even existed.

The exception was my unit, which by this time was a little enclave of dedicated students of animation. Shane Miller's penchant for odd camera angles was having a decided influence on the whole picture. I believe this was because the layout drawings were hung on a wall and were available to the casual passerby. This was not true of the animation.

We didn't influence anybody, because there was hardly ever an exchange of pencil tests from one unit to the other. In fact, as we neared the end of the picture, I had seen less than half of the film in pencil-test form. My animators had seen even less. It was as if showing the film in progress to all the units was a waste of time that was better used in churning out animation.

During the early months of 1941 I had been mulling over my plans. I decided that it would be good for me to have a kind of sabbatical at the drawing board. I had very little opportunity to animate during the time I was at Fleischer's. On the other hand, I had no wish to find another job. I had saved eight thousand dollars, a huge sum in those days, so I didn't need to worry about making a living for at least two years.

I applied to the Guggenheim Foundation for a grant to do some experimental animation. A man with the improbable name of Henry Allen Moe answered my letter by sending me the information that my request was under consideration, but I would need two sponsors. When I wrote to Don Graham for advice, he suggested that I use Jean Charlot and Walt Disney. Charlot had readily agreed, but I had best approach Walt myself.

Still smarting over the omission of my name from the screen credits on *Pinocchio,* I was reluctant. Finally, I sent him a stiff little note. Back came a memo from Walt's secretary, Dolores Voght, enclosing a copy of the letter of recommendation from Disney to the Foundation. It was an enthusiastic summation of my skills, talents, and prospects as an animator. Anybody would be proud to get such a recommendation. If anything, I had expected a very businesslike letter or no answer at all. What a mercurial son-of-a-bitch!

In spite of the reputation of my two sponsors, I did not get a grant from Guggenheim. But I guess I broke the ground for John Hubley. He produced *Adventures of an* * on a grant in 1957.

The layout department overcame the difficulties in showing insects and people in the same film. Here the insects are fleeing in panic as a bulldozer wrecks their habitat. *Mr. Bug Goes to Town,* 1941, Fleischer Studio. *Paramount Pictures. Museum of Modern Art/Film Stills Archives.*

Hoppity, the grasshopper lead in *Mr. Bug Goes to Town.* Fleischer Studio, 1941. *Paramount Pictures.*

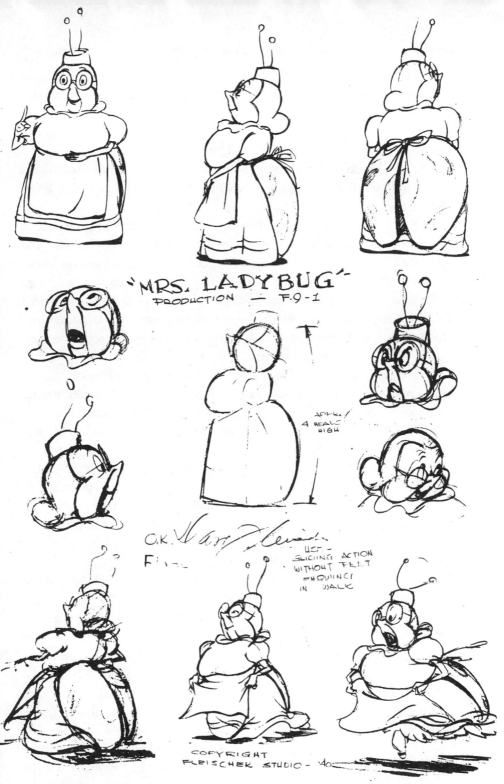

"MRS. LADYBUG"
PRODUCTION — F.9-1

APFL/
4 HEALS
HIGH

O.K.

USE
SLIDING ACTION
WITHOUT FEET
—QUINCI
IN WALK

COPYRIGHT
FLEISCHER STUDIO - 40

Mrs. Ladybug, one of the leading characters in *Mr. Bug Goes to Town*. Fleischer Studio. *Paramount Pictures.*

In 1941 almost everybody agreed that it was just a question of time before we were in the war. My wife, Bettina, had a brother-in-law who was a rear admiral, and her father was a retired colonel. The year before we had visited them in Washington. One of our tours led us to the animation department of the Signal Corps.

To my astonishment they were using a camera and camera stand that was a duplicate of the rickety equipment we had at J. R. Bray's in 1924. The animation was to match.

As I walked down an aisle I became separated from the group. One of the workers sidled up to me furtively. "You Jimmie Culhane, the animator?" I nodded. "This place stinks," he whispered, and slid back into his seat as the party caught up with me. The major who was in charge of the studio was very hostile, and I began to understand why. The studio was obviously incapable of producing the most simple type of animation. Much of the work seemed to be adorning still photos of machinery with arrows pointing at various features.

Back at the colonel's house I launched into a diatribe about the stupidity of the military in not exploring the possibilities of educational animation. The colonel said quietly, "Why don't you make them an example?" This fired me up and, by the time I returned home to Miami, I was determined to make an instructional film about the Battle of Chancellorsville. It was the colonel's idea to use this battle between the armies of General Hooker and General Robert E. Lee. He pointed out that General Lee had used Stonewall Jackson's men in an encircling movement not unlike the Germans' use of armored divisions during the current blitzkrieg. It was probably the most complicated battle of the Civil War in terms of movement. If we could make a film that explained the strategy and tactics of this fight, we would certainly have opened the way to a use of animation as a teaching vehicle.

I enlisted Shane Miller in the project to do layouts and backgrounds. What I planned was to animate a military map showing geometric shapes signifying army corps, brigades, and regiments filing along roads and taking up positions. In the right-hand corner of the field would be a clock and the date, so that an observer could tell when the maneuvers happened.

Tom Moore, who was now an animator in my unit, was also a captain in the Army Reserve. He volunteered to read the maps for me so that I could plot the movements of the troops. Max Fleischer allowed us to use the recording room and cutting equipment. None of us realized what a monumental job this was. Very soon we were working forty hours a week on *Mr. Bug* and more than forty hours on *Chancellorsville*.

Many of the inkers and painters gave hours of their time too. Most of them were paid, but others worked for nothing with the proviso that if we sold the picture they would be paid double wages. Even with this help I had to pay three thousand dollars for materials and services, making a sizable dent in my savings.

The Battle of Chancellorsville was finished just before my contract with the Fleischers ran out, which was the main reason we had all put in so many long hours. It was a very dramatic moment when we screened the film and watched units break their geometric shapes and assume new ones as the battle progressed. We called it *The Strategy and Tactics of the Battle of Chancellorsville.* I was sure that we had an impressive picture to show that constipated major in the Signal Corps. Not only that, nobody had ever made such a teaching film before.

While I had spent hours reading numerous history books that described the battle, not ten minutes had been set aside to examine the sales possibilities. I had a vague idea that this film would be used as a sample, and orders would be forthcoming for use in officers' training.

Bettina and I had bought a trailer, and we set off for Washington after the usual farewell lunch with my group. I had a long talk with Max the day before, and I had explained to him that what I really wanted to do was some experimental animation without the pressure of deadlines, just for my own satisfaction. Max shook his head in disbelief.

At lunch the next day, Max sat with his usual group, and I heard later that he was discussing my quitting such a good job. "The trouble with Jimmie," Max said sadly, "is that he is an artist."

In Washington, my father-in-law set up a screening of *Chancellorsville* for a few friends who were in various branches of the military. The film finished to an enthusiastic round of applause and congratulations. The next step was to arrange for a showing with our dyspeptic major. He was remarkably reluctant to view the picture, but at length agreed to see it.

Most of the audience were engineers from Fort Benning; a very few people were from the Signal Corps. When the lights went on, I beamed at the loud applause. It came to a stop as the major got up shaking his head in disapproval. "Sorry," he said grimly, "we never use color films in our training programs. Color hurts your eyes." With that he stalked off.

The colonel had been fairly powerful in G2 (Army Intelligence), so he had a certain amount of clout, but not enough. We had many screenings, and most of the people who viewed the film thought that it was an amazingly useful tool for teaching strategy and tactics, but inevitably we came back to the fact that the churlish major was head of visual training for the whole army, and there was no way to get around him.

The large film companies had been wining and dining him for months, so he wasn't about to promise work to a pipsqueak who hadn't even invited him for a beer. Several five-percenters came around, hinting delicately that if I had some money to spread about things could be arranged. My refusal was always loud and never delicate. The fucking hyenas! Any minute we were going to be embroiled in the worst war that ever happened, and here they were sipping martinis and talking about bribes.

Finally, in the spring I gave up the whole venture and started west in my trailer. The overwork all those months, and the fact that the picture was being ignored like a fart in a sulphur mine, left me in a deep depression.

11

The New Wave

For several years before World War II, there was a group of younger artists in the business who chafed at the restrictions of the traditional approach to designing layouts and painting backgrounds. In a large sense there was only one style of cartoon, and it encompassed all the studios in the country. The only difference was in the degree of craftsmanship.

The heavy-handed design and murky painting of the Fleischer Studio and the deft handling of design and backgrounds in Disney's were not all that divergent. They both were attempts to bring to the screen a type of art that was prevalent in children's books at the turn of the century. Walt, especially, admired the English illustrators, Arthur Rackham and his followers, who all drew and painted as if modern art did not exist.

For the most part the older animation designers and background painters did not question the fact that two diverse kinds of textures were being lumped together on the screen. It had been that way since Bray and Hurd patented the use of cels more than twenty years before.

Characters were drawn in the round, moved in space, but were painted flat like posters. On the other hand, the backgrounds were usually rendered in transparent washes, allowing for delicate transitions between light and shade, with an emphasis on interesting textures.

The direct antispasis between the flat characters and the realistic backgrounds was readily accepted by the older artists; but to the youngsters, better educated in modern art, it was an optical insult.

Oddly enough, the first full-scale revolt against this textural potpourri was started at Columbia's animation studio, that catafalque of mediocrity, Screen Gems.

In 1941, Frank Tashlin had been hired as a writer, but was soon given creative control of the studio. He took advantage of the Disney strike to pluck a covey of brilliant young artists off the picket line.

His catch included men who very soon would exercise a profound influence on modern animation, an influence that continues to function to this day. They were Zack Schwartz, Dave Hilberman, John Hubley, and Ted Parmalee. Other ex-Disneyites were Bob Wickersham, John Ployart, Sam Cobean, and Bill Shull.

They all shared Frank Tashlin's iconoclastic feelings about traditional cartoons as epitomized by the Disney films. For a year this group had a riotous time turning out cartoons that were highly experimental, not only in appearance but in story content as well. Tashlin encouraged them to indulge in their wildest fantasies about filmmaking.

Tashlin himself started off with a blockbuster. The first cartoon he made as a writer-director at Screen Gems was called *The Fox and the Grapes.* It was composed of a series of blackout gags, a technique that was well known on the burlesque stage, but never before used in an animated cartoon. It foreshadowed Chuck Jones' Road Runner films, not only in the blackout formula but also in the type of gags. Chuck freely admits to the Tashlin influence on his work.

As a writer-director-cartoonist, Tashlin's creativity is so great that even if he had concentrated on any one of these talents, he would still have to be considered as one of the giants in animation history.

The others, for the most part, went through a period of fumbling for ways to combine new kinds of graphics with new kinds of humor. The graphics were radical departures from academic layouts and background paintings.

There was a great use of flat areas of color in the backgrounds, and sometimes there was no background at all, just a colored card. No attempt was made to create a feeling of air, and objects like trees were often symbols, rather than even remote attempts at reality. This kind of film delighted in the fact that the audience was being presented with moving drawings and was quite the opposite of the Disney attempt to create characters who moved and spoke like little live actors.

The stories were often not as successful as the graphics in that they sometimes seemed a little self-conscious, but at least they were breaking away from the traditional humor of Disney and his need to create lifelike characters.

Frank Tashlin was responsible for giving the group this unique opportunity to experiment, but I believe that if it hadn't happened in Screen
Gems it would have happened somewhere, in any case. Throughout the
business the balance of power was swinging away from the older character designers, layout men, background artists, and animators, into the
hands of younger, more educated and sophisticated artists.

The older artists tended to socialize with each other, while the younger
men had a social strata of their own. Long before there was a chance to
use these new graphics, they had been bruited about during evenings
where the youngsters got together to listen to jazz records, sip Bourbon,
and talk shop.

It was a source of great satisfaction to Tashlin as he looked back at that
period later. "We showed those Disney guys that animated cartoons don't
have to look like a fucking kid's book. We dumped their whole background department on its ass."

Ironically enough, Tashlin was in the process of writing and illustrating a children's book himself. *The Bear That Wasn't* is a delightful story
about a bear who wakes from hibernation to find that a wartime manufac-
turing plant has taken over his territory.

When he is confronted by an impatient foreman who insists that he
is not a bear, he is just a lazy worker in a fur coat, the poor bear can't
win. He is shunted from one pompous executive to another. Nobody
believes that he is a bear.

The illustrations and the story charmed adults as well as children, and
the book made Tashlin a lot of money. It also showed that his vast
contempt for the corporate mentality struck a sympathetic vein in the
public's attitudes.

Frank had a healthy respect for his own talents, and no respect whatsoever for those who profited from his work. When he approached Screen
Gems' producer Ben Schwalb for a raise, Tashlin was turned down. He
promptly quit, and the studio hired Dave Fleischer, late of the Fleischer
animation studio in Miami.

It took only a few weeks of exposure to Dave's antiquated "Gotta
gag?" technique, then all the talented New Wave boys fled as if from the
pox. That ended Screen Gems' brief flash of glory.

Bill Shull, who had been Bill Tytla's assistant for many years at
Disney's, was one of the animators who left Screen Gems shortly after
Dave Fleischer arrived. Instead of looking for a job in another animation

studio, he joined the faculty of U.C.L.A. There he founded an animator's workshop, as a part of the school's motion picture division.

Under Shull's guidance the pupils were encouraged to experiment in avant-garde styles and materials that were never in use at Disney's, and probably never will be. Until his retirement several years ago, Shull provided the only animation school in the United States that rivaled the Canadian Film Board in the quality of the students' work, and the wide range of the subject matter.

Although the strike had been long over when I returned to Hollywood, the Disney Studio was still in a ferment.

The emotions of strikers and non-strikers are often very complex. Some people who did not join the picket line were guilt-ridden because they were not sure whether they had remained loyal to Walt from conviction or cowardice. Others who had been in the strike were equally unsure. Had they been wise to pursue a course that had so disrupted the studio?

A group of militants felt that their focus was on the traitors to brotherhood among the workers who had refused to strike, rather than Walt Disney, who at least was a legitimate enemy.

All these bitter feelings were not assuaged by the legal steps that ended the strike, and because they weren't, the esprit de corps that made possible all the brilliant films of the 1930s was as dead as a dodo.

Walt himself was a victim of his own paternalistic self-image. In a suit brought by Art Babbitt for reinstatement and back pay, Disney tried to persuade the court that he had fired Babbitt because he was not a good animator! The creator of the wicked Queen in *Snow White,* expert animator of Goofy, and the mushroom dance in *Fantasia,* a poor animator? The idea was so preposterous that Babbitt won the case.

The two tragic heroes had butted heads together like moose in rutting season, and Walt lost. Looking wildly around for some reason why his paternalism had been attacked and defeated, he pounced on the most obvious answer for that period . . . communism.

Appearing before the House Committee on Un-American Activities, Walt stated: " . . . I definitely feel that it was a communist group trying to take over my artists, and they did take them over." This was another preposterous idea.

The fact that he still wanted to practice Victorian paternalism (which he obviously believed to be the proper relationship between employer

Sylvester, one of the most popular characters in the studio. Drawn by Shamus Culhane, 1943. *Warner Brothers.*

A quick sketch of Sylvester by Shamus Culhane. *Warner Brothers.*

and employee) is evidenced by his repeated use of the term "my boys" when he referred to his staff.

In actuality, many of his "boys" were a lot older than Disney was, semantic evidence of his need to see himself as the benevolent father, not just an employer. Fleischer and Disney had this Victorian trait in common. Max always referred to his staff as "the kids."

Art Babbitt, in his role of tragic hero, sacrificed his career as a great animator; after winning his job back at Disney's, he found the atmosphere too oppressive and hostile, so he left, and for many years he seemed unable to find a position suitable to his enormous talents. He worked for a time at UPA, then as director for Hanna–Barbera's television spot department. He won many awards from Madison Avenue, but it wasn't until he started to work on Dick William's feature picture *Raggedy Ann and Andy* that he was able to find some animation worthy of his abilities.

His work on the Camel with the Wrinkled Knees, one of the stars in the picture, leaves no doubt that even in 1976, Art Babbitt was still one of the world's great animators.

Bill Tytla, the comic hero, was a victim of the strike, because when work was resumed he felt that he was the target for a great deal of hostility from those members of the staff who had resisted the strike. After a few years he left Disney and went to work at his old haunt, Terrytoons. Then he worked at Fleischer's for six years, where he found that there was really no use for his talents as a director, so he started a small business in New York making television spots. He proved to be an inept businessman and never succeeded in making more than a bare living.

As a result of the strike, Disney lost two of the men who had been prime movers in his meteoric rise to greatness; and in addition many others who might have been able to explore new heights. Artists like Sam Cobean, John Hubley, Walt Kelly, Vip Partch, Bill Hurtz, Zack Schwartz, John Ployart, and Dave Hilberman never came back.

Hubley, Hurtz, and Engels went to work for Bosustow, Hilberman, and Schwartz when they started UPA. Cobean and Partch became famous magazine cartoonists, and Walt Kelly created "Pogo," one of the most popular comic strips ever.

While the remainder of the Disney staff included many artists of incredible talent, they were not innovators. Instead, they brought the viewpoint and style that had already been set to an astonishing degree of perfection.

From an artistic standpoint there is very little difference in the approach to *Snow White, Pinocchio, Fantasia,* and the other features that followed, except that they became more polished, especially the special effects and acting.

For example, in a review of *The Fox and the Hound* in *The New York Times* of July 10, 1981, Vincent Canby writes, "One of the nicer things about *The Fox and the Hound,* which opens today at the Guild and other theaters, is that it breaks no new ground whatsoever."

Historically there were two attempts to break out of Disney's personal brand of humor. The first was instigated by the Kinney brothers. Dick was a staff writer, and Jack, a former animator, had made his debut as a director with one of the best Pluto shorts of all time, *Bone Trouble,* in 1940.

The Kinneys teamed up on a series of shorts that featured Goofy. Heretofore, Goofy had been cast as a good-natured, simpleminded oaf. The Kinneys used him as the star of a series of satiric attacks on the bombastic writers of "how-to" books.

They may have been influenced by a group of short films that Robert Benchley had created in the 1930s. Benchley, a nationally known humorist, appeared on the screen as a bewildered duffer who was trying to improve his proficiency in various games. A very pompous instructor on the sound track led Benchley through a ridiculous and complicated analysis of his movements as he swung a croquet mallet, golf club, etcetera.

From their first venture, *How to Ride a Horse,* the Kinneys went on to make a series of highly successful satirical films: *The Art of Skiing, The Art of Self Defence,* and *How to Play Baseball* were all enormously funny. Interrupted by World War II, they were resumed in 1949.

Dick's acerbic writing style, and Jack's fast-paced direction, competed successfully with Warner Brothers' brash humor, which dominated the 1940s. The satire in these Goofy shorts was the only new approach to humor in many years, and the only lasting diversion from Disney's personal brand of humor.

There was another attempt at rebellion when Ward Kimball, Dick Huemer, and Nick Nichols put together a charming high-style short, *Toot Whistle Plunk and Boom,* which won an Academy Award in 1953.

It has been said that Walt was less than enthusiastic about the picture because it used a very avant-garde type of graphics which rivaled the style of UPA. Whatever the reason, there were few attempts to follow it up with pictures with similar concepts.

It might be that Walt had reached a point where he was producing shorts that were as far as he could go artistically. Another avenue of speculation is the possibility that the whole studio, which had started so humbly, then flowered brilliantly, was entering into a long period of decline, with the strike merely hastening the wilt that seems to be inevitable in any artistic point of view.

This may account for the fact that Walt, perhaps recognizing that he had reached the limit of his creative resources in animation, became increasingly interested in Disneyland as a new and more vital expression of his talents as a showman.

For this extraordinarily inventive mind, it was just a small step to begin thinking about the structure of our global environment. When he died, Walt was planning a whole new project, an experimental prototype community of tomorrow.

In 1942, Chuck Jones, then a very successful director at Warner Brothers, produced *The Dover Boys,* a spoof on Victorian stories. It was a high-style film so radical in concept that it influenced many of his films from that point on. According to John Hubley it inspired many of the graphics later used in the UPA cartoons and started a whole new trend in filmmaking.

An interesting by-product of the New Wave pictures was the dislocation of the animators as the most important factors in filmmaking. Animation of characters as facsimiles of live actors was no longer a prerequisite, so the long years of study and training to achieve this expertise went by the board. With the stylized background came equally stylized animation, much more simple in execution. Relatively untrained animators, if they were good draftsmen, could readily produce satisfactory animation. The star of the animator sank as that of the designer rose.

With that came another departure from custom. Heretofore, a director was a man who rose from the ranks of the animators. Now there was a new breed . . . the director-designer (like John Hubley), who had never animated at all.

The years 1941 and 1942 saw the pecking order of the whole industry slowly start to become rearranged. Nobody realized the implications of this new approach to filmmaking at the time; and it took many years before the work of pioneers like Frank Tashlin and Chuck Jones had any

Chuck Jones when he was directing at Warner Brothers. His *Dover Boys* started the trend away from lifelike animation. UPA followed this approach and a whole new school of animation was born. © *1983 Karsh, Ottawa.*

Paul Julian, 1958.

real impact on the business as a whole. However, once started, the movement of the New Wave was inexorable.

Recently (1981), I wrote to Paul Julian, asking for some information about his work at Warner Brothers as a background painter during these experiments in the 1940s.

This is part of his reply:

> I didn't do anything that involved overtly contemporary design until I got to UPA, during the last two war years. What I was doing with Friz Freleng was damn well what Friz wanted to see. The innovating I did was mostly sly, furtive, and sneaky, and it was hidden by a definitely theatrical effort to expand the environment I was given as staging.
>
> I was working with Hawley Pratt's layouts, very rough, and I spent some time adding descriptive material. Turning a roughly-staged, nowhere house in blue pencil into one of the tacky decrepit old houses on West Eighth Street (in Los Angeles) with up-the-wall wiring and tin patches outside; cheek-by-jowl with leftovers of furniture from earlier inhabitants.
>
> Or the ordinary nowhere street became a late afternoon street, where it had rained earlier. I remember rebuilding fences now and then, using boards from a dismantled boxcar. None of this was allowed to get too junky or to distract too much from the staging of the animation, for which I have the *greatest* respect. I still do, as I think on it.
>
> I did occasionally get involved with some Cezannery or Picassery, but I made sure that Friz didn't notice it. Some people grinned, but they promised not to tell. So I was not an innovator at all, and not much of a rebel.
>
> If I have an attitude about traditional background painting it comes to a head, or becomes a painful abscess mostly from someone's overstatement, or the wrong kind of self-indulgence. Most of the time this is the result of disregard for the characters we are staging. If we are planning around a gray and white rabbit made of garden hose, we learn rapidly what *not* to do. Another thing that

gets me in the gallbladder is a disregard of the scene as *light*.

A refusal to notice how a flow of light up there has a dramatic value of itself. I have been preaching this gospel to dewy-eyed little kids now for a number of years.

This is a characteristically modest self-evaluation of his work. In truth, during the early 1940s Paul Julian was recognized as one of the most talented background artists in the field. No doubt that some of his ideas would have been very acceptable at Disney's. However, his "sneaky" bits of Cezannery and Picassery would not have been very well received by Walt, who had no appreciation of modern art.

It was just as well that Julian stayed at Warners, with his comparative freedom to interpret layouts to his own satisfaction, making a notable contribution to the art form in the process. Later, Julian went to UPA where his feeling for modern design was more than welcome.

There he worked with John Hubley on *Rooty Toot Toot* and the animated main titles for Stanley Kramer's *The Four-Poster*. He also was the designer for Ted Parmalee's version of Edgar Allan Poe's horror story "The Tell-Tale Heart." These were some of the best animated films ever made.

When I arrived in Hollywood, one of the first things I did was go to the Screen Cartoonists' office to apply for membership. There was only one person in the office, a slight, dark little man with a heavy Latin accent. With visible reluctance he admitted that he was Pepe Ruiz, assistant business agent.

I launched into an enthusiastic babble about how pleased I was that the guild won the strike and how happy I was to become a member. Ruiz cut me short. "We doan wan' jou as a member. We got too many goddamn members out of work already." I was so stunned I didn't even get mad. I thought he was simply quoting the official union policy.

When I talked to my friends they assured me that no such restrictions existed. Back I went to the office in a fury. Ruiz was out. Instead I met Bill Pomerance, the business agent. Bill was sympathetic. It seemed that I was not the only victim of Pepe's *mala leche*. A short time later he vanished, only to pop up a few months after as the business agent of the New York animated cartoonists' union.

One day my friend Marc Davis telephoned me. I had not seen him since my return. He told me that he was bringing a message from the Disney Studio. There had been a meeting and the consensus was that I should be allowed to come back. For Chrissake! I damn near blew a gasket! *Allowed* to come back!

Whether it was a loose interpretation of the actual conversation I never did find out. I just hung up rather abruptly. I would have had to be a masochist to go back to Disney's as if I were being forgiven for some crime. I had intended to go back to talk to Walt as soon as my depression lifted, but not to eat crow.

What Marc had not explained was that there was a new situation at the studio, under which matters of policy were acted on by a newly created board of advisors. They were independent of Walt to a great extent. The group consisted of Les Clark, Woolie Reitherman, Eric Larson, Ward Kimball, John Lounsbery, Frank Thomas, Milt Kahl, Ollie Johnston, and Marc Davis. They were later known as the Nine Old Men. This was probably *their* offer.

Once again, as in the case of the doctor who had advised me to have my teeth "checked" instead of X-rayed, a probable semantic mix-up ended any possibility of my resuming a career at Disney's.

Shortly after the Disney incident I went to lunch with Chuck Jones. We had known each other for a long time. I had first met Chuck when he used to drop in at Iwerks to pick up his girlfriend, Dorothy Webster. They had now been married for many years. Chuck had started in the business as a cel washer at Iwerks. From there he drifted to Screen Gems, stayed a few weeks, then got a job with Walt Lantz, as a writer.

After a short time with Lantz, Chuck took a job as an able seaman on a cruise ship, but the trip had ended in a shipwreck. Chuck next became an itinerant caricaturist on Olvira Street, drawing tourists for a dollar a head.

The year 1933 found Jones at work as an inbetweener at Warners. He went on to become an animator and had the invigorating experience of working in Tex Avery's unit, when Tex's crew included such talents as Bobo Cannon and Bob Clampett.

In 1938, when director Frank Tashlin left Warners, Chuck Jones took his place. Within four years he had established himself as one of the outstanding directors in the business. He looked dashing and confident, and gave me an enthusiastic sales pitch about the joys of working at Warners.

As he explained it, Schlesinger, the producer, was too lazy to come into the studio to look at the pictures. Every director could do pretty much as he pleased. After two years of Dave Fleischer breathing down my neck, it all sounded good.

When I went into the sorrowful litany of my tribulations with my *Chancellorsville* film, he insisted that I should see Schlesinger at once, because Chuck was sure that the studio was about to be given a contract for some navy pictures. With my experience I would be just the man to direct them. I agreed.

Frank Tashlin told me a story about Leon Schlesinger, which illustrated his character very well. Tashlin always had two sources of income; he worked in the studios all day and, in his spare time, made even more money selling gags to magazines and newspapers.

Tashlin had worked for a while at the Van Beuren Studio and disliked the man so much that he created a comic strip about a cruddy little character named Van Boring. By the time Frank went to work at Warners as an animator, the strip was selling very well.

When Schlesinger heard about it, he called Tashlin into his office. Since Frank was his employee, Leon insisted that he was entitled to a percentage on *Van Boring* or any other creative idea that Frank might sell. The reason he gave was that Tashlin could not prove that he wasn't thinking up gags on the company's time!

Before Schlesinger could go on to tell Frank what he considered to be a fair percentage, Tashlin was out of the door and out of the studio.

Now, several years later, Frank was back in Warners, this time as a director. The war was making such inroads on the available man power that Schlesinger discreetly made no claims on Tashlin's outside income.

When Frank heard that I was coming in for a job interview, he was very concerned. "Look Jimmie," he said, "Watch this Schlesinger bastard. Whatever he says, just keep thinking, "You're full of shit!' "

With my usual naïveté I discounted Tashlin's advice in favor of Chuck Jones' enthusiasm. Schlesinger turned out to be a dapper little man, who had the powdered, coiffed appearance of a man who had just stepped out of a barber's chair. His office was to match. Every item of furniture was polished and gleaming.

When I explained that I was the only animation director who had produced a military training film, and I intended to pursue this career, Schlesinger assured me that he already had a commitment for some navy films. He was going to Washington in a few months to sign the contracts. As soon as the deal was consummated, I would be directing.

In the interim he suggested that I work in Chuck's unit as an animator. It would give me a chance to get acquainted with the staff. That sounded reasonable, so Chuck was called in and Schlesinger outlined the arrangement.

Chuck was very pleased and ushered me into the animation department to meet his group. When he opened the door we stepped into a slovenly area, broken up by little cubicles of rough beaverboard. Each cell housed an animator and his assistant.

The unpainted pine floor gave off a smell of rancid oil, and the stench mingled with a foul odor of rusted radiators. The place looked and stank like the hold of a slave ship. This was in sharp contract to Schlesinger's impeccable office.

I was given a very friendly greeting by Chuck's animators, Ben Washam, Ken Harris, Phil Monroe, and Bobo Cannon. Craggy-faced Art Heineman was the layout man. I could tell that they were very impressed by meeting a real, live, ex-Disney animator.

Although I had not done any animation for almost four years, I still had the Disney snobbery, that is, these were nice fellows, but after all . . . what could they really know about fine animation? This job was going to be a pushover.

Chuck announced that Bobo Cannon and I were going to split the animation on his next film, *Inki and the Minah Bird.* This did nothing to deflate my high opinion of my prowess. My first impression of Cannon was that he was a timid, ineffectual-looking, chunky little man. "No competition there," I though smugly.

We all went over the storyboard and layouts with Heineman, and I was surprised at the fine quality of his drawing. Inki, a little black kid, was going to be delightfully cute and easy to animate because the design of the character had been very well thought out.

The minah bird was a weird character. He would enter a scene, interrupting a confrontation between Inki and the lion by simply hopping past them to the music of "Fingal's Cave." When they followed him he

Inki and a surprised lion. Drawn by Shamus Culhane. The picture *Inki and the Minah Bird* was directed by Chuck Jones and animated by Bobo Cannon and Shamus Culhane. 1943. *Warner Brothers.*

Drawings of Inki by Shamus Culhane for *Inki and the Minah Bird*, 1943. *Warner Brothers.*

would do a trick, like jumping into a large haystack. The hay would start hopping, getting smaller and smaller until it vanished. They were simple gags but for some reason very funny. Perhaps it was that strange hippity-hop beat which structured the music.

Bobo and I were both given a fairly long sequence to start with. Chuck's instructions were very much in the Disney mode, a detailed analysis of each character's actions, thought processes, and reactions. No Fleischer slapdash. The pace of the picture was carefully built up to the various climaxes. No doubt about it, Jones was a damn good director.

I started my animation in a state of enthusiasm. By Jesus, I was going to show the provincials what Disney animation was all about. Unfortunately, the four-year hiatus had taken its toll. For about a week, I sat there fuming and throwing away drawings, vainly trying to get back my expertise. One day I decided to see what Bobo Cannon was doing.

He was sitting at his desk like a little chubby Buddha, effortlessly turning out some of the most dazzling drawings I have ever seen. As I flipped one scene Bobo watched me anxiously. "You think it's going to be okay?" he asked timidly. I hastily reassured him and scuttled back to my drawing board, my self-aggrandizement replaced by blind panic.

That night I took the model sheets home and drew for hours. I did the same thing the next night and all the following weekend. After drawing hundreds of Inkis, lions, and minah birds I slowly began to draw with more facility and could start to use my high-speed technique. Until then I had managed to refuse to show my drawings to anybody.

Bobo had to be the most modest, self-deprecating person in the business. He generously gave Chuck Jones all the credit for teaching him the fine points of animation. This may be true, but Bobo brought to Warners a prodigious draftsmanship and that innate feeling for action and acting that cannot be taught. Without the benefit of Disney training, he was easily one of the best animators in the business.

Cannon and I had a rollicking time together exchanging ideas on bits of acting for the various situations. I especially enjoyed working on the lion because he was a dumb, raggedy coot who didn't remember that he was supposed to be the king of beasts. Chuck pretty much gave us carte blanche on the details.

The end result was a very funny picture. Some critics think it is one of Chuck Jones' best. Chuck recalls that one feature of the picture was

Storyboard sketch by Bobo Cannon for an Office of War Information film, 1944.

Drawing by Shamus Culhane for *Inki and the Minah Bird*. Directed by Chuck Jones. 1943. *Warner Brothers.*

the fact that I animated the lion's hind legs correctly, a problem that seems to have defied the rest of the studio.

I remember *Inki and the Minah Bird* as a painful lesson in hubris and ego deflation.

Several months went by. Schlesinger had gone to Washington and returned with no visible result. One day I happened to go into the camera room and saw that a very technical drawing of a submarine was being photographed. The cameraman mentioned very casually that this was part of a series of navy pictures.

When I stormed into Schlesinger's office, he waved my furious complaint aside, explaining that I was too valuable an animator to waste on that navy crap. When he denied he had promised that I would direct the military films as soon as they came in, I called him a liar.

Like a cardsharp who had just had his five aces called, Schlesinger blandly ignored the insult and suggested that I continue to work with Chuck Jones until a really interesting military film came along.

There are times when one becomes aware of the main weakness in the English language, that is, colorful invective. We cannot match the Yiddish, "You should be rich, you should have a fine house, in the house a hundred rooms . . . and you should be found dead in every room!" Or the Cantonese: "Thrust your unfragrant stalk up your ghastly gully."

I had to make do with the Anglo-Saxon, "Go fuck yourself!" which really didn't have the scale suitable for the occasion.

Five minutes later, I had packed my gear, shaken hands with my startled fellow workers, and stomped out. I was damn mad because I had enjoyed working with Chuck and the unit. There was a good esprit de corps in Warners and a very healthy feeling of competition among the various directors.

Aside from Jones, Warners had Friz Freleng, Frank Tashlin, Bob Clampett, and Norman McCabe, all talented directors. Since Schlesinger was so completely disinterested, every director followed his own bent, which was why the humor and construction of Warners' pictures varied so widely.

I had been looking forward to the time after the war when I would have a chance to direct my kind of pictures, with a heavy emphasis on pantomime. "Shit!" I thought glumly, "Every time I get a good job, some goddamn thing happens and I lose it." The circumstances surrounding my leaving Van Beuren, Disney, and now Warners seemed to bear this out.

I had heard through the grapevine that Walt Lantz was looking for a director and had started a series of navy films, so I decided to call him up.

12

Walt Lantz Studio

ess than two hours later, I was surveying my new office at Walt Lantz Studio. It was a strange feeling. I had not seen Walt Lantz since 1928, when the J. R. Bray Studio closed down. At that time I had been an inker and errand boy, now, thirteen years later, I had just been hired to direct all of Lantz's cartoons. I vaguely wondered about the kind of psychological problems our former relationship would cause, but, as it turned out, there weren't any.

We had a long talk about the type of pictures he was producing. Walt explained that in addition to stories about Andy Panda and Woody Woodpecker, the studio was making a series of jazz films called Swing Symphonies.

Darrell Calker, the studio musician, knew all the top people in the jazz world, performers like Nat King Cole, Jack Teagarden, and Meade Lux Lewis. Musicians of their stature could be coaxed into making a sound track for a film either because it was a novelty, or they were broke, usually the latter.

I kept nodding in agreement, as if I knew what Walt was talking about, but the truth was that I had never heard of any of these people and had no knowledge of jazz whatsoever. At Fleischer Studio, Willard Bowsky handled all the jazz cartoons, using recordings made by the Mills brothers, Cab Calloway, Louis Armstrong, and other great entertainers. Bowsky did some very good pictures in this genre because he loved jazz.

Rudy Zamora, Al Eugster, and I had worked on the old standards like

"Alexander's Rag-time Band" and "Please Go Away and Let Me Sleep."
As a devotee of classical music I found both kinds of music to be junk.

I had four days to find out what jazz was all about, because on Monday
I was going to start on a Swing Symphony as my first assignment.
Fortunately I had a good friend, Jack Weir, who was a jazz buff. Not
only did he have a great collection of records, but he also had many books
on the history of jazz.

As soon as I left the studio I called Weir, arranged to borrow some
books and records, and accepted an invitation to go to a jam session. By
Sunday night I had read four books and had been subjected to an ear-
shattering three hours of New Orleans–style jazz in a dingy dance hall
near Watts. (We sat in the first row.)

Monday I met the Lantz crew. Bugs Hardaway and Milt Schaffer were
the writers. I had worked with Bugs at the Iwerks Studio, and Milt had
been in the story department at Disney's. Paul Smith, Emery Hawkins,
Pat Matthews, and La Verne Harding were the animators. I had never
met any of them before.

Darrell Calker, our music composer, had a very interesting background. He had studied classical music before he went on to compose jazz.
Calker had written a symphony which included a section in which the
musicians were expected to extemporize as if they were in a jam session.

Darrell was very pleased to find that I was a former musician. When
I confessed to my meager knowledge of jazz, he proceeded to give me
an education. Every few days Darrell would bring in some classic jazz
records. While I listened to the music he would point out the various
features of each selection.

The usual format for a Swing Symphony was a music track divided
into two recording sessions. The first was the hard core of the track,
several minutes of jazz by a featured performer. This part of the track
was always recorded before we started the animation, because the action
often followed the music note by note.

When the animation was completed, Darrell wrote and conducted the
incidental music in a second recording session. The orchestra for this part
was often made up of musicians who played classical music in the Hollywood Bowl, so Calker was using the best talent from both the jazz and
classical music worlds.

During the recording sessions, Walt Lantz and I sat in the control booth reading the basic score from Darrell's notes on my lead sheets. We needed to make sure that the music was properly interpreting and accenting important actions. When we thought it didn't, Darrell was so expert that he could devise a new orchestration in a few minutes.

Schaffer never came to the recordings, but Hardaway often did. He couldn't read music, but Bugs had firm convictions about what he liked or didn't. One night we were doing a session with Bob Zurke. He was vigorously thumping out a bit of boogie-woogie on the studio's battered upright piano.

Hardaway grew more and more restless as the boogie theme unfolded, and finally ended in a brilliant cascade of notes. Bugs got up muttering, "There's too damn many places where the music stops." With that he stalked out to the stage to have a lengthy talk with Calker and Zurke. There was a long argument, which neither Lantz nor I could hear.

Finally, Bugs stomped back to the booth shaking his head. "You know what?" he fumed. "That sum-bitch can't even read no music, an' he says that he already forgot what he just now played. What the hell did Calker git in a dumb guy like that for?"

We both assured Bugs that everything was going to be fine. He subsided into disapproving silence for the rest of the session. It was very fine music indeed, made for *Jungle Jive,* a picture that featured a cocky crab rambling up and down the keys of a castaway piano.

La Verne Harding did the animation for that sequence and it was some of her best work. At that time she was the only woman animator in the field, a distinction that she ignored. La Verne was quiet, reliable, and businesslike. She worked as an animator for twenty-four years. Recently (1980), she was given the Winsor McCay Award for Lifetime Achievement, which she well deserved.

The relationship between Milt Schaffer and Bugs Hardaway was useful as well as comic. Schaffer was a quiet man who had long before given up any attempt to argue with such a curmudgeon as Bugs. However, since Milt drew the storyboards, in his own unobtrusive way he managed to keep some semblance of a story line in the pictures.

Bugs was essentially a gagman, and like Dave Fleischer, had a disdain for the niceties of character analysis. To him a gag was a gag, and if it didn't fit all that neatly into a story . . . what the hell. He loved bad puns. When Hardaway started a picture he usually opened with thirty or forty feet of bad puns lettered somewhere on the backgrounds.

During a production meeting, as he read the puns off the storyboard during a presentation, Bugs would laugh until the tears rolled down his cheeks. Schaffer would look moodily at the ceiling, and I would start to figure out which of the more atrocious puns I would excise.

We usually had to leave some of them in the film. Since puns involved little or no character animation, it was cheap footage, and it was needed because we worked on a very small budget. The liability was that starting with puns, lettered on road signs or shop windows, prevented me from getting off to a good start with some attention-grabbing action.

When we ran a pencil test, and Bugs saw that I had cut down the number of puns to a minimum, he would look at me reproachfully. "Jeezchrist, you cut them gags half in two!" he would growl.

Another source of irritation was the fact that I added many of my own gags as I worked on the lead sheets. Often this meant that I could junk some dead spots in the original storyboard. I abandoned the practice of making story sketches for this new material because Bugs would wander into my room and see them. This would lead to an argument because Bugs never liked my brand of humor.

Since adding material to a script is the perogative of a director, Bugs' heated complaints fell on deaf ears. Walt Lantz had a policy of leaving the director entirely on his own, so Bugs could not complain to him.

As one picture after the other was previewed and my gags were well received, Bugs stopped his resistance to my additions, albeit damn reluctantly.

Art Heineman left Chuck Jones' unit at Warners and joined us shortly after I was hired. He was just as interested in experimentation as I was. His work as a designer and layout man radically changed the appearance of the Lantz cartoons.

For example, in *Boogie Woogie Man* we related the colors of the backgrounds to the structure of the music. The picture was basically painted in cold colors, until there was a riff in the music. When that happened I cut, in sync, to a scene painted with vivid orange, red, or yellow. After the riff I cut back to a series of scenes with cold colors, then repeating this process on the following riff.

Some years after *Boogie Woogie Man* was released, I came upon an article in S. I. Hayakawa's magazine, *ETC.*, a periodical devoted to semantics. The writer analyzed in scholarly terms our use of color to interpret music in the film. Our experiment did not go unnoticed.

Another innovation for the Lantz Studio was Heineman's idea of using colored paper instead of paint to create backgrounds. A good example of this technique is in *The Greatest Man in Siam*, a Swing Symphony. The result was a very unusual-looking picture whose brilliantly colored flat format rivaled some of the high-style pictures that Bernyce Polifka and Gene Fleury were designing in Chuck Jones' unit at Warners.

The best animation in the picture was a sensual dance by the Sultan's sexy daughter. Pat Matthews, at that time a comparative novice, animated the sequence without benefit of rotoscope of live-action, or any other form of research. It was a tour de force, which showed that Pat had joined the small group of professional animators who could draw convincing human movement.

The most popular character in the Lantz stable was Woody Woodpecker. According to Walter, his favorite character was created when a rambunctious woodpecker persisted in pecking away at the roof of the Lantz house.

Both Walter and his wife Gracie tried various ways to get rid of this pest, but he stubbornly refused to leave the roof alone. The bird's antics were so funny that Gracie suggested that he would make an amusing cartoon character.

So Walter sketched a rough drawing of Woody, Alex Lovy drew a model sheet, and Bugs and Milt Schaffer used him as a foil for Andy Panda and his father in a zany film called *Knock Knock*. The film, released in 1940, was such an instant success that Walter recognized that he had a potential star in the frenetic bird. From 1941 on, Woody Woodpecker was featured in his own series. The studio starred Woody until Lantz ceased operations in 1972, a long career for an animated cartoon character.

The most distinctive aspect of Woody was his raucous voice. Walter Lantz supplied the idea for his oddball delivery, which was mechanically contrived. The actor would speak his lines very slowly during the original recording of the sound track. At a second recording session the track was speeded up. This accounts for the mechanized quality of Woody's voice, and a certain lack of nuances.

Mel Blanc, known as The Man of a Thousand Voices, was Woody's voice in some early pictures. Hardaway and several others have been used at different periods; but oddly enough, the most successful voice was Walter's wife, Gracie. She was the voice of Woody Woodpecker for many years.

*   *   *

In my early days in Hollywood, in the 1930s, the town was really a cultural desert as far as the graphic arts were concerned. There were a few art galleries in Beverly Hills and in Hollywood, but they confined themselves to offering tidbits from the turn of the century: small paintings of little old ladies crocheting, while girls in flowing skirts gravely played with hoops; and large paintings of fish on ornamented platters, surrounded by bunches of grapes, glasses, and silverware. All were meticulously painted down to the last highlight, but who the hell cared?

I used to flip the pages of *The New Yorker* magazine, looking wistfully at the list of dozens of exhibitions in the galleries and museums, and marvel at the riches so casually offered.

Suddenly the arid climate of Hollywood changed, due to the enthusiastic efforts of one ex-New Yorker, Clara Grossman. In 1942 she opened the American Artists Gallery right in the middle of Hollywood. Clara was a statuesque brunette with a flat New York accent, a typical Greenwich Village Bohemian. She had an almost inexhaustible knowledge of modern art, but more important, Clara brought to the film capital the first opportunity to see great foreign motion pictures and old American classics.

Every Friday night she had a film show, a picture that she rented from New York's Museum of Modern Art Film Library. For the first time I saw documentary films by John Grierson, Robert Flaherty, and Joris Ivens; Russian pictures by Sergei Eisenstein and V. I. Pudovkin; the work of D. W. Griffith, Fritz Lang, and Jean Renoir.

In addition to the films, Clara had an uncanny knack for finding people who had actually worked on the pictures, so after the show we would often be treated to question and answer periods. One time we had a Russian émigré who had been Eisenstein's wardrobe mistress. Another evening Jean Renoir told us about his struggles in Hollywood. He commented wryly that he had no trouble in the local film business until he learned how to speak English. Moholy-Nagy gave us a lecture about Cocteau and Marcel Duchamp's "theory of accident" as the basis for his compositions.

Most of the audience was composed of young people who were working in minor jobs in the film business. Years later I found out that Faith Hubley, who at that time was a music editor, was one of the enthusiastic youngsters who never missed one of Clara Grossman's film shows.

As a result of this stimulating environment, I reread Pudovkin's book *Film Technique* and bought Eisenstein's *Film Sense*. I began to look for a suitable picture to try out some of their ideas, especially fast cutting. While I was at Fleischer Studio I had thought to try some experiments, but somehow the material did not seem suitable.

Looking over the screwball antics of Woody Woodpecker on the storyboard for *The Barber of Seville,* I knew right away that this was my opportunity to use the theories that had so excited Frank Tashlin and me back in 1937. Frank had gone on to do a whole series of pictures using fast cutting.

One of the joys of being a director is that fact that he is the only artist who has a captive audience. A person can wander through an art gallery, always at his own speed or the lack of it, never controlled in any way by the artist's concept or his subject matter. To quote Jean Charlot in *Art from the Mayans to Disney* (Books for Libraries Press), "The main difference between immobile painting and cinematic drawing lies in the fact that the element of time, which is artificial in the former, becomes one of the essentials in the latter. In this sense animated drawing partakes of the qualities of music, poetry, and the dance."

A cautious director will naturally cut at a slow pace. That way there is no possibility that the audience will fail to understand the action. Many of Fleischer Studio and Terrytoon's cartoons are examples of conservative cutting.

The danger in fast cutting, where the director is weighing the screen time for each shot within a twenty-fourth of a second, is the risk of miscalculating the ability of the audience to assimilate the material, thus evoking irritation and the possible rejection of the picture. But what a fascinating gamble!

The Barber of Seville got off to a lumbering start with the usual collection of Hardaway's bad puns written on signs in the barbershop window. When Woody finds that the proprietor is away he decides to become an amateur barber.

His first customer is an Indian, complete with an eagle-feather warbonnet. Woody wraps a hot towel around his head and when it comes off the warbonnet has shrunk to a shuttlecock. Things really heat up when the next customer arrives.

He is a burly hard hat. Woody, at this point, starts to sing the "Largo el Factorum" while wielding a shaving brush. He lathers the hapless customer right down to his shoes, then, flourishing a wickedly gleaming razor, Woody starts shaving in a sprightly but not unusually fast speed.

The tempo more than doubled in the reprise, and following the phrasing note for note, I had Woody repeat all his former antics at a frenzied pace. Some of the shots were six exposures long, or a quarter of a second. In one scene the tempo was so fast that I split Woody into multiple images, all yelling, "Figaro!"

When we showed the pencil test to the crew, I had to admit that some of the action was hard to follow as a line drawing. Hardaway was disgusted because this whole fast cutting sequence was not in the original script. "Looks like a fucking Chinese goulash," he grumbled, but Walt agreed with me that when the animation was painted the action would be understandable. From the audience reaction at the preview, there was no doubt that we were right. *The Barber of Seville* is one of my most satisfying achievements as a director.

In *The Beach Nut,* which featured Woody Woodpecker and Wally (a walrus with a Swedish accent), I had a chance to conduct another interesting experiment. Woody at one point is being chased by Wally. The walrus ends up at the edge of a pier. Woody, who is underneath, pulls out one of the piles. The whole structure slowly collapses bit by bit, and the entire pier tumbles into the water like a pile of jackstraws. The sound effect was several feet long.

For once, Milt Schaffer had not fully defined the action on the storyboard. He had a few drawings, the beginning of Woody's tugging at the piling, a shot of the startled walrus, and a long shot of the wrecked pier.

I listened to the sound track for a long time, playing it over and over until I could differentiate between the various sounds that made the breakup. It was something like following a melodic line in music for a string quartet. Without trying to think about the actions I was going to depict, I replayed the track and swiftly drew a series of scribbles.

When I examined them I saw that they were all geometrical—circles, parallel lines, pyramids, etcetera—about a dozen seemingly meaningless doodles. Scrupulously adhering to the sequence in which they were drawn, I began to analyze them in relation to the components I had to work with, namely, Wally, Woody, and the various parts of the pier.

One scribble became Wally's startled face in a close-up. Another doodle developed into beams falling, a triangle turned out to be Woody's beak. In a very short time I had an interesting montage that was such an accurate interpretation of the sound track that I didn't have to revise a drawing. I got the idea of this technique from Eisenstein's writings. What I had done was to tap my unconscious just as I had done in my animation.

Like many zealots I have often met with a profound rejection when I have tried to discuss this aspect of filmmaking with my associates. They seem to equate it with crystal gazing or tarot cards.

I remember in 1968 Dick Williams asked me to give a lecture to his staff on my approach to animation. I talked for about an hour, and much of that time was devoted to my method of tapping the unconscious. During the question and answer period that followed, nobody addressed a question to my theory of creativity. The subject was delicately ignored, yet it was the only really provocative part of my lecture.

In my research on the subject I began to find plenty of material to back up my amateurish gropings. In one study of the human brain, the author commented wryly, "Contrary to our Calvinistic reverence for hard work, the brain functions best in a state which is called pejoratively 'a daydream.' "

Rollo May, in his book *The Courage to Create,* wrote of his personal experience of the creative process. "The moment the insight broke through, there was a special translucence that enveloped the world, and my vision was given a special clarity. I am convinced that this is the usual accompaniment of unconscious experience into consciousness.

"I define this unconscious as the potentialities for awareness or action which the individual cannot or will not actualize. The potentialities are the source of what can be called 'free creativity.' "

Rollo May goes on to supply what seems to be a valid reason why so many creative people have rejected this approach.

"Here again is part of the reason that the experience scares us so much: the world, inwardly and outwardly, takes on an intensity that may be momentarily overwhelming. This is one aspect of what is called ecstacy —the uniting of the unconscious experience with the conscious, a union which is not in abstracto, but a dynamic immediate fusion."

One of the amusing things I have discovered about my method of calling up free creativity is that my unconscious has very strict and independent standards of its own. For example, I was least interested in

Drawing by Emery Hawkins for *Fish Fry*.
Walter Lantz Productions, 1944.

A Wally Walrus rough by Emery Hawkins. Walter Lantz Productions.

directing the Andy Panda series. To me they were too goddamn sweet and cuddly.

Although I tried very hard to give these pictures my best efforts, for the most part I was unable to do more than reproduce what was on the storyboard. My muse remained aloof. The sole exception was *Fish Fry*, which was nominated for an Academy Award in 1944.

The original story seemed not to have been very inspired, and I made a lot of changes and additions. As usual I was doing this work over a weekend when the studio was quiet, because normally I had scarcely fifteen minutes to myself during a business day.

There was one sequence in which a scruffy tomcat tried to steal Andy Panda's newly acquired goldfish. The fish was a standard cutey-cute character whom I found especially irritating. In one scene on the storyboard, the fish bit the cat and he reacted slightly. In a fit of impatience at the lackluster story, I added a sequence in which the fish looked very contrite. She patted the cat's injured finger and lisped, "Poor pussycat!"

The cat was mollified and watched with satisfaction as the fish produced a large first-aid kit. Suddenly she opened the case, took out an enormous set of false teeth, crammed them into her mouth, and bit the bejeezes out of the injured finger.

The cat had an incredible reaction. I cut to an aerial shot hundreds of feet in the air. The cat soared up like a rocket, accompanied by a cacophony of police sirens and whistles.

The gag was a smash because Milt and Bugs had created such a sickly-sweet goldfish that this sadistic side of her nature came as a satisfying shock to the audience. I had the same feeling because, until I wrote the action down, I had no idea that the fish was going to bite the cat again.

Unlike Disney Studio, where there was no footage quota, Walt Lantz expected each animator to do twenty-five feet a week. Emery Hawkins had great difficulty in meeting that figure. He had his own standards of quality and would often throw out a whole day's work, just after I had assured him that it was a beautiful piece of animation.

Emery was never satisfied with any of his work and suffered more agonies of anxiety and frustration than any other animator I have ever met.

The most important thing he did at the Lantz Studio was to redesign Woody Woodpecker. Hawkins made him more compact with a neater and more satisfying combination of his various parts, just the way Fred Moore had redesigned Mickey Mouse. Art Heineman then made a new color scheme for Woody, not quite so garish, and the final result was a much more modern-looking character.

Emery Hawkins' dedication to his education was fantastic. One day I gave him a copy of a marvelous book on drawing, *The Natural Way to Draw* (Houghton Mifflin & Co.) by Kimon Nicolaides. This is the only textbook about drawing that I have ever found to be of real value, except for Don Graham's *Composing Pictures* (Litton Publishing, Inc.), which was written many years later.

Emery and I left Lantz Studio in 1946, and I didn't see him again until we met at a party at Gil Miret's house in 1975. Ignoring my effusive greetings, he glared at me. "You stuck me with that goddamn Nicolaides book," he snarled. "You know what? I spent twelve years working with that son-of-a-bitching book! And it's all your fault!"

To a large extent Emery Hawkins is one of the unsung heroes of the profession, because for long years of his career he has been bogged down animating television spots. It's like hitching a racehorse to a hay wagon.

In 1944 my old friend and mentor Grim Natwick joined Lantz's staff and contributed some beautiful animation to one of our best Woody Woodpecker pictures, *Ski for Two*. One important sequence featured Woody skiing to an old standard, "The Sleigh."

Shortly before the picture was about to be released, Walt Lantz found out to his horror that the music was not in the public domain. Darrell Calker or the copyright research staff in Universal had goofed.

To write another composition would have been difficult because the animation followed the music note for note. In addition, a new recording and remix would have cost a small fortune, yet the music could not be used without a release from the publisher who owned the rights.

It would seem that Walt was over the proverbial barrel. He solved the problem neatly by sending a telegram offering fifty dollars for the use of the music. Back came an indignant letter from the publisher. He wouldn't take a cent less than a hundred dollars. A sigh of relief rustled the eucalyptus trees in front of the Lantz Studio.

Compared to Disney's budgets of $35,000 to $75,000, we made Lantz's films for $15,000 to $25,000, usually the former. Unlike the nerve-racking pursuit of quality at Disney's, Walt Lantz made no such demands

A revised version of Woody Woodpecker by Emery Hawkins. Walter Lantz Productions, 1944.

A scene from *Ski for Two*. Written by Bugs Hardaway and Milt Schaffer, directed by Shamus Culhane, designed by Art Heineman, animated by Grim Natwick. Walter Lantz Productions.

Model sheet for Woody Woodpecker by Emery Hawkins, 1944. Walter Lantz Productions.

on his staff. He wanted good pictures of course, but he knew the business well enough to realize that there was no possibility of competing with Disney. Lantz made no stringent demands on his staff.

The atmosphere was relaxed, and as a group we had genuine fun at our work. The small budget did not entice Lantz to create an oppressive atmosphere like Harrison and Gould's Krazy Kat Studio.

Even my arguments with Bugs Hardaway were conducted on a very friendly basis. After a ferocious quarrel over a story point we would end up eating lunch in our favorite spaghetti joint, having another argument. This time it was about the course of the war.

One of the standard questions I am often asked during an interview is, "Do you make films that you think will please the audience, or do you choose stories that give you personal satisfaction?"

In a way the question is semantic nonsense. How could anyone possibly envisage a typical audience? A group of moviegoers in Kansas City is going to be different from one in New York City, and they both will be different from one in Bangor, Maine.

Excluding hacks, directors, like any other creative people, need to find emotional satisfaction in their work. That kind of hunger is not served by turning out potboilers aimed at the "general audience," whatever that means.

Can anyone imagine crusty old Cézanne toiling up the slopes of his favorite mountain for perhaps the fiftieth time because he was hoping that this time he would create a painting that would be accepted by the Salon?

As a director, I do take the audience into account in one area, editing. When I am doing fast cutting, I know that audiences are not trained to see the difference between one-twelfth of a second and a twenty-fourth, but I make them try for it. I also anticipate the possibility that I will step on a gag if I cut away too soon. That's a sure way to lose a laugh.

Except for those two aspects of directing, the whole process is geared to my pleasure, instincts, and experience. Since I am an animator as well as a director, my rule of thumb in evaluating story material is whether or not I would like to animate that particular sequence. If I find it doesn't excite me, it is subjected to severe examination and usually revised or discarded.

When the war started Don Graham had left Disney's and taken a job in an airplane factory as a designer. He had been educated as an engineer. Soon he was working very long hours at the plant.

Marc Davis and I talked about the fact that we missed his support and encouragement. We discussed this with several other former Graham pupils. They all felt the same way, so we approached Don with the idea that we could muster a class at the Chouinard's Art School, if he was willing to teach us one night a week. In a way it was very insensitive of us because Graham was being severely overworked.

To our intense satisfaction, Don agreed. However, we found that it was impossible for us to get an extra ration of gas for the thirty-mile round trip to Chouinard's. I was turned down by the Ration Board, even though my neighbor was given gasoline for his lawn mower. By using car pools and public transportation a few of us managed to attend classes. Marc and I, Bill Hurtz and Les Clark worked with Don Graham for over a year. Sometimes he would show up in a complete state of exhaustion, but he never missed a session, and neither did we.

Finally, what with Bill Hurtz going into the army, and the increasing pressure of work on us all, the class was abandoned. Yet it is indicative of the value we placed on Graham's teaching and his dedication that we had all made prodigious efforts to keep our relationship as long as it was physically possible.

The beginning of World War II found all branches of the armed forces totally unprepared to cope with even a small visual education program. The army and the marines had no visual aid units, and the Army Signal Corps in twenty-five years had produced only a handful of training films, which for the most part were long since outmoded.

Furthermore, the upper-level brass, in all branches, firmly rejected the idea that visual aids in the form of slides and films could play an important role in the conversion of civilians into fighting men.

Nevertheless, when the war did come, by some miracle, a faction in war planning managed to bypass these fossilized bumbleheads. A vast program was launched to train civilians by the use of slides, films, and three-dimensional mock-ups of enemy installations.

The science of warfare had come a long way since the comparatively simple destructive devices used in World War I. The uses and maintenance of new and intricate weapons and equipment presented an awesome problem. The nation was faced with the need to convert hundreds of thousands of civilians into military specialists. Not only was it imperative to teach but the lessons would have to be learned quickly.

It was the biggest problem of mass education ever attempted, and from a standing start. Most of this heavy responsibility fell on the movie industry. The army set up two film production units, one in Long Island City, the other in the Hal Roach Studios in Culver City, a few miles from Hollywood.

Men from every branch of the movie industry, from grips and electricians to prestigious writers and directors, were rushed into uniform. In an amazingly short time the units on both coasts were turning out more footage in a month than Hollywood had produced in a year. In addition, other pictures were farmed out to studios like Disney, Lantz, and Warner Brothers.

Many of my friends in the animation business were shunted through boot camp and found themselves at the Roach Studio. Bill Hurtz recalls that his company commander was "that great military mind of the twentieth century (complete with swagger stick), Captain Ronnie Reagan."

A constant battle soon developed between the regular army personnel assigned to the post and the Hollywood filmmakers. The regular army's idea of using the motion picture medium was usually a cross between the army field manual and *The Perils of Pauline*. While the Hollywood people resisted such obvious corn, nobody really knew the mentality and the emotional attitudes of the average G.I. Joe.

For many years, especially during the Depression, Hollywood had churned out pictures that studiously avoided any resemblance to real life. The hero always won the girl; the villain was always foiled; and any script with an unhappy ending was rejected as bad box office.

The only studio that attempted to make films with social significance was Warner Brothers, but even they turned out their fair share of potboilers. Most of the film people were not psychologically equipped to make films for the tough-minded, cynical realists who comprised our civilian army.

They soon found out that any picture that tried to "sell" the army audience with a suave, unctuous approach was quickly rejected. Any hint of talking down to the troops with high-flown hyperbole was promptly greeted with catcalls and Bronx cheers. In some instances, especially in the war zones, rocks were thrown at the screen.

As news of these incidents reached the film units, the former makers of escapist movies realized that if the training films were going to do the job there were going to be some radical changes in their basic concepts.

This realization resulted in a much more honest, direct approach to the whole information and education process. For the most part the use of the stilted English in the field manual was abandoned. Instead the writers used simpler terms and often larded the facts with soldiers' slang and scatological humor.

Now, when private Joe Doaks (still sweating from a thirty-mile hike) lowered his aching butt to a seat in the camp theater, he didn't know that his mental and physical condition had been anticipated and evaluated by the makers of the film he was about to see. The style of the presentation was carefully calculated to overcome indifference and fatigue.

He and the rest of the tired audience were going to receive an essential bit of information about soldiering, not by standing in the hot sun listening to a raspy-voiced sergeant, or learning the hard way in a hastily dug foxhole, but by sitting in the quiet of the theater. He was going to absorb some important facts that might save his life and they would be free of gung ho slogans and hypocritical appeals to this or that ideal. He would see a film narrated in soldier's English and salted with soldier's rough humor.

Very often the film was an animated cartoon. To the astonishment of the live-action writers and directors there were many subjects that proved to be more effective in cartoon form than they would have been in live-action.

For example, John Hubley directed a cartoon for the navy called *Flat-Hatting*, which was a huge success. Flat-hatting was air force slang for the custom of putting a plane into a screaming dive at some innocuous target, animal, architectural, or civilian, sometimes with fatal results.

Flat-hatting was motivated by sheer high spirits, and official reprimands seemed to have little effect on the custom. Hubley's picture showed, in a series of very funny gags, just how stupid and useless this form of braggadocio really was. Instead of being a colorful hero, the flat-hatter was dangerous. It totally demolished the image of flat-hatting as an admirable feat of derring-do.

In any group of men there is always some loudmouth who scoffs at authority, has his own unorthodox way of doing things, and often has enough charisma to attract a following. Frank Tashlin, directing at Warner Brothers, made the first cartoon that caricatured this kind of personality, *Private Snafu,* the guy who fouled up everything.

The script was written by Ted Geisel, a cartoonist already famous in civilian life under the nom de plume of "Dr. Seuss," and Phil Eastman, who later wrote most of the Magoo pictures at UPA. Psychologically, the script must have been an accurate portrait of a type of troublemaker, because Snafu became so popular that the two writers went on to do a whole series of scripts featuring Snafu as a klutz in various aspects of training. Snafu is soldier's shorthand for Situation Normal, All Fucked Up.

Still another problem was solved by a combination of animation and sex. Life jackets were one piece of equipment that evoked considerable resistance from the troops. They were bulky and uncomfortable. The job of convincing the men that life jackets were a necessary evil was given to an animation unit.

During the war, Mae West was one of the most popular pinups. Photographs displaying her formidable potrine were to be found in every barracks. When the writers decided that there was a similarity between Mae West's figure and a soldier wearing a life jacket, Bill Hurtz was given the assignment of meeting Mae and drawing her caricatures.

Bill recalls going to her lush apartment and while waiting for La Belle West to make her appearance, he was enchanted by a life-sized statue of Mae in the nude, which dominated the decor. On close examination, Hurtz decided that even without a life jacket her remarkable topography would make it impossible for her to drown.

Mae was very cooperative (Hurtz never discussed the full extent of her cooperation), sat patiently for her caricature, and later did some dialogue for the picture. As she put it in her inimitable drawl, "I'm happy to think that the life jacket is gonna be called the Mae West. It kinda gives the woman's touch while the boys are flyin' around nights."

As motion picture producers, the animation unit was a great success, but from a military standpoint this conglomeration of talent was a disaster. After staggering through boot camp, the lads paid scant attention to the niceties of military conduct per se.

They irreverently called the installation "Fort Roach," and the inmates "The Foreskin Fusileers." There were no barracks so everybody went home after work, appearing in the morning just in time for roll call, in a state of disarray that would have given General Patton the vapors.

The infrequent attempts to give "Fort Roach" a military appearance usually were a miserable failure. The drilling looked like something from a Mack Sennett comedy. Instead of a snappy salute, a casual wave was usually forthcoming when a private from the animation unit encountered an officer.

Rudy Ising, ex-producer at Harmon-Ising Studio, was sent to Officers' Training School. He emerged as Major Rudolph Ising, U.S.A. Trim, impeccably uniformed, with a military bearing that resembled the "brace" of a West Point plebe, Major Ising cut an impressive figure.

When he strode into the animation unit, for once the group was so overawed that the boys acted with a semblance of military decorum. They gathered respectfully around the major listening to the litany of harrowing experiences at OTS.

But the military atmosphere didn't last long. Another animator entered the room and interrupted the spit-and-polish major by slapping him on the back. "Hiya there, Rudy!" he said brightly, "I see they took some of that lard off your ass." The soldierly aura was fragmented right then, and Major Rudolph Ising, U.S.A., went back to being just plain Rudy for the rest of the war.

There was consternation when a latrine rumor was confirmed. There was going to be a real U.S. Army old-line, hard-nosed colonel in charge of Fort Roach. The whole garrison was assembled to hear Colonel R. M. Jones' introductory speech. When he appeared, the boyos steeled themselves for the worst because he looked every bit the hide-bound professional army officer.

Then Jones made the following speech: "Gentlemen, I want you to know that I understand your problem very well. I have a 16mm camera of my own and often take pictures of my family. I send the film to Eastman-Kodak for developing, and it always comes back with a note that the whole roll has been underexposed. That, gentlemen, is all I know about the movie business."

Despite his confessed ignorance of filmmaking, Colonel Jones was responsible for the idea of exchanging films with all the other motion picture units throughout the country. Screenings were held for the staff, and the teaching techniques for each subject were evaluated and discussed.

In a misplaced fit of enthusiasm for the new regime, two animation writers (lieutenants) requested a personal white-glove inspection by the colonel. When he agreed, there was a frenzy of dusting and mopping. The whole unit scrubbed ashtrays, pencil sharpeners were emptied, erasers lined up in serried ranks, and all visible surfaces polished until they shone.

Exhausted but happy, the group waited for the inspection with smug satisfaction.

The colonel and his aides entered the room with an air of gravity suitable for the occasion. Jones flourished a pristine white glove. Instead of applying it to the nearest available surface, he reached under a drawing board and swiped at the underside. His glove came out with a dark smudge of dust. The back of a storyboard added still another black streak.

There was a horrified silence while the crew waited for a blast of rage from the colonel. He studied the glove for a moment, then turned to his aides. "Does anyone here have a black glove?"

With that he turned and walked out. While he was still in earshot, one of the animators (a private) turned to the two crestfallen lieutenants and snarled, "You and your fucking big mouths!"

Jones went on to the next room and opened the door on an astonishing tableau. Private Paul Fitzpatrick was lying on the floor, hands comfortably tucked behind his head. From this vantage point he was delivering an irreverant evaluation of a story point to two lieutenant–writers who were standing abjectly in front of a storyboard. Jones quietly closed the door.

One of the problems that developed on the West Coast during the war was an acute shortage of assistants and inbetweeners. Up to that time these two categories of production were completely filled by men. The Screen Cartoonists Guild asked me to train a group of inkers, all women. Within a few months I managed to teach most of them how to draw inbetweens; and one of them, Joyce Weir, became Bobo Cannon's assistant at Warner Brothers. Later when Cannon moved to UPA, Joyce followed him and eventually became an animator. She was the third female animator in the business.

During the same period I became a member of the executive board. At the first meeting I attended, I broached an idea that I had been mulling over for some time. The ancient guilds had existed for centuries as virile supervising bodies. They had strict rules about the quality of the work, and the passage from apprentice to master could only be made at the sufferance of the ruling members of a guild. Since we were a guild why should we not adopt some of the regulations of the guilds which had protected the level of craftsmanship?

I suggested that our members should be promoted from one category

Story sketch designed by Gene Fleury for *Lend Lease*. Office of Information and Education, 1944. Walter Lantz Productions.

Hair follicles and skin highly magnified. A layout for *Enemy Bacteria* by Art Heineman. Walter Lantz Productions, 1943.

to the next not at the whim of the employer but by a test given by the guild. After all we were more concerned with keeping the quality of the pictures on a high level than the employers.

The group listened to me in stony silence. I had scarcely finished when somebody at the far end of the table said, "You sound like a fucking fascist." The remark must have seemed appropriate because nobody argued the point; we just went on to the next part of the agenda.

Looking back at the decline of craftsmanship more than thirty years later, I believe I was right. Now the business world has the animation profession by the throat, driving the quality down with no scruples, to the point where some of these same people who sat with me at the table, highly creative people, are now working on a level that is not far removed from factory hands.

My first training film for the Lantz Studio was a navy medical film, *Enemy Bacteria*. It was twenty-four minutes long, and combined live-action and animation. Art Heineman had an unusual problem with the design and layout in that he was having to depict leukocytes, bacilli, bones, and highly magnified areas of muscle tissue.

There was a great deal of research involved because the animation section of the picture had to look authentic. In one sequence we had to animate a human heart beating. Nobody in the studio knew what it looked like or how it would move, so we sent a request to Washington for a medical film that would give us a clear picture of this specific action, a heart pumping, preferably in color.

When the film arrived, Heineman and I, along with several animators and assistants, attended a screening. We had no idea of the subject matter, other than the fact that somewhere in the film was a good shot of a human heart.

The first scene showed a patient being prepared for surgery, then the picture cut to a close-up of the patient's chest. A knife sliced it open and was followed by a pair of shears, which neatly snicked the ribs away from the sternum, exposing a wildly beating heart.

The surgeon reached into the chest cavity, extracted the heart and started to probe it with a small knife while it was beating in his hands. Finally a piece of shrapnel was removed and the heart sewn up. All these shots were in glorious and gory color. When the lights went on, Art

Heineman and I were the only survivors. Everyone else had fled. The animators had to work from my verbal description of the action.

Enemy Bacteria was a picture about the tragic results of inadequate scrubbing up before taking part in an operation. The facts were presented in such a dramatic way that the film was still being used in medical schools all over the country many years after the war had ended.

In 1944 we began to produce pictures for the Office of War Information. The OWI was, in effect, the public relations agency for the government. Its job was to explain to the armed forces and the civilian public various aspects of the war, namely political, strategic, and economic.

By this time there was such an efficient system of film distribution that one picture, *Two Down, One to Go,* about the defeat of Italy and Germany, within five days after its first screening had been shown to 85 percent of the eight million men and women in the army, and within three weeks had been screened for twenty-five million civilians. The films I directed were distributed on this scale.

The first OWI picture we made was *Lend Lease,* whose title is self-explanatory. All OWI films were written and the storyboards drawn at Fort Roach. When I went to pick up the script and storyboard on *Lend Lease* I found Gene Fleury, who had designed the storyboard, and the writers all in a fury.

Following the usual procedure they had sent a copy of the script and storyboard to Washington for approval. *Lend Lease* was a touchy subject because, after all, we had an uneasy alliance with two potential enemies, Russia and China. The script had been a very frank examination and appraisal of our Lend Lease program. It mentioned the fact that Russia was receiving enormous quantities of military equipment of every discription. China was getting a meager stream of supplies, mostly small arms.

When the script came back from Washington, to everybody's rage, many of the salient facts had been deleted, and the whole text so bowdlerized that it was little more than a framework for artful dodging and downright propaganda.

For example, the statement that China was not getting much vital equipment now read, "All that we could do, we did for China." Other statements were equally castrated. Compared to the honesty of the original script, this version was a basket case.

In keeping with the new mode, there was no animation in *Lend Lease*. It was a series of beautifully designed still shots, which were embellished by zooms and pans. When it was finished *Lend Lease* was a very handsome film, but for anyone who had worked on it, the term "information and education" was ironic.

By the end of 1944 I was getting very tired. We had turned out eleven cartoons and about ten minutes of animation for *Enemy Bacteria* since I had started at the Lantz Studio. I was glad when Walt told me that he had hired Dick Lundy to direct half the pictures.

Dick had started working at Disney's as a cel painter in 1929. Two months later he was doing simple inbetweens, and then went to work for Burt Gillett as the first assistant animator in the business. In 1930 Lundy did his first animation, in a scene were Mickey played the piano. A few months later he found his métier when he animated a dancing dachshund in *The Shindig*. From then on Lundy choreographed all of his own dances and became the studio dance specialist.

He used real dance steps, whether it was a waltz, Charleston, or a dazzling imitation of Fred Astaire. When a story called for a dance, there was usually a terse note on the storyboard, "Dance a la Lundy," and Dick would take it from there.

Donald Duck's first appearance on the screen was as a bit player in *The Wise Little Hen* (1934). Lundy did the animation. The acting was so good that Walt realized he had a new star on his hands.

The Orphan's Benefit had three hundred feet of Donald Duck. With that much footage to play with, Lundy started to develop some of the duck's mannerisms that have become world-famous. One of them, Donald hopping on one leg as he spars angrily, is worthy of Charlie Chaplin.

Dick Lundy is a very tense person with a quick fuse, so in a way, it was a perfect bit of typecasting. However, unlike Donald Duck, Dick Lundy's bursts of irritation never lasted for very long. For the most part he was very good-natured.

We worked together very well at the Lantz Studio. As in the halcyon days at Disney's, we gave each other suggestions and gags for stories without reservation. I was pleased to find that Dick preferred to work on Andy Panda films because I had much more empathy for Woody Woodpecker.

Lundy also brought to the studio an impressive background of more than two years of directing complex technical films for the navy while he was at Disney's. He knew a lot more about the intricate techniques of filmmaking than I did. He told me about one film in which the negative had been exposed thirty-two times! Another picture was shot on three separate negatives, then combined in an optical printer. I had never even seen an optical printer.

We produced so many films for the military in 1945 that between us we only managed to produce eight cartoons. One of them, a very fine Andy Panda, which Dick Lundy directed, *Poet and Peasant,* was based on the familiar overture. It was nominated for an Academy Award. I think it is one of the best pictures ever produced at the Lantz Studio.

The war was winding down when I was assigned to direct a film called *The G.I. Bill of Rights.* Driving to Fort Roach, I wondered what the picture was about. It sounded like a new version of the Magna Carta.

As I sat through the briefing, I realized that I was about to direct an historic document. From the end of the Revolutionary War, when thousands of ex-soldiers were cheated out of the land grants that they were promised as a reward for their services, through every war after that, our ex-service men had been treated with callous indifference and chicanery.

Here was a script promising that the G.I.s would not have to make an adjustment to civilian life unassisted. Some ex-service men would want to go back to school, others might want to learn a trade, set up a business, or buy a house. All these activities were going to be backed up with hard cash, from the government, unlike the cruel indifference that motivated the veterans' desperate march on Washington during the Depression.

We rushed the film through production, it whizzed through OWI's distribution facilities, and in a few weeks *The G.I. Bill of Rights* had been seen by eight million in the military, and it had been shown in every motion picture theater in the country.

We barely finished the picture on time. Suddenly the war was over, and just as suddenly the whole structure of visual aid to the military was gone. Pictures were stopped in mid-production, scripts and storyboards were abandoned, and all the equipment put up for sale. Fort Roach closed down.

The only active film unit was an army group making medical pictures, especially a number of very good films about the grim business of adjusting to an amputation.

Even the most vociferous opponents of visual education had no arguments that would hold up against the motion picture industry's incredible performance. For example, from January 19 to August 1945, one hundred men had produced 246,862 feet of film for 576 army projects. The navy, by the end of the war, had a film library of over 10,000 educational films, averaging two reels each.

A few people in high places in the government tried to switch the expertise that had helped the military into the academic world, with no luck. Congress cut off the funds, and the most gigantic visual education effort ever mounted simply vanished.

To this day, to my knowledge, nobody has attempted a serious study of the films that were so important in the transition of our civilians into fighting men.

With worldwide distribution of commercial films completely wrecked by the war, Hollywood entered into a period of intense dislocation. The Walt Lantz Studio did not escape unscathed. The supply of film was limited, and the studio was only allocated enough stock to photograph eight cartoons. There wasn't enough work for two directors so Walt suggested that since I was not married at the time and Lundy was, it seemed fair to lay off my unit.

I was not overly dismayed at the prospect because I had finally arrived at the point where I wanted to own my own shop. I did not want to produce theatrical animation; rather I was sold on the value of film as a teaching tool.

Working for Walt Lantz had been a tremendous learning experience, chiefly because Walt had given me a free rein to conduct any experiment that struck my fancy. It also had been a chance to renew our friendship, which goes on to the present day. Lantz is unique in the business. He has been an employer most of his life, yet I have never heard anybody say a negative thing about him.

Sketches by Bernard Garbutt, 1941. *Collection of Shamus Culhane.*

Tony Rivera and Shamus Culhane, drawn by Pat Matthews. 1944.

"WHAT'S THIS SOUND LIKE?"

Dick Lundy and Shamus Culhane, drawn by Pat Matthews, 1944.

13

The Beginning of Television

During the war years I kept up a steady correspondence with Arthur Turkisher, former music composer at Iwerks Studio, now a sailor on the *Enterprise*. The fact that his ship was engaged in just about every major battle in the Pacific did not diminish his interest in animation. As I wrote him about the various new methods we were using to produce films for the Office of War Information at Lantz's, he became more and more excited about the possibility of starting an educational film studio.

We exchanged a number of letters about the feasibility of such an operation and the kind of equipment we would need. The body of our letters was mostly about business, with a paragraph or two containing more personal matters and some trade gossip. However, at the end there was always a parting shot, usually an ethnic jibe about sex. We discussed the advantages of circumcised penises as against uncircumcised, etcetera.

This kind of give and take continued throughout the war. I wrote to him that "A Hungarian is only an Albanian with shoes," and "A cock without a foreskin is like a window without a shade." Turkisher replied in a like vein.

At the end of the war the *Enterprise* was docked in Honolulu and was slated to go on to Philadelphia, where Turk would be officially discharged. Only if he could produce a valid reason would he be allowed to change ships and get his discharge in Los Angeles.

He requested transfer on the grounds that he had a business opportunity in Los Angeles. When the captain demanded evidence, Turkisher had to sheepishly produce my letters.

Half a dozen letters were read right down to the last bawdy line, including remarks about his probable fornication with empty shell cases, his masturbation with a pair of eyebrow tweezers, and so on. Turk had to stand at attention while the captain gravely read one letter after the other.

Finally he looked up with a perfectly straight face. "This gentleman seems to know you very well. Pack your gear."

When he arrived in Hollywood, Arthur and I had long discussions about our prospects, ephemeral as they were. Our talks ended when he received a wire from an old family friend offering him a junior partnership in a very prosperous diamond company. Turkisher had a natural flare for business. He became a very successful diamond salesman; later he owned a fleet of taxicabs in New York.

Moviemakers are daft! They fiercely resist any new technical development in the entertainment field with xenophobic vigor. They seem to think that if they ignore it, it will go away. Most of them had to be forced into the use of sound films. When television began to do a brisk business in New York, Hollywood, as usual, dragged its feet, in spite of the fact that the foreign markets were in a turmoil and thousands of writers, actors, and directors were unemployed.

I didn't share this apathy. I was impatient to try this new medium, so I started a new company with the somewhat flamboyant name of "Television Art Enterprises." The headquarters of this notable addition to the corporations of America were in my garage.

I was convinced that my future was double-barreled, that is, television production and educational films. I believed that if educational films were entertaining as well as informative, they could attract a wide audience on television.

The results of the training films made for the armed forces had been so spectacular that it was only going to be a short time before all schools used film for such varied subjects as arithmetic, geography, science, and history. (Loud derisive laughter at this point.) I didn't know anybody in the educational field, so I hadn't the slightest notion of how I was going to enter this market.

The *Motion Picture Daily* carried an article that seemed to be the answer. Cecil B. De Mille was going to create a national network for the sale and rental of educational films. I immediately called his office and arranged for an interview.

I didn't meet the Great Man himself. He was probably on a set shooting some houri in a bathtub full of ass's milk. His assistant, who seemed to be in charge of the project, was impressed with my background and urged me to join in this marvelous venture. It was going to keep me busy because Mr. De Mille was going to need hundreds, nay thousands of educational films.

I proposed that my first picture would be about geology, using both live-action and animation to explain the formation of rivers from the mountains to the sea. He crowed with delight . . . a first-rate idea!

When I delicately mentioned the possibility of some front money, he froze. De Mille wasn't about to buy a pig in a poke. When I finished the film, I was to bring it in for a screening. If it was of good professional quality I would receive a good price, plus royalties.

With my usual business acumen, I neglected to get any details in writing, nor did I remember to ask him about such trivia as the amount of the initial fee or the percentage of the royalty payments.

I went home at once elated and dejected. Throughout all the years of the Depression I had fed six to nine people, so I was broke. Here was a golden opportunity and no way to utilize it.

At the time I was squiring Maxine, the daughter of Chico Marx. She promptly came to the rescue with fifteen hundred dollars, and became a full partner in Television Art Enterprises.

With the aid of a half-dozen library books I soon had a script that bristled with impressive terms like deltas, monadnocks, and alluvial deposits. The Vocational School for Boys had omitted even rudimentary geology from our studies, so it was all great fun.

Then I made a very carefully rendered storyboard, which included every kind of shot I was going to need in the picture, tracing the formation of a river from its beginnings in the mountains, its serpentine wanderings on a plain, to its entrance into the sea. There were asides about the Egyptians' dependence on the annual flooding of the Nile, and a sequence on the civilizations on the Tigris and the Euphrates rivers. All of it was good graphic material.

I planned to start shooting in the Kings River area and end up at the mouth of the Sacramento. The subject was a rather shrewd choice for a low budget film. No actors, no sets, one narrator, and canned music, shot on 16mm stock. I intended to do all the artwork myself.

We hired an oddball cameraman named "Spots" Leppert, who had shot newsreels before the war. When I told Spots that I had no money for hotels, we would have to either sleep in the car or on the ground, he just shrugged it off. Leppert had just come out of the army.

Off we went one morning, in high spirits. Spots had a rickety tripod and a battered camera, which was taped like a prize-fighter's hands. On our way to the Kings River we managed to pick up shots of small streams that miraculously coincided with some of my story sketches. This impressed Spots no end. He realized that we could almost shoot on a one-to-one basis because my storyboard was so comprehensive.

By the end of the second day most of our mountain sequence was in the can. In the late afternoon we came to a part of the Kings River Canyon where the river had narrowed to a fast-running stream swirling around huge boulders. The late sun was making intricate patterns on the rocks. We simply had to get some shots down there, but the walls of the canyon were almost three stories high.

Camera in hand, Spots nonchalantly stepped backwards over the edge, and I followed gingerly, clutching my script and storyboard. Most of the climbing area had an angle of forty-five degrees, so it was easier to get down than I had expected.

The water was flowing so fast that it was making a great roar. Even from a few feet away, we had to yell to be heard. We rolled up our pants legs and started shooting happily, even though the water was ice cold.

Pretty soon we forgot about wet clothes and scrambled thigh-deep around the elephant-sized boulders. Spots got some spectacular shots, including a lovely little rainbow, a very welcome addition to my storyboard. When we finished, we were so excited by the quality of the shots that we stood there in the freezing water and hugged each other.

Then we slipped on our shoes and started up the face of the canyon. I wore new leather-soled shoes, and scrambled up clumsily. Spots, with rubber-soled Army shoes, went up the wall from rock to rock with the agility of a mountain goat. I was less than twenty feet from the top when I saw that Spots was already stepping nimbly over the edge.

Then my foot dislodged a rock just as I had put my full weight on it. For an instant I was flat on my belly against the rock face, both legs flailing wildly. Slowly I started to slide down, right hand holding the script and storyboard, my left scrabbling for a new handhold.

Just as I was beginning to pick up speed, I went by a little bush about a foot high. I was watching my hand reach out for it, feeling a kind of wry objectivity. If this shrub wasn't well-rooted I was going to die.

It held, but I could see the earth loosening around the roots. There was no point in yelling for Spots. Even fifty feet away the water made too much noise. Nothing to do but hang on. There was a big firm rock near my right hand, but the thought of releasing my papers never entered my head. We didn't have any copies.

Finally, I saw Spot's face as he leaned over the edge. He was wearing a big grin, but when he saw me dangling he went into a horrified expression that would have done credit to Pluto. In a few minutes he had scrambled down and hauled me up. Off we went, chattering gaily about the shots, as if nothing had happened. We were simply two workaholics at play.

Kings River was still a wilderness in those days, no gas stations or restaurants, so we had to drive to Yellowstone National Park. We reached there in the middle of the night. A trooper told us the bad news. The restaurant would open the next morning at seven. We drove wearily over to a grove of pine trees and flung ourselves down on a luxuriously soft bed of pine needles.

Suddenly we sat up, wide awake. There was an infernal row going on behind us. Chains were rattling, heavy metal clanged, with an obbligato of hair-raising snarls and growls. It was pitch black. I could hardly see Spots.

The thumping of metal grew louder, then the animal sounds went into a crescendo. Just as we started to get up, we heard a sound like the Charge of the Light Brigade! Heavy bodies hurtled by us, all uttering gutteral snarls and mind-numbing roars. We were being overrun by bears. They missed us by about six feet!

We listened for a while but they seemed to have gone. By this time we were so tired that we wouldn't have cared if the Four Horsemen of the Apocalypse used our pine grove for a racecourse.

The next morning a waitress told us that the bears raided the garbage cans behind the restaurant every night. When they fought over the food they were very dangerous. The garbage cans were secured by heavy chains, but they had been tossed around like tenpins. Spots and I were too ravenous to think about bears. We were almost doing a little growling ourselves.

There were no further adventures until we were in the San Francisco area getting a great shot of the Golden Gate Bridge. We were arrested by a navy shore patrol. It seems that we were in a restricted area. They bundled us into a jeep and we were taken to see the commander.

Two-day beards and hair still matted with pine needles made our appearance far from impressive. The climate was frigid until I thought to produce a business card. President of a television company? The commander thawed visibly, gave us a very respectful admonishment, and ordered the patrol to take us back to our car. Business cards should be standard equipment for spies.

To the shore patrol's annoyance, Spots finished our shot of the bridge before we left. He hated MPs.

Back in Hollywood, I whipped through the animation, raced through the editing and recording, and two months to the day I was once more facing De Mille's assistant. He looked at me as if I was a leper whose nose had just fallen off. No, Mr. De Mille didn't have time to see the picture.

It seemed that the Great Man's plans had changed. He was busily directing twenty thousand extras through forty tons of strawberry Jell-O, for the parting of the Red Sea sequence. Too busy to get involved in educational pictures. Perhaps next year? The minion waited somewhat nervously for my reaction. Assault, battery, or murder? But the Age of Chesterfield is not dead. I merely invited both De Mille and his assistant to perform an acrobatical sexual act, and stalked out.

My next step was a dreary round of the few companies in Hollywood that sold or rented educational films. I found the biggest collection of thieves since Ali Baba. Yes, they would accept my film. No, there was no money up front. The contract would stipulate that they would be paid for sundries like advertising, exhibition prints, postage, and packaging. I'd receive 30 percent of the remainder. What could I make in a year? Hard to say, maybe two or three hundred dollars. Just sign right here.

I didn't. I put the negative and print on a shelf in my garage, and like Achilles, went into a monumental sulk. Fortunately, before my mouth settled into a permanent pout, I was given a reprieve.

A friend, Sobey Martin, was one of the first directors in Hollywood to make television pictures. He and some of his fellow workers had formed a production company to make their own pictures for the new medium. One project was to make a film for the children's market—a pilot for a series. He wanted to know if I could make a ten-minute animated cartoon for five thousand dollars.

We scribbled out a contract, and as I signed it, I thought that some day we might make enough money to buy an old typewriter, and even some letterhead paper with Television Art Enterprises on it in fancy lettering.

In those days, five thousand dollars wasn't enough money to produce a silent cartoon, much less a film with dialogue, music, and sound effects. Some of the usual conventions of filmmaking would have to be discarded.

This was going to be the first animated children's show for TV, so we had no precedents to guide us. Obviously it was out of the question to make a picture that would have to be photographed exposure by exposure, so synchronized mouth action was the first casualty. Next, we figured that if the film was not going to show mouth movements, it followed that we could cut down the action during dialogue to a few basic poses in each scene, changing the position of the speaker only if we needed a new pose to express a change of thought.

By eliminating these expensive elements we were able to spend more money on a good story and an elaborate sound track. More important, where we really needed action it was going to be full animation, not the limited style of movement that Grim Natwick calls "spastic animation."

The producers of series for children's Saturday morning TV shows have taken quite the opposite approach. They do have synchronized mouth action, which means that the whole picture is shot exposure by exposure. Compared to our idea, the many mouth drawings and painfully slow photography are so expensive that it leaves a much smaller percentage of the budget for scripts; and the animation, of necessity, is severely limited. From an aesthetic point of view I think we had a more imaginative approach.

I chose Robin Hood as the subject of our pilot. Since all the characters are so well known, we had a pre-sold audience. I did enough research into thirteenth-century England to uncover dozens of quaint laws and customs, enough for an indefinite number of scripts.

With the aid of Maxine, who was herself an accomplished radio actress, we assembled a cast of very good young actors. I directed in radio style, in that the music and sound effects were added to the track as we did the dialogue. It was a very good session, and the actors enjoyed the rollicking style of my script.

Spencer Peel made the layouts and backgrounds. He was a draftsman with remarkable virtuosity, especially in his handling of dramatic light and dark. Pat Matthews, one of the few men in the business who could animate a human figure without the aid of rotoscope, worked with me on the animation. With this advantage we decided to draw realistic-looking people rather than use cartoon characters.

Spencer had an idea which saved time and gave our film an unusual appearance. Normally, animation is painted flat like a poster; we used cels with a slightly rough surface so we could render light and shade on the figures with lithograph crayon.

Photography was our next problem. The picture was going to have many long panoramic shots. Conventionally, they are shot on a standard animation camera by shooting one exposure, moving the artwork slightly, taking another exposure, and so on, ad infinitum. Such a procedure would have taken days.

We had a spring-wound Kodak 16mm camera, with a tripod. We bought a kid's wagon, loaded it down with rocks, mounted lights on the tripod, buttressed the legs with sandbags, and presto! We had a mobile camera.

Spencer painted the backgrounds on long strips of heavy paper, which we nailed to the wall of the garage. One of us would stand on the wagon looking through the eyepiece; another would pull the rig, while the third would time the shot with a stopwatch. We shot at twenty-four frames a second, and if the scene was too long or too short, it was no problem to take it over. We were able in minutes to photograph a shot that would have taken many hours on a conventional camera stand.

At one point I found, to my horror, that I had inadvertently written us into a booby trap. Robin Hood was walking to Nottingham with Giles the cook. I couldn't make them stop to talk because we had footsteps on the sound track. If we animated a normal walk and shot it exposure by exposure it would have taken us days to finish.

We got around our difficulty by making cutouts of Robin and Giles, then mounted them on long, flat sticks, like Balinese puppets. The characters were going to be shot waist-high, so we didn't have to worry about animating legs.

The photography proved to be easy. While we played a record of the sound track so that I could synchronize the action with the footsteps, I crouched under the long background, holding a stick in each hand. When the camera and sound started, I gently bobbed the characters as they advanced across the background. I had to walk like a duck to keep out of the camera range, and when we were finished my legs ached for a week. But when we saw the shots, there was no hint that the scenes had not been shot on a conventional camera stand.

There were some scenes that demanded full animation, and these we shot exposure by exposure, swearing and cursing at our crude camera setup.

When we screened *Robin Hood,* Sobey and his friends were delighted. The first children's cartoon for television was a very beautiful and entertaining film. Sobey went off to sell it with high expectations.

Sobey's group was entirely composed of creative people. None of them had ever tried to run a business before, still, anybody with the intelligence of a mongoloid chimpanzee would have found out a few details about the market. What kind of a deal might be forthcoming, ten pictures, twenty? What could we expect to earn, and how long would it take to recoupe the negative cost?

Creativity and business sense seem not to be compatible, because none of us thought to investigate these basic questions. We just put down our heads and charged.

There were no customers for *Robin Hood* because the market was glutted with old animated cartoons. Some of them were renting for fifty dollars a broadcast.

We were stunned because we were all sure that what television sorely needed was good children's programs, specifically designed for their vocabularies and age levels. It was a case of being too early with too much.

Adults and children alike had enjoyed the picture every time we screened it for a test audience. Nobody had questioned the lack of conventional mouth action. Everybody loved the sprinkling of archaic words in the dialogue, and especially praised the voice of our lusty Robin Hood. Why not? He was played by a rising young actor named Telly Savalas.

At most it would have taken a few phone calls to find out that there was no market. What psychological factors impelled us to waste five thousand dollars and weeks of hard work? Was it sheer stupidity? I doubt it. I think it was a compelling urge to create, to the exclusion of any practical matters.

Henry Ford built his first car in a small brick building near his home. After spending months at work, he finally finished his prototype, only to find that he had forgotten to measure the door of the building. It was too small to get the car out. Fortunately the back wall was made of wood, so he could dismantle it without destroying the building. Was Ford a simpleton? Any jerk would have measured the door before he started building his car.

The creative urge can be so strong that it becomes an idée fixe, and logic goes by the board. That seems to be why creative people are usually such poor businessmen. In our case we were quite right. Children should be exposed to good art, good stories, and good music. If Sobey had met a broadcaster with some imagination, the results would have been different. There might have been no need for the present situation, where outraged parents and teachers are attacking networks for presenting children's programs of poor quality. Contrary to the old adage, there's some use in crying over spilt milk.

After duly commiserating with Sobey and his friends, I put my print of *Robin Hood* on the shelf next to *The Formation of Rivers,* sat on the toolchest, and went into the serious business of counting the knotholes in the nearest wall.

I was interrupted by the vice-president, who came in beaming. It was time to meet the family, so she had arranged a dinner date with Chico! Christ! I had visions of blowing fifty dollars at Chasens, or maybe more at the Brown Derby. I decided to take Maxine and Chico to the best Japanese restaurant on the Sunset Strip, where we could get a sumptuous meal for five dollars apiece.

When we met in the restaurant, Chico gave Maxine a perfunctory kiss and offered a limp hand to me, then he went back to a profound study of a racing guide. Maxine sprayed us with nervous chatter, but Chico never looked up. He was in the process of losing a million dollars on horses. It looked like hard work.

When the kimono-clad waitress came, Chico waved the menu away. "Just bring me a medium steak with French fries." The waitress almost popped her obi. The manager came, and one could tell by the way he hissed and bowed that he recognized Chico.

They, of course, had no steak and potatoes, but if Mr. Marx would kindly wait, the chef would send somebody to the nearest steak house. Chico agreed, and the manager went off, his face saved. He wouldn't have to commit hara-kiri.

While waiting for the steak, Chico began to ask me questions about my interest in racing, boxing, and baseball. At that moment all I remembered about boxing was that Benny Leonard parted his hair in the middle. I'd never been to a track, and my interest in baseball waned when I stopped running the daily pool at Bray Studios long years ago. Chico went back to his racing guide. He wasn't disgusted, just sad.

When the sukiyaki arrived I could tell that Maxine wished she had ordered a steak, too. As for her chopsticks, they might just as well have been a pair of oars. The meal ended on a dour note when Chico found out that fortune cookies are not served in Japanese restaurants.

While I was paying the check, Chico asked me if I would drop him off at Pickfair. Mary Pickford was throwing some kind of a bash. I was happy to oblige, but dubious about my car.

At the beginning of the war I owned a very snappy Studebaker roadster. When it broke down I couldn't get new parts, so I sold it and bought Pat Matthew's fifteen-year-old Chevy. The felt lining of the ceiling was hanging in strips like Spanish moss, both fenders were tied to the hood with baling wire, and the door on the passenger's side had fallen off and was now secured with lengths of clothesline.

Chico laughed all the way to Pickfair. We entered the driveway and I tooled around a collection of Cadillacs, Bugattis, and Rolls-Royces to the entrance. The doorman went into a state of shock, but he pulled himself together and came to open Chico's door. Chico waved him away. "Don't bother," he said with a straight face, "I'll open it myself. I've got the can opener."

Things went from bad to worse, as they say on Madison Avenue, finance-wise. Along came Chet Huntley with a brand-new project that looked like a steady income at last. Chet was a popular radio newscaster, considerably more of a left-winger than was healthy on the West Coast. He was anxious to get into television, but he wanted to do more than just be a talking head.

He proposed that we team up on a television news program that combined Chet telling the news with the spice of caricatures of politicians and other public figures. Sometimes I might even make a drawing that had editorial impact, like a newspaper political cartoon.

It sounded like a hell of an idea. Nobody was doing anything remotely like it, so we picked a date at random, and Chet wrote a sample script of a television show. I plucked my cameraman Spots Leppert off the line at the unemployment office, and we went into a studio and shot Chet in 16mm color. There wasn't any color television yet, but we thought it would make a more impressive pilot.

It ran fifteen minutes, and I inserted about six or seven caricatures and a political cartoon about Truman and the Russians. This was all a dry run to see if we could do a show a day. I kept track of the man-hours and figured that with a staff of three artists we could turn out a handsome product.

When it was finished, Chet took the print around to the networks. (This must be getting boring.) He hadn't checked out his idea with anybody, with the usual result. Nobody wanted to spend $225 a day for graphics. Of course Chet went on to become one of the most famous newscasters in the country, but that did not pay my rent.

I know it sounds familiar. I put the print on the shelf with the other two bombs.

The Screen Cartoonists Guild asked me to attend a meeting of the executive board. (I had dropped out when I became a producer.) It was a heartwarming meeting because the subject was, "What can we do to help you get started?" At the moment a nice ten-pound ham and a rye bread would have been useful, but I didn't want the discussion to reach such a primitive level. Really there was nothing that they could do, but it was a hell of a nice attitude.

Large parties bore me into a semicoma, and I usually manage to avoid them. On one rare occasion I found myself in a group of ex-New Yorkers who were entertaining some refugees. This was not an evening of idle chitchat. Some of the refugees had stories of hair-raising escapes.

As the evening progressed I realized that these people, unlike the refugees I had met before, had all been in positions of wealth and power in Europe. From their clothes and jewelry it was obvious that they had fled Europe with enough money to live here very comfortably. The term Jet Set had not been coined, but it would have been applicable to this group.

One of the guests was the Baroness Rothschild, easily the most striking woman in the room. I was introduced to her as an ex-Disney animator. This sharpened her attention, and she asked me a number of questions about the studio. She insisted on taking my address, and gave me an effusive good-bye when she left.

A few days later I received a very impressive invitation from the baroness. Would I come to a party? Since I found her very attractive, I went. She lived in a huge house in Beverly Hills. When I followed the butler to the garden, I noticed that the baroness had some good color prints. All the walls of the foyer and adjoining rooms had at least one fine reproduction: a Cézanne, several Degas, a Renoir, and other standard stuff.

The garden was exquisitely furnished with white tables and gaily striped umbrellas. There were about a hundred people chatting and sipping champagne. The baroness all but fell on my neck with happy chirps of hospitality. She pressed a drink into my hand and led me back into the house.

We ended up in the library and sat together on an elegant settee. I began to wonder what this effusive welcome was all about. It didn't take long to find out.

She had written the most charming script about some flowers, which would make the most marvelous cartoon, surely! Since I was such a good friend of the great Walter Disney, would I not take the baroness to meet him? Then she could sell him the script.

When I protested that Disney rarely bought story material from the outside, she brushed that fact away with a be-ringed hand. I shouldn't worry. Walter would love this script. I had just to arrange a meeting. Also, she was selling the story for a mere trifle . . . ten thousand dollars.

It was time to dam this Niagara, prick the bubble, so to speak. It wasn't easy. The baroness was launched into a nonstop sales pitch. Finally I managed to stop her with a large hand held up like a traffic cop.

"Baroness," I said sadly, "you are asking for too much money. Even if Disney liked the script, he never would pay ten thousand dollars."

"Ah well," she tinkled, "I don't mind. Why not ask for seven thousand five hundred?" I hated to do it. "Disney did buy one very popular children's book, *Ferdinand the Bull.* I believe he spent seven hundred dollars for the movie rights."

The lady had class. She managed a brief smile, then stood up. "I must get back to the guests, of course." I agreed. I got the message. Following a brief handshake, I started for the foyer. Halfway through, a glint of light on a rough patch of paint caught my eye.

I stepped closer, then realized that I was not looking at color prints! These were all originals. In this small room was a fortune. Any one of these paintings could be sold for enough money to buy this house and everything in it. I stopped feeling sorry for the baroness.

One day I was in the garage counting knotholes, and was well up into the triple digits when I got a phone call. The gentleman introduced himself as a New York agency rep. Now if he had said that he was a yellow-bellied sapsucker it would have made as much sense. What in be-Jesus was an agency rep?

He went on to say that he represented Sherman & Marquette Agency, which in turn handled the advertising for Colgate, Palmolive & Peet. They had a product called Ajax Cleanser, which they wanted to advertise on television. I had been highly recommended by a former assistant at the Fleischer Studio in Miami as a first-class animator.

Could I make them an animated spot? I hadn't the foggiest idea, so of course I said yes. We met, and I was shown some copy and a little jingle. They needed a one-minute advertising film. That's what a spot was. When asked for a price, I came up with a nice round figure, five thousand dollars.

What I didn't know was that they were already using spots on television in New York, but the going price was around one thousand to fifteen hundred. At those prices they were getting junk. The Ajax people wanted a very fine piece of animation, so the gent didn't bat an eye.

At this time the employment situation in the animation business was in a desperate condition. People of the caliber of Grim Natwick and Arthur Babbitt were unemployed, so was Art Heineman, one of the best layout designers in the business.

I hired all three. We were expected to design a film that would show the efficiency of Ajax in the bathroom. I cooked up a storyboard using three little elves, one small, another tall and skinny, the third big and fat.

When the storyboard was approved, we made a track, using June Foray, Joe Silver, and Hans Conried, three very talented people. The track was a smash. June had an enchantingly piping voice, and Joe Silver had a basso profundo that made Chaliapin sound like a castrato. The others would sing, "Using Ajax," and Joe would come in with a "Boom Boom" that almost shattered the mike.

Art Heineman designed three elves that had very good intrinsic acting ability, so Babbitt, Natwick, and I had an easy time of putting them through some very amusing antics.

The Ajax elves advertisements, with their combinations of live sets and actors, portrayed a new approach to advertising. This is a shot from a 1949 spot written, directed, and animated by Shamus Culhane.

Tiny handled most of the visual gags on the Ajax commercials. His personality was enhanced by the voice of June Foray, an outstanding radio actress in Hollywood during the 1940s.

I had set up shop in our spare bedroom, and we worked jammed together in this small space. The work we did was real Disney-quality animation, including the inking and painting. The unemployed labor pool was so large at the time that I got the best possible talent in every facet of production.

Everyone was so grateful for the work that there was an atmosphere of almost hysterical gaiety in the crowded room. Everybody wanted to know when there was going to be more of these strange pictures, but, since Sherman & Marquette were in New York, and the rep had gone back, I had no idea.

We shipped *Ajax #1* and waited for a reaction. The check came and with it a terse note thanking us for the work. This was followed by silence. We had made a small profit on the spot, but months went by without new work.

Finally, I had to sell my car. Once in a while Maxine would pick up a radio job with Ronald Colman or Orson Welles, but it wasn't enough to keep us going, even after we got married and shared our expenses.

If anything the unemployment situation worsened, so there was nothing to do but take a bold step. I decided to go to New York to see if there was any more work like the Ajax spot.

One important change happened. On the advice of our lawyer, Morry Coopersmith, we incorporated a new company, Shamus Culhane Productions, Inc. Shamus is Gaelic for James. My father always called me Shamus, but in the business I was always known as Jim or Jimmie. Maxine, quite rightly, pointed out that Shamus was much more memorable than Jimmie. Now only very old friends forget and call me Jimmie.

We needed three hundred dollars to go to New York, and we didn't have a sou. We decided to ask Maxine's mother for a loan. It took a lot of chutzpah. Betty Marx had the usual aspirations for her daughter, probably expecting her to marry some nice Jewish director. Then I came on the scene. A goy, twelve years older than Maxine, twice divorced, and without visible means of support—not exactly a catch. My only asset was that I was not a gambler like Chico. Betty was used to adversity, having had to cope with Chico's organized propensity to lose all their money.

She had one outstanding quality. Betty was the best originator of malapropisms that I have ever heard. She "took the rump to her right," worried about "the autumn bomb," was "knocked from pillow to post," and loved to hear the "Moonlight Sinatra." There was at least one classic a day.

Betty had given us a sumptuous house for a wedding present, a little jewel box, which she furnished with exquisite style. In spite of having been raised on Bleecker Street, where she slept on two chairs in lieu of a bed, Betty had the taste of a duchess, and this house was by far the most luxurious place I had ever lived in.

When I outlined my plans, Betty agreed totally. Some of her best friends, high up in the industry, were also hurting. It was time to make a radical move. She gave us the money and her best wishes.

When we arrived in New York, I hated the place. It was even dirtier than I had remembered . . . and the people in the streets didn't have the manners of a starving sow. We had arranged for an exchange of our beautiful house in North Hollywood for the use of a friend's New York apartment. Every morning when I woke up, the first thing I saw was a coffee table that had legs made of upended bowling pins. Yeeegh!

Neither of us had ever been in an advertising agency, so we approached the Sherman & Marquette offices with some trepidation. Carl Brown was head of the company and gave us a very friendly welcome.

Brown turned out to be a character out of a William Faulkner story. In spite of his many years on Madison Avenue, he was a very simple, straightforward person, who still kept his Missouri accent. His ordinary style of conversation was so colorful it sounded like a mule skinner driving his team up a steep hill.

Brown was very bewildered by the whole television business and the technical jargon, which was completely beyond his understanding. Carl often longed, with appropriate curses, for the old days of printed copy.

Instead of a formal written contract on the first Ajax commercial, Brown had ordered it orally. Now he merely said, "Shamus, make me three more of them silly goddamned cartoons." I promptly fell to work in the kitchen. I couldn't stand to look at the bowling-pin table in the living room. After the storyboards were approved, I sent them out to my friend Bill Hurtz for layouts and backgrounds. This was his first venture into television and he did a beautiful job.

Norman Ferguson was reputed to be the fastest animator in the business, but I set him a dizzying mark to shoot at . . . three one-minute spots with over twenty-five hundred drawings, animated in four weeks. Being flat broke is a marvelous incentive!

I farmed out the inking and painting, and while that was going on Maxine and I started looking for more work. It was a weird experience. We would go into an agency and inform the receptionist that we made television spots. Often she didn't know what we were talking about. When we finally made a breakthrough, we were told that the "television specialist" would see us.

We would be ushered into the shipping room. There on a pile of packing cases would be an antiquated projector. The "television specialist" would, more often than not, prove to be a gawky kid wearing a well-worn suit, which he was rapidly growing out of. Inevitably he would ask if we knew how to run the camera. The poor bastard didn't know the difference between a camera and a projector!

Since I knew nothing about loading a 16mm projector, usually a flustered young girl from the steno pool would arrive and, after some fumbling, manage to thread the machine.

The fact that we were about to show our Ajax commercial was always electrifying. People came from all over the shop to meet the originator of the most popular spot on the air. We hadn't seen it on TV yet, because nobody we knew owned a TV set. In spite of the fact that the film was usually projected on a bilious green wall, the agency people were amazingly enthusiastic.

In a few weeks we were asked to bid on more work than we could possibly handle. One of our first jobs was from Compton Agency, and it almost sank us without a trace. When I was asked if I also produced live-action, I answered gaily that I did. Since I came from Hollywood, nobody questioned my expertise. In truth I had no more idea of how to assemble a crew and build sets than the average man in the street.

These were Rinso commercials, and animation was a very minor part of the project. For thirty-five thousand dollars we were to complete six one-minute spots and six thirty-second spin-offs. There were sixteen sets involved, including a full-scale mock-up of a large part of a supermarket. The whole complex of sets filled both stages of Fox-Movietone to overflowing.

Luckily I had met a young live-action director, Jules Schwerin. He recommended a good propman, who in turn found me a reliable set

Fatso was the slow-witted elf in the Ajax spots. Joe Silver supplied his basso-profundo voice.

A model sheet drawn by Art Heineman of Skinny the straight man in the Ajax Cleanser spots.

builder. He told me about an excellent cameraman. He had an electrician who worked with him a good deal. Bit by bit, I put together a very good crew.

In order to have us build an authentic replica of a supermarket, Compton hired an architect whose specialty was markets. He was a nervous little man and drove our set builder slightly crazy. Although there was only going to be one long shot in each spot, of a housewife taking a Rinso package from a shelf, the architect was making a set only slightly smaller than Grand Central Station.

The propman got us several hundred prop boxes, jars, and cans. When it came to the area around the Rinso boxes I went to the account executive and asked for other products that were made by the parent company. He looked at me as if I were daft. "For Chrissake," he said crossly, "do you think for a minute the guys are going to loan me products, and then this goddamn housewife walks right by them and only takes the Rinso?"

Instead we set up a section of Rinso boxes about twelve feet long, filling all the shelves from top to bottom. So much for authenticity.

I made no effort to hide my ignorance from the crew (which would have been futile anyway), but when I talked to the agency people I dropped esoteric words like "flats" and "inkies." This made a profound impression. Casting was easy; from Maxine's experience in radio she already knew many capable actors and actresses in New York.

I had made a careful set of storyboards, and that first morning the lights and camera were set up very quickly, in spite of the fact that I was always in the way. I was always just where the crew wanted to place a light or put down a cable box. The camera was a monolith encased in a huge blimp. I made very sure that I watched the cameraman look through the lens so that I would do the same without fumbling.

I found that rehearsing the actors was just about the same technique as directing animators, so when the lights went on and the actors were in place I was very relaxed. Suddenly I realized that everybody was looking at me expectantly. Obviously I was supposed to say something. What?

I leaned over to the cameraman and whispered, "What the hell do I do now?" He hissed back, "Say, 'sound.'" Like a parrot, I yelled, "Sound!" After the boy with the clap-stick retired, there was another uneasy silence. "What the Christ is the matter now?" He muttered, "Say 'action,' just say 'action.' " I bellowed "ACTION!" in my best De Mille manner, and we started shooting.

By midmorning I felt like an old veteran. Don Graham's action analysis classes paid off because I began to make suggestions to the actors that were gaining me growing approval from the crew. They were watching me with the fond look that parents get when their precocious offspring is reciting for the company.

Technically, directing live-action is a lot easier than directing animation. In live-action production the editor is usually cutting a one-minute spot from five to seven minutes of material. Animation directors have to pre-edit their films. There are no key scenes and various covering shots. The footage left on the cutting room floor is usually a few exposures.

The Rinso spots were very successful. The live-action was well composed and the movement very clear; the animation was my usual careful job. Compton gave me more work, most of it live-action. In a very short time I was walking onto a set with great confidence. My knowledge of composition and acting made the switch from animation to live-action comparatively easy.

We did have to overcome a reluctance on the part of some agencies to give us a chance to bid on live-action. They tried very hard to pigeonhole us as an animation studio, but after we had compiled an exhibition reel of live-action spots with excellent compositions, lighting, and acting, we gradually overcame the resistance. From that point on we grossed more money from our live spots then we did from animation. They usually made us a substantial profit, which was never true of the animation.

Unlike Carl Brown, who would not have cared if we produced his pictures in the Gobi Desert, Compton and the other agencies we worked for were adamant about our doing all our production in New York. Reluctantly, we put our house on the market and shipped our furniture and equipment to New York. Our studio was a back room of a wholesale stocking salesman. He was convinced that I was mad. He used to watch openmouthed as I acted out the scenes I was about to animate.

When I was leaving for New York, Bill Hurtz had asked me to carry out a confidential mission for the guild's executive board. There had been so many contradictory reports about the condition of the animation industry in the East that the Hollywood group needed a good detailed analysis of the business conditions.

It was going to have to be extremely confidential, because it would be very embarrassing if the New York local ever found out that it was being evaluated. Hurtz assured me that whatever I reported was not even going to be entered in the minutes.

Within a few weeks after I arrived in the city I managed to talk to the half-dozen owners of animation studios. When I compared my contract with theirs I found an astonishing thing.

Every contract was different. Some had more holidays, a few had a trial period for new employees before they had to join the union; even sick leave did not conform in all the contracts. They had been issued by Pepe Ruiz, who was now the local's business agent.

Whether it was just slipshod attention to details, or some form of favoritism, the fact was that these inequitable contracts made it impossible for the studios to compete with each other on a fair basis.

Practically all spots were allocated by asking from three to six studios to submit bids. While agencies did consider the quality of the work important, the bidding price was often the deciding factor. It is interesting to note that this group of entrepreneurs was so naïve that they had never thought to check each other's contract.

Tempo, Transfilm, and Bill Sturm Studio were the three largest animation studios at the time. Tempo's owners were Dave Hilberman, ex-president of the Hollywood Screen Cartoonists Guild, and Bill Pomerance, ex-business agent of the guild. Before going into business for himself, Bill Sturm had been an active union member, and Jack Zander, head of Transfilm's animation unit, served several terms as the New York local's president. Later on, we probably accounted for more than 75 percent of the animated spots business in New York.

A more ideal group of employers can scarcely be imagined, yet they were the target of implacable hostility from Pepe Ruiz. He made no secret of his vast hate for bosses. At union meetings his terms for employers were always pejorative. He hinted darkly that the studio owners were a bunch of exploiters of the hapless union membership. Ex-president, ex-business agent be damned. Somehow, anyone who rose from the ranks was instantly transmogrified into a robber baron.

I dutifully sat down and wrote a very detailed letter, noting these complaints and the skewed contracts, as well as an excited evaluation of the TV spot market as a huge source of employment which might flower very soon.

At the next meeting of the executive board, the members were sworn to secrecy before my report was delivered. The following morning I received a spluttering, almost incoherent phone call from Pepe Ruiz. I had been telling the guild lies! All lies! So much for the security measures of the executive board. The result of this incident was that Pepe Ruiz and I began a feud, which continued without letup for fifteen years, as long as he was in office.

To me, he epitomized what was basically wrong with this particular union. There was a hard core of the membership who had gone through a traumatic experience during the strike against Max Fleischer, so it was no accident that a boss-hater like Ruiz was elected to the office of business agent. He symbolized their reaction to a bitter scarifying experience, and Pepe made sure that the abscess did not heal. Using a kind of Pavlovian semantics, he made sure that the membership was constantly reminded that bosses were inherently brutal, greedy villains.

The studio owners all believed that some day the union membership would accept the fact that they intended to supply decent working conditions and the best possible wages. There would come a time at a union meeting when Ruiz's usual tirades against bosses would be challenged by a clearheaded member who would break through to the mesmerized audience with some facts and figures that would dispel the image of the employers as exploiters.

This was naïveté in its purest form. As it was explained to me by some of the union membership, that challenge was never going to happen. The main reason was the fact that Pepe Ruiz controlled the source of job opportunities. If a producer needed more employees, he had to telephone Pepe to find out who was available. Very few people had the courage to oppose Ruiz on any subject.

None of the neophyte employers had ever run a business before, but as far as I know I was the only one who tried to make a systematic evaluation of my new role. I began to read books about business management, especially the writing of Peter Drucker. Some of it made for dismaying reading. Especially dismal was the fate of most entrepreneurs.

Throughout the history of American business it seems to have been a definite pattern that when a new industry started it was usually begun by people who had great knowledge of a similar field, but no business experience. By a combination of a particular skill, better than average intelligence, and foresight, they would become employers.

When the new industry was finally stabilized, ironically enough, they often lost control to outsiders who came into the field with better business acumen.

The worst aspect of the entrepreneur's role was the fact that he was often the target of intense envy. Psychologically, many of his employees, who had been his fellow workers, could not accept the new relationship. Outsiders were much more acceptable as employers.

On the West Coast this envy, if it existed, played no dominant role in the relationship between the producers and the union. In New York it certainly must have been a factor that enabled much of the membership to see the employers as hostile, even though there was no evidence to prove it.

In spite of my reading I had some serious psychological problems of my own. My father was a follower of Eugene Debs, and he had a cynical regard for both of his employers, Western Union and the Interborough Rapid Transit Company. While I had been a major executive for years in various studios, I had not been the boss. Now that I was one, I tried to hide this fact by a number of subterfuges.

For several years after I opened my studio I worked at an animation board, cheek-by-jowl, with the other animators. I had no private office. I wanted to be like everybody else, so I was a kind of pseudo-employee.

In the beginning I was a soft touch. As we started to hire employees, it seemed that almost everybody had some reason to come in late or leave early. One had to take her kid to school, another had to catch a certain train, there were sick mothers, dental appointments, etcetera. Nobody seemed able to put in a nine-to-five day. Since I wanted to be a nice, well-loved boss, I let them all do it.

An ink and paint department, with an all-female crew, can be a hotbed of petty jealousy and backbiting. Every few days another vendetta would erupt. There were tears and bitter accusations.

This situation was remedied when I hired a gum-chewing kid about nineteen years old, just out of a minor job in Woolworth's art department. Ruth Gench was a ninety-pound dynamo and the best natural executive I have ever met. She learned the rudiments of the business in a very short time and became head of the ink and paint department. Very soon she was promoted to studio manager.

Ruth had a velvet hand in an iron glove, and soon straightened out the crazy schedules and endless quarrels. We had our share of eccentrics, and as long as they did good work Ruth allowed them a certain leeway. For example, we had a very efficient assistant animator who needed to unleash a primal scream every day to relieve her nervous tension. Ruth didn't mind it at all, as long as she yelled near the back elevator.

In the beginning we had no bookkeeper, and our finances were a mess. Certainly we had made a good deal of money, but it was going through our hands so fast, to finance new jobs, that we didn't know what was going to be used for bills and what was profit.

We found that Carl Brown and Compton Agency's prompt payment of monies due was not normal procedure in the rest of the industry. The more work we took on, the more working capital we needed, and it wasn't coming in fast enough. Some of our trouble was the fact that we had no time to do the necessary bookkeeping and mailing out of statements.

A friend of ours mentioned that she knew a black secretary who was working for an insurance company. She was allowed to eat in the company commissary, but behind a screen! I was so incensed at the story that I hired her sight unseen. Cynthia Walker proved to be a marvelous secretary, very well organized.

Within a few days she told us firmly that we had to have a bookkeeper. There was no way to get the billing out and keep up with the books without help. She had a friend, Cecil Brathwaite, who was studying bookkeeping at night. Since he wasn't a professional yet, he would probably work for a small salary.

Cecil was a chunky, jovial black from the West Indies. After he stopped answering the phone by saying, "Hoy," instead of "Hello," he was a great addition to our staff. Brathwaite worked for a few days and then announced that we could not operate on the cash flow we had. In fact, we were going to have to borrow twenty thousand in order to pay current bills.

I timidly went to a bank with my agency contracts. When they saw that they all included a cancellation clause, I was ushered out, not too politely. Again we had to call on Betty Marx for help. She thought that we were absolutely mad when we were unable to even guess at the amount of money we had made. All we knew was that it was a lot. Betty agreed to loan us the money with the proviso that we take on her brother-in-law, Joe Rosen, as our accountant.

Things were happening at a dizzying pace. Our equipment arrived just as the stocking people announced that they were moving out. This coincided with the expansion of our staff. We hired Rod Johnson, a former West Coast animator, to take care of some of the animation that was pouring in. Johnson was later to become one of our most valuable employees, but at the moment, he made our cash problem even tighter. We needed additional space desperately, so when the stocking company left we leased the entire suite for three hundred dollars a month.

I hated the idea of nepotism, but finally I had to consent to a meeting with the mysterious Joe Rosen. He arrived one evening after work, with a cigar that looked like the barrel of a French 75mm gun. I gave him a tour of the place, showed him some of our contracts, and gave him a quick lecture on the intricacies of animated films.

I couldn't tell if Rosen understood a word I said because he kept reflectively looking at the tip of his cigar. Finally, he looked up to the ceiling and announced that he was very familiar with our problem. The studio was just like a lumberyard, and he had great experience in that business. I almost fell out of my chair. What kind of a schlemiel was I saddled with?

Joe went on to explain that in a lumberyard no two orders were alike; not in price, quality, or delivery date. Since a TV studio had the same working conditions, it followed *ipso facto* that we should organize the business accordingly.

He countered my feeble protests by pointing out that some spots were bringing in $5,000; others as little as $2,500, which meant that they shouldn't all cost the same to produce. Some cost-control system would have to be devised for each phase of production. I reluctantly agreed to do this on each spot—reluctantly, because it was a time-consuming job which took me away from the drawing board.

Here is where I made my first major mistake. I should have immediately started to train a business manager. I never did, and I lived to rue my lack of foresight.

The cost-control system I devised worked very well in theory. Each department was given a budget for its work on each spot. Every morning Brathwaite added up the figures from the time cards, so that before noon I knew what we had spent the day before, and how much work was still to be done on every spot in the studio. That was the theory. The practice was something else.

14

The Madison Avenue Environment

he first year we were in New York we grossed $165,000, but there was no profit because we equipped a cutting-room, had a dozen desks built, installed a projection room, and expanded our space. Our staff at year's end was fifteen people.

It was a grueling year. I worked seven days a week. On Sundays the building was unheated. I spent many hours at my drawing board wearing a muffler and my overcoat, trying to animate with gloves on. I don't recommend it. Maxine and I each took seventy-five dollars a week, almost the lowest paid employees in the studio.

Rod Johnson became head of our animation department. He often directed pictures as well. During World War II he had been an officer in the Signal Corps animation unit in Astoria, so he knew how to handle people. He was deliberate and not easy to ruffle, so I very often sent him to conferences at agencies.

He and snappy Ruth Gench made a funny combination at production meetings. Johnson would slowly unfold the details of some hang-up that was bothering him, and I could see Ruth's size-three shoes drumming on the floor in impatience.

In spite of the difference in pace, Ruth and Rod got along very well. When I hired an editor, Irwin Wallman, all three made a solid core of efficiency. In addition, they all had a fierce love for our studio; and they all understood and respected my insistence on the highest quality of work on every production no matter how inexpensive.

Unlike Disney, we could never work without a footage quota because of our rigid air dates, so depending on the cost of a job, each animator had a definite amount of footage to do every week. For ego gratification we tried very hard to have an animator do a complete spot by himself. Although it would have often been easier to turn the work over to two or three men, I wanted the animators to enjoy their work and have the feeling that they had each made a unique contribution.

Not every animator basked in this kind of atmosphere. One animator that we had just hired was making a miserable drawing as I passed by, at least terrible by our standards. When I pointed this out he replied gaily, "Ah, those agency guys will never see it." I grabbed the drawing off his desk, crumpled it up, threw it in the wastebasket and snarled, "Maybe they might not be able to see it, but I can!" He didn't last long.

Rather to my astonishment, since I don't fancy myself as a designer, in the first year we were in business, a Tetley Tea commercial, which I designed and animated, won an Art Director's Award. I was relieved when we were able to hire Lou Keller, a Hollywood designer who had drifted East because of a lack of job opportunities on the coast.

Lou had started out as a designer at UPA, then for a short time became a director. We had just begun a series of Halo Shampoo spots, using fairy-tale motifs like "Goldilocks," "The Three Bears," and "Red Riding Hood." Keller proceeded to give these spots a very distinctive look, because he was using a typical UPA style.

As we grew more expert in evaluating the TV spot market, I began to see that the story idea was still the most important element in creating a good spot, but almost equally important was the design of the film. While good animation was a necessary requisite, design and story seemed to carry more weight. In effect, it was the same situation as the entertainment business; in making high-style animation the designer had become more important than the animators.

Keller worked for us for more than two years, then went home to Hollywood for a vacation. He suddenly decided that he had missed his friends and Hollywood so much that he was not coming back to his job. While the short-term results of his defection were little short of disastrous, it did give me an opportunity to adjust my sights.

I started to realize that ad agencies have a tendency to pigeonhole commercial artists, and they were beginning to have the same tendencies in the spot business. Being labeled a follower of the UPA style might very well be the kiss of death. I could just imagine an art director looking at a storyboard and deciding that this particular job was not suited for high-style animation, so the work would go to a studio that had a more eclectic approach.

I decided that we would never fall into this trap, and looked for a designer whose talents were more versatile. Bernice Rankin became our new designer and accepted the challenge. She had so many different styles at her fingertips that we were able to offer a wide range of artwork to Madison Avenue.

I have never agreed with the American belief in the intrinsic value of specialists in any area. Specialists, to my mind, readily fall victim to a kind of tunnel vision. In my case, I worked as a Pluto specialist at Disney's for several years, to the point where I could draw a perfectly acceptable Pluto with my eyes shut. But I can't imagine drawing the dog as a career. Specialization enevitably puts a clamp on one's sense of adventure and the normal need for exploration.

We never acquired a Shamus Culhane Productions style in our animation or our live-action. Instead we were constantly looking for new techniques. For example, we were the first studio to design painted backgrounds for our live-action. Another innovation that we were responsible for was the use of animated stills.

We were asked to produce a series of live-action spots for Phillip's electric razor, but the budget was too low to pay for a crew. We hired an actor, put him through a series of shaving actions in stop motion. Each time he moved we shot a still. Then we blew up each shot the same size as animation paper. With an airbrush, we added a three-day beard onto the cels. When the actor's razor passed over a given area, the cameraman scratched off a corresponding part of the airbrushed beard. The spots were highly successful and started a whole new trend, animating still photography. Had we been less resilient in our attitude about techniques we would have turned down the job. As it was we made a modest profit and created a new approach to filmmaking.

One day Clark Agnew, a brilliant art director from Lennon and Newell, came to the studio with some drawings for Muriel Cigars' first venture into television. Agnew had taken a cutout photo of a cigar and drawn a sexy face on the ash, topping it off with a big cloud of smoke, which looked like a wide-brimmed hat. He envisioned the character as a Mae West type, even down to a drawling, "Come up and smoke me some time."

It was such an exciting idea that I decided to do the animation myself.

Luckily there was an old Mae West film playing in town and I must have seen it a half-dozen times. Each showing I concentrated on some aspect of her acting, one for her walk, another her hands, then her voice, and so on. The spots were a smash. There was such an overwhelming demand for Muriel Cigars that the factory fell far behind in its orders.

Mae West was furious and threatened to sue, which would have made Lennon and Newell very happy. The publicity would have been priceless. When Winston Churchill came to the United States he was asked what he thought of American television. He replied that he didn't think much of it except for the dancing cigar.

One of the difficulties that the television studios faced was a shortage of talent. The experienced animators for the most part worked in Terrytoons or Famous Studio. Taking a cue from Walt Disney, I started an animation class after work for my assistants and inbetweeners. One night a week I taught for three hours, then the class was given about another three hours of homework.

It puzzled me for a long time that many of my people did not like to attend the classes, because I remembered my excitement as my drawing improved at Disney's. Here, in one of the best studios in the business, with a chance to learn from an ex-Disney animator, they shirked the homework or tried to avoid attending classes.

The fact is that the average person is not ambitious enough to do more than a good day's work. He is simply not emotionally equipped to put out extra effort. It was no accident that three of the top people at Walt Lantz Studio, Pat Matthews, Emery Hawkins, and I, were the only ones out of a staff of fifty people who were working on a planned course of self-improvement.

I was studying at night with Don Graham, and Emery and Pat were both using Kimon Nicolaides' book to teach themselves better drawing. The rest of the staff forgot that they were supposed to be artists after five o'clock.

It was the same ratio at Fleischer's, Iwerks, and Warners. Only one or two people would be studying at night. Chuck Jones was one of the few people I knew outside of Disney's who appreciated the Nicolaides book and used it to improve his draftsmanship.

It was no wonder that Disney thought of his staff as separate and distinct from the rest of the business. In his studio everybody was learning all day long.

Like Disney, I found that, for the most part, eastern artists would often have to go through a long period of indoctrination to get rid of sloppy drawing habits. It was better to train new people, even if it was a time-consuming process.

A negative factor in my training program was that no other studio was working on a similar project. In many cases I found that after I had taught an inbetweener to be an assistant, he would very often go to a shlock studio as an animator. This kept happening over a long period of time, I began to realize that my school was training more people for the rest of the industry than I was retaining. The lure of more money in a higher category was too much, and I refused to promote people who were not yet qualified to work according to my standards.

The last straw was supplied by a very timid youngster who had brought in an impressive portfolio. He had one big advantage in that he was a complete novice, so he had no bad habits to eradicate. However, when he was given a job as an inbetweener, he froze. He sat for hours like a catatonic, staring at a blank paper on his drawing board. He averaged not more than one drawing a day for weeks!

In a normal studio the poor kid would have been fired in two days, but I knew that he could draw very well so I accepted the challenge. I coaxed him, Rod Johnson wheedled him, and gradually he overcame his funk. Nevertheless, it took many weeks.

He was very enthusiastic about my classes and did his homework so diligently that within a few months we promoted him to assistant, with suitable congratulations all around. Our patience had paid off. For several months he worked very hard.

Working late one night I looked up to find this big lunk gingerly approaching my desk. "I guess you won't like to hear this," he quavered. I stared at him openmouthed. "I got an offer to become an animator." He didn't even ask me to try him out myself, because he knew damn well that he was not qualified to do animation according to our standards.

It took a lot of self-control not to throw him out bodily. In disgust I closed down the school. That was the last son of a bitch I was going to supply to the other producers.

Since Cynthia Walker, my secretary, and Cecil Brathwaite were such good, intelligent workers, I became interested in the possibility of employing more blacks in the studio. Brathwaite had become our head bookkeeper with several other people under him. Maybe I was spurred into action by the fact that at this time Cynthia died. Maxine tried valiantly to supply her with nurses around the clock, but white nurses didn't want to go to a Harlem hospital. When we went to see Cynthia, the doctor explained that she needed penicillin, but the hospital had no money to buy it! We bought some, but by that time it was too late. We lost not only a good worker, but a dear friend.

Many left-wingers are inclined to sentimentalize about minority groups, but I have what might seem like a hard-nosed view. My philosophy was, and still is, that no human being wants special attention from his society just because he belongs to a group that has been labeled inferior. Mollycoddling is no more welcome than hostility because it is basically an act which implies a lack of normal self-sufficiency in the recipient.

I proceeded to hire young blacks between the ages of seventeen and twenty. They usually started as errand boys and moved up from there to camera work, or became assistant editors. One of the youngsters turned out to be a positive genius at repairing equipment. In a very short time Irwin had him in charge of the maintenance of all our equipment, projectors, cameras, and everything else.

Newcomers were always brought to me for a talk. I would explain that there was no racial prejudice in the studio. In fact, it was so nonexistent that they would get no special attention at all. I don't really think any of them believed it. It was just another ploy by whitey. The only stipulation I made was that, in turn, they would not bring racist feelings into our organization.

Not everybody was able to handle this unfamiliar situation. I would say roughly a third of the blacks were already so bitter that they could not cooperate. The ones who stayed said later that it had been the most happy period in their lives. The rest of the staff accepted the blacks completely, and we never had any problems that were a result of a direct confrontation between the black and white employees.

Up to that time I don't believe that there were more than two or three blacks in the whole union. At the present time there are a few designers, assistants, and animators in the local, but the percentage still remains small.

* * *

This caricature of Eddie Cantor was used in a Halo Shampoo TV commercial in 1948. It was designed by John Ployart. Cantor made the voice track for the film, marking the first time a major movie star worked in a commercial spot for television. Produced and directed by Shamus Culhane.

DESIGNED BY
JOHN PLOYART

A Halo Shampoo model sheet. Designed by Lou Keller, 1948.

In 1951 we created a new series of spots which received favorable attention from the public. They were spots for Quaker Puffed Wheat and Puffed Rice. We animated the Little Quaker man who has appeared on Quaker boxes for decades. We decided to use him in live-action scenes playing with a small child.

By the use of mattes we were able to have the little man jump off the box and do tricks, like picking up a real spoon, dipping it into a cereal bowl, and giving the kid a mouthful; or he would push a real bowl of cereal over to the child and add cream and sugar as the youngster watched. This combination of live-action and cartoons had never been used before in the spot business, so it created quite a sensation on Madison Avenue.

The spots were difficult to direct, and the child actor had to be very imaginative because he was reacting to a character who wasn't there. The animation was added later.

These spots were all black and white. We did no color TV until 1956. It was too bad because in our first Quaker spots we used a boy with marvelously red hair. Jackie was an endearing little tyke with freckles and a big grin that featured the fact he had a front tooth missing. He very quickly mastered the technique of reacting to an invisible man, so what might have been a nerve-racking directing job became lots of fun. This lad was just about the best child actor I had ever worked with, a miniature Marcel Marceau.

The next year we did another series for Quaker with the same format and the same boy. Jackie lived far out of town, so we gave him the job sight unseen. When he came on the set I saw with a sinking heart that one year had made some drastic changes in our little pantomimist. He had lost so many front teeth that when he smiled his mouth looked like a picket fence. There was a change too in his manner. He swaggered around the set while we were tooling up and ignored his mother's attempts to sit him down.

The worst thing was that his simple reactions to the invisible man were long gone. He was now the biggest ham since Adolph Menjou. Nothing I said stopped him from overacting.

After wrestling with his mugging for an hour, I took his mother to one side and asked what the hell had happened. "Oh," she said brightly, "I forgot to tell you that Jackie has been studying the actors on television all year." Then she dropped her voice to a whisper. "I just don't know what to do with that boy. He bit a nun last week!"

When I was a child I had several years in a Catholic school, so I reflected that any kid who would bite a nun can't be all bad. With this renewed respect, I managed to wring an acceptable job out of him.

A few years later, Carl Brown, who was still my favorite client, opened his own agency and took the Colgate account with him. Carl hired a production manager, Joel Malone. Joel had been writer-director on the famous "The Whistler" series both on radio and television. He had a very irreverent attitude about the whole advertising business, however, he also had some good, solid ideas, especially for Halo Shampoo, which was Carl's biggest account.

I wish I had taped some of Malone's dialogue during our conferences with the "Colgate Brain-Trust," as he called the account executive and his minions.

His style was informal to say the least. Joel would go through a storyboard making pithy comments like, "The gal picks up the Halo crap. . . ." What with Carl Brown's mule skinner vocabulary, Malone's disrespectful allusions to the product, and my usual flamboyant beret, red silk shirt, and espadrilles, the Colgate group (all in gray flannel suits and narrow ties, hair *en brosse*) must have felt as if they were in the middle of a three-ring circus. The saving grace was that we were turning out some highly successful spots, usually a combination of animation and live-action.

During one casting session Joel and I were excited by a delicate, elfin child with a profile like a cameo. To our dismay we found out that Carol Lee was only fourteen. Since she was under age, we would have to have an observer from Child Welfare on the set, and probably a schoolteacher. Colgate would never agree to this additional expense.

We decided not to mention her age to the Brain-Trust, and Carol Lee's mother agreed. Carol had never been in a film. The other girls were all models, whom we had picked not for their acting ability, but because they all had lovely long hair.

Apparently their agent had instructed them to look sexy, because they all walked around the set taking little bites of air, in what they fondly hoped was an authentic imitation of Marilyn Monroe. Instead they looked like guppies and drove me crazy.

Carol, on the other hand, did her spot like an old trouper. She didn't look like a guppy, she looked like a movie star, and a few months later she was—that is, after she changed her name to Carol Lynley.

A Shamus Culhane version of "The Sleeping Beauty," designed by Lou Keller for Halo Shampoo, 1952.

Joel Malone, creative director for the Carl Brown Advertising Agency, whose irreverent approach to TV spots was responsible for the success of many of the TV Halo Shampoo films.

A Culhane version of "The Three Bears" for a Halo Shampoo TV spot. Designed by Lou Keller, 1952.

* * *

The term "culture shock" is a phrase that has been bandied about a good deal these days, but to me it is more than a cliché. Imagine the psychological trauma involved in switching from a career of more than twenty years in a complicated art form like animation, then suddenly being dashed into a mutation of this long familiar environment.

In a studio, the lowliest person in the pecking order has at least a sound grasp of the principles of animation, and certainly a knowledge of the professional jargon. For fifteen years I had worked in the upper echelon of the animation business, surrounded by my peers, who were able to understand any aspect of filmmaking, no matter how complicated. Suddenly, I was propelled into an atmosphere where the most important people I had to deal with were absolute amateurs.

Not only that, they controlled the situation. Many agency executives we had to deal with in the early days were primarily skilled in office politics and only interested in getting on the TV spot bandwagon. Most of them had no intention of really learning about the intricacies of filmmaking. It was enough that they had managed to squirm into a cushy job in what was obviously going to be an important facet of the advertising industry.

The distinguishing thing about them was their facility in learning the technical terms of the business, often without the slightest idea of their meaning. I had account execs glibly ask for one-exposure dissolves, barn door wipes in the music track (when they meant a segue), and then they'd vent loud irritation when we were unable to deliver a completed live-action spot the day after it was shot.

One art director made us change all the backgrounds in a spot which featured an elephant in a house, on the grounds that an elephant would not have that kind of furniture.

Early on, I learned about the Machiavellianism in meetings, and began to understand how a perfectly good idea could be sunk for political reasons. The person we had to fear the most was the character with the least clout. More often than not he would pipe up, after we had all agreed on some story point, with an objection.

This gave him a chance to become the center of attention. His suggestion was usually inferior to the original idea, but such was the climate of insecurity at those meetings that the others would sometimes accept it. Not me! I indulged in no diplomatic circumlocutions when such a

Muriel murmuring her famous, "Come up and smoke me some time." A 1953 TV
spot written, directed, and animated by Shamus Culhane.

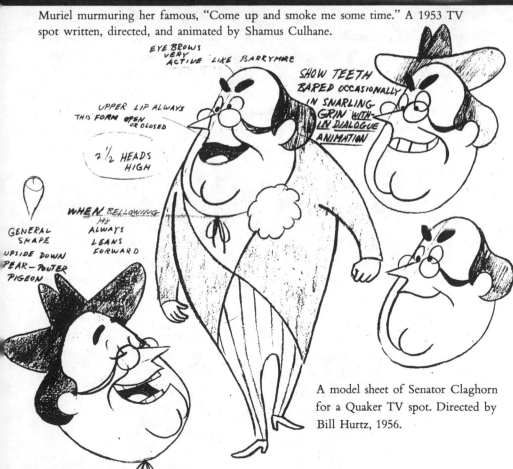

EYE BROWS
VERY
ACTIVE LIKE BARRYMORE

SHOW TEETH
BARED OCCASIONALLY
IN SNARLING
GRIN WITH
IN DIALOGUE
ANIMATION

UPPER LIP ALWAYS
THIS FORM OPEN
OR CLOSED

2½ HEADS
HIGH

GENERAL
SHAPE
UPSIDE DOWN
PEAR— POUTER
PIGEON

WHEN BELLOWING
HE
ALWAYS
LEANS
FORWARD

A model sheet of Senator Claghorn
for a Quaker TV spot. Directed by
Bill Hurtz, 1956.

situation arose. I would bluntly protest and try very hard to steer the group back to the original concept if it really was better.

In this way I achieved two negative results. One, I made an enemy of the pipsqueak. Two, I often found that I was suspected of trying to discard the new idea because it was more expensive.

Maxine very cleverly used my bluntness to advantage by assuring the boys that I was a true genius. If the agency wanted the benefit of my talents, it would be better not to irritate me, because like all geniuses, I had a short fuse. It very often worked because in a few months I had built up a formidable reputation both as a filmmaker and curmudgeon.

The other aspect of advertising that I found enraging was the atmosphere of fear in which we were expected to operate. Very often when I suggested some innovative approach to a spot, there were loud cries of, "J. B. would never go for that!" or "The client might not like it." Since the mythical J. B. and the client were never involved in these discussions, I refused to believe that these poor frightened bastards could guess so accurately their superior's mind. I began to feel that working with an agency was potentially a castrating process unless this creeping, mindless fear of unseen higher powers was vigorously resisted, so that is what I did.

I soon acquired a reputation on Madison Avenue as a very difficult person to work with. On the other hand, in agencies like Carl Brown and Compton, where I was given comparatively free rein, I was very well liked. Nobody in these agencies tried to make me into a compliant vehicle for putting other people's ideas on film.

Another problem that arose was that agency personnel resisted all our efforts to charge for a retake when it was the agency's fault. If it was a large sum, we insisted on collecting, knowing full well that we were going to lose an account in the process. When small sums were involved we tried to include them in the cost of the next batch of spots we did for that agency. This wasn't always successful, because in an open bid we had to compete with studios that were not trying to recoup a previous loss.

One could never, never ask for money to cover a studio loss. No matter how successful a spot was, if we lost money it was irretrievable. If, in a burst of artistic enthusiasm, we added something to the spot that made it outstanding, there was no way to wring additional money out of the agency, even if we just wanted to get back our basic costs.

Another pain in the arse was having to turn down requests for so-called "experimental" storyboards or character sketches. These were supposed to be done gratis, in the fond hope that a job for pay would be forthcoming. Some damn fools went along with the practice, but I was adamant, and flatly refused to work for nothing.

We actually lost the Muriel Cigars account because I would not agree to shoot a live-action spot for nothing. As the agency producer put it, "Since you are on the set anyway, one more spot shouldn't cost us anything." He was new on the job and determined to make a good showing. When I refused, not only did we lose the account, we never worked for Lennon and Newell again.

Finally Maxine devised a very good answer to the requests for "freebies." She would explain that if we did work for nothing it increased our overhead, thus penalizing the agencies who paid for all their work.

This seemed so reasonable that we usually managed to extricate ourselves without losing a potential customer, but it didn't work in every case.

Maxine tried very hard to make me accept all these facets of the advertising business as annoying but unimportant. There was no way I could be persuaded, because I felt that these were attacks on my integrity as an artist, or my profits as a businessman. I was too stiff-necked to bow my head meekly just because the other fellow had the money.

She completely underestimated the depth of my feelings about my principles. Maybe a soft answer turneth away wrath, but you might find that your balls have dropped off in the process.

In the early 1950s many agency people were frightened by the crackpot threats of Joe McCarthy and put on a lickspittle performance that would make a hyena puke. Maxine and I decided to give blacklisted actors work whenever it was possible. It was fairly easy when we recorded for animation, because we often used trick voices and the actors were not recognizable. Of course we had to do this with the secret connivance of the casting director; not everyone was a spineless coward.

One of our friends, an animation writer in Hollywood, was called before a McCarthy tribunal. When asked about his antecedents he replied that his ancestors had been in this country during the first witch hunts. The resulting uproar was so great that he was forced to resign from his job. Then he found that he was blacklisted. At the time we were tooling up for a huge job, eighty spots for the air force, so we hired him to write the stories and do the storyboards. For months he was hidden away in a back room in the studio. It was a dangerous move.

The owners of Tempo Studio, our greatest competition, were called down to Washington to face a McCarthy investigation. They proved to be "hostile witnesses." The next day they were the victims of a scurrilous attack in Walter Winchell's column. The following day every client canceled the spots that Tempo had in production. A week later their equipment was sold at auction.

Despite that example we continued to help blacklisted actors whenever we could. An informer in our studio could have blown us out of the business overnight too, but we had confidence in our staff and it wasn't misplaced.

We managed to get the air force account in a curious way. I did a lot of work for Dancer, Fitzgerald & Sample. Through the grapevine we heard that they had a new account executive who was unbelievably cantankerous. He was new to the television business and was making a name for himself as a scourge who demanded work at impossible schedules.

One day I was called by his office and ordered (not asked) to present myself at the agency in half an hour. I was inclined to refuse, but, rather than risk skewing my pleasant relationship with the agency, I went along.

When I walked into Charlie Fitzmaurice's office I found myself in a situation that looked like a comedy. Charlie had a phone in each hand and was carrying on two separate conversations at once. When he saw me he jerked a massive jaw in the direction of a chair, so I sat down and watched this curious performance with amusement.

After a while he stopped talking long enough to shout for his secretary. She came in cringing and fawning. Fitzmaurice told her brusquely to fetch me some storyboards from the file, then went back to his dual conversations. The poor girl came back, literally wringing her hands, to tell Charlie that the stories were not there.

Fitzmaurice rapidly turned purple. He screwed up his face as if he were going to cry. Ignoring the fact that he was still holding both phones, he launched into a tirade about the slovenly workers he had to contend with, having to do everything himself right down to the last goddamn detail. Why couldn't he get people around him with brains?

Since he was addressing his complaints to the ceiling, he didn't notice

A TV spot for Black Forest Beer. Written, designed, and directed by Shamus Culhane, 1950.

Character for a Red Heart TV spot, designed and animated by Shamus Culhane, 1948.

Romeo and Juliet in a Bab-O spot, designed by Lou Keller. Written and directed by Shamus Culhane, 1951.

that the girl was now pointing at a pile of papers under his elbow. Finally she timidly interrupted, "Mr. Fitzmaurice, they're right there." He stopped bellowing and looked down at the welter of papers on his desk. Then he switched to the kindly tone one might use on a congenital idiot.

"My dear girl, why don't you pick them up and give them to this man. That's all I want. Just pick them up." She snatched the storyboards off the desk, thrust them into my hands, burst into tears and fled.

Charlie looked at me for the first time, and quavered, "Oh God!" Then he went back to his two phones, and I studied the spots. They were pretty pedestrian, and I quickly saw several places where they could be much improved.

Finally Charlie hung up both phones and turned to me, frowning ferociously. "Well, what do you think?" I carefully put the spots back on his desk and said very casually, "They're no good." He almost fell out of his chair. "I like them," he growled ominously. Ignoring the gathering storm, I went on to tell him what was wrong, and how they might be improved. Charlie was beaming when I finished.

"You're right, I didn't really think much of them myself." He shoved the papers in my direction. "Here, fix them up and let me know how much they're going to cost. I need them all in three weeks."

"Six," I said, starting to fold them into my briefcase. Charlie started to turn magenta. "Look," I said, reaching for my jacket, "I'd have to slop them out in three weeks. You don't look like a man who wants slipshod work. Six weeks."

Charlie switched to a broad grin of sheer pleasure. "By God, you know your business. What was your name again?" For the next two years Charlie and I had a marvelous relationship. He took every suggestion I made as gospel and refused to put out any of his spots for competitive bids, which must have irked the management no end. The result was that we made him a steady stream of very successful spots.

Fitzmaurice was the original Terrible-Tempered Mr. Bang, but he was highly intelligent, and a very good account executive who quickly adjusted himself to the television business. In the whole period that we worked together Charlie never uttered a cross word to me. However, in the agency he was considered to be a cross between Attila the Hun and Jack the Ripper.

Without warning, he was gone. Charlie had accepted the presidency of a large chain of supermarkets in the Midwest. We lost about a $150,000 guaranteed annual income, which was the reason that Joe Rosen, our accountant, called this business Russian roulette. In addition, I missed the challenge of having to deal with the crabby old bastard; it had been great fun.

In 1952 we hired Zack Schwartz as layout man, designer, and storyman. Zack and I worked on a lot of pictures together, and he became practically a co-director.

Zack had to be just about the most unlucky man in the animation business. He, Dave Hilberman, and Steve Bosustow started UPA. After doing a fair amount of work during the war, the studio started to flounder as the postwar depression set in. It was a tense time, and they couldn't get along with Bosustow, so Zack and Dave sold their stock and quit.

Shortly after, UPA was given a very lucrative contract by Columbia and went on to become the hottest new studio in the country. In the interim Hilberman and Schwartz teamed up with Bill Pomerance, the ex-business agent of the Hollywood Screen Cartoonist's Guild, and started Tempo Productions in New York.

They were too early. Television was in its infancy. They were soon reduced to doing lettering jobs just to pay the rent. Zack quit again and became a commercial artist. A few months later my Ajax spot hit the air and the boom began. Tempo was soon swamped with work, but Zack had to come back into the business as a freelancer.

In spite of his bad luck, Zack still had a great sense of humor, and like me was an enthusiastic workaholic. We became very good friends, and together created some successful spots. Zack was a well-educated artist in both the classical and commercial sense. His sense of design was much more sophisticated than was usual in New York animation studios.

When we were asked to create a main title for Billy Rose's new television show, Zack created an intricate montage of electric signs, spelling out "Billy Rose" in every conceivable manner. As usual we were given the assignment at the last minute, so Zack and I rushed through a storyboard. Next the whole staff plunged into a whirlwind of animation and other components of the film. For some reason we all seemed to relish working in an emergency situation, so the job, which would have normally taken six weeks, was done in two.

We rushed the titles through the lab, and at last, late one afternoon, a red-eyed, exhausted crew sat in the projection room with a nail-biting account executive. We watched an intricate pattern of trucks, pans, and dissolves with "Billy Rose" blinking on and off in every shot. There was not a single mistake in spite of the rush.

The account exec scurried off to show the film to Rose, after assuring us all that we had a possible award winner. About a half-hour later I received a spluttered, almost incoherent, phone call. We had made a horrendous mistake. Throughout the whole montage we had spelled Rose's name *Billie!* The irony was that Billy Rose was one of the country's biggest egomaniacs, who spent a fortune every year on his publicity, yet none of us, including the agency people, had noticed the misspelling.

Around 1953 we began to be asked to bid on storyboards that had been designed and written by agency personnel. Most of them were piss poor and many were downright unworkable. We had a new problem, namely, how to fix some of these abominations without stomping on somebody's ego. There were some exceptions; the most notable of course was Muriel Cigars, which had been a brilliant conception. However, once the trend started it spread inexorably.

The reason for it is fairly obvious. By getting into the creative area of production, the agencies were in an almost invulnerable position. If the spot was a success, they could claim a major part of the credit. If it was a failure, it could be hung on the producer. It certainly was a shrewd business move, but from a creative standpoint the spot market lost a lot of quality. The most important part of the films was taken away from expert filmmakers with years in the business and put into the hands of amateurs. These amateurs didn't really know the possibilities of either live-action or animation.

A case in point was Halo Shampoo. Since 1951 we had been making a series of animated and live-action Halo spots. The animation was always the main part of the story; the live-action was only used to show the actual shampoo bottle. They were amusing spots, usually a funny version of a fairy tale, like "Goldilocks," "The Three Bears," et cetera.

One day I was talking to two members of the Brain-Trust about the fact that animation wasn't intrinsically the proper medium for showing beautiful hair, which after all was the main sales point. I had come up with a fantastic idea. Why not find a ballet dancer with lustrous long hair, and shoot her in slow-motion so that the audience could watch her beautiful hair undulating as she danced.

I was pacing back and forth in my office, talking with earnest excitement. As I passed a window, reflected in the glass were the two executives grinning at each other. One of them elbowed the other in the ribs. They were both laughing at this silly artist and his dumb idea. A few years before I would have gotten the copy from the agency and drawn up the storyboard with no restrictions whatsoever. My evaluation of the best medium for this particular product would probably have gone unchallenged. Now I had to answer to two meatheads who had never had a useful sales idea in their lives.

Very soon it became a rarity to be allowed to create a spot from the basic sales points as we had been doing. It took all the fun out of the work, because that is really the most creative aspect of spot production.

We did have a chance to show what we could do in competition with agency creative people when Peter Paul, Inc., decided to change agencies. The Mounds/Almond Joy account was worth $8,000,000. Six agencies were given three months to develop presentations for a new advertising campaign. Dancer, Fitzgerald & Sample was not included initially, but less than a week before the presentations were due, Peter Paul relented, and DFS was allowed to compete.

Two days before the deadline, Dancer gave us some copy, and a plea for us to come up with an idea that would win the account. Chris Ishii, one of our new designers from the coast, Zack Schwartz, and I designed storyboards around the theme, "Indescribably Delicious!" Working around the clock, we managed to complete three storyboards showing two sprites making candy bars in various trick ways.

Dancer won the account. It was the only ad agency in the competition that had gone to a production house for a basic idea.

During the early 1950s Maxine and I found that it was impossible to take a vacation during the summer. June, July, and August were a period of intense production, because in those three months we made almost half our annual gross.

Ocean Beach on Fire Island in those days was the favorite vacation spot for show business people. This was before *The New Yorker* magazine did several documentary articles about the fact that some of the most famous stars of stage and screen vacationed there with their families. After that the island became a bedlam of gawking tourists, and a rutting ground for the singles set.

While it was still unspoiled, it was a marvelous place to relax. We would spend Friday afternoon, the weekend, and Monday morning at Ocean Beach all through the summer. Maxine would huddle with her actress friends, exchanging bits of gossip about the racier aspects of show-biz, and the sturm and drang of getting parts, subjects I found less than earthshaking. So I would wander down to the far end of the beach, dragging a go-cart full of books.

Under a huge beach umbrella I would sprawl on a blanket and set out my books. I was trying to learn Attic Greek, and it was a bitch of a task with my slapdash knowledge of grammar. Greek grammar is so complicated that I had trouble finding out if Helen's face had launched a thousand ships, or if they were still at anchor in the wine-dark sea.

It took so much concentration that I quickly forgot the problems of air dates, money, and even the ranting of Pepe Ruiz about the evil producers. Slowly I was beginning to appreciate the richness of the Greek language.

As a producer I have been involved in casting sessions all these years, but I can never get used to the task of telling people that they missed out on a part. The hurt looks of the newcomers to the business are only a little more heart-wringing than the quick professional smile the more seasoned veterans use to mask their feelings of defeat. "Making the rounds" has to be the most frustrating part of the acting profession. In this area they have my full sympathy. But not on Fire Island.

I suppose if people knew how desperately I needed this time to relax, they might have withstood the temptation to make a pitch, but I doubt it. The lure of catching a producer all by himself was too great. So the first summer I was often approached by some blithe young thing with a great ploy like, "Oh, you're reading Greek! How fascinating!" The reaction was something like sticking a red-hot poker up a sleeping lion's arse.

After a while the news got around, at least among the more permanent vacationers. Don't go near the big red umbrella at the end of the beach. Never!

One Monday morning as the old *Fire Island Queen* lumbered up to the wharf like a tired elephant, Maxine and I were standing anxiously at the rail. The boat was late and we might miss our train. A man next to her stretched out an imperious finger at the crowd of waiting taxi drivers, and called out, "Who wants to drive me to New York?" There were several volunteers.

Maxine turned to the stranger and asked him how much the fare was. Instead of answering he curtly said, "Get in. I'll take you," and scuttled down the gang plank. He was obviously surprised when, as he got into the back seat with Maxine, I opened the opposite door and climbed in. From his sour expression I could tell that he had thought that he'd made a pickup.

Maxine, oblivious to his frustration, introduced us. There was no reaction. After a few minutes he muttered that he was Charles Revson. There was no reaction from us either. We'd never heard of him.

A few miles later he asked what we did, and Maxine went into a very sprightly spiel. I sat moodily in the corner suffering from my usual prebellum depression, gearing up for the weekly onslaught of perilously approaching air dates, studio conferences, agency meetings, etcetera.

Revson brightened up as Maxine talked, and leaned over to get a better look at me. "You people are pretty damn smart," he said, smiling. "I'll bet you get more business out here on a weekend than you could get in a month on Madison Avenue. All the important guys are here taking it easy. You must make some great connections."

I brushed aside his admiration and snarled, "Connections? The only connections I have here are a bag of books and a bottle of Scotch. If people want to talk business they can see me at the studio. I come out here to rest. Anyhow, we have more business than we can handle."

After that sullen outburst Revson fell silent, and all of Maxine's valiant attempts to resume the conversation on any level were a failure. He dropped us off in front of the studio, ignored our thanks, went off, and was promptly forgotten.

A few weeks after that episode, my secretary Jo-Ann told me that I had an appointment at Revlon. This was odd, because the drill was to send a salesman to an agency, show our exhibition reel, then pick up some storyboards to bid on. If we were given the job, then I went to the agency for a production meeting and would meet the client.

I was mystified. Jo Ann could supply no further information. Someone had called, told her to have me appear at a meeting, and had hung up. All we knew about the account was bad. Revlon was one of the most lucrative accounts in the spot business, good for at least $200,000 a year, but we had heard that the company's demands on producers were beyond belief. They included rat-race schedules, revisions at the last minute, and constant verbal abuse.

After some reflection, I decided to attend the meeting. I was intrigued by the idea of bypassing the advertising agency and coming directly to me. But one thing I was not going to do was make a sales pitch. I couldn't have done it if I wanted to, because psychologically it is impossible for me to evaluate my work objectively. With a few rare exceptions, when I look at my work on the screen I can always find something about the film that is unsatisfactory, something I wish I could do over.

I am one of those unfortunate neurotics who will never enjoy success. I could easily qualify as the world's worst salesman.

At the Revlon office I was met by a haughty young lady who cast a disapproving eye at my open shirt, mismatched pants and coat, and espadrilles. I followed a neatly revolving set of buttocks through the usual labyrinth of halls, and found to my amazement that the Minotaur was none other than our acquaintance from Fire Island, Charles Revson.

Obviously pleased at my amazement, he leaned back and waved a casual hand toward a group of about twenty people seated at a conference table. In front of each person was a glass of water, a yellow pad, and a row of pencils. "This here's my creative staff, come on in and sit down." There was only one vacant chair, at the far end of the table, so I sat down and confronted Revson at the opposite end. Nobody said a word, a few bobbed their heads almost furtively, and the others just flicked me a quick look and turned back to look fixedly at Revson.

He steepled his fingers and smiled. A vagrant thought flashed through my head and almost made me giggle. Revson looked like a praying mantis about to strike. What the Christ was he up to? "Shamus," he said gravely, "tell us about yourself."

Well, there was a lot Revson and I could have talked about. We had very similar backgrounds, which I was not aware of at the time. We had both known extreme poverty as children, raised in cold-water railroad flats, ate food cooked on woodburning stoves, and took baths in the laundry tubs in the kitchen.

His first working space was so small that four people were crowded into it, filling bottles of nail enamel by hand. My first studio was a small bedroom, which barely had enough room for four artists.

Both of us earned about twenty-five dollars a week during the first two years we were in business. Here the comparison ends. After five years our gross had grown to a half million dollars; in the same amount of time his company was earning over two million. We had a solid, permanent staff, and the joke on Madison Avenue was that all of Revlon's executive offices came equipped with revolving doors.

Tell them about myself? What a question! I looked at the double row of blank faces and said flatly, "I make good pictures, what's your problem?" Apparently that wasn't what the group had expected. There was an audible gasp from them, then they all turned to look at Revson.

His smile was gone. "Show him the boards," he said curtly. The two young men on my right whipped out identical briefcases. Each extracted a storyboard and laid it gingerly in front of me. Before they had landed on the table, I had my stopwatch out. The first thing I was concerned with was the length of each spot. They were supposed to be fifty-eight seconds, but in those days at least half of the storyboards I was expected to bid on were overlong.

It was so quiet in the room I could hear my watch tick. For me this was always a moment of intense concentration, especially in timing live-action spots. In a cartoon one can whisk a character across the screen in three drawings, but there is no such malleability with live actors. I forgot the watching group and visualized the action in each sketch, going over and over each shot until I felt that the pacing was as tight as possible.

For almost ten minutes there hadn't been a sound except the pages of the storyboards flipping over. I looked up. "This first spot is sixty-three seconds long, the other sixty-four."

The two young men were in a panic, and protested in unison that all the action had been carefully timed. I shook my head. "You timed the dialogue correctly, but what about the dissolves? You have five in this spot and six in the other. They can't be left out because the cutting would be too choppy."

Revson stood up, his face grim. "All right, that's enough. We get the idea. I can't sit around here while you guys try to fix the fucking things up." He left through one door, and I took the other.

What a son of a bitch! This kind of mistake was very common, but it was always resolved in the privacy of the agency office. Finally it dawned on me . . . the whole thing was staged. We didn't need all those people at the table. They had been brought in to witness the humiliation

of those two youngsters. It was some kind of a lesson to the group. The
kids were probably getting their last checks before I was back at my
studio.

As for me, he must have disliked my rejection of using my vacation
to drum up business, because that's the very thing he would have done
in my place and made himself a mint. For a gung ho person like Revson,
my outburst must have been an affront. In retaliation he used me as his
hit man in his little drama. Anybody who thinks I am being paranoiac
should read *Fire and Ice,* a book by Andrew Tobias, a very good biography of Charles Revson, financial genius and prize putz.

In spite of several years of psychoanalysis it took a long time before I
was able to accept the fact that I was a boss. For at least three years I had
a drawing board in the animation department, and directed and animated
pictures alongside my "fellow" workers. I was finally forced out of the
area when we had to hire more animators because of the increased flow
of work.

I decided to rent a room next to my office staff and furnish it with
a secondhand desk and some rickety chairs. The general effect was one
of monasticism or grim poverty, depending on one's viewpoint. This
illusion of being a kind of non-boss was shattered very suddenly when
an account executive and an art director from a Montreal agency came
to see my exhibition reel.

They were ushered into my office for a short visit, after which I turned
them over to a salesman who showed them the film in our projection
room. I must say that the projection room matched my office in meager
equipment and a general air of shabbiness. A short time later they came
back and we discussed a deal for a half-dozen spots and we agreed on a
contract.

The account exec left for Canada, leaving the art director to mop up
the details. He seemed so nice that I impulsively asked him out to lunch.
Usually I ate an austere lunch by myself, but on this occasion we went
to the Bistro, where I knew we could talk a long time without being
rushed by an officious waiter. We chatted gaily about Montreal, which
at that time was much more interesting than Toronto. I had been going
there since the early fifties, knew most of the top agency people and all
the good restaurants.

I liked the Canadians. They seemed to have inherited the honorable business ethics of the English, and the ability to come quickly to a decision like us—a very agreeable combination. Very often I would accept an order by phone from the Canadians, a thing I quickly learned not to do on Madison Avenue.

On our third bottle of wine the art director became quite garrulous. He confessed that the account exec's evaluation of the shabbiness of my office and the sleazy projection room made him want to leave immediately. It was only at the insistence of the art director that he stayed to see the exhibition reel. It was so good that they both agreed to give us the work they had brought from Montreal, without visiting another studio.

This oblique compliment set me to thinking. How many times had the shabby atmosphere turned away a prospective customer? The lunch was scarcely over when I was back at my office with a stack of color cards and a sketch of the office layout. I decided that New York had so many sunless days, the colors should be cheerful enough to overcome the gloom outside.

The next day I sent for the building's painter. He was a wizened little man, so covered with spots and drippings of various colors that he looked like a walking Jackson Pollock painting.

"I'm de paintner," he announced proudly. "Good, here's the color sketch." I handed him a completed sketch of the office and some color cards. The little man looked with growing horror, then pushed the papers back firmly. "Never I'm seeing such a meshuggeneh office. "I'll paint a nice off-white de whole thing. You'll love it."

"No I won't," I said curtly. "Do it exactly like this or I'll tell your boss to get me another painter." The sketch showed two opposing walls cocoa-colored, and the other two bright yellow. The three doors were black, red, and blue, respectively. The ceiling was a light blue. Mondrian would have approved; the "paintner" didn't.

He started his work reluctantly, making feeble protests as the days went by. "Maybe a nice vite de ceiling," or "How about de doors de same color from de walls?" I was adamant and he went around muttering to himself.

In the interim I bought two Matisse lithographs, nudes, a Braque pigeon, also a litho, and two Picasso etchings from his "artist in the studio series." A friend told me about a new type of Italian furniture made of black lacquered wire and foam rubber. I bought a settee, some chairs, coffee table, and a large free-form rosewood desk, and some Swedish rugs.

I also brought in some items from my collection of antiques, Greek toy horses from Athens, 400 B.C., and some Egyptian ushabtis, almost three thousand years old. The place looked more like a museum than an office.

I didn't neglect the projection room either. We had it wallpapered. Irwin bought several rows of chairs from a motion picture supply house, and suddenly we had a snappy-looking room where the salesmen could bring a client without being ashamed by the lack of decor.

In addition, I gave myself a raise, bought silk suits and handmade shirts, shaved every day and looked every inch a boss. I don't credit this all to a chance visit by a stranger. Probably the psychoanalysis was the main factor, with the slightly drunken lunch just tipping the scales.

For once, Joe Rosen didn't complain about the expense. The "paint-ner" took to dropping by occasionally, ostensibly to check his work, but in reality to look around at his glorious creation. As he once confided in me, "You know what? If I never seen it, I wouldn't believe it!"

I am fairly sure that I have a slight case of dyslexia because I make an inordinate number of mistakes on my exposure sheets. One day Ruthie Gench came storming into my office waving a scene I had animated. Since I missed being an animator I was still, almost surreptitiously, taking interesting scenes home to animate at night. Often I was too tired to attend to the details of my exposure sheets and would leave them for the assistant. This was contrary to my own house rules. ·

Ruth was reminding me with some heat that I couldn't go around making rules and then breaking them, just because I was the boss. Usually I would take these tirades very meekly, because she was quite right.

This time as she clacked off down the hall on her three-inch heels, I rebelled. "Shit!" I thought. "I have plenty of people on the staff who make very neat exposure sheets, but they can't come up with campaign ideas that are good for thousands of dollars' income to the studio. My kind of brains are just no good for details, and I might as well accept it. To hell with feeling guilty."

From then on I continued to animate small scenes at home, made mistakes on the exposure sheets in spite of my best efforts, but stopped worrying about them.

This might sound like a small victory but in truth it was the beginning of my maturity. I had a long way to go but this was the start. It was a little late, I was forty-six at the time.

I didn't ignore my mistakes, and they were not confined to exposure sheets. A producer is in a position to make some very expensive errors of judgment, and I made my share. Early on, I formed the habit of discussing them in executive meetings. I would explain in detail to Ruth, Rod Johnson, and Irwin Wallman what had gone wrong and what underlying principle I had violated. I felt it was important to point out my boners because at times they were all going to have the same kind of responsibility.

In a way it was good psychology, because there is nothing more demoralizing to a group than to have the top executives try to hide behind rank or shift the blame to a scapegoat. It made it possible for the others to discuss their shortcomings too, without being defensive. Sometimes these sessions must have sounded more like self-help groups than business meetings.

Some very valuable insights came out of these bull sessions. One example is memorable. Every TV spot at some point has an especially important shot of the product. In those early days we were dealing with package designs that were not conceived for television, so these were often the least interesting shots in the film. While the object was duly retouched, we never attached much importance to it.

At one of our meetings I got a brainstorm. We had been missing the psychological implications of product shots. I explained to the group that we had been looking at the package as just a pain in the arse because of the usual poor design. For the agency people this product represented a payment on a mortgage, or the money to send a kid to Yale, or maybe just plain job insurance. We had to show the agency people that we had the same respect for the product that they felt.

From that point on we were careful to exhibit products in the best possible way, and the agency people were grateful when we suggested better package shots, more interesting than the agency storyboard artist had designed. I believe that this appreciation of the psychological factors involved increased our sales.

15

Riches to Rags

In the early days of our work in television I was lulled into a feeling that this was an honest business because of our good association with agencies like Carl Brown, Dancer, Fitzgerald & Sample, and Compton. For example, during the twelve years we worked for Brown, we never had a written contract.

We soon found out that other agencies were not quite this honest. When we sent in bills for extra work on a film, some smart ass in the business office would notice that it wasn't spelled out in the contract. Usually we only had a verbal order to back us up. Sometimes the agency producer would welsh, making a loss for us.

My original contract, which was less than a page, was soon expanded to five pages bristling with production items in neat rows. That straightened out most of the problems, but not all.

One time we received a contract from a new agency for a large package of spots, both live-action and animated. We decided to make the animation look like a series of cutouts with shadows cast by each drawing. In reality it was conventional drawing with double-exposed shadows, and just a few cases where we did cut out paper patterns and glue them on the cels.

The agency people were delighted with the concept because it was a new approach to a spot design. It was a big account, and we would probably make a great deal of profit on the live-action because it was very simple. For that reason I decided to use this technique although it was more expensive than we had budgeted for.

As production progressed, I noticed that the two agency boyos were making determined efforts to add various expenses to the original concept. We let a few slip by, others I fended off. It was annoying because they were already getting more than their money's worth. They didn't seem to appreciate it.

The live-action was so easy that Irwin assured me he could direct it all in two days. The first day's shooting went very smoothly, but at noon on the second day I received a call from the secretary of the manager of the sound stage.

"Mr. Culhane," she began tentatively, "I hate to tell you this, but I was standing behind a flat, and I overheard those two agency men talking . . . well it's about your studio."

"What about my studio?"

She gulped. "Well the big one asked the little one if Irwin was going to finish on time. The little one said yes. So the first one said, let's give the goyim a little overtime. Then they both laughed. Should I tell Irwin?"

I thought for a moment, then I decided to tell him myself. When I did, Irwin hit the roof. "The goddamn pushcart peddlers!" he fumed. We decided not to say anything, just go ahead with the job. Since spots, like most movies, are shot out of sequence, the two schlemiels (who obviously had never been on a set before) didn't realize that Irwin was finished until he suddenly yelled, "That's a wrap!" Whatever they had in mind to delay the shooting hadn't worked because Irwin was finished long before five o'clock.

I did a lot of thinking that day. We had over a month's work on the animation, and we would have to deal with those two hostile bastards. Finally I decided that the best thing to do was to put everything in writing. Even phone calls were to be translated into memos. Any changes in the contract, no matter how trivial, were to be handled the same way. We'd agree to them all, but the agency would be sent a memo covering the extra expenses the next day.

When we finished the job I was sorry to see that we had done some of our best spots of the year, because the agency didn't deserve it. I had also garnered about two dozen memos. As I expected, when we sent in the final billing, it was rejected because of the extras, which had kited the initial sum. I didn't waste time talking to the two jerks, I went right to the head of the agency. He turned out to be another pushcart peddler.

He had the gall to tell me that everybody was dissatisfied with our work. I didn't remind him that we were still holding the negative and sound track, I just tossed him the memos. From his reaction I could tell that those two damn fools hadn't even mentioned them. He read every memo, then looked at me over his glasses. "Real smart, aren't you? I guess you have me over a barrel." He gave not one word of apology. I went on to tell him that he would get his pictures when I received a certified check. No company check would do. He paid, but it was a bad experience. After that, even for old clients, we never did work that was not covered in the initial contract without a covering memo.

Our gross was now well over a half million dollars a year, but we had a working capital of less than $30,000. We were forever in hock to the factors. The first time we needed working capital, Joe Rosen had taken me to see three handsome old men, dressed in traditional black hats and suits. They had long beards and looked as if they came right out of the Old Testament. They seemed to have complete confidence in Joe and gave him whatever sum he asked for without question.

He used them reluctantly because they charged 10 percent interest. Since the banks were still refusing to extend credit on television spots, we had no choice.

Joe and I had been going to the three men for years, but they never talked to me except for a very formal greeting. They laughed and talked to Joe quite freely, but I was completely ignored. I wasn't angry about it, I just felt frustrated. Their attitude was easy to understand, because during the 1950s there was a great deal of anti-Semitism. They were just reacting in kind.

Once Joe Rosen gave me a very stern lecture about the future of the business. "A big overhead on a regular basis, and no fixed income of any kind is just Russian roulette. All the profits are being skimmed off by the union because the wages are too high and are not related to the market. You can't change that because you and the other producers have no clout.

"So build this company to a million-dollar gross and sell it for two hundred thousand. Then go out and buy yourself a potato farm in Idaho and forget this whole goddamn business. Otherwise, one day the law of averages will make you go broke."

I remembered Pepe's famous line during a heated contract negotiation, "We doan care if you go out of business. There is always some other damn fool who wanna be boss and take your place."

A few months after I arrived in New York I had started a producers organization. I thought that in addition to presenting a united front at contract time, we would be able to exchange information about the business and help each other. The latter idea never came about. As for negotiations, we couldn't stand even one week of a strike, so the negotiations were a charade. We were completely at the mercy of the union. Every year the wages were raised. When we tried to raise the price of spots, there was always some producer who put in a bid based on the old format, and took the work away from somebody who was trying to raise prices. There was absolutely no solidarity.

I took a good long look at the whole group at our next producer's meeting. We were a pack of ragtag entrepreneurs, doing millions of dollars worth of spots a year, yet I doubt if there was even $125,000 working capital in the entire group.

Here we were starting our annual fuming and swearing, saying that somehow, this year, we were going to make a firm stand against excessive union demands. Yet we all knew that the organization was a paper tiger caught between the union and the hard-nosed agencies who refused to allow us to raise prices.

Suddenly this atmosphere of impotent rage and frustration was too much for me. I decided to open a West Coast studio. At least there we wouldn't have to contend with Pepe and his goddamn jingoism. Eventually I would let Ruth Gench, Rod Johnson, and Irwin Wallman run the New York branch. Let them tangle with Ruiz. I already had a bellyful.

When I approached Joe Rosen with the idea, he thought I was mad. It would take at least $10,000 to gear up a new studio, leaving us with less than $20,000 to run the business in New York.

But I had good arguments on my side. We were always turning down work because there was no labor pool in New York. Everybody who was any good was working on a permanent basis.

From a psychological aspect, we could entice many agency people with the magic name of Hollywood. Once they started to travel there, the climate, the exotic atmosphere, and the extraordinary talent available would keep them coming back.

Grudgingly Rosen agreed to take the gamble. He went off to see the factors, and I opened negotiations with my old friend Bill Hurtz. Bill had gone to work at UPA as a designer, working with John Hubley and Bobo Cannon on such outstanding pictures as *Robin Hoodlum* and *Gerald McBoing Boing*. Hurtz's first film as a director was *A Unicorn in the*

Garden, from a story and illustrations by James Thurber. Bill, with great sensitivity, had managed to retain the charm of Thurber's drawings and his oddball humor. Altogether it was an amazingly fine job for a novice director.

UPA itself was amazing. Here was the greatest assemblage of talent in the country. Many of the stars on the staff were veterans of Frank Tashlin's great experiment at Screen Gems. Tashlin ran the studio in such a way that everybody had a free rein to explore the possibilities of new graphics and story material. However, he was running a business, not a playground, and the films were made within the budget and on schedule.

UPA was the same kind of environment, except that the talent had run amok. Neither Steve Bosustow, the executive producer, or Ade Woolcry, the production manager, could control the creative staff. At that time the studio had a contract with Columbia, which provided UPA with a 25 percent share of the profits. In the welter of pictures made with no consideration for the budget, frantic loans from banks, and weeks when there were no paychecks for the principals in the studio, Bosustow had to arrange loans from Columbia, which were in reality the loss of participation in the profits.

The studio was lumbering from chaos to catastrophy at a time when the rebellious staff was producing some of the most brilliant cartoons in the history of the business. This infantile disregard for money was inadvertently fueled by Steve Bosustow's greedy efforts to acquire more and more of the company's stock.

He must have been the only man in the organization who had a coat that matched his pants. So he took on the role of greeting guests, made speeches at various functions, and saw to it that when the studio won an award, it was he who strode to the podium and modestly thanked the donors in the name of UPA.

It may be that all this contributed to the need to overrun the budgets and watch Steve running around frantically trying to raise more money. The resulting danger to the studio was ignored by the artistic members of the staff. They were drunk on creativity, like a band of moths doing a Dionysian dance around the hot flame of reality. There never was a more mad juxtaposition of talent, anger, avarice, and infantilism.

When I offered Bill Hurtz the job of producer–director of our new studio, he was very hesitant. He wasn't sure that he could handle the work of running a business. I assured him that we would do all the bookkeeping in New York, make out all the salary checks, and pay the bills. In short, he was going to be free from all mundane business matters. All he would have to do was be creative, so finally he accepted.

We opened a very small studio, financed a camera for Bill (to Joe Rosen's anguish because it cost $15,000) and Shamus Culhane Productions, Hollywood, was an ongoing establishment. It couldn't miss. We sent Bill a steady stream of work from Chicago, Montreal, Toronto, and New York, enough to keep a small staff busy.

Almost immediately the studio started to bring in a fat profit, 10 percent, sometimes more. We were getting East Coast prices for our spots, but the salaries were lower in California, and the workweek five hours longer. It looked as if we had turned the corner at last. Hurtz even managed to pick up a few local spots. One series was from Saul Bass, the internationally known designer.

Bill was in his element. He and Bass turned out some of the most innovative spots on the air. Bill also won an Art Director's Award for a very inexpensive spot for Mitchell Beer which he designed as well as directed.

My gamble was a success in live-action too. By this time I was recognized as a very good live-action director, and we received more and more work in this area. I began to go out to Hollywood every few weeks with six or eight spots to shoot, with an agency account executive anxious to see and sample the fleshpots of Hollywood. If he did, it wasn't on my time. We were on the set before eight, worked all day, checked the rushes about seven, then redrew the storyboards when it was necessary, and rarely got to dinner before ten o'clock.

We had found that even with the added travel expense we could bring in live spots cheaper in Hollywood. In spite of the fact that the basic union crew required two more men than New York crews, the work was done faster and more efficiently. The East Coast people were already beginning to slow down in the afternoon in order to force the producer into overtime. There was excessive drinking at lunch, and other behavior calculated to drive the motion picture business out of New York.

We usually made a profit of 15 percent or more on our live-action. In all the years we worked on animation in New York our annual profit was never over five percent, usually we broke even, and in the early years before we settled down to a methodical approach to our work, we lost money.

* * *

During the decade of the 1940s, the United States was suffering from a severe shortage of scientists. In 1951 the Bell Telephone System, which is made up of eighteen or twenty separate companies, decided to do something to foster interest in science among the young students in school as well as the general public.

Bell turned to its advertising agency, N. W. Ayer, for some advice on the best way to mount such a project. Harry Batton, a veteran adman, thought of the idea of producing a series of hour-long science films. After they were shown on TV, the prints would be made available gratis to the school systems of the country as a public service.

All three networks turned down the project, and even in the agency nobody seemed enthusiastic except Don Jones. Therefore, he was assigned to the project and the job of assembling a production unit to produce the films. His choice of Frank Capra as producer–director was particularly astute, because in addition to being one of the most famous directors in the world, Capra had graduated from Cal Tech as a chemical engineer.

A board of advisors was selected from among the most outstanding scientists in the country, and Frank Capra chose Dr. Frank Baxter to star in the series. Baxter, a former science teacher, had just come into the spotlight in a low-budget series on local TV in Hollywood. He was an impassioned teacher with a very attractive personality. Soon his science programs attracted national attention.

Capra's first film, *Our Mr. Sun,* was an artful combination of stock shots from observatories, live-action, and a large section of animation. Bell had no trouble in getting access to prime time after it was finished. *Our Mr. Sun* received rave reviews. The animation had been done at UPA, and was almost a year in production. During that time Frank Capra had worked very closely with UPA and especially Bill Hurtz.

By the time Capra's staff had written a script for the next Bell Science special, Hurtz had already moved from UPA to our studio. The UPA crew had done an excellent job on *Our Mr. Sun,* and normally this next film, *Hemo the Magnificent,* would have gone to them. But Capra had especially liked Hurtz. He had so much confidence in Bill Hurtz's direction that he awarded our company the contract for the animation of *Hemo.*

The picture featured Hemo as a Greek God who was worshiped by the animals as the essence of all life. He jeered at the possibility that Dr.

Dr. Frank Baxter and Richard Carlson are amused as Hemo ridicules the idea that humans could ever understand the complexities of the human body. From *Hemo the Magnificent. Bell Telephone System.* Produced and directed by Frank Capra.

Professor Anatomy lectures the audience on the mechanism of the heart. From *Hemo the Magnificent, Bell Telephone System.*

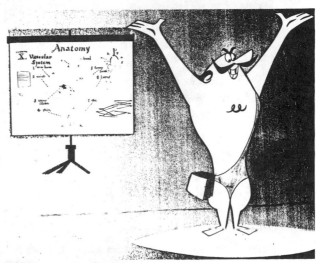

The nervous system responds to an emergency in *Hemo the Magnificent. Bell Telephone System.*

Baxter and actor Richard Carlson understood the functions of blood in the body. Capra very clearly made the two men answer Hemo's jibes by offering in rebuttal vital information in the form of slides, highly magnified motion picture photography of the blood stream, and of course many animated examples of the bodily functions, lungs, kidneys, heart, et cetera.

Some of the best teaching material was animated, especially one sequence that explained the function of the valves of the heart in such a simple yet amusing way that a six-year-old child could understand it.

About half the picture was animation, so suddenly Hurtz's small staff zoomed to forty people. We had to move the studio to a two-story building with its own parking lot. The news of our association with Frank Capra enabled us to attract some of the best talent in Hollywood. Ben Washam, a star animator, formerly with Chuck Jones' unit at Warners, Tony Rivera, one of the top storyboard artists in town, and well-seasoned workers in every department . . . with the exception of management. I repeated the same mistake I had made in New York. Hurtz did not have a business manager. Neither did he have an advisor at his elbow like Joe Rosen. I left him up the creek without a paddle. Without even a Peter Drukker book.

The first time I met Frank Capra he was sitting in front of a moviola in our new cutting room, looking at some pencil tests of *Hemo*. He had started in the business as an editor, and he was running the machine as if he were in the Indianapolis 500. Every movement was twice as fast as normal.

When Bill introduced us I was struck by the fact that Capra had a pair of eyes as black and piercing as Picasso's, but he had a very relaxed and informal manner. Afterward we went to the story department, and Bill briefed us on Tony Rivera's latest storyboards. Hurtz has one of the smoothest deliveries in the business. He made a Sotheby auctioneer sound like a street hawker.

Through Bill's lecture Capra sat very quietly. He was looking at the drawings with evident admiration, nodding his head in approval as Hurtz pointed out salient graphic ideas he had added to the script.

In the discussion that followed I could tell that Capra was very familiar with the terminology of animation. Not only had he spent a great deal of time at UPA during the production of *Our Mr. Sun,* but he had also used various types of animation in his training films during the war. He

Dr. Frank Baxter (left) fingers a puppet caricature of Dostoevski held by master puppeteer Bil Baird as Richard Carlson looks on. In the background are puppets of Charles Dickens and Edgar Allan Poe, and the set used in the production of *The Strange Case of the Cosmic Rays*. A Frank Capra Production. *Bell Telephone System.*

Producer–director Frank Capra (center) discusses with Richard Carlson (right) and Dr. Baxter details for a scene in *The Strange Case of the Cosmic Rays. Bell Telephone System.*

is the only director of world stature who has such a sound knowledge of animation.

Capra was very popular with our crew because he never threw his weight around and always remained relaxed and very informal. However, there was a latent intensity about him which indicated that when it was necessary, Capra had an explosive Sicilian temper. He never had to use it in our studio because everybody was doing the best possible work. Obviously we were competing with UPA, and the outstanding success of *Our Mr. Sun*.

Hemo was a very difficult picture in that the production was full of crowd shots. Hemo trailed a large group of animals after him, and no matter how skillfully Hurtz composed the film, these animal shots could not be avoided. In spite of many technical problems the picture was finished on schedule.

When *Hemo the Magnificent* was shown on television the film received an avalanche of favorable criticism. Enthusiastic articles were written about the possible use of this format of entertainment and information in every branch of education. In every way it was a better picture than *Our Mr. Sun*. The Bell System began to be deluged by requests from schools for the use of prints. Years later I learned through Bell's publicity department that the film had been seen by more than a hundred million schoolchildren.

There was one difficulty in that Capra and Hurtz had worked out a bonus system in addition to the flat sum we received in the contract. It was obviously an attempt on Capra's part to see that we were not underpaid. We were given additional money for footage with three characters, a higher rate for shots with four, and so on. It looked fine on paper, but it deprived us of the day-by-day analysis of our financial position which Rosen and I had worked out for TV spots.

It was only when the final accounting was made, weeks after the picture was finished, that we found that *Hemo* had lost a great deal of money. By that time we were well into our second picture for Bell, *The Strange Case of the Cosmic Rays*. Over Joe Rosen's loud protests, I decided not to talk to Capra about our losses on *Hemo* even though the same system of bonuses was going to be used again. On Madison Avenue, asking for additional money to cover production losses was verboten. Although we had been hired by Capra, recoupment could only have been arranged by N. W. Ayer, so the possibility of getting additional money was miniscule. Besides I believed that Bill Hurtz was entitled to learn by his own experience. I felt that it was enough to tell him how much we had lost without recriminations.

Capra decided that he would try another format in *Cosmic Rays,* a combination of live-action, stock shots, animation, and puppets. Not stop-motion puppets—these were going to be puppets on strings.

Bil Baird, one of the world's greatest puppeteers, was given this assignment. I was fascinated when I visited his studio on New York's West Side. He owned a brownstone which he had converted to a puppet factory. He made his own puppets, and his wife designed their clothing, so the studio looked like a weird combination of machine shop and dressmaking establishment.

There were rooms with racks full of puppets of every size and shape, looking so lifelike that one expected them to be chatting away and gesticulating. One little figure impressed me very much. He was in a very acute stage of tumescence. I never did find out what role he played.

Baird designed three of the main characters in *Cosmic Rays:* Charles Dickens, Edgar Allan Poe, and Fedor Dostoevski. They acted as a jury to evaluate the methods used in the solving of the mystery of cosmic rays as good story material.

The choice of Bil Baird as puppeteer was greatly influenced by the fact that Bil and his wife, Cora, had just completed a nine-part television series on arithmetic. *Adventures in Numbers and Space* was far from being an academic course in math. The ideas that the Bairds presented were enlivened with gags, music, and the antics of two of Baird's puppets, Sparky and Gargle. In spite of the witty approach, Baird managed to expose his audience to a whole spectrum of math, starting with simple numbers and going on to very complex ideas, like the function of computers.

The series was successful to the extent that any science programs can be successful on television. Broadcasters know that science programs will never draw as large an audience as a straight entertainment show. This makes for a reluctance on the part of the networks to accept programs with educational value, since their yardstick is the size of the audience rather than its quality.

Then, too, Baird's approach, and Capra's for that matter, is not popular with a large number of educators in this country. The old idea that knowledge can only be gained by suffering and discipline is still prevalent in educational circles in this most Puritanical nation. Baird's unique talents as an educator and entertainer are not welcome in Academia.

In a recent talk with Bil Baird, I asked him why he had no interest in stop-motion animation. "Stop-motion animation is not subtle enough for me. For example, when a character stops, it becomes dead. Working on a figure with strings, even when it is quiet, there is always a certain amount of movement, however slight, which keeps the figure very much alive."

Then I remembered that when the puppet jury was on the screen, Poe and Dickens seemed quiescent, but Dostoevski listened with mounting impatience as the actors talked. This was accomplished by a minimum amount of movement, which was followed by a burst of sardonic Slavic comment with very brusque gestures. It was a perfect example of what Baird was talking about, because in spite of a lack of movement on the part of Poe and Dickens, they were projecting a feeling of quiet intensity.

Again Richard Carlson worked with Dr. Baxter. Together they tried to convince the jury that the manner in which the cosmic rays were tracked down was worthy of their attention. This was done by Baxter demonstrating various scientific instruments, and Carlson calling on a magic screen to illustrate his part of the information.

Unlike *Hemo,* where the designers had functional parts of the body to illustrate, the information about cosmic rays was almost completely abstract, so Capra fell back on a dizzy assortment of characters. There were bank robbers and a symbol of ultraviolet rays who looked like Mae West, bowing to Dickens. Cosmic rays were depicted as Fagin, the archthief; and a number of equally bizarre figures. In this aspect alone, the designing of this film was probably the most difficult job of its kind ever attempted. Animation proved to be the right medium to cope with the examination of abstract ideas and invisible forces.

While the picture was still in production, we had an offer from Saul Bass. He wanted Bill Hurtz to produce and direct the credit titles for Mike Todd's feature film *Around the World in Eighty Days.*

Todd had gotten himself into a bind by hiring a bevy of movie stars to do cameo bits in his picture. When he finished the shooting he was faced with a mind-bending situation . . . who was going to get top billing? Movie stars are notoriously implacable about credits; their position in relation to other stars, and even the size of the lettering on the titles, is of utmost importance to them.

Todd solved his dilemma by hiring Saul Bass to design animated titles in which the names appeared in chronological order, thus saving everybody's face and his neck. As usual the schedule was too short. Besides we would have to jury-rig our animation camera with a special lens in order to shoot in wide-screen. Bill thought he could handle all the difficulties and still get Capra's film out on schedule. Anyhow, it looked too intriguing a job to pass up.

Everybody in Hollywood knew that Mike Todd had made the picture on a shoestring (probably somebody else's) and was very short of money at this point. He also had the reputation of not paying his bills on time, if ever.

Soon I received a phone call from a very excited Bill Hurtz. Todd had come to the studio, looked at Bill's guileless face, and offered to do the titles with us without a contract. Just a "friendly handshake." I would have preferred to shake hands with a giant squid.

We settled for a less friendly arrangement. Todd was to send us cash every Monday for the payroll for that week. The contract bristled with penalties, including the stopping of all work on the project if cash (not checks) was not forthcoming every week before the close of the business day on Monday.

We made the titles, and Todd dutifully sent the money on time. When the composite print was finished, it was delivered to Mike Todd's office, but not handed over until the messenger had the last cash payment in his hand. Then some idiot in the cutting room sent Todd the negative before we, in New York, discovered that the rascal had not included the sales tax in the payment. Of course he blandly ignored our subsequent billing. Under California law, if the buyer does not pay the tax, the seller is liable, so the bastard beat us out of almost three thousand dollars!

Many years later I met S. J. Perelman. He told me that when he was working on *Eighty Days,* every night he held the finished pages in one hand until Todd put the requisite cash in the other. We both agreed that a pirate like Mike Todd should have been ridden out of Hollywood on the end of a pointed stick.

In spite of my fury at being screwed out of the money, I was pleased with the result. The titles were so well received that they opened up a whole new area of the movie business. Saul Bass and Bill Hurtz had set a new standard for titles. Heretofore, the titles had been some of the cheapest footage in a picture. Now, when one sees the lavish artwork in

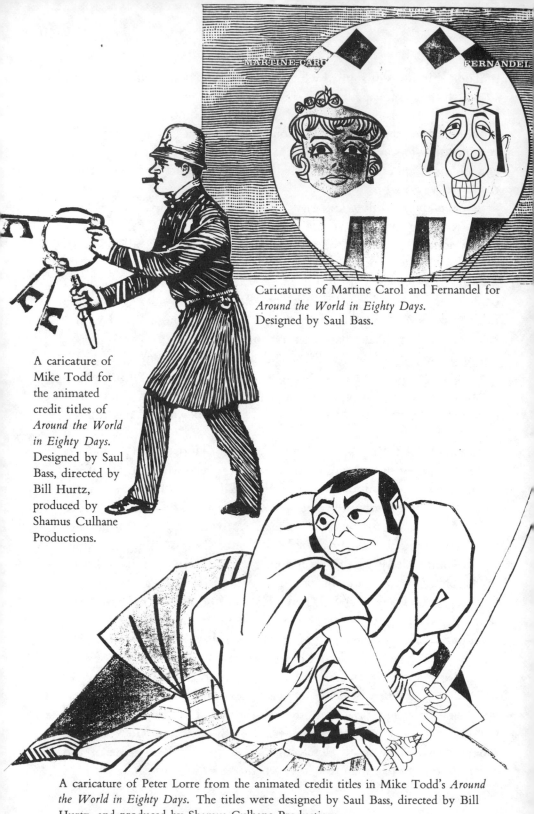

Caricatures of Martine Carol and Fernandel for *Around the World in Eighty Days*. Designed by Saul Bass.

A caricature of Mike Todd for the animated credit titles of *Around the World in Eighty Days*. Designed by Saul Bass, directed by Bill Hurtz, produced by Shamus Culhane Productions.

A caricature of Peter Lorre from the animated credit titles in Mike Todd's *Around the World in Eighty Days*. The titles were designed by Saul Bass, directed by Bill Hurtz, and produced by Shamus Culhane Productions.

the James Bond titles, for example, it is interesting to remember that all this started with a con man's dilemma.

While Bill Hurtz was producing his blockbusters with Frank Capra, our New York studio was producing live-action and animated spots of such fine quality that we dominated the field. A trade paper took a survey among the twenty most active spot buyers, asking each one for their choice of the six best producers. Our company was the only film studio to be listed by all twenty buyers.

One of the tactical errors I made at this time was to allow the Hollywood studio to stop making television spots. All of our income from the coast had to come from the Bell series, or special projects like Mike Todd's titles. Joe Rosen was very uneasy at this turn of events and kept reminding me that this was not our original plan.

One day during a production meeting, Rod Johnson mentioned idly that he had heard that Norman Ferguson was no longer at Disney's. My jaw dropped. I remembered with a pang that Fergie once said that when he became too old to animate, he'd take a job in the Disney parking lot.

I called Bill Hurtz on the teletype immediately and told him to hire Fergie if he was available. A few hours later I received a call from Fergie, a scarcely recognizable voice, tired and listless. He timidly asked if he could have two hundred dollars a week. I was stunned! The greatest pantomimist in the business asking for two hundred dollars?

I told him that his starting salary was three hundred, and he was going to head a special unit producing TV spots. In fact I had a special spot for him to begin with. It was a highly experimental job using animated paper cutout figures, and we'd have to jury-rig our camera to get a multiplane effect. The film was part of a series of Alka Seltzer spots, which I would be shooting in Hollywood the following week.

Alka-Seltzer was one of our exclusive accounts. We did all the pictures for their television campaigns without having to submit competitive bids, a gross of at least $175,000 a year. Since the account was all ours we broke our necks on every spot. The cutout paper technique was my idea, and because it was far removed from anything the company had tried before, I was anxious to make it another award winner.

When I arrived in Hollywood I was shocked at Ferguson's appearance. He was extremely lethargic and without enthusiasm. I attributed it to the psychological jolt he must have received when he left Disney's. I decided that it must be too painful a subject to discuss, because Fergie never mentioned how he came to leave, so I never asked him about the circumstances. We got right down to business since I was going to start shooting the next morning. The spot was already laid out and the track made, so with a minimum of instructions I left him to his own devices.

Even in those early days I was making a shooting storyboard, which enabled me to turn out as many as four to five minute-spots in a day. Because of my editing experience in animation I never leaned hard on the editor. What I drew was pretty much what we ended up with in the final cut.

It took me two weeks to finish my spots, and when I got around to Fergie it seemed to me that he had accomplished little except for rigging the camera. Since he had another four weeks to go, I wasn't worried. However, before I left for New York I asked him to send me some sample rushes as soon as possible.

Two weeks went by and I hadn't seen a foot of film, so I called him up. To my horror nothing had been shot. Besides, Fergie sounded confused, almost irrational. He couldn't promise me a completion date. The whole Alka-Seltzer account was being jeopardized, but to my consternation Fergie didn't seem to be able to rise to the emergency. He was in a fog.

Reluctantly, I told him he would have to go. Fergie wasn't surprised or resentful. It was as if he expected it. The next day he had a heart attack and died. I only learned a long time later that Fergie had been a diabetic for years. He must have been very close to going into a diabetic coma all those weeks, a sad end for a great artist.

After Fergie's death I made no effort to establish a TV spot department, in spite of Rosen's repeated warnings that we needed the spots as a kind of insurance. Hurtz had months of work ahead of him, so I ignored Joe's advice.

One aspect of Madison Avenue that I chose to ignore was the practice of bribery. Almost from the beginning of the spot business we heard rumors that this accountant executive or another was "on the take." Some of these people were very well-known figures in the business.

Not all of them wanted money. For some, a luscious hundred–dollar–a–night whore would do the trick (no pun intended). I heard of one agency producer who was on a shoot in Miami. He blandly informed the director that he had come without a wardrobe.

The Shamus Culhane Productions Christmas card for 1958. Designed by Chris Ishii.

Carl S. Brown, head of Sherman and Marquette Advertising in the 1940s and 1950s.

He proceeded to go through the most expensive men's shops on Miami Beach, bought clothes and two suitcases. The bill was forwarded to the director, a fairly modest $1,500.

The first instruction I gave any salesman we hired was that under no circumstances was he to consider giving bribes, not in the form of presents, women, or cash. If he didn't believe that our exhibition reel was good enough to earn him a living he shouldn't accept the job.

Several job applicants scoffed at this stiff-necked attitude, pointing out that it wouldn't cost us anything. My rejoinder was that in effect we would be stealing the money from the client, and the interview would end right there.

The only time I was involved in a direct confrontation with a bribe taker came about when I was called by an agency producer in one of the largest ad agencies in town. He asked me to bid on a series of spots. He was sending the storyboards by messenger. When I had arrived at a figure I was to go over to discuss the bid.

When I arrived, he was very cordial, looked over the numbers and announced that I could raise my bid by a thousand dollars and still get the job. I was very pleased at his honesty. Here was an agency man who was looking out for the creative people.

During the next few months he gave us several more jobs, and in each case told me to raise my bid by a substantial amount. I began to be puzzled because I was bidding within my usual price range, and we were one of the most expensive studios in town.

I guess he must have finally become impatient at my obtuseness because he invited me to lunch. After we finished our meal and some desultory shoptalk, he broached the subject, that is, what did I think of kickbacks?

I gave him my opinion with some heat. A few days before I had fired a salesman for disregarding my house rules; he had hired a whore for a client. When I recounted this incident he nodded sympathetically. He agreed that buying whores was a very disgusting practice.

By this time we were out of the restaurant and had arrived at his corner. We shook hands and instead of the usual farewell, he hurriedly said, "I agree with you. Most of the guys are hogs. Me, I only want six percent." I looked at him with such disgust, that he spun on his heel and went into his building.

A few days later, I called in my top salesman to find out why he was having such a bad month. He burst into a furious tirade. "What are you

asking me such a dumb question like that for? Of course I'm having a
bad month. How the hell can I compete with the Good Guys?"

"Good Guys? Who are they?"

"My God! Do I have to spell it out? Good Guys pay off, Bad Guys
don't, and believe me you are on everybody's shit list."

He assured me that if I would agree to payola he'd be back before day's
end with at least five spots; when I turned him down, he quit.

I sat there for a long time after, wondering if the whole world was
out of step except me, or vice versa?

A few days later I was sitting in a corner of a very posh restaurant near
Madison Avenue, waiting for a client. The World Series was on, and a
group of men at the bar were enthusiastically reacting as they watched
the game on television.

Suddenly I was hit by a wave of anguish. I had been in this business
more than ten years, but I wasn't a part of it. The whole room was full
of men dressed in medium gray suits, white shirts and narrow dark ties,
and everybody had a short haircut. I wore my usual mismatched sport
coat and pants, an open-collared silk shirt, and espadrilles. I must have
looked like a freak.

In a way I was. I hadn't made a serious drawing in years. I couldn't
remember what it felt like to stand in front of an easel waiting for that
sudden burst of energy. Instead I was an imitation businessman scurrying
around the country making deals.

Joe Rosen couldn't believe it when I told him that I was going to stay
home one day a week and draw. I tried to explain that a part of me was
starving. I needed to be an artist once again.

Rosen brushed my arguments aside as sheer self-indulgence. I was
going to need all my energies to cope with an increasingly desperate
situation. We had grossed well over a million dollars but our profits had
been dented badly by another huge loss. This time on *Cosmic Rays*.

I should immediately go to the coast and talk to Capra about an
adjustment, then stay there and direct the next picture. I refused. We
never had been able to recoup a loss from an agency. In fact we lost
several accounts that way. Here was a series that was going to go on for
years and I wasn't about to jeopardize it.

As for Bill Hurtz, if I took the work away from him he would
probably quit; not only was he a good friend but he was too valuable

to the organization to lose. Anyhow I was sure that he would be able to control his money on the next Bell Science picture, *The Unchained Goddess.*

Rosen curtly prophesized that if we lost money on this third picture, all the profits we made in New York would not be enough to save the company. I didn't believe him. After all, we had gone through some hazardous times before and always managed to survive.

Soon after, Joe Rosen quit. It was a mortal blow to the studio. He was much more than an accountant, Rosen was a highly creative businessman. For eleven years Joe had rescued me from one rash act after the other. He loved the studio because he had helped to create it, but, as he told me bluntly, no company he ever worked for had ever gone out of business, and he wasn't about to spoil his record.

Joe's leaving did not change my plans. Every Wednesday I hired a model and worked at home for eight hours. I refused to accept any calls from the studio, no matter if an emergency arose. One time my secretary, Jo-Ann Cuff, had made a time study of my work. We found that I had to make a decision about every eight minutes. Now for 20 percent of the workweek I was not available.

The Strange Case of the Cosmic Rays, while it was hailed as a very good picture, did not have the appeal of *Our Mr. Sun* or *Hemo the Magnificent.* Possibly, cosmic rays were too esoteric a subject for the television audience.

The Enchanted Goddess was a return to the old format of live-action and animation. The film was about the weather, and it featured a sultry little sexpot goddess who flirted with Dr. Baxter and Richard Carlson. Without the crowds of animals we had to draw for *Hemo,* and the intricate designs of abstract animation which made *Cosmic Rays* so difficult, it looked as if we could make a good profit for the first time.

There were rumors that Frank Capra and the N. W. Ayer agency were not getting on very well. Capra had made it very plain from the start that he would brook no interference from the agency. There would be no holding up production while an agency man looked through the camera, and certainly no control over the script.

Capra was used to working in an opulent manner. He would call Don Jones, the agency producer, and casually mention that he had need for another day's shooting. He always had a good reason, a new lab shot had been found, which was going to necessitate a change in the script, or whatever. Like Walt Disney, Capra believed in keeping the picture malleable right down to the finish, until he was satisfied with it.

Many times Don Jones would have to go back to all the Bell companies and ask for more money, usually ten or twenty thousand dollars. He might just as well have asked for a pound of bone marrow from each chairman of the board. While Jones managed to get the money, there was grumbling on both sides.

In 1957 we almost started to produce a feature picture. Several years before, a group of motion picture exhibitors had banded together to go into the business of producing feature pictures themselves. Their first venture was buying the rights to produce *Finian's Rainbow* as an animated cartoon.

Their choice of a production house was John and Faith Hubley's Storyboard Productions. By this time John and Faith had racked up a number of awards for TV commercials in addition to some outstanding short subjects, and John's background as the top director at UPA, when that studio was at its height.

The Hubleys accepted the deal with great enthusiasm. Not only were the songs in *Finian's Rainbow* unusually good, but the main character was a leprechaun, ideal for an animated cartoon.

The contract they were offered was a step deal, that is, one sum of money was advanced for the production of a sound track and storyboard. If they proved to be satisfactory, the Hubleys would be advanced additional monies toward the production, which, however, would not cover the entire cost. The Hubleys would have to raise some of the money themselves.

Ade Woolery, former production manager of UPA, ruefully recalls that the directors used to go far over their budgets at the start of a picture. By the time the office found out about the situation, there was no choice but to raise additional money for completion. It was either that or junk the picture, which of course could not be done.

One of the chief exponents of this budget-busting technique seems to have been John Hubley. According to the exhibitor's representative, he did it again on *Finian's Rainbow*.

When I was given the story sketches and the sound track to evaluate I found that the Hubleys had created a remarkably concise version of the play in motion picture form, and the design of the characters was an animator's delight.

Furthermore, the drawings were as nothing to the sound track. The Hubleys had managed to hire Frank Sinatra, Ella Fitzgerald, Louis Armstrong, David Wayne, Barry Fitzgerald, and Oscar Peterson—far better talent than Walt Disney had ever assembled for a feature picture.

The exhibitors became so alarmed at Hubley's disregard for the limitations of the budget for this material that they canceled his contract. Now they were stuck with a storyboard and sound track, so they were looking for a producer to finish the picture. They had one stipulation: the Hubley's were not to have anything to do with the production.

At face value it looked like a dazzling opportunity. However, when my attorney began to unfold the complications of the contract, we found that it was a nightmare of percentages. If the picture grossed a certain amount, Sinatra got an additional percentage. If the profit was higher, he received more. The same held true for all the other people involved. They had all been hired at a very low salary, so low that it must have been a pittance compared to their normal income on a picture. Nobody would say who had entangled the potential profits in such a bizarre fashion.

The exhibitors proved to be remarkably reluctant to give us all this vital information. Every few days (after assuring us that we had all the figures), we would get a phone call and still another stipulation was revealed. Finally we pried all the facts out of them and began to look for the additional production money, the sum we would have to raise ourselves.

Our first prospect was a young Greek shipping magnate. He came to a meeting, my accountant rattled off the percentages, and the Greek did all the equations in his head. In a few minutes he was satisfied that the figures were favorable.

He asked if we had been in touch with a distributor. I was in the process of explaining that we hadn't because we wanted to go in with a production deal all wrapped up, but my salesman interrupted, "Oh, that reminds me, I was talking about that this morning, but I forgot to mention it. The exhibitors want to distribute the picture themselves."

Our erstwhile investor stood up and reached for his Borsalino. "Do you people realize that Paramount, Warners, and the other majors supply exhibitors with films all year around. These damn fools are going to come into the market with just one feature? Hell, they don't even know their own business! Forget it." We did. Somewhere on a shelf in somebody's office is a marvelous collection of story sketches and the best sound track ever recorded for an animated cartoon.

Nobody realized it, but we were about to enter a period in the economy that has been called the Eisenhower Depression. In the early days of 1957 a wave of uneasiness swept through the business in New York. There were persistent rumors that clandestine groups of employees were secretly bidding against the producers, and animating spots at night and on weekends.

Any investigation of this blatant breach of the union contract proved to be impossible. The producers were unable to get any employee to give solid evidence, names, dates, etcetera. The Producers Organization sent a delegation to Pepe Ruiz to complain about this undercover work which, coupled with a sudden drop in the number of TV spots in production, was threatening the very fabric of the business in New York. Pepe smiled like a Cheshire cat and assured us that "Nobody in the union is taking jobs away from you."

The agency boys put up a solid wall of secrecy about their relationship with the clandestine workers. What the hell, they were getting first-class spots for cheap.

One month we bid on $30,000 worth of spots and didn't get one. A few months later they appeared on the market. When I checked with the other producers, several of them had bid on the same spots, but none of the studios with union contracts had produced any.

I called a meeting of our entire staff and talked about this underground work force and the amount of work that was being siphoned off from legitimate channels. They looked at me with miserable faces, but were tight-lipped. Nobody was going to be a stool pigeon. It was a weird situation.

In a misguided feeling of solidarity with their fellow union members, they were confused enough to take a passive position in a situation that threatened their jobs. On the other hand, there still was the strong emotional bond between us. They expected me to get the work that paid their rent and fed their kids. Somehow, since I was the authority figure, I should be able to cope with this or any other situation. Psychologically, they could not accept the fact that I was helpless.

I blew up. Angrily, I pointed out that the only new work we had picked up in the last month was a $1,500 job from Canada, which was not enough to pay our phone bill. They remained silent, so I curtly closed the meeting and they filed out sullenly.

Months later, after the harm was done, one of the animators who had worked at the now defunct UPA branch in New York told me of one example of this kind of piracy. Without the knowledge of the executives, almost the entire staff of UPA had worked one weekend around the clock. They finished a TV spot using the company's equipment and supplies, and made a huge profit. Why not? In this way there were no welfare payments to the union, no taxes, vacation, sick pay, or other trivia.

Frantically we turned our efforts to getting more live-action business, but even in that area the market was drying up at a frightening rate. Out of the blue we were given an offer that seemed like every producer's dream. The *Saturday Evening Post* was in serious difficulties. It had acquired the reputation of being a "barbershop magazine." In spite of valiant efforts, such as hiring better-known writers and featuring articles that were aimed at women as well as men, the advertising income was dwindling.

The new manager of the *Post* realized that he would have to do something startling and effective to coax old clients back to the magazine. He approached me with a plan. For $100,000 we were to write and produce a film that would be the perfect image of the *Post* as a revitalized magazine. We would be given carte blanche with the proviso that we include in the script a number of technical sales points, namely, how many people read the magazine, cost of a page of advertising, and the like.

It all sounded too technical for the average scriptwriter to cope with, so I hired an economist, Peggy Kenas, to see to it that the script duly promoted the sales points.

We decided to make a film that was a spoof on the usual way that magazines drummed up business. Normally a salesman was given a territory to cover. He would hire a restaurant in the area, invite all the local advertising managers to a free lunch, and carefully dole out drinks. Then in a happy haze of calories and alcohol, they would be treated to a sales pitch, which was usually accompanied by slides. I even went to such a presentation just to see what it was like, and it was pretty dull.

Our film was far from dull. We hired Orson Bean as the lead. I had seen Bean in the nightclubs and enjoyed his act because he played the role of an earnest but incredibly stupid young man. Our picture opened with

Bean struggling into a buckskin suit, at the same time that he was being briefed by the sales manager in Philadelphia. He was explaining that every time the *Post* had sent a salesman out west to Ulcer Gulch, he was shot. This was going to be a golden opportunity for Bean to become a star salesman.

You could see Bean's brain trying to equate the bullet holes in the suit with a dazzling career. Finally he clapped his coonskin hat on his head and off he went to the Far West. The Ad Club in Ulcer Gulch is a saloon full of cowboys, Indians, and assorted hoodlums. Bean is mistaken for a local bandit, and soon finds himself making his sales pitch from the top of the bar, with a hangman's noose chafing his neck. From that vantage point he proceeds to give a perfectly legitimate pitch about the advantages of advertising in the *Saturday Evening Post*.

We used Mike Todd's approach for *Around the World in Eighty Days*. There were cameo bits by various movie stars throughout the film. Salome Gens was a luscious tart, who took a fancy to Orson Bean. Chico Marx played tunes in his own inimitable way on the tinny piano. Edie Adams acted an irate housewife as she dragged Ernie Kovaks away from the bar, and at one point the sales pitch was illustrated by a little skit by Bob Hope and Bing Crosby. Even Groucho Marx added a few bad puns to the script.

The crowd in the saloon is so mesmerized by Bean's earnest delivery that he is cheered to the echo. Indians, cowboys, barflies, and roughnecks start to write out checks for double-page spreads. The film ends with Bean clasped to Salome's ample bosom as a shower of checks rain down on him.

The *Saturday Evening Post* people had a screening of *Showdown at Ulcer Gulch* at the Plaza Hotel. The audience was composed of the top advertising managers in the New York area, as well as many presidents of large corporations. It was a blue-chip crowd.

The script was full of trade gags that would have been lost on the average audience, but had these professionals rolling in the aisles. I counted thirty laughs in twenty-five minutes of screen time.

When the film was over the ad manager of Texaco walked over to the *Post*'s producer and clapped him on the back. "I wasn't sure whether we should set up our next campaign with you people or *Life*, but by God you've sold me on your new approach." The Texaco campaign more than paid for the film.

People in the ad business have told me that *Ulcer Gulch* was one of

Peggy Kenas, head of the studio's sales department, Maxine Marx, Shamus Culhane, and Dave Easton, the company's attorney, at the premier screening of *Showdown at Ulcer Gulch*. 1957.

the most successful promotional films ever made. It certainly opened marvelous prospects for our studio. It also was an opportunity to show just how foolish and reckless I was. In spite of the fact that we were very short of cash, I lavishly spent money on *Ulcer Gulch* because it was going to be our sample reel in a whole new business. When the picture was finished I had used up all the profits in the production.

This is a sample of the recklessness that had driven Joe Rosen to quit. Our cash position was terrible, yet I ignored the reality of the situation in favor of looking into the future, as if somehow there was a guaranteed happy ending for every crisis we confronted. We should have made at least $20,000, instead we had nothing in the bank to show for our work.

If we had been in a different cash position there would have been more than a grain of truth in my decision. With *Ulcer Gulch* as a sample, we could now compete for large promotional films. These were the most lucrative jobs in commercial filmmaking. Our studio had a tremendous advantage over most of the studios in the field because with the exception of Jam Handy, in Detroit, none of them had animation departments. We could offer ideas that were suitable for live-action, animation, or a combination of both.

Our run of good luck wasn't over. Early in the year two ex-MGM directors, Bill Hanna and Joe Barbera, had made a deal with Columbia for a series of children's TV shows. They were now in the process of hiring a huge staff. My salesmen were looking for a similar deal. They found one at Interstate Television. We were offered $800,000 for 195 five-minute cartoons.

There was a catch. The first ten pictures would have to be financed by our company. Joe Rosen would never have agreed to this stipulation, but I did. When I went to our old factors, they turned me down. Joe they trusted, but not a meshuggeneh goy in a beret.

Next I went to a bank. The bank manager, in a fatherly tone, told me to close down while I was still solvent. Then our newest salesman said that he knew two factors who would put up the money, but the interest was going to be 25 percent.

It didn't sound too bad because as soon as we finished the first ten we would be reimbursed, plus $75,000 advance production money.

I disliked the two new factors on sight. One looked like a broiled lobster, and the other like your friendly neighborhood troll. They insisted on a deal that supplied us with money for the payroll of $13,000 a week, but not one cent for overhead. As the troll archly put it, "That way, Mr. Culhane, you will be personally involved.

Unless we made a profit on *The Unchained Goddess* or brought in some other work, my savings were going to vanish like piss on a hot rock. What the hell, I had gambled before, so I signed a contract with Interstate and closed a deal with the factors.

Of all the attempts to write children's shows for TV, Jay Ward's *Crusader Rabbit* was by far the best. Shortly before we met, Ward had sold the rights to *Crusader Rabbit* and was looking for work. We hired him to develop a series about two bumbleheaded detectives . . . no violence, rather a Laurel and Hardy approach.

Ward had just started to work on his scripts, and Bill Hurtz was in the final stages of production on *The Unchained Goddess,* when Frank Capra inadvertently pulled the rug from under us. He announced that he was retiring from the Bell Science series. What the hell was I going to do with forty or fifty employees, to say nothing of my parking lot!

I rushed down to Philadelphia to put in my bid for the remainder of the series. When I arrived at N. W. Ayer, instead of discussing the situation with Don Jones, the producer, I had to talk to a man I had never met. He was a pompous pipsqueak who obviously knew nothing about the films, or the role we had played in their production. He flatly refused to even consider us as a part of the realignment.

The work was going to a large studio that had facilities for both live-action and animation. I finally pried out of him the news that the series was going to Warner Brothers. When I pointed out that I had a larger staff of animators than Warners he obviously didn't believe me. Three years of experience on this highly specialized animation was brushed aside as of little consequence. I doubt that he had ever seen the pictures.

N. W. Ayer did give the work to Warners, and they turned out a turkey. Later they gave the work to Disney, but nobody seemed to be able to cope with the combination of live-action and animation as well as Bill Hurtz. *Hemo the Magnificent* was never topped. To this day it is the most popular film in the Bell Science series.

To add to our problems *The Unchained Goddess* lost another huge sum, and Jay Ward and I did not agree on his approach to the Interstate series. There was absolutely no work to be had in New York. I was faced with a painful problem, lay off the staff in New York, or close the Hollywood studio.

There really wasn't too much choice. The New York staff had worked for me for twelve years and had put us in the forefront of the spot business. I couldn't close the shop down. It would have been a hell of a reward for their efforts.

In November 1958, my Hollywood studio closed. I was glad that I was three thousand miles away when it happened, because the emotional factors involved were too great to handle face-to-face.

There was no chance that I would put anybody on the dole. Hanna-Barbera was hiring everybody who could hold a pencil. Jay Ward got himself a contract for a new series, and Bill Hurtz works for him as a director to this day.

We sent for the half-completed artwork for our series and settled down to the grim business of survival. Could we finish the ten pictures before my money ran out? This Hair's-Breadth Harry situation was intensified by a sudden move by the Lobster and the Troll.

They used to come in every Monday morning to give me a check for the payroll of the previous week. The last week in December they arrived with a dried-up little fellow who looked like a Talmudic scholar. He proved to be a lawyer with less than theological ideas.

The three of them sat in my office in uneasy silence. Finally the lawyer blurted out, "We want half of your studio!" "Aw, don't say it like that," chided the Lobster. "It's just that we like you, and we want to help you with some advice."

I said curtly that I didn't need their company or their advice, just pay me the money and forget the whole idea. I'd close the studio rather than give away half of my stock. I must have sounded convincing because they gave me a check and grumbled off.

Scarcely had they left when I received a call from Maxine. A well-known Hollywood producer was interested in buying our studio. I had never met him, but I did know that when Mussolini's son-in-law visited Hollywood he received the bastard with open arms. This monster had written about his delight in bombing spear-carrying warriors during the Ethiopian War, how the explosions caused them "to blossom like a rose." He was a lyric houseguest.

Maxine and I had long since separated, but she still was a full partner in the studio. When she insisted that we have a meeting with this toad, I reluctantly agreed. The offer was simple. He would pay all my debts and give me a large salary, but I had to sign a five-year contract.

He pictured our association in glowing terms. One of the first things we would have to do would be to furnish some of the back rooms for clients and willing starlets. Also, he would take care of the payola to agency people. We would all make a fine living. I couldn't see myself running to the back rooms with the soap and towels, so I turned him down.

I was within less than two weeks of finishing the ten episodes when the three ghouls arrived the next Monday. We all knew damn well that once the pictures were finished I would be out of their clutches.

This time they brought a contract ready for signing, and put it on my desk. I threw it on the floor. We glared at each other. Then I told them brusquely that they had five minutes to think it over. It was either the payroll check, or I'd close the studio. It was quite a gamble for them, because by now we owed them $80,000.

Obviously I had much more to lose, so they all sat there looking very confident. Even when I picked up the phone and called Pepe Ruiz, they were very calm. It probably looked like a desperate bluff. When I told Pepe that we couldn't meet the payroll it must have been his finest hour. His archenemy brought down at last!

The trio watched in a state of shock as I hung up the phone. I didn't feel anything. A year of overwork and worry had left me with no adrenaline to pump. After they were gone I had a hasty meeting with my secretary, Jo-Ann, and the bookkeeper to check our financial situation, which was just about zero. The company had grossed $1,300,000, but we were broke, because the gross for the last quarter had been almost nothing.

I wasn't licked yet. I called the whole staff into my office and began to outline a plan. We would finish the pictures without pay. Two weeks without pay would put none of us on the breadline. Here was at least a year's work if we just finished two remaining pictures. Before anybody could answer, a white-faced Jo-Ann brought in a telegram. Interstate was canceling the contract as of this date.

Who pulled the plug? I leave even my most naïve reader to correctly guess who made the fatal phone call to Interstate.

The farewell to my staff must be one of the most painful experiences of my life. There were tears and convulsive embraces. Suddenly I was alone. I was dully aware that I was even feeling a sense of relief that it was all over. I never really wanted to be a tycoon. I had just wanted to be a good artist, yet I had allowed myself to be caught up in a whirlpool of economic forces that had spun me far from what I expected to be my life's work.

In addition I had dragged Bill Hurtz, one of my best friends, into what must have been a harrowing experience.

The weeks before the auction of my equipment were a nightmare of angry creditors, phone calls, visits from professional bill collectors (who have to be the scum of the earth), and a flood of legal papers every morning. Looking at the litter of mail one day I said to Juana, my new wife, that we were using up all our bad luck at an alarming rate.

There was one small ray of hope. Rudolph Weiss, my landlord, decided to go into the movie business. He had watched me zoom from a subleased back room to a business which rented three floors of his building. If I agreed to work for him, Weiss was willing to start a studio. I prepared a list of the basic equipment he would need and bought everything at the auction at a tenth of its value.

For the factors the auction was a disaster. The Eisenhower Depression had struck hard, so there were very few buyers. I had paid more than $150,000 for our equipment and it went for $30,000. Not only did they lose $50,000, but I had the grim pleasure of watching one of the auctioneer's assistants buy my Picasso, Braque, and Matisse pictures because he liked the frames. He paid $20. I was the only one present who knew they were originals worth almost $3,000!

Soon after the auction I declared personal bankruptcy. When I left the court building I jingled less than two dollars in change in my pocket, my total assets.

I never saw the Troll or the Lobster again, or the salesman who suggested that we use them as factors. I understood his role a little better when I heard from the Hertz Car Rental. He'd used the company credit card for months after we were out of business. A short time later I received a call from the police. My former salesman was wanted by the District Attorney in Brooklyn. I hope they found him.

Transfilm had been the biggest TV spot producer in New York, with a gross of several million dollars a year. Yet from time to time Marvin Rothenberg, Transfilm's best live-action director, would call me up. "Listen," he would ask, "how the hell do you guys make a profit on your animation? We're losing our ass over here."

I would quote him Joe Rosen's evaluation. The wages were too high for the market. There wasn't anything to be done about it, except to consider animation as a service to the customers. I suspect that Marvin thought I was kidding.

Transfilm closed down a few months after we did. UPA's New York studio had already been abandoned in late 1958. By the end of 1959 every large animation studio in New York had collapsed. The Hubleys survived, probably because John and Faith were not only in the spot market, but were making short subjects as well. Also, unlike the rest of us, they had no permanent staff.

Significantly enough, no such debacle occurred in Hollywood. Even the smaller studios did not go bankrupt, and there were no clandestine raids on the producers by their employees. The Depression did cause a drop in the spot business, but the new expansion of children's TV programs took up the slack. There was no widespread unemployment.

The exception was UPA. The long period of reckless spending left the company with no financial resources. The collapse of the New York studio, plus the fact that all of the original crew had gone, left Busostow with the majority of the stock and little else of value. He sold the company to Henry Saperstein, a producer whose aims were both practical and commercial. UPA as a major creative force had vanished.

If we had gone forward with the Interstate series, New York might now have a studio as large as Hanna-Barbera's, with five hundred employees, and millions of dollars would have enriched the membership. The call that tipped off Interstate to our financial emergency might very well be the most expensive phone call ever made in the animation business.

In place of the large studios, dozens of two- and three-man studios sprang up and engaged in a desperate struggle to survive. Few of them did. Most of them lasted for a short time, then the lack of business acumen and the unstable market would force them to close. For more than ten years the animation business had enjoyed steady employment; now the majority of the workers had to be content with a gypsy existence, working for a few weeks, then living off unemployment insurance for long periods. They still do, and the membership of the local has dwindled to less than a fifth of its former number.

Of course the basic question one must ask is why I reacted in such a passive way to the managerial problems in my Hollywood studio. Why did I not move in on the problem as soon as we found that *Hemo* had lost money? If not then, why not after *Cosmic Rays* went way over the budget? Certainly it looks like the height of folly to have continued with Capra's basic fee and bonus arrangement on *The Enchanted Goddess*.

It took many years of self-evaluation and contemplation before I had the true answer to these questions. At best the spot business was an exercise in trivia, even when we were given a free rein in creating the scripts. Still it was endurable, until the agencies decided to handle the creative end themselves. After that, for a creative person, it was the dullest and most unrewarding job imaginable. Within a very short time, under the agency yoke, I grew more and more frustrated. My creative spirit rebelled against the idea that I was little more than the mechanical extension of some art director's fumbling attempts to create an animated film.

In effect Bill Hurtz became my surrogate free spirit. With wings unclipped, he was soaring into the heights of creative euphoria. He was doing all the things I wanted to do but couldn't, because I had Joe Rosen at my elbow like a Jiminy Cricket, scolding, prodding, watching every move I made. It became a self-reinforcing circle. The more money we lost in Hollywood, the more I was forced to be a businessman in New York. The more I hated the role, the more Hurtz became a symbol of creative freedom. He became a kind of safety valve for my mounting feelings of frustration and rage. This was why I subconsciously avoided curtailing his actions. Once this premise is accepted, it can be seen that however illogical it must have seemed, the artistic spirit in me refused to be completely annihilated. Since I couldn't escape from the restrictions of my own job I used Bill Hurtz as my doppelgänger.

As for Bill, he really had no experience in handling large projects in a sensible way. After all, he had worked at Disney's, where there seemed to be limitless funds and projects were explored until Walt was satisfied, no matter what the cost. After that, he worked in the most infantile atmosphere in the business at UPA. When he left there the studio was miraculously still functioning, so he did not have the sobering effect of seeing it go broke. As far as he could tell it was possible to ignore budgets and still continue to remain in business because the pictures were so good.

The bankruptcy did have a happy ending. Bill and I realized that our friendship was too valuable to founder. We just pushed the whole mess to one side and continue, to this day, to be the best of friends, as if the whole ordeal had never happened . . . or better still, that it did happen and our friendship survived.

Pepe Ruiz, business agent for local 841 Screen Cartoonists in New York. *Collection of The Montreal Museum.*

Bill Hurtz in 1938. Hurtz joined the staff of Jay Ward twenty years ago, and still works there. *Collection of Shamus Culhane.*

*   *   *

It took about a month for Rudolph Weiss to tool up his new company, Shamus Culhane Films, Inc. During that time I received no salary. For a month Juana and I lived on rice and beans. I was as poor as I had been when I first started in the business, thirty-five years before. In a grim way I enjoyed it, because I wanted to find out if I really didn't care about money, or if that was all a poseur's philosophy.

To my satisfaction I found that for the most part I had lost the studio without a qualm. It was true that I had a badly damaged ego, but artistically the studio had become a trap, and I had escaped. Now I had to find out what kind of atmosphere I could create in which I could make a living. That was all I expected from the business world. My artistic needs were going to be nourished after work. I wanted a small studio, no more teletype machines or quick trips to the West in drawing rooms on the Super Chief. I wanted to have some energy left after work so that I could draw, listen to music, and read. Screw the tycoon business.

Mr. Weiss was a whiz at real estate. He came to this country after escaping from a concentration camp, arriving almost penniless. Within ten years he owned three office buildings, but in the spot business, as Betty Marx would say, "he was a bull in a Chinese closet." He expected me to peddle our exhibition reel door-to-door. When I explained to him that I had never, in all the years I was in business, sold a single film, he reluctantly consented to hire a salesman. The most he would put up was fifty dollars a week against a ten percent commission.

This dazzling prospect attracted a number of amateurs and failed neurotics. They were up against an understandable reluctance on the part of the agencies to give work to a bankrupt. None of the big agencies would even invite me to bid. The work I got was from small out-of-town agencies who hadn't heard that my studio had failed. I did have the same address and phone number.

After almost a year of foundering around, I realized that as far as the large agencies were concerned I was on the shit list. All the accounts I had saved, the new ones I had dreamed up for the agencies, with multimillion-dollar billings, didn't mean a damn thing. I had been chewed up and spat out.

Finally I dropped the last amateur salesman, thanked Mr. Weiss heartily for his good intentions, and closed the shop. I needed time to think things out, and I found that even Mr. Weiss' small shop was too frantic an atmosphere for calm and contemplation. Besides I really didn't think I wanted to stay in the spot business. Famous Studio and Terrytoons were turning out such miserable lackluster films that I didn't want to work for them either. On the face of it, I seemed to have some very good options.

There is no doubt that I could have gone back to Hollywood and made a good living as an animator or director. If I had set up shop in Toronto or Montreal I would have had a virtual monopoly, since at the time there was not one good animation studio in Canada except for the Canadian Film Board. We had made about $200,000 a year from our Canadian clients. However, there was no way I could take advantage of any of these options. A domestic problem made it impossible for me to leave New York.

In an ironic turn of events, just as I closed Weiss' studio I was notified that three spots—the Ajax elves, animated in 1948, an Esso of Canada spot, which Bill Hurtz had directed, and Muriel Cigars, animated and directed by me in 1951—had all won Clio Awards in the category of "The U.S. Television Hall of Fame."

Many of the members of my New York crew went on to carve out successful careers on their own.

Ruth Gench continues to work as a production manager on various projects. Rod Johnson joined the Bray Studios as animator/director.

Chris Ishii continues to be one of the outstanding designers in the business; Zack Schwartz now teaches animation in Israel; and Harvey Seigel, one of the mainstays of our background department, now owns a very successful animation studio in Mexico City. Rudy Tomaselli and Sal Buta, who came to work for me when they were in their teens, now own Cel-Art Productions, one of the most important production centers for TV spots in New York.

Fred Wolf likes to recount the story about how he parked his truck outside of our studio and changed into a clean shirt, which he had bought for his interview with Rod Johnson. Fred quit the trucking business when Rod hired him as an inbetweener. He went on to become one of the most facile animators in the profession.

Wolf teamed up with Jimmy Murakami, and their Hollywood studio has turned out a steady stream of award-winning TV spots and specials. In 1968, Murakami–Wolf won an Academy Award for a short film, *The Box.*

All of these people had worked for me for from eight to ten years. Rod Johnson once told me that after the studio closed, many of my ex-employees had such a sense of loss that they often had lunch together in an effort to keep up the relationship.

16

Freelance

he Eisenhower Depression was in full swing during 1959 and 1960, and its impact on the advertising business completely altered the flow of work in the production of live-action and animated television spots in New York.

Heretofore, large studios like mine had steady work all year around, and usually had between five and twenty spots in production in any given month. We had several large accounts, like Ajax, Halo Shampoo, Alka-Seltzer, and Quaker cereals, which we handled on an annual basis, without having to make competitive bids.

Now the work was being doled out, one or two spots at a time. The bidding was frenetic because very often these hastily formed two- and three-men studios were not even trying to make a profit. They needed the work to pay the rent.

Small studios would open, operate for a few months, then the team would split up. Its members would join with other groups, which in turn would divide like amoebas.

In addition, the quality of the work suffered. Animation is such a group effort, and the production methods so complex, that comparative strangers working together, often in makeshift quarters, created an atmosphere that invited misunderstandings and retakes. The agencies began to send more and more of their quality spots to the well-established studios in Hollywood.

This drain on an already dwindling supply of work caused New York studios to make even more desperate bids, until there was a time when some TV spots were being made for less money than we had been getting ten years before.

If Carl Brown still had his agency I probably would have been getting all the work I could handle. He wouldn't have cared if I set up shop in the men's room of Grand Central Station. But Carl had already decided to leave the profession. Most of the agencies liked to send art directors or production executives to inspect work in progress. The days of animating on a kitchen table were long gone.

Such were the prospects I faced in the winter of 1960, with no capital and the credit rating of a Bowery bum, plus the fact that I had no business address.

I was rescued from the latter situation by Lou Bunin. We had never met, but I knew that he was considered to be one of the top stop-motion puppeteers in the world, and certainly the best in America. Bunin called me up, introduced himself, then went on to say in a diffident voice that he had a large studio on lower Fifth Avenue, and in one corner was a desk that nobody used. Would I care to avail myself of this old piece of furniture, rent free?

When we did meet, Lou brushed aside my effusive thanks, explaining that he had always admired my work, and he was simply offering the help that one artist should give to another. Now I had a new business address, a new friend, and an introduction to a fascinating aspect of animation.

As a puppeteer, Lou Bunin was following a career in an art form whose origins go back into antiquity. Puppets have been animated by many methods. The buffalo-hide mythological puppets of Bali are mounted on thin rods; Japanese life-sized puppets are moved manually on stage; marionettes, animated by strings, have been in use for centuries, from the Orient to almost every country in Europe.

The invention of the motion picture camera opened still another possibility. Three-dimensional figures could be animated by photographing them one exposure at a time, just like drawn animation, with the movements plotted out on an exposure sheet. The big advantage was that there was no need for strings, rods, or other apparatus in moving these puppets.

As a teenager in the 1920s, Lou Bunin had no interest in puppets. He studied painting and drawing at the Chicago Art Institute; then, following the usual pattern of the period, he went to Paris. There he fell under the influence of Modigliani, which caused him to abandon some of the academic precepts he had learned at the Institute.

After several years in France, he returned to Chicago and had a one-man show. He had arrived home penniless, but the show was so successful that Bunin made three thousand dollars. The turning point in his career was when, shortly after his exhibition, he met Meyer Levin, who later became a well-known writer. Levin at that time was more interested in puppets and his puppet theater than he was in writing.

Bunin became so excited by the potentials of puppetry that he joined Meyer Levin in the co-production of several important plays, like *Dr. Faustus* and *The Crock of Gold*. They were so involved in the complexities of building sets and designing marionettes that they ignored the more mundane details like advertising and promotion. Needless to say, they went broke after a year.

Bunin decided to go on with his career as a painter. His work interested Diego Rivera, so Lou was hired to assist Rivera and Pablo O'Higgins on fresco paintings that they were making in Mexico City.

While he was there, Bunin became friendly with an Austrian count, Rene D'Harnoncourt, who later became the head of New York's Museum of Modern Art. He was a striking man, almost seven feet tall, thin as a Giocometti figure. At that time he was working as a humble clerk in a small shop that sold pre-Columbian artifacts and local folk art.

Bunin was fascinated by the humorous little carvings that the Indians brought to sell to the store. They inspired him to make a series of puppets of D'Harnancourt, some of the Indian craftsmen, and various customers who frequented the store.

Using these figures, they put on a highly successful puppet show at the American embassy. D'Harnancourt supplied the voice for his own puppet, and Bunin recalls that one of the assistant puppeteers was Anne Morrow, later the wife of Charles Lindbergh.

Unlike Pablo O'Higgins, who settled down in Mexico for the rest of his life, Lou Bunin decided to go to New York. There he met Meyer Levin again, and his interest in puppets was rekindled. They decided to mount a marionette production of Eugene O'Neill's play, *The Hairy Ape*.

The show was so successful that it attracted the attention of important critics like John Martin and Brooks Atkinson. Both wrote glowing reviews. They marveled at the dramatic impact and force that could be achieved by puppets.

Due to this favorable publicity, Paramount sent a newsreel team to photograph a portion of the play. Lou Bunin remembers that when he saw the footage on a screen, the long shots looked very impressive; but in the close-ups the marionette strings were so magnified that they spoiled the enjoyment of the action. This convinced him that stop-motion puppets were the proper way to use the medium for motion pictures.

Shortly before World War II, Bunin and some fellow artists, including Arthur Turkisher, who had been the music director at Iwerks Studio, made an anti-Nazi film entitled *Bury The Axis,* using the stop-motion technique.

Following an all too familiar pattern, the group had invested its own money, produced the film, and then looked for a market. The State Department, for one, turned down the film on the grounds that a serious subject like Nazis had been handled with too much satire!

As a business venture it was a total loss, but it supplied Bunin with a marvelous opportunity to display his talents. Executives from MGM happened to see the film and promptly offered Bunin a contract to produce a prologue for a musical feature film, *Ziegfeld Follies.*

The Bunins were given a small stage on the MGM lot and a lavish budget. Florence Bunin designed and sewed the costumes, and Lou created a cast of puppets that were caricatures of some of the great musical stars who had appeared in Ziegfeld shows on Broadway: Fanny Brice, Will Rogers, Bert Williams, and Eddie Cantor.

The *Ziegfeld Follies* was not a particularly memorable musical, but the animation was a real tour de force. In this one picture Lou Bunin established himself as a great stop-motion puppeteer. When the film was completed, the Bunins looked around for work with a similar scope.

Many of the film companies had been hard hit by the collapse of the world market because of the war. Walt Disney was no exception. In 1948 an article appeared in the *Hollywood Reporter* in which Disney explained that his income had been so drastically cut back by the chaotic conditions of the postwar market that it was necessary to lay off a good part of his staff and to abandon the production of a feature picture based on *Alice in Wonderland.*

There is a curious custom in Hollywood, practiced by an association called Motion Picture Producers and Distributors of America, Inc. In flagrant disregard for the principles of the Copyright Act and the Geneva Convention, once a producer registered a title with the association, the others adopted a hands-off policy, even when the title was in the public domain. They even "sold" each other the rights to books and plays in the public domain, as if registration with the association made the works private property.

To Lou Bunin, who was not a member, *Alice in Wonderland* presented a very intriguing vehicle for a combination of Alice as a live child, working with the White Rabbit, the King and Queen, and all the other characters in the book as stop-motion puppets. The technical facilities of the time were advanced enough to make such a combination possible.

Bunin had no trouble in finding financial backing. A French government-subsidized company invested half the production money, and the other half was supplied by the J. Arthur Rank Organization.

In spite of difficulties in postwar Paris, like a shortage of electricity and heating, the first stages of animation production were soon under way, and the English live-action unit began to cast *Alice* and to assemble a crew.

Some remarkable talent worked on the picture. Art Babbitt, ex-Disney animator, drew individualized walks for each character; Florence Bunin designed the costumes; Gene Fleury and Bernyce Polifka, the man and wife team who had worked for Chuck Jones at Warners, designed the sets and puppet characters; and the cameraman was Claude Renoir. Lou Bunin gathered together a group of puppeteers, mostly European, and intended to direct them, as well as animate a number of the key shots himself.

Walt Disney was not pleased at this turn of events, because in the interim he had decided to resume working on his own version of *Alice*. Despite the fact that Bunin was not a member of the producers organization, it was expected that he follow the "code," and respect Disney's claim to *Alice*. When he refused, retribution was swift and sure.

Just before the animation unit was about to commence photography, Bunin was hastily summoned to London for a meeting with J. Arthur Rank and the head of the London branch of Technicolor. Orders had come from the main office in Hollywood to deny Bunin access to Technicolor stock for his picture. J. Arthur Rank exploded, "Don't you have antitrust laws in America?" It was explained that Walt Disney was an old and valued customer, so the decision was final.

There was only one other color stock available, Ansco. It was not like Technicolor, which was completely reliable. It was necessary to test every can of Ansco film before it was put in the camera. Even with this precaution, the best the J. Arthur Rank lab could do was to deliver a very uneven negative.

The prints had another problem. The film had a blue dye which affected the sound track. The only way to circumvent the static the dye produced was to use a specially tinted blue bulb in the projector. Compared to Technicolor, Ansco was a disaster.

In spite of these tribulations, Lou Bunin's *Alice in Wonderland* opened in the Mayfair Theatre on Broadway in 1951. Walt's version of *Alice* was showing at the Criterion two weeks later. Disney had filed suit against Bunin, asking the court to stop the exhibition of his film for three years, while Disney was recouping the cost of his picture. The case was dismissed in forty-five minutes.

Ironically enough, Disney's *Alice in Wonderland* is considered by many critics to be one of his least successful features. Some thought that the quality of the entertainment was spotty; others thought that the frenetic pace of some of the sequences was foreign to the dreamlike quality of the book.

The charm of Lewis Carroll's story is the fact that once Alice has popped down the rabbit hole, she is a stranger in a world of fantasy. In Disney's version Alice is an animated girl surrounded by animated animals; in effect they are all creatures of fantasy.

Bunin's film shows Alice in an almost surrealistic environment. A live girl associating with talking animals, birds, and playing-cards is a concept that is visually much nearer to the feeling of unreality in the book. Discounting the miserable quality of the color and the muddy sound track (which is admittedly not easy to do), one can see that Lou Bunin and his crew had created an outstanding motion picture.

Bunin is such a great animator that the first time I saw the film (on a moviola) I had no difficulty in picking out the scenes that Lou had animated. His characters move with the intensity that distinguishes the work of great artists in conventional animation: the Tytlas, Babbitts, Natwicks, and Fergusons.

Of course Bunin's *Alice* was a colossal financial failure. When we met in 1959 the Bunin Studio was producing TV spots for Brill Cream and Utica Beer. Bunin was making a comfortable living.

Recalling his controversy with Disney, Lou is remarkably philosophical about it. He thought that Walt had done what any good businessman would have done in similar circumstances.

He went on to explain that if Walt had approached him as one artist to the other, the clash might never have occurred. I think so too, because Walt had an enormous respect for unusual talent. Who knows? If the

In this scene from Lou Bunin's *Alice in Wonderland*, the White Rabbit is accusing Alice of stealing the Queen's tarts. Lou Bunin Productions, 1951.

John and Faith Hubley enjoyed a unique relationship in the filmmaking industry as the only husband and wife team in the animation field. This picture was taken in 1975.

circumstances had been different, Disney and Bunin might have entered into a joint venture, and the art of puppeteering would have taken a great leap forward.

During a discussion with Bunin about the basic difference between stop-motion puppets and drawn animation, he made these observations:

> Think how impossible it would be in an animated drawing to duplicate the lighting of a Giacometti figure. The figure actually is in space, and you light it in the way you do a form that displaces space. The thing that Giacometti is concerned about.
>
> To animate that figure calls for another side of experience, a feeling of life, because you exploit what is there. Lighting is itself an enormous contribution. How impossible it would be to draw animated cast shadows, highlights, and halftones. [Note that Bunin's interest in light, as a dramatic resource, parallels Paul Julian's (see page 242).]
>
> Drawn animation tends towards shapes that are simple . . . a simplicity that is not wanted in the sculpture of stop-motion figures. We look for textures that are not usable in drawing . . . like shiney shoes, a checkered suit, bushy hair. Think how each hair, if the lighting is good, has its own reflected light, its own cast shadow.

In talking about acting, he agreed that great acting can't be an intellectual effort.

> If you interpret somebody else's acting ideas, the result can't possibly be important. If you have no inner reaction that you can express by becoming the puppet, then you have no way to transmit vital elements to a performance. You have to be the character in order to make it believable.
>
> Suddenly as a performer, if you have the good sense to follow the performance of the puppet while you are that character, you sense what is right, what is funny or dramatic. You can't anticipate that on your exposure sheets.

Then you get that creative feeling that is so familiar to
every good animator I know; you become the performer
in a strange shape, and become the audience at the same
time. You are amazed at what is happening, the thing that
you yourself are doing. I don't know of another art form
that gives such a dual experience to the artist.

Bunin's observations show how puppet and drawn animation basically
have the same goal for the animator, that is, to reach that intensity of
concentration where the characters seem to move of their own volition.

After decades of comparative obscurity, Lou Bunin is at last being
recognized again as one of the great animators. In June 1981, at the
international animation festival in Annecy, Bunin was honored by a
retrospective screening of his work and an exhibition of many of his
puppets.

In September 1981, The Mid-Hudson Art Center in Poughkeepsie
mounted a huge show of Bunin's work as a painter, sculptor, and
filmmaker. It is heartwarming to know that this gentle, modest man is
finally being assigned an honored place in animation history during his
lifetime.

The Eisenhower Depression lasted into 1961, and this period must have
been the worst. For weeks I went from one advertising agency to the next
looking for work, without getting a chance to bid on so much as a
ten-second spot. There were plenty of others in the same fix, but that
didn't whet my appetite when I sat down to eat rice and beans for the
fourth time in a week.

One night when I came home from my usual fruitless rounds, my wife,
Juana, told me that I had received a phone call. The name was not familiar
to me, but that meant nothing. I have an incredibly bad memory for
names and faces.

The next day was bitterly cold, and as I trudged along Madison
Avenue, I suddenly remembered that I had stuffed Juana's memo in my
pocket. I went to a phone booth and started to dial. The index finger of
my worn-out glove fell off. "Shit!" I thought. "That's my last pair of
warm gloves."

A very cheery voice answered the phone. While we had never met,
he was well aware of my brilliant career in the spot business and was

acting as an emissary for a very large agency. He had been instructed to offer me a prestigious job as a creative director, answerable only to the president, and in complete control of some very important accounts. He was not allowed to name the agency unless I was interested.

While this was going on, I was groping on the floor of the booth for the missing finger of my glove. I said that I wasn't interested. I was recalling Zack Schwartz's experience in a similar job. "The job pays thirty thousand dollars a year," he prodded. I reiterated that I wasn't interested.

The voice became more persuasive. "Well, how much would you consider to be a proper salary? Remember that there are a number of fringe benefits, stock options, Christmas bonuses, a pension plan. Name your price, and if it's reasonable, I'm sure that we can take care of you." I never even pressed him for the name of the agency, just thanked him and hung up.

Considering our miserable financial condition, my answer might be considered the height of folly. I look back at the incident as a milestone in my maturity as an artist. It is easy for people to live with their skills, especially if they are better than average, but damn difficult to admit that there are areas in which they are totally incompetent.

Zack Schwartz had been lured into a similar job a few years before. He was supposedly only answerable to the president. Zack and I are very much alike, both workaholics, both blunt and undiplomatic in our relations with other people. The upper echelon of the agency made mincemeat of him, because he steadfastly refused to align himself with any of the various power groups. Consequently, he was a prime target for his more politically adroit peers.

They advanced themselves by stealing his ideas, attacked his projects for political reasons, and deftly undermined his relationship to the president. Unable to cope with the intricacies of internecine warfare, Zack, hurt and bewildered, dropped out of the business.

With this new insight on my personality, I knew that I wouldn't have fared any better than Zack. Anyhow such a job would have taken me further and further away from my drawing board, which was my big mistake in the first place.

Not everybody was doing so badly. The largest production house to fail in that fateful year, 1959, was Transfilm. While it had specialized in live-action TV spots, the company had also maintained an animation unit headed by Jack Zander. When Transfilm closed, Jack started his own animation studio, Pelican Films. Unlike people like me, Zander did not have the stigmata of bankruptcy, so his business started to flourish immediately.

Another studio that was doing well was Hal Seeger Productions. The company was started by Hal with a loan of five hundred dollars and a borrowed desk and typewriter. Seeger ran what was essentially a service house, supplying other companies with titles, mattes, and sometimes bits of animation. For a long time he had only one employee, Susie Blaney. When he had more work than the two of them could handle, he hired other artists on a day-to-day basis. This Spartan approach was so successful that within two years Seeger made enough money to buy an Oxberry camera and an optical printer.

While Hal never was a really topflight animator, he was an astute businessman. In 1961 he made a deal with Max Fleischer to make a series of short subjects for the TV market, featuring Koko the Clown. When Seeger offered me work on the project, I was glad to accept because it meant a surcease from the interminable tramping around looking for work on TV spots.

The Koko series had a budget so small that the animation had to be very limited. The resulting pictures bore no resemblance to the entertaining cartoons that Max Fleischer made in the early 1920s. Even so, it was more interesting than doing one-minute TV spots.

Like Walt Lantz, Hal Seeger was able to work with small budgets without yielding to the temptation to wring more work out of his employees than their salaries were worth. But working with Koko after these long years, I remembered with nostalgia when Dick Huemer's animation of the clown was matchless, and Koko was the most popular character on the screen.

It is one thing to do a primitive type of animation from ignorance, and quite another to deliberately turn your back on knowledge painfully acquired. For my own satisfaction, I spent far more time drawing good poses of Koko than the job called for.

In my heyday as a live-action director, I made a practice of using the same crew as often as possible. One of my regular crew members was a woman who was an excellent propman. She was indirectly responsible for one of the most alluring proposals ever made to anybody in the animation profession.

I didn't know that her husband was one of the outstanding producers on Broadway. One day he called up and introduced himself, suggesting that we meet to discuss a project that might interest me. His wife had recommended me as one of the top animation directors.

We met in a bar near Times Square, and he began to talk about Pablo Picasso. He had never met the great artist himself, but he had a close friend who was one of Picasso's intimates. He went on to give me a vivid picture of the court of friends and sycophants that surrounded Picasso, like the nobles in the court of a king.

It was impossible to reach Picasso directly. He had set up a phalanx of people between himself and the rest of the world, because he sat in a state of siege. Hundreds of people tried to see him every week. Some were curious tourists, others art lovers, gallery owners, and businessmen with every type of commercial idea. Picasso's talents had become a kind of ambulatory gold mine.

He could rough out a salable drawing in one minute, and that drawing could earn him more money than all the facilities of U.S. Steel could make in the same amount of time!

After giving me this picture of Picasso's ambience, the producer finally came to the reason for our meeting. The idea was breathtaking. Picasso's love for American comic strips was mentioned in Gertrude Stein's book, *The Autobiography of Alice B. Toklas*. He was now thinking about making an animated version of *Don Quixote*! Since he knew nothing about the intricate processes of making animation, Picasso had left it up to his courtiers to find someone who could help him to make the picture.

One of those people was a friend of the producer, so here we were sitting over a beer as I faced this mind-jolting possibility. A stream of thoughts were jostling each other through my head. Imagine working with Picasso on a storyboard! Since my Spanish was terrible, perhaps Juana could act as our interpreter. Where could I get an animation crew in France? Would Picasso do more than just draw a storyboard? Could he learn to animate?

There was something very cloak-and-dagger about this whole business. The producer refused to tell me the name of his friend in Picasso's court. Instead, he carefully wrote down a list of my screen credits, and went off, saying that after he had checked my background, if it was satisfactory, we would get together again and plan the next move.

A few nights later we met again. He had investigated my credentials, and they were impressive enough to satisfy him. He was going to get in touch with his French connections the very next day. I went home so elated that I couldn't eat or sleep.

The following morning as I scanned the newspaper, I got the shock of my life. There on the obituary page was a headline. My erstwhile go-between had dropped dead shortly after our meeting. From what he had told me, it was useless to send a letter to Picasso. A letter from a stranger would not be seen by him.

I had no money to go to France on what might easily be a fool's errand. Perhaps Picasso's notion of making an animated Don Quixote had been just a passing whim. Anyhow, how to get past the barricade of courtiers?

The most wonderful opportunity in the history of animation faded away. When I think of it, my toes curl with frustration.

John and Faith Hubley's Storyboard Studio had survived the 1959 debacle in New York, probably because they did most of their animation and camera work on the coast, and kept their overhead low by owning a minimum amount of equipment. Aside from a secretary, they had no regular employees.

I had never worked with Hubley in Hollywood, but I had heard a good deal about his brilliance from Bill Hurtz. Bill had been designer and layout man on some of Hub's best pictures. In my opinion Hubley was the outstanding director in the New Wave, which had begun under Frank Tashlin's guidance at Screen Gems back in the 1940s.

Together John and Faith represented a formidable array of talents. Hub was a writer, director, layout man, character designer, and background painter. Faith was a painter, music and sound effects editor, writer, and production supervisor. In addition, she often would ink whole pictures herself, when she felt that the work was too personal to be farmed out to regular inkers.

I was delighted when John called me up to find out if I was available to animate a dog food commercial. One TV spot led to another, and then to one of the most satisfying animation assignments of my career.

In 1964 the Hubleys wrote a short subject called *The Hat*. It was subsidized by an international peace organization. The picture featured two sentries marching on opposite sides of a boundary line. A clash occurs when one soldier's hat accidentally rolls into enemy territory, and the other soldier refuses to return it until he has checked on the necessary protocol. During the ensuing discussion the two men become friendly, and the film ends on an optimistic note.

Although there were other characters and animals in the picture, the two soldiers accounted for about 80 percent of the footage. When Hubley asked me if I could do all of the animation of the sentries myself, I jumped at the chance. The last time I had drawn full animation, other than one-minute spots, was about twenty years before, when I worked with Chuck Jones at Warners.

The Hubleys were exciting to work with because they had a strong sense of adventure in their filmmaking. John was never tied down to techniques that he was already familiar with. Each picture was a new experience, because the appearance of the film was always dictated by the content. *The Hat* was no exception.

The design of the two sentries presented some odd problems in animation, in that the action was going to be normal, but the arms and legs were not attached to the bodies. Although we had detailed model sheets of each soldier, Hub's layouts paid scant heed to his original designs. As the picture progressed his drawings of one of the soldiers became more and more Christ-like.

While I animated the picture at home, Hubley and I worked very closely together. Whenever I had a few scenes finished, we would have a conference on this work and the following scenes. Hubley was a very enthusiastic director. He would pick up the newly animated shots with obvious excitement, flip the drawings, and burst out laughing. His pleasure was so infectious that I would laugh, too. We shared a feeling of joy in the whole process of filmmaking.

The animation of *The Hat* took many months. During that time, with my usual curiosity about the working methods of great artists I have worked with, I studied Hubley's approach whenever I could. In the first place he worked in a room that was crammed with the largest collection of art books I have ever seen in private hands. The subjects ranged from prehistoric cave paintings to Picasso, Klee, Chagall, and other modern artists. There were books on the art of every culture imaginable, Aztec, Mayan, Chinese, Persian, Greek, etcetera.

At the beginning of a picture Hubley would pore over a random selection of art books. Seemingly they had no relationship to each other, but he was using them to inspire his own sense of design. However, the final appearance of a Hubley film was never blatantly derivative. In *The*

Hat, for example, I have the feeling that he was influenced (if that is the right term) by Chinese scroll painting, but that is just my own intuition.

Since Hubley was going to paint his own backgrounds, the layouts were usually little more than a vague series of scrawls with little or no detail, unless the background and the animation were going to be closely related.

Unlike Disney Studio, where the dialogue is broken down for the animator in meticulous detail, Faith gave me a very loose track analysis. Neither Faith nor John seemed to be concerned with precise synchronization of the mouth action and the dialogue track.

John's instructions for the movement of the characters were also very loosely indicated on the exposure sheets. It seemed to be his feeling that the pace of the animation should be the shared responsibility of both the director and the animator.

The Hubley children had to be the luckiest kids in New York City. Not only were they encouraged to draw, write, and paint, but in their Riverside Drive apartment the Hubleys had built a small stage, so it must have been easy for the family to create the sound tracks for such imaginative films as *Moonbird, Windy Day,* and *Cockaboody.*

Like John Cassavetes, the Hubleys believed in the value of ad-libbing sound tracks, so a good deal of the children's dialogue in these pictures was completely spontaneous material.

Whatever his formal education had been, Hubley was a very well-informed person, with a sophisticated view of life. One Saturday morning I dropped in to find John working alone, and in a very depressed mood. It happened that I was on the down side myself that morning. After we had talked over the work in the new scenes, our conversation drifted off into a very open discussion about the problem of being an alienated personality. We exchanged anecdotes about incidents that had happened to us because of alienation.

Somehow our talking acted as a catharsis, and we both found our moods lightened. We ended up laughing, and agreed that being alienated in our kind of society had more merit than most people realized. It was a very stimulating discussion.

On the other hand, I have seen Hubley get up to give a talk at a meeting and present himself to the audience as a kind of homespun shit-kicker. In reality Hubley was about as homespun as a Gobelin tapestry.

The Hubleys used a backlighting technique in photographing *Windy Day*. Note that this resulted in some areas of the background showing through the characters. *Windy Day* was hailed as one of the Hubleys' most successful films. Produced in 1968.

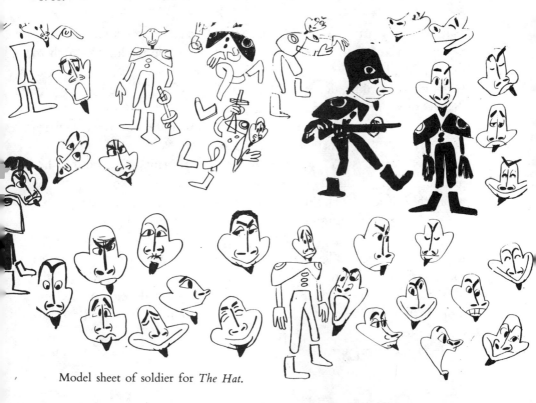

Model sheet of soldier for *The Hat*.

What psychological factors within him made it necessary to offer this kind of facade to the public will probably never be known. John, during working hours, would present his views very succinctly, with no hint of becoming an incipient Jimmy Stewart.

While Hub often appeared moody and depressed, Faith was just the opposite. She always seemed to have an ebullience, a zest for life, and a dazzling smile. Both John and Faith were energetic, with an enormous capacity for long hours of hard work. Faith took over the task of supervising the interminable details, which plague every production, no matter how well thought out the original concept. John was left free to indulge his creativity to its fullest extent, without being interrupted by tiresome details.

For years Faith worked under the shadow of John Hubley. Most people, unless they worked closely with the Hubleys, thought of Faith as a good wheelhorse, a capable editor and production supervisor, yet through all those years of their association, she worked side-by-side with John on initial concepts, scripts, and sound tracks.

Before they were married, Hubley's pictures were outstanding because they contained strong elements of sardonic humor. *Mr. Magoo* is a good example.

It was only after Faith and John started to work together that they began to make picures with a lyric quality, a subtle tender approach to filmmaking, like *Windy Day, The Moonbird,* and *Cockaboody.* Nothing in Hubley's UPA films suggests such a poetic approach. To me it is obvious that Faith supplied the missing ingredient.

As long as he lived, John continued to gather the kudos, with Faith modestly accepting whatever honors were left. Now that John is dead, Faith has blossomed into a more aggressive personality. She exhibits her paintings, and produces, writes, and directs her own films. It will be interesting to see just how far Faith will go on her own. My guess is that she will make a significant contribution to animated films.

In 1965 Hal Seeger offered me some more work. He had sold the idea for a series of children's shows about a charcter called "Milton the Monster." At a time when the average show for children was nothing more than a collection of insensate violent actions, Milton was refreshingly different.

He was a huge, amiable klutz, who puffed smoke out of the top of his head when he became excited, but never really scared anybody. Like Seeger's Koko series, the Milton the Monster series had a very small budget. There was no possibility of doing anything but very limited animation.

While the series represented months of steady work, I was reluctant to tie myself down to this restrictive kind of animation. I had just completed many exciting months on *The Hat*. After some reflection I decided to take on the work and to focus on one area of production which I had hitherto ignored . . . layout.

On each picture I made an extensive study of the possibilities of unusual compositions and camera angles. What might very easily have been a routine job became a very interesting learning process. By the end of the series I felt that I had become a capable layout man.

However, in the summer of 1966 I realized that I was getting very bored by this aimless existence. While I cared very little about my sharply curtailed income, I did miss the excitement of leading a group of filmmakers in the production of entertainment films.

This was the environment in which I was the most comfortable. Pictures like *Milton the Monster* were not broad enough in scope to satisfy my need to use all my talents. As for TV spots, by this time the creative aspsects of production were almost completely controlled by agency people.

For seven years I had been nursing a severely wounded ego by leading a very hermetic existence, working at home, not mingling with my peers, spending endless days reading instead of working. Psychologically, I probably needed this period of hibernation, but suddenly it was over, and I had a compelling need to reenter the mainstream of the business.

For personal reasons I was still confined to New York City, and the prospects for working in the entertainment area were bleak. Only Terrytoons in New Rochelle and Famous Studio in midtown Manhattan were still producing shorts.

Terrytoons I promptly discarded as a possibility, mainly because a friend of mine told me about a job interview he had with Paul Terry. The opening lines of the meeting were certainly succinct. Terry said, "We do shit here, compared to the rest of the business, but it makes me a lot of money. If you don't like to do shit, don't ask for a job." My friend took the next train back to Manhattan.

Ironically enough, Paul Terry and Walt Disney, on opposite ends of the spectrum, were the two richest men in the business. It says a lot about the structure of the industry when a cynic like Terry could amass so much money by deliberately turning out potboilers. Many talented people worked for him, among them Bill Tytla and Art Babbitt, but even their prodigious talents could not elevate the quality of the Terry films one iota. I wasn't about to try.

Paramount was something else again. After Max and Dave Fleischer had been tossed out of their studio by Paramount, in a move that had some questionable legal aspects, the studio was renamed Famous and put into the hands of three executives.

Sam Buchwald, one-time accountant and watchdog for Paramount while the Fleischers ran the studio, handled the money. Seymour Kneitel, Max Fleischer's son-in-law, was in charge of production. Izzy Sparber, once head of the Fleischer camera department, has been given credit as director on 135 pictures! Knowing Izzy's creative abilities, or rather the lack of them, I do not take these credits very seriously.

During the late 1940s and early 1950s, the West Coast studios were still operating with their usual high standards, while Terrytoons and Famous were churning out some of their worst films.

History repeats itself. Just as Frank Tashlin had done at Screen Gems in 1941, when he had lifted the quality of the studio's films to a remarkable height for a brief period, Gene Deitch did the same for Terrytoons fifteen years later.

Gene had started in animation as a designer in the Hollywood studio of UPA. When the studio opened a branch in New York to compete for the TV spot market, Gene was made the principal director. His most outstanding commercials were the Burt and Harry Piel's beer spots, which are considered to be some of the most popular commercials ever produced.

The main characters were caricatures of the two brothers who owned the brewery. One was a talkative, confident fellow who made a pitch for the beer, and the other was an ineffectual klutz who tried to add his comments, but was usually unable to get a word in edgewise. It was a whole new brand of humor on Madison Avenue, and the brewery's business soared as a result.

In 1956 Deitch joined Terrytoons after a brief stint with John and Faith Hubley, and had the satisfaction of taking the Piel's Beer account to his new job.

Under his guidance Terrytoons turned out some excellent pictures. Many of them were written by Jules Feiffer, who was making his living as a writer in the animation business. His newspaper cartoons were still only a part-time work.

One of the best ideas to come out of Terrytoons during Deitch's regime was a series of short films that were shown daily on "Captain Kangaroo," the most popular children's television program at the time. It was a tongue-in-cheek adventure series featuring a small boy, Tom Terrific, and Manfred the Wonder Dog.

The cartoons were produced on a very small budget, so Gene designed the two characters very simply. They were rendered with a heavy black line, without color. Often they played against a solid color background whose only detail was a horizon line.

Feiffer wrote scripts which were sophisticated and artful jibes at the overblown superheros and the insensate violence which cluttered the air on the Saturday morning children's shows. The literary quality of Feiffer's humor and the avant-garde design of Deitch's characters were not welcomed by the old-timers on the Terrytoons staff.

Gene's blunt manner was often mistaken for arrogance, and he had frequent fights with Bill Weiss, the studio manager. Bill was no artist, but he had definite ideas about the kinds of pictures that made money. The fact that Tom Terrific was so successful did nothing to change his mind. Terrytoons had flourished on making traditional pictures, and Weiss thought that Gene was setting a dangerous precedent. In 1958 Weiss fired Deitch, and the studio sank back comfortably into the familiar production of mediocre cartoons.

Famous Studio in the mid-fifties really hit the bottom. The cartoons suffered from Seymour Kneitel's idea that the determining factor in making animated cartoons was the lowest expenditure possible.

The studio staggered from elephantine efforts to capture UPA's style, to some feeble attempts to build scripts around the space age. Even the Popeye stories were the victims of formula writing.

The studio made no attempt to join the other studios in the spot business. In one particularly bad year for Paramount, the company buttressed its falling income by selling its enormous backlog of animated cartoons to television programmers.

Under the leadership of Max and Dave Fleischer the studio's cartoons always had a lusty, if crude, humor. At one point Popeye had been even more popular than Mickey Mouse. Many of the animators had stayed with the studio through its various stages of popularity. Now these same artists were content to work in an atmosphere of complete surrender to the Nepenthe of formula cartoons.

In 1960 Gene Deitch joined Bill Snyder's Rembrandt Films as director, and the company started a tenuous relationship with Famous Studio. Rembrandt Films was a small company, but made films of very high quality. Luckily for Deitch and Snyder, they were completely independent of Paramount and Famous in their choice of subject matter.

During all the years that the studio had been run by Max and Dave Fleischer, their pictures had only been nominated for three Academy Awards, and they had never won an Oscar.

The first film that Paramount bought from Rembrandt Films, *Munro,* directed by Gene Deitch, won an Oscar in 1960. To show that it wasn't a fluke, Deitch directed *Self-Defense for Cowards,* which was nominated for an Academy Award in 1962. In 1964 Rembrandt had two films nominated, *How to Avoid Friendship,* and *Nudnik No. 2,* both directed by Deitch. Paramount neglected to buy any of them.

Paramount aroused itself from its torpor at this point and arranged a contract with Rembrandt Films for a series of cartoons based on Nudnik, a downbeat character, as the name implies. Deitch, by this time, had moved to Prague, although still under contract to Rembrandt. He started to produce the Nudnik series using the state-owned animation studio there.

In spite of the fact that they were all comparatively young men, by 1964 Buchwald, Sparber, and Kneitel were dead. When Kneitel died, the sensible thing would have been for Paramount to lure Deitch back from Prague and put him in charge of the studio. Instead, a comparatively unknown writer, Howard Post, was hired as studio head.

Unfortunately Post's experience in the animation area was very meager. He had worked at the studio some years before as an inbetweener, then left to write comic books. When Seymour Kneitel started to make TV cartoons for King Features, Post was hired as one of the storymen. A less stimulating education in filmmaking can scarcely be imagined.

Post's first move in his new job was to create a character named Honey Halfwitch. Honey was ostensibly a little girl, and followed the usual heavy-handed attempts at cuteness which had bogged down the studio since the days of Betty Boop.

There was only one light in this murk, and it soon glimmered out. Jack Mendelsohn, an ex-newspaper cartoonist, was hired as a director-writer. His first picture was called *The Story of George Washington*. This clever little film was an entirely new approach to animated films.

The characters were drawn very crudely, the kind of primitive artwork that a five-year-old child might have done. The sound track, narrated by a child, was full of misconceptions about the adult world. It was a delightful idea, and should have been the basis for a series. Instead, after making one more film in the same vein, *The Leak in the Dike,* Jack Mendelsohn quit.

Post, left to his own resources, ignored the possibilities of Mendelsohn's concepts, and went on with his lumbering Halfwitch pictures. In addition he tried his hand at making a pilot for a TV series, which was to feature the voice and humorous material of a nightclub comic, Bill Dana.

Dana, a fairly successful stand-up comic, had, oddly enough, become the court jester for the astronauts in the space program. They particularly enjoyed the jokes Dana created about a little Mexican character named José Jiménez. Post decided that what convulsed the austronauts must be good enough for the American public.

Somehow, whatever humor Dana possessed was filtered out of Post's script. What remained was a typical, clumsy Famous story and a pedestrian storyboard.

Shortly before these problems arose, Post had incurred the wrath of some members of Paramount's board of directors when he produced a film about Noah's Ark that seemed to have antireligious overtones.

So it looked like a fitting time for me to ask for an interview with Burton Hanft, who had the thankless job of managing Famous Studio. At least I could let him know that I was available, if he was contemplating a change.

The fact that I had not been an executive for eight years did not worry me a jot. I remembered the physical and mental strain of being a producer with the surging excitement of an old athlete who gets a whiff of the stale smell of a locker room.

17

Famous Studio

Burt and I had never met before, but his greeting was so warm that I soon relaxed. I spoke quite frankly about my bankruptcy and the eight subsequent years, wandering aimlessly . . . a loner.

I told him of my sudden realization that I had thrown the baby out with the bath water. I was not using some of my major talents: direction, organization and teaching.

The more I talked, the more I felt that Burt was sympathetic, understanding, and a good listener. I found out later that he was a lawyer, in addition to his other skills. His questions were neatly designed to draw me out.

Then I came to my evaluation of Famous Studio. The place needed somebody who was familiar with other markets besides theatrical shorts.

My plan was to start with the theatrical films, modernizing the direction, stories, and animation design. During that time we would be looking for stars to replace Popeye and Casper the Ghost.

Later, we could set up a television unit, perhaps two. One possibly producing television spots, the other creating half-hour specials. The spot unit would include a live-action crew, in order to produce combinations of live-action and animation when called for.

Finally, I believed Famous needed a separate division of live-action people to start competing for large business films. Depending on the needs of the client, our sales force could also make deals involving the whole animation unit, which could drop theatrical production long enough to make a commercial film.

All this would take time. Maybe three or four years. I had learned from my bankruptcy never to expand too quickly. It should be a program of steady but controlled growth.

However, with the prestige and resources of Paramount behind us, we could make a huge success in each field. There was a potential annual gross of millions of dollars with such a multi-faceted company. With my background I was sure that I could make it all happen.

Neither of us mentioned the present difficulties of the studio. The salary Burt offered, I accepted without hesitation. To my surprise, he added that he would include some type of profit participation in my contract. I realized that it was an oblique way of letting me know that he approved of my plan, and this was his way of ensuring that I was suitably rewarded if it all came about.

Burt chuckled at my obvious happiness and wished me luck very warmly. I left his office feeling that I was going to work for a very understanding and supportive boss, and an odd premonition that I had just made a good friend. I was right on both counts. Burt Hanft remains, to this day, one of my closest friends.

Within a few minutes, any trained observer can tell if a studio is functioning well. The morning I arrived at Famous Studio to take over my new job, I was appalled at the atmosphere of depression and weary indifference that hung like a miasma over the whole place.

I knew many of the people in key positions. Winston Sharples, the music composer, had worked with me at Van Beuren. Al Eugster, Nick Tafuri, and Bill Pattengill had been in my unit in Fleischer's Miami studio. Lennie McCormick, one of the cameramen, had been with the organization for over thirty-five years. In the ink and paint department, I recognized several people who had worked in my own studio. It gave me a feeling of security to know that I wasn't going to be working with total strangers.

Everybody greeted me very cordially, but underlying the enthusiasm was a certain constraint and a visible uneasiness.

I made a brief talk to the staff, in which I outlined my plans for more modern stories, better animation, and a general uplifting of the quality of the films. When I finished there was a scattering of applause, then the whole group drifted back to work very slowly, like sleepwalkers. I thought wryly that they must be drinking the waters of Lethe at the coffee break. Never had I seen such mass sluggishness in an animation studio.

OLIVE

← OPEN TOE

A model sheet showing the comparative sizes of the principals in the most popular series the Fleischer Studio ever produced. For a time, in some markets, Popeye, Olive Oyl, and Bluto were more popular than the Disney short subjects.

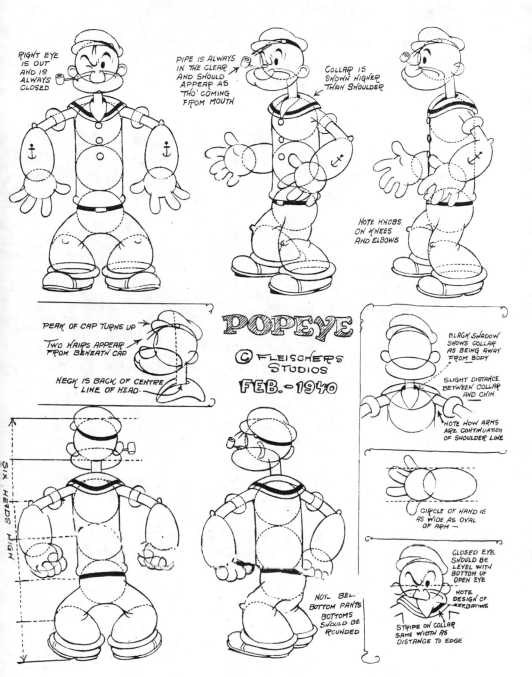

This Popeye model sheet dated 1940 shows that the lack of education in draftsmanship was still a serious problem in the Fleischer Studio. One of the basic tenets of figure drawing is to avoid using symmetry. Here, it would seem that the artist considered symmetry an advantage. Popeye stands solidly on both legs, his hands mirror images of each other, as are his pants and shoes.

That afternoon Nick Tafuri and I had a very revealing discussion in my office. Nick was never one to mince words. He said bluntly, "The trouble is that after Paramount fired the Fleischer brothers, all the Hollywood guys left, except Eugster, and they moved the rest of us up here.

"At least Max and Dave wanted to make the pictures funny. I know you never thought much of Dave's gags, but at least for Crissake he tried. After, when Seymour Kneitel, Izzy Sparber, and Buchwald took over, they just wanted to turn out cheap pictures. Maybe Buchwald didn't, but he couldn't do much about it.

"We started doing this formula shit. It got so you couldn't tell one picture from the other. We just ground them out like sausages, and nobody seemed to give a fuck except Buchwald. But he died, then Sparber. When Seymour died too, they got in this kid, Howard Post. He used to write stories for Kneitel, so it's just been some more of the same old crap.

"I know you like to do good pictures, but I think Paramount doesn't give a damn either way. Just get the fucking pictures out on time, and in the budget. I'll pitch in, but I don't know how far you're gonna get with this bunch. They're kinda knocked out."

My only rebuttal to this sour evaluation was that Burt Hanft gave a damn or I wouldn't be there.

Nick had scarcely left when one of the inkers asked to see me. She was an ex-employee of mine, and a very sincere, hardworking person. Almost tearfully she explained that there was a clique in the department led by a woman who was very powerful in the union. She and her friends made a practice of waiting until the head of the department left his desk, then riffled through the piles of animation drawings and picked out the easy scenes to ink or paint.

The rest of the women hadn't dared to complain, because the clique might get them in trouble with the union. The leader was a very good friend of Pepe Ruiz. I assured her that I'd do something about the situation right away, so she left somewhat mollified.

Rather than talk to Hal Robbins, the department head, I decided to beard the dragon herself. She came into my office looking very defiant and slouched into a chair without waiting for an invitation.

I said bluntly, "I notice that you weren't very impressed by my talk this morning." She shrugged. She hadn't been. I had noticed her making sotto voce asides to her friends. They couldn't have been complimentary, because the group was smirking and twittering.

I went on, "Some people have natural qualities of leadership, and I would guess that you are one of the lucky few." Now she was looking puzzled, but interested. "Usually these few people go on to become valuable executives. On the other hand, others become what I call anti-executives. They use their power of leadership to rally other people against authority, whether the antagonism is warranted or not. They even use it against their fellow workers." She made no move, just looked stony-faced.

I leaned over my desk and glared. "Why don't you go back and tell your friends what a tough son of a bitch they now have for a boss; because I am going to fire the first one of you that I catch looking for an easy scene instead of taking the one on the top of the pile."

She flounced out of the office without a word. I went home that night with my enthusiasm slightly dented. It didn't sound like the beginning of a beautiful friendship.

It might have been a coincidence that a few days later Pepe Ruiz stalked into the studio, looking every inch the efficient business agent. We glared at each other as we passed in an aisle. I went on to my office, and a few minutes later Ruiz burst in without knocking and announced (with poorly feigned indignation) that he was closing the studio. Two of our inkers were behind in their dues!

The idea was so preposterous that I fervently wished that he'd try it. Instead I invited him to talk it over with Burt Hanft. Of course nothing ever came of it. Pepe just wanted to raise my blood pressure a little. It worked, too.

Although I was itching to get to work on the job of assembling a new group of writers, I decided that I should look over the work of the individual animators for a few days. To my astonishment, Seymour Kneitel, usually such a penny watcher, had saddled the animators with the computations of camera moves that traditionally were the work of the camera department.

Not only that, while the rest of the business had been using the metric system, this studio, years behind everybody else, was still laboriously calculating in inches and fractions. Animators were spending hours every week using this clumsy method. The cameramen who used metrics could do the same work about five times faster and cheaper.

During my first production meetings with the animators, I announced that they were going to be freed of this onerous job, leaving them more time for their own specialty, animation. To my consternation, several of the animators objected vociferously. They were used to it. They had always done it (which certainly was not true).

I ordered (rather brusquely) that the practice was to stop as of that day. Willy-nilly, Famous Studio was about to enter the modern world, even if I had to carry it kicking and screaming! I'll be damned if one of the animators didn't stay after the meeting to see if he couldn't argue me out of my decision. When he couldn't, he left in a fury.

Somehow his anger seemed too great to be consistent with the relative triviality of the incident. I began to realize how anything that disturbed the somnambulistic nature of their routine was going to be fiercely resisted. It was going to be necessary to jar these Rip Van Winkles awake. The opportunity came very soon.

I spent the rest of the morning looking over recent pictures. Most of them were about Howard Post's brainchild, Honey Halfwitch. She was drawn like a little girl, had the voice of a child, and the personality of a fire hydrant. After lunch I came into animation row, straddled a chair, and looked around quietly until I had everybody's attention.

Then I smiled and said, "I've been looking at some of your latest pictures." Since I was smiling, everybody relaxed. I went on in the same casual tone, "I feel very good about them." They all smiled in relief. I stood up. "The reason I feel so good is that dead drunk I couldn't turn out such a piss poor pile of crap." Without waiting to see the effects of my bombshell, I walked out.

Unfortunately, we were saddled with other Howard Post Honey Halfwitch scripts. He had a deal to write six more in 1967. You could embellish them with better camera angles and good cutting techniques, but the films were bound to be like all the other pictures that had been made since the Fleischers had left . . . about as funny as a dead horse.

The first thing we did for the story department was to raise the price of scripts from $300 to $800. The fallacy of spending only $300 for a script, then making a $15,000 picture out of it, is too obvious for further comment. I wrote up a spec sheet as a guide for new writers, and some of its contents show how radical our new point of view was going to be:

> Remember that we are now doing high-style animated films, with modern story ideas, offbeat characters both in design and animation, and backgrounds using materials like Zippatone, colored papers, and other aids to textures. We are willing to use puppets or any other new technique for a good cinematic result.

We did have some problems with the salesmen. Unlike Burt Hanft, who was heartily in favor of my attempts to revitalize the studio, I met nothing but unyielding hostility from the salesmen. There were five of them, who looked so much alike it was startling. They were all about fifty, with comfortable paunches, triple chins, and pursey mouths clamped over half-chewed cigar butts that I never saw them light.

The first picture I had to screen for them was a Honey Halfwitch, directed by Howard Post. When the lights went on again, they turned to me indignantly. "Waddaya say? Ya gonna do better than this crap?" I assured them that I would. "How about something funny like Bugs Bunny? Yeah, why can't ya copy him . . . just some funny fuckin' rabbit or something?"

When I tried to explain that cartoon stars were just like live movie stars, they could not be manufactured on request, I could tell that they rejected this concept and trundled out, disappointed and disgruntled.

When Burt Hanft showed me the books of the company, going back several years, I saw that Famous Studio was on a collision course with disaster. For the last five years the income from the exhibition of our cartoons in theaters had gone inexorably down. At the same time wages and other costs had gone up just as inexorably.

There was no additional income, except when Kneitel made some pictures for King Features' television programs. Ironically enough, many of them were Popeye cartoons. King Features had revoked the studio's license to use Popeye and the other characters from Segar's comic strip several years before. These television shorts earned Famous a pittance.

Under the leadership of Max and Dave Fleischer, Popeye became so popular with movie audiences throughout the world that for a time he

1945

There is no comparison between the 1940 stilted model sheet and this group of drawings by Carl (Mike) Meyer. Unlike most storymen, Mike drew his own storyboards. Since he was an ex-animator, his poses were usually an inspiration for the layout men and animators. *King Features Syndicate.*

Opposite page: This model sheet of Little Lulu is an example of the East Coast's preoccupation with measuring characters by the size of their heads. In truth, every animator has his own interpretation of the construction of a given character, although the public is not aware of these differences. A well-trained animator can tell at a glance that Freddy Moore, not Norman Ferguson, has animated a Pluto sequence, and the same is true of other animators and characters.

Mike Meyer was also responsible for this new version of Bluto in 1945, leading the way to better animation. Unfortunately, this more modern approach to the construction of the characters coincided with a sharp decline in the quality of the story material. This slide into mediocrity ended when King Features refused to renew the Popeye contract.

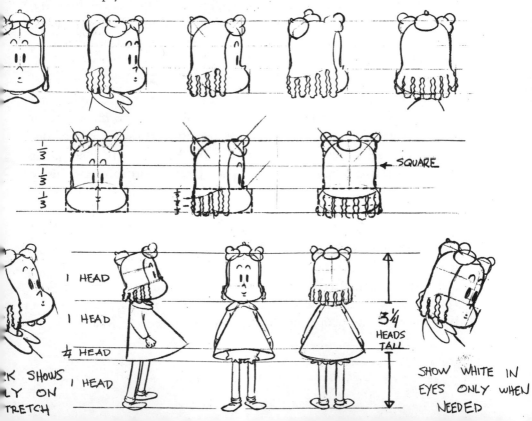

had equaled or even surpassed the popularity of Mickey Mouse. Under the aegis of Kneitel, Sparber, and Buchwald, the quality of Popeye cartoons sank to an incredible low. The TV shorts made for King Features dragged Popeye down even more, because in addition to inept stories, Kneitel used extremely limited animation.

In examining the books of the company it was obvious that we could expect nothing but a dwindling income from the theatrical shorts. Even if we improved the stories and the animation, we could never get back the prosperous days before block booking was abolished.

The practice had been stopped by a court decision in 1950. Under block booking, a production company could send out a salesman to an exhibitor with a package of feature films. With each feature was a rounded out program which included a newsreel, a cartoon, and a two-reel film, which might be a live-action comedy, a nature study, or another type of documentary.

Why it was declared illegal was because the hapless exhibitor had to take the whole package of features, although he and the salesman both knew that some of the films were very inferior. After block booking was banned the death knell sounded for all the short subjects. It didn't pay for a salesman to go to an exhibitor to sell him a short film. Traditionally, they rented for very little money. The exhibitors refused to pay more on the grounds that the public came to the theater to see the feature, not the short subjects.

Within a few years of the elimination of block booking, two-reel production was dropped, the newsreels were headed toward oblivion, and the cartoons seemed to be on the way out as well. The income from animated cartoons was so low that it was hardly worth while to send out a salesman. The government had rescued the exhibitor from an unfair situation, but had sounded the death knell of the short subject industry in the process.

Based on the figures I saw in the books, Famous would have to be revitalized very fast. I explained the situation to the staff, but I could tell that there was an underlying disbelief. It might easily be just another ploy to wring more work out of them.

About a month after I started working at Famous, a disaster hit New York City. We had a transit strike that tied up all buses and subways for days. Many of the people in the studio lived outside of Manhattan, so it was impossible to get to work. A few tried thumbing rides, but it took so long that after a few attempts they gave it up.

A small group elected to stay at the studio and sleep on chairs or couches. Traffic was so congested that I set out from my home in Washington Heights at five in the morning in order to reach the studio by nine. Driving home was even worse.

After the strike was over, Famous paid everyone their full wages whether they had been able to come to work or not. The schedule had been seriously disrupted, so we had to work overtime, which meant an additional loss. It was necessary to hire several animators and assistants on a freelance basis, i.e., time and a half.

At the end of the first day of this accelerated schedule, I was still in my office when the door opened and one of the new assistants came in very timidly. She was an ex-employee of mine and very talented. Under our training program she had gone from painter to assistant animator in a few months. My interest in her as a good artist was about to pay off.

She told me indignantly that one of the new assistants had gleefully announced that this was a golden opportunity to make extra money and advised everybody to work as slowly as possible.

What had shocked her was the fact that nobody had disagreed with him, at least not verbally. It shocked me, too. The next morning I summoned the bastard to my office and told him what I had heard. He didn't deny it; what seemed to stun him was the fact that somebody had "ratted"! I assured him that he was the only rat in the studio, and he was fired. Furthermore, I was restraining a great urge to beat the shit out of him.

After the miserable creep had gone, I sat there fuming. What crazy "code of honor" made it possible for an outsider to come in and suggest that the whole group should steal from the company. Why didn't they throw him out bodily?

Was it possible that there was no gratitude for Famous Studio's payment of all salaries, when more than half the staff had been unable to appear for work for days? Was it more important to protect a union "brother" even when he was a crook?

I began to recall many years before, when I gathered my staff together and tried to explain the economic ramifications of clandestine, unaffiliated groups stealing work from the legitimate union studios. I remembered, from their taut faces, how I could tell that some of my staff knew something, but were not about to tell. When the chips were down they would rather have the company lose business than "rat" on their fellow unionists.

It was true that before the unions the animation business was utterly lacking in the most basic economic rights. There were no vacations, no sick leave; Christmas, New Year's, and Thanksgiving were the only paid holidays, and almost all of the studios did not pay overtime. The cartoonists' unions had to drag the business into the twentieth century.

However, what had become of the feelings of solidarity, the enjoyment of working together that I had experienced at the Bray Studio; the feeling of embarrassment the staff had because Krazy Kat was not as good as Felix; the loyalty to Max, and the excitement when Betty Boop became a hit; our earnest efforts to make Flip the Frog a star because Iwerks was our boss and we liked him; the togetherness that caused the boyos to meet at the Metropole after work, to spend hours in discussing the problems of Burt Gillett at Van Beuren's; the pride we all took when Lundy and I started to invigorate the Walt Lantz pictures; and of course, the immense feeling of an elite corps that suffused the Walt Disney Studio before the strike.

As far as I knew, we had the same attitude in Shamus Culhane Productions . . . or did we? Would a staff from the old days have kept silent when the survival of the company was at stake? Or listened to a suggestion to blatantly steal from the company?

At Krazy Kat Studio I think the staff would have voted yes without a qualm because the management was so openly exploitive. Otherwise, I think not. There was loyalty to fellow workers, and a commonsense evaluation of the fact that this company was where one's living came from, and as such must be defended from all forces that might threaten its existence.

Now all these healthy emotions seemed to have been bypassed in favor of a blind loyalty to the union. It must be that the incessant ranting about the "cruel bosses" and the "exploiters of the masses" had succeeded in brainwashing the union members. Mindless hostility was replacing the healthy concern for the welfare of the company that was supplying the members a living.

I sat there in my office for long hours musing about what had happened. The best that I could conclude was that something valuable, some spiritual asset, had been lost in the transition from exploited individuals to union members.

One of the first artists I hired for my modernization program was Gil Miret. He had been a successful book illustrator, who wanted to abandon his profession and learn how to design and lay out animated cartoons.

Oddly enough, his father, Raymond Miret, had been an animator in Spain during the 1920s. He made advertising spots for movie houses, just as Walt Disney had done in Kansas City. Unlike Walt, Ramon Miret left the business after a few years. Even when he came to America with his family, at a time when the animation business was thriving, Miret made no effort to reenter the profession.

Gil's enthusiasm and respect for animation were infectious, and his style of drawing and painting was both modern and fresh. None of his work resembled the lackluster design and painting which had characterized the output of the Famous Studio for many years.

People began to drop into the layout department to see what Gil was developing. He was working on the very first picture under the new regime, *A Balmy Knight.* The animators began to get excited at the prospect of working with these new and odd-looking characters.

Nick Tafuri recalls that at one point I assured him that his work on the knight was the best animation he had ever done. Al Eugster snapped out of his torpor and became the reliable animator I had known years ago. He was always able to add some little touch to a commonplace bit of action. His was the kind of showmanship that distinguishes the top-flight animators from the hacks.

One day I was walking down the hall, and many people were walking past me on various errands. Suddenly it struck me! They were moving briskly and smiling. By Jesus, the gloom was gone. This was a happy studio, except for one problem.

The most painful aspect of revamping the studio was the growing awareness that some of the key people were not able to adjust to the new methods I was installing. I tried switching them to other jobs; Burt tried to find them positions in other areas of Paramount. Neither of us succeeded.

When we both realized that they would have to be laid off, Burt and I went into a series of meetings, which would have been hilarious if the issue wasn't so tragic. One day I would come bursting into Hanft's office, in a fury because of some incredible bit of ineptitude. I'd demand that the perpetrator be fired. Burt would calm me down and gently suggest that we should not act hastily.

The next time Burt would be the heavy. As I listened to his iritation, I could only imagine the stricken faces of the victims. Some of them had worked for the studio for over thirty years. When I pointed this out, Burt would stop, and we would just sit there looking at each other in frustration.

We did this for months, until the day came when we mutually agreed to take action. The union had very specific rates for severance pay, but Burt ignored them. Some of the people left with more than six months' severance. Even so, it was a bitter experience all around. We must have looked like two hardhearted bastards. In truth, we had no choice. There was no way we could allow old-fashioned work methods to exist cheek-by-jowl with modern production systems.

Every week I went over the bills, looking frantically for some way to cut down the overhead. I noticed that most of the staff left their lights on when they went to lunch, so I sent around a memo asking people to turn off their lights in the interest of economy.

Everybody complied except our anti-executive. One day I caught up with her at the door. "You forgot your lights," I said patiently. She looked at me sardonically. "What's the matter? Afraid that Paramount won't make a profit?" I was overcome with fury. Here she was getting her weekly paycheck, while the poor bastards in the television spot business were working three weeks, then out of work six; and she didn't have the common sense to want to protect her job!

"What the Christ do you think this studio is, a charity organization? Turn off those goddamn lights, and do it every day or I'll report you to the shop steward." Sullenly, she switched off her lights in a series of venomous snaps.

Some months later she had gone on her vacation. When she returned, I met her in the hall. She had a red nose and a bad cold. "What's the matter with you?" I asked. She looked at me distastefully. "I was sick the whole time I was away." As I walked past her I snapped, "Take another vacation, you're entitled to sick leave." I just glimpsed her jaw dropping in amazement as I walked by.

There was nothing in the contract about sick leave while on vacation, but I knew that Burt would back me up. I had no illusions about her. We would always be the enemy. But that was her problem.

Overseeing the cartoon studio was not Burt Hanft's major job. He was in charge of renting all of Paramount's old features to the television networks. I would often come into his office when he was on the telephone haggling about the price of a dozen features. Figures like a quarter of a million dollars for this, half a million for others, the terms would be bandied back and forth.

Finally he would make a satisfactory deal, hang up, and turn to me. Burt would gravely listen to my suggestion that we give one of the employees a ten-dollar raise, with the same kind of concentration he had just used on a big deal. We both knew the delicate condition of the budget, so sometimes he would ask that the subject be shelved for a few weeks. I would rarely object, but I did joke with him about the fact that he was the only person I knew who could juggle iron and feathers at the same time.

As months went by I knew that Burt was giving me his full confidence, in spite of the salesmen's open hostility. I was sure that he was taking a lot of flak from them, but he never mentioned it.

Once a month we screened a new Honey Halfwitch or one of Gene Deitch's Nudniks for the sales force. They all would get up and walk out without a word. None of them were able or willing to accept the fact that we had to finish all of Post's pictures before we could complete one from the new regime.

Meanwhile, I was always on the lookout for new material from outside sources. When John and Faith Hubley invited me to a screening of a new picture, *Herb Alpert and the Tijuana Brass*, I was so impressed with the film that I asked Burt Hanft to screen it.

Burt was impressed too, and made a deal with the Hubleys to release the picture through Paramount. As in the case of Gene Deitch's *Munro*, *Tijuana Brass* won an Academy Award. Again Paramount had won an Oscar through osmosis.

The fact that the Nudnik series was not funny was a great puzzle to me, because it was not consistent with Deitch's track record. I had been a great admirer of his work at UPA and Terrytoons, so I was sure that he could create a better character. In the interim, we had to wait until the Nudnik series was completed, and I was just as impatient as the salesmen.

Finally, after seven months, my first picture, *A Balmy Knight,* was screened for the sales force. When the lights went on all they could do was curse and splutter that it was worse than that UPA shit! Much more important to me was the fact that Burt Hanft liked it.

All this time I had been building up a staff of writers. The lone survivor of the Old Guard was Joe Szabo. For the most part he made his living writing and drawing gags for magazines. A new writer, Howard Beckerman, had been in the animation business but drifted away into designing gags for Hallmark cards. Now he was back with some very offbeat story ideas. Possibly the most valuable new employee was Cliff Roberts, an ex-Hollywood veteran, a first-class writer, and equally proficient as a character designer, layout man, and background artist.

We even discovered some latent talent in the assistant department. Dante Barbetta had been an assistant for years at Famous Studio. At one point he had tried to do some animation, but Seymour Kneitel had been such an impatient tutor that Dante lost confidence and decided to return to assistant work.

I had paid no attention to him because he had been working on the pedestrian characters for Honey Halfwitch pictures, which were still in production. At that time, there was no hint of his extraordinary talent. One day I happened to pass his desk at lunchtime and found Dante amusing himself by drawing some remarkably funny doodles. I promoted him to layout man and character designer, and he soon was one of the most valuable artists in the studio. Yet he had languished for years as a lowly assistant.

One of the most imaginative cartoonists in this country is Bob Blechman. By 1966 he had already distinguished himself in newspapers and magazines with his distinctive technique of drawing everything in a wavering line.

I happened to buy a book he had written and illustrated. It was a small book of short stories. They seemed ideal for animation. The modern themes that Bob had used seemed to be exactly the contemporary wit I was looking for. In fact, I was already visualizing the possibility that he might become one of the writer–directors on our staff.

I showed the book to Burt Hanft and he agreed that several of the stories would make for very funny animation. Accordingly, I called

Blechman and arranged for a meeting in Burt's office. Bob arrived with a lawyer, and in a very short time a deal for a film was consumated. All that was necessary was to prepare the papers. However, just as we were all about to disperse, Blechman asked if he could add one proviso to the contract.

Our meeting had gone so smoothly that nobody was prepared for his proposed stipulation. Blechman explained that he thought that Paramount pictures were of very poor quality. Could there be some arrangement made whereby his cartoon would not appear on the same programs as Paramount features? The meeting and the proposed contract ended right there.

Some years later Blechman opened up his own animation studio, and now makes some of the most distinctive spots on the air.

The biggest money-maker we made was a cartoon called *My Daddy the Astronaut*. It came about because Joe Szabo brought in a dreary story idea that was a throwback to the unfunny pictures of the former regime. I peevishly told Joe that he should be thinking about more modern ideas.

At that time there was an intense public interest in the space program. There was even some speculation that some day we might land a spaceship on the moon. To give him an example I began to concoct a theme about a small child's version of what happened to his father who was an astronaut.

Besides taking his point of view, why not design the picture in the style of a five-year-old child's drawings? Within a few minutes I had given Szabo the entire structure of the film. The father goes to a space school for lessons; lands on the moon; is picked up by a warship when he lands; has a sleep-over at the White House, and is given a ticker tape parade. This latter event puzzles the kid because the adults are littering.

After all the excitement the astronaut takes his son to an amusement park. They eat a lot of junk food between dizzying rides on the roller coaster and other forms of torture. The child has great fun, but the father gets sicker and sicker from the junk food and the rides. Finally, when they are on the carousel, he falls off and breaks both legs. Then, as the child relates, "The ambulance came just like the movies, and we had a nice ride all the way to the hospital."

The film ends with a shot of the astronaut in bed with both his legs in traction. The boy, standing by the bed, addresses the audience very sagely, "If at first you *do* succeed, don't try again."

Character sketches by Howard Beckerman for *A Balmy Knight*. Written by Joe Szabo, directed by Shamus Culhane, animated by Al Eugster, Nick Tafuri, and Howard Beckerman.

A drawing by Gil Miret for *My Daddy the Astronaut*. Famous Studio, 1967.

The child-narrator of *My Daddy the Astronaut*. Designed by Gil Miret, animated by Al Eugster, directed by Shamus Culhane. Famous Studio, 1966.

Indignation must be a wonderful catalyst, because I reeled off the story in about five minutes without hesitation. A very chastened Joe took the idea home and added some very funny embellishments of his own.

A common custom when recording a child's voice is to fake it by using a woman who can speak in falsetto. However, I decided to use a five-year-old. During the recording I purposely fed him the lines so fast that he became very confused.

He made some marvelous bloopers, like saying "suspoosed" instead of "supposed," "firkst" instead of "first," and repeated himself, faltering through the longer sentences.

We ended up with more than an hour of sound track, so it took us several days to whittle it down to six minutes, retaining as often as possible the many awkward pauses and mispronunciations. The end result was a very authentic-sounding track, with the child giving his halting interpretation of the puzzling adult world.

Oddly enough, nobody in the studio had the sense to tell us that Jack Mendelsohn had made two pictures just two years before with the same approach. Had we screened them, it would have saved us from doing a great deal of fumbling.

Gil Miret was designing the characters and making layouts, and he was having a lot of trouble. He simply could not make a drawing that looked as if it had been done by a child. Several of us tried to help, even drawing left-handed. They all looked phony.

Finally, in desperation, I asked my wife, Juana, who was teaching kindergarten at the time, if she would give us a stack of drawings made by her class. After that, we had no difficulty. Gil was able to glean enough information about proportion and poses to make a very convincing crude set of characters. The raw colors, made with children's crayons, also looked genuine on the backgrounds.

Al Eugster animated the entire picture. He faced the same problem that had stumped Gil Miret: how to draw with naïveté, while using his expertise to keep the action funny.

He succeeded very well, adding some subtle touches of his own, while presenting what seemed to be a very primitive animation.

I shocked Win Sharples, our music director, when I rejected the idea of using our usual fifteen-piece orchestra in favor of getting the best harmonica player in New York. Then I stunned the musician when I told him to deliberately make some mistakes in his playing. He reacted with the same indignation that Heifitz would have exhibited if I had asked him to put a few clinkers in his favorite concerto.

The completed cartoon is what I believe to be one of the best pictures I ever produced. *My Daddy the Astronaut* was booked with *2001: A Space Odyssey,* so it probably was one of Famous's largest money-makers.

To this day I have never seen Jack Mendelsohn's *The Story of George Washington* or *A Leak in the Dike,* but I have read rave reviews about them in trade magazines, and Leonard Maltin's book, *Of Mice and Magic* (Van Hoffman Press).

Several years before, when I was animating and directing Hal Seeger's children shows, I worked with a young layout man and character designer named Hal Silvermintz. I found his ideas much more imaginative than most of the designers in New York. The best designers in New York at the time were all artists with a Hollywood background. Hal was a notable exception.

Silvermintz had never worked in Hollywood. He had studied at the High School of Arts and Design, the National Academy, and Cooper Union. His first job in animation had been at Electra. When that studio closed he began to freelance in the spot business.

His first assignment was working with Dante Barbetta and Gil Miret on one of our more offbeat stories, *Think or Sink.* They designed the characters as linear figures with no body color at all, playing against monochromatic backgrounds.

The story was about a dog and an elephant who were great friends. The dog invites the elephant to the beach, but he refuses because he can't swim. The dog persuades him to come anyway.

The dog is swimming contentedly until he suddenly spies the elephant happily skating on the water. Then the elephant explains that while he can't swim, he always has been able to walk, dance, or skate on water. The dog, very sure that something is terribly wrong with his friend, convinces him that he should see a psychiatrist. The doctor tells them that anybody can walk on water if he knows that he can.

The next time the two friends go to the beach they both skate on the water, that is, until the elephant begins to get dubious. Suppose they only *thought* they could stand on water. With that they sink like two stones, and the dog has to save his friend from drowning.

Even on the beach the elephant is troubled. Suppose, he queries, that

A sketch by Dante Barbetta from the storyboard of *Think or Sink*. Produced in 1967, it was the only Paramount cartoon ever to appear in the Annecy Film Festival. Directed by Shamus Culhane.

This is a layout drawing by Dante Barbetta, who also designed the characters for the film *Think or Sink*. Famous Studios, 1967.

"HEART GENTLE."

we are standing on the ground only because we think we can? With that the two friends sink in the sand up to their necks. While they are helplessly looking at each other, the doctor comes in, collects a fee in advance, and makes an appointment to see them the following week with this new problem. He exits, and we iris out on the dog looking furiously at the crestfallen elephant.

Think or Sink was shown at the ASIFA animation festival at Annecy, France, in 1967. It was the first time in the history of the studio that had happened.

My Daddy the Astronaut had been so successful that I decided to do several more cartoons in the same vein. The first one was a story, which I wrote with Cliff Roberts, called *The Stuck-Up Wolf.*

This was a child's confused version of Little Red Riding Hood and the Wolf. He adds contemporary details like the Wolf planning to go to the movies to see *Wolf Man.* The film ends with Red Riding Hood enticing the Wolf to compete with her in a bubble gum contest. She gives the wolf a huge wad of gum, and he blows such a big bubble that he is entrapped in it. Then she calls the FBI and they cart him off to jail. Quite a different story from the classic Prokofiev version.

Instead of using a box of crayons to color the backgrounds as Gil Miret had done, Roberts used finger paints. The result was just as charming as the crayon drawings.

Again, we recorded a small child's voice, and the piping voice stumbling over the big words made for an amusing sound track. Several months later I saw the film in a theater and the audience reaction was very gratifying.

The other film was called *The Stubborn Cowboy.* The child narrator confuses the story line of a Western with the television commercials. He can't understand when the cowboy hero, while having a harrowing running battle with some Indians, refuses to succumb to the blandishments of a salesman for a nerve medicine.

The child is further perplexed when the cowboy is losing all his money in a crooked poker game, and turns down an unctuous offer of a bank loan. When his girlfriend is dragged around by the hair by a local "bad man," the cowboy does not buy a shampoo from an earnest huckster. The child decides that this cowboy is about the most stubborn cowpoke ever.

The audience reaction to these stories was so good that I decided to make a full series of this kind of picture as soon as the Honey Halfwitch series was finished.

The Plumber, a very offbeat musical written and designed by Cliff Roberts is about a plumber working in the cellar of a building, trying to clear a pipe. When everything else fails, he blows into it. To his astonishment and pleasure, it sounds a deep musical note. He experiments with other pipes and very soon is blowing a jazz composition that has people dancing in the streets overhead.

The plumber becomes wealthy and famous as he gives similar concerts in building after building. The apex of his career comes when it is announced that he is going to blow the pipes of the Empire State Building.

He arrives in a limousine, graciously acknowledging the wild cheering of his fans. When he settles down in the basement, among a maze of pipes, the plumber has all the hauteur of a master musician. However, he has barely started to play when an annoying fly makes him blow a sour note. The sound shatters all the windows, wrecks the building and his career.

The picture ends on a night shot of a deserted street. The plumber, now an unkempt bum, sneaks into the scene, furtively lifts up a manhole and enters the sewer. He begins to blow a plaintive blues as the picture fades out.

The reaction of the salesmen to these screwball stories was predictable. They finally were so disgusted that they wouldn't even say hello if we met in the hall. The screenings each month were painful events. At first they pleaded with me to mend my ways and copy some fucking character like Daffy Duck, or even Mickey Mouse. After all, Terrytoons had a Mighty Mouse, why couldn't we copy too, for Chrissake!

Finally, they lapsed into gloomy silence, looking at the screen with wounded eyes, then trooping out in dignified silence.

On the other hand, Burt Hanft liked what we were doing. The only time he vetoed an idea that I was enthusiastic about was when he rejected a Sholom Aleichem story on the grounds that it was too ethnic. Burt never criticized the kind of graphics we were using, even though we had radically changed the appearance of the Famous cartoons.

It wasn't that I had effected a renascence in the studio, because that would imply that I was reviving something that was there before. The new films were diametrically opposed to Max Fleischer's credo that animated cartoons should be "cartoony, not arty or psychological."

What I had done was more on the order of Frank Tashlin's impact on Screen Gems in 1941 when he hired Disney strikers off the picket lines, or Gene Deitch's campaign against the Old Guard at Terrytoons, which resulted in a dramatic if short-lived period of quality production.

Every creative person in Famous had the chance to use his creativity to the fullest. I had no desire to emulate Walt Disney in organizing a studio where everyone was like a microcosm of one huge macrocosm, like the various cells that make up a jellyfish. The only pictures that reflected my taste were the films I wrote and directed myself.

Disney had the need to express his own personality to the exclusion of anybody else's ideas about humor. He had the combined iron will and seductiveness to bring his artists to accept his needs and relinquish their's.

This is not a unique situation in art history. Peter Paul Rubens put together a stable of specialists who worked on his paintings. They were outstanding artists in their own fields, such as landscapes, drapery, and still life. Others could paint the figure so well that they could follow Ruben's own sketches up to a point. Then the master would step in and swiftly add the requisite details to the contribution of each specialist. The details that made the painting a "genuine" Peter Paul Rubens.

Taking into account the vast number of films produced by the Disney Studio, there are only a few examples, like *Toot Whistle Plunk and Boom*, that are counter to Walt's personal taste. Nobody in the studio had total freedom of expression.

In a basic sense there was creative deprivation, which must have aroused vague feelings of hostility among the more innovative people in the studio.

In an article in *Funnyworld* magazine, Wilfred Jackson, a director in Disney's almost from the beginning of the studio, recalls an incident during World War II, which has obvious undercurrents:

> Directing *The New Spirit* was a unique experience, in that, for once, meeting our deadline took precedence over *all* other considerations—even including making sure we got exactly what Walt wanted in the picture, or making sure Walt knew how *his* picture was going to look in time for him to do anything about it, if he did not like something in it. This was perhaps the only time I was completely in control of a large part of one of the cartoons I directed for Walt.

Looking at the evidence it can be postulated that Walt's decision to educate his staff by hiring such outstanding teachers as Don Graham and Jean Charlot was not altogether altruistic. It may be that like so many self-educated men, Walt had the capacity to evaluate his talents or their shortcomings very dispassionately. Since he was not capable of producing a picture by himself, and the rest of the staff were his surrogates, he would want the group to have the best possible education.

The carrot on the stick was the fact that each artist was permitted—nay, commanded—to do his best possible work. The whip was applied only if an individual showed signs of wanting to express his own artistic needs and they did not coincide with Walt's. Although *Toot Whistle Boom and Plunk* did win an Academy Award, it is significant that there was little effort to make other pictures using the same techniques.

If you leaf through the pages of Ollie Johnston and Frank Thomas' book *Disney Animation, The Illusion of Life* (Abbeville Press), the many illustrations of backgrounds used in various pictures reveal that there were no Fauves among the artists in the background department; no Paul Julians with sly, discreet Picassoid details.

These are the negative aspects of working at Disney Studio. The positive sides are not to be brushed away lightly. One worked in clean, modern surroundings, with the best art materials and equipment, exchanging ideas with some of the most talented men in the profession, with the satisfaction of pushing every day for one's best possible achievement.

While we will never know what some of the Disney directors would have accomplished in other studios, neither will we know about the potentials of the directors in these studios, because if Disney dominated his directors to the point of restriction, the others were equally restricted by smaller budgets and fast schedules.

We, in the animation field, are not loners like Picasso, Cézanne, Degas, and Renoir because of the nature of the field in which we work. Animation, for the most part, is a group effort and uses expensive machinery and materials. We are attached to the business world like a pilot fish clings to a shark.

People in the animation business are more like Renaissance artists, who were willing and able to design anything from a finger ring to a tank, paint an altarpiece or a portrait, or work on the costumes and motifs for a costume ball. Each master unabashedly ran a commercial business.

Unlike my reckless approach to spending money in my own studio, we never ran over the budgets for our pictures at Famous, because, happily for me, we had no budget-busters on the staff, and besides, I had learned my lesson.

No more helter-skelter approach to expansion either. I was slowly solidifying the staff into a well-run unit. Only when that was accomplished did I intend to go to my next step, television spots. However, my plans were radically changed when Steve Krantz came to Famous Studio with a proposal.

Krantz, an entrepreneur in children's programs in television, wanted us to produce thirty-nine five-minute cartoons as part of a half-hour superhero show that he was putting together. He had gotten an option on several of the standard comic-book characters like Captain America, the Hulk, the Mighty Thor, etcetera. Krantz had signed up the four available studios in Hollywood, and needed a fifth to produce *The Mighty Thor*.

From an artistic viewpoint the series was garbage. Krantz was using Xeroxed illustrations from the comic books, only animating the eyes and mouths of the characters. By adding special effects like death rays, explosions beefed up by camera moves, he had put together a sample film of a Captain America story which had been accepted by the networks.

It was a typical plot of the period, i.e., insensate violence and simplistic characterizations of good guys and bad guys. It was indicative of the kind of film that finally aroused a group of concerned parents and teachers to make an organized attack on the type of junk that was being served up on the Saturday morning children's shows.

My ambition was for Famous to produce television entertainment with sophisticated whimsy, like Jay Ward's *Bullwinkle* shows. However, even if Krantz's whole approach was diametrically opposed to our own plans, it was an opportunity for our staff to learn the basic production techniques used in making a series for television.

Burt Hanft invited me to a meeting with Steve Krantz to discuss the details of the contract. Krantz was a tall, lean man who would have been quite handsome except for a slightly overshot jaw. He seemed to radiate a scarcely controlled energy which kept him constantly shifting about in his chair. By contrast Burt Hanft sat very quietly, only occasionally leaning over to make short notes on a memo pad.

I watched with fascination at the parry and thrust that went on between Hanft and Krantz. Never have I seen such a nimble exchange of offers and counteroffers. The discussion took more than an hour.

Finally, a satisfactory deal was arrived at, and Krantz, smiling triumphantly, rose to go. Before he reached the door, Hanft reminded him of an important omission. He had forgotten an important clause, which was for his own protection. Somewhat chagrined, Krantz admitted that he had, and the clause was duly entered in Burt's notes.

After Krantz left I began to praise Hanft for his honesty, but he brushed it off with the remark that he never entered into a contract where one side was not going to get a fair deal. In his opinion such arrangements were usually worthless in the long run. In the cutthroat world of motion pictures, Burt Hanft is a rara avis.

We had to enlarge our staff in preparation for this additional work, because we still had to produce our shorts on schedule. About a dozen art school graduates were hired. Under the guidance of Ida Greenberg, who was now head of the ink and paint department, the enthusiastic youngsters were initiated into the intricacies of animation production.

Chuck Harriton, an ex-employee of mine, had long wanted to move from animation to direction, so I gave him the opportunity to direct the majority of The Mighty Thor films. In addition, I hired two other veteran animators who were slated to do most of the animation on the series, as soon as we had a few of the pictures finished.

It was very easy work; the comic-book illustrations were Xeroxed directly onto cels and painted like normal animation drawings, so the animators had nothing complicated to do except for the special effects. The rest of the animation, the eye movements and mouth action, were so simple that even a novice animator could have finished a whole picture in three weeks. To give Harriton lead time on his first episode, I decided to allow the two animators to direct and animate the first two pictures.

The trick in turning out limited animation films is to compile a morgue of stock shots of the main characters as soon as possible. These drawings can then be used in subsequent pictures. It is only necessary to change the sequence of mouth-action drawings to synchronize with the new dialogue, make a different background, and perhaps change the camera field from a long shot to a close-up, to make a stock shot look like a brand-new scene.

Krantz was supplying dialogue tracks for each film, and we made careful storyboards covering each shot. Long before the first two pictures were finished, Harriton and I had selected dozens of shots from the two storyboards to use in the next five episodes, which he had already put into production.

Because the action was so simple nobody bothered to examine the drawings of the first two pictures. Animators took the stock scenes as soon as they were animated, noted the drawing numbers of the characters, mouth actions, and special effects, and returned them to the inking department as quickly as possible, because as long as they were in reuse the first two pictures were being delayed.

I had screened the *Captain America* sample reel for all the animators, pointing out the judicious use of blinks and the perfect synchronization of mouth action and dialogue tracks. The animation was so basic that I elected to dispense with the normal routine of checking each scene before photography. It seemed a needless expense. I also omitted shooting a pencil test for the same reason.

When the first two pictures were ready to be screened, I sat in the projection room with complacence. The two films had been done within the budget and on schedule. A few seconds after the first picture started, I was jolted into shock. The mouth moves were a mess; often they were completely out of sync. In some cases the mouths were so distorted that the characters looked as if they were in a class for speech therapy. All the eyes blinked and blinked. Thor looked like a junkie in great need of a fix. Practically nothing was usable except for the basic Xeroxed cels of the characters. Even the special effects were terrible!

The second picture was only different in that the mouths, in addition to being out of sync, slid all over the face. Needless to say, there was no usable animation in this one either.

I moved from complacence to panic in ten minutes! I broke out in a sweat as I realized that these horrible scenes were already distributed through the next five pictures, and Harriton was already planning to use them in a sixth.

What followed was a mad scramble to find the stock shots (some of them had already been photographed in the subsequent five pictures) and re-animate them. After that the first two pictures were completely re-drawn. The summation of our dismal situation was that we were now two pictures behind schedule, and the loss was more than $10,000.

Chuck Harriton proved that he had the potential to become a very competent director. The pictures he turned out were very well paced and professional-looking, in spite of the limitations of the technique. The new inkers and painters learned quickly to do very clean work; and none of

Nick Tafuri, drawn by Shamus Culhane, 1967.

Howard Beckerman wrote the script for *The Trip,* designed the characters and layouts, and animated the entire film. This was part of a long-range program to create a group of self-sufficient artists capable of doing an entire film from script to screen. 1967. *Paramount Pictures.*

the remaining films ran over the budget or fell behind schedule. However, it proved to be impossible to made inroads on that $10,000 loss.

When he saw the first pictures, Steve Krantz was very pleased, and at no time during the remaining episodes was he disappointed in the result. Naturally we did not show him the first two pictures until they had been repaired.

When *The Mighty Thor* was about halfway through production I realized that we needed two more animators to work on our theatrical shorts. The difficulty was that we had no available working space. The entire area was so crowded with new people and equipment that there wasn't room for even one more desk. I was very excited to find that both Grim Natwick and George Bakes were available. They would be a formidable addition to the talent we had already attracted. I offered them as much work as they could handle with the proviso that they work at home until we finished the Krantz series.

Bakes, a Disney-trained animator, and Natwick, one of the foremost animators in the profession, would need a modicum of supervision. The terms would provide them with a very good income. In fact, Natwick would make a higher salary than any other animator on the staff.

Since we had revitalized an almost moribund studio, added many new members to the union rolls, and raised some of the older Famous employees to more responsible positions with higher salaries, it would seem logical that the union hierarchy would be eager to give us support and encouragement whenever it was possible. Logic proved to have nothing to do with the situation.

My bête noire, Pepe Ruiz, jumped into the Natwick-Bates deal with shrill cries of outrage. "Culhane is trying to turn Famous into a sweatshop! Animators doing piecework!" Natwick and Bakes were commanded to appear before the executive board and made to stand in the hall for an hour, until their case came up on the agenda. Then they were severely reprimanded.

To his devoted followers Ruiz looked as if, once again, he had protected the workers from exploitation. The reality was that Natwick and Bakes had to go back to the financial vagaries of the spot business, we lost the services of two of the best animators in New York, and our theatrical films stayed behind schedule.

When we completed the thirty-nine episodes of *The Mighty Thor*, Krantz came in to tell me that our staff, in comparison to the Hollywood studios who were producing the other segments of the series, had consistently done better work. This was high praise for a hastily assembled group of untried art students, Ida Greenberg, who taught them, and Chuck Harriton, on his first assignment as a director.

The $10,000 loss Burt and I were forced to dismiss as part of the educational process. Although the two animators involved certainly used poor judgment in doing such slipshod work, the basic fault was mine. I should have remembered that there is no such thing as a foolproof picture. Mea maxima culpa!

We retained most of the enlarged staff and went to work on the process of catching up on our schedule. Ironically, now that we had room neither Natwick nor Bakes were available.

The spring and summer of 1967 were a highpoint for us all. The studio was turning out three pictures a month, yet the quality did not suffer. The staff was too enthusiastic to let that happen.

As for me, with the exception of my years at Disney's, I had never been happier. Freed from the constant talk about estimates and contracts, which had plagued me when I had my own studio, I could concentrate on my work as a filmmaker.

After Harriton completed his work on *The Mighty Thor,* he began to direct some of our theatrical shorts, which released me to work more closely with Roberts, Miret, Beckerman, and Barbetta in the design and writing.

One big advantage our layout men and designers had in common was the fact that they were artists who knew a great deal about modern art. The exception was Barbetta, but even he had managed to escape from the influence of the Fleischer and Kneitel designers, so his drawings bore no resemblance to the dull, crude figures that had characterized New York design from the earliest beginnings.

Hal Silvermintz, Gil Miret, and I began working on a zany story: a spoof on the feature pictures about carefully planned robberies, like *Rififi.* Three crooks plotted to saw a hole in the Paris Opera House roof during a concert by a buxom singer who was billed as "The Golden-Voiced Soprano."

Her voice would emerge from her mouth as a transparent stream of bars, measures, and notes, and the golden notes would twinkle in the spotlight as they rose in the air like smoke.

There would be some funny sound effects when the crooks yanked on

428   *Talking Animals and Other People*

the vaporous stream of music as it rose up through the hole in the roof. Every time they pulled the strand of music, the singer's voice would speed up.

Miret was doing some research on the opera house, and we planned to make a very high-style version of its rococo architecture.

The Opera Caper was interrupted by two events, which happened almost simultaneously. Gulf and Western bought Paramount, and Krantz arrived with a proposal to have our studio produce thirty-nine half-hours on *Spider Man,* another comic-book hero.

It looked as if Krantz's offer could not have come at a more fortuitous time. It would give us a whole year of work in addition to our theatrical shorts, giving me time to develop our own series for television.

But before we could enter into a discussion with Krantz about the new contract, a covey of Gulf and Western accountants began to go through the books of every department in the Paramount organization. The animation studio was particularly vulnerable if one just wanted to look at the current income.

If we still had the four hundred *Betty Boops, Popeyes, Little Lulus,* and *Caspers,* Famous Studio would be showing a handsome profit. The new owners of these films were making a fortune renting them to the TV networks. There was a rumor that they had recouped their initial investment in two years. On the other hand, our cupboard was bare, except for the trickle of income from the theaters.

It was so obvious that we should take on the *Spider Man* series as an integral part of our expansion program that I couldn't believe it when the new management turned it down. It was because of the small profit we had made on *The Mighty Thor.* As one snippy accountant put it, "We can make more profits by just leaving the money in the bank."

When I protested that the small profit was due to the fact that we were learning to work in a highly lucrative but very different field from theatrical cartoons, my excuse was brusquely rejected. None of the accountants even wanted to hear about my plans for expansion.

Ironically, just when Famous was emerging from the doldrums into a bright future, these number-happy accountants were about to destroy the studio, an establishment whose roots went back for fifty years. Since I didn't want to be around for the funeral, I quit.

When I gathered the staff to announce my resignation, many eyes filled with tears, and it wasn't just the women who were so moved. I was pretty choked up myself. We had all been having such a happy, exciting time!

Burt Hanft arranged for Ralph Bakshi, a young director from Terrytoons, to take my place. He only produced four pictures before Famous Studio closed down.

A few months later, Terrytoons stopped operations, too, and that was the end of theatrical production on the East Coast. During the same year, 1967, MGM and Disney stopped making shorts. Two years later, Warners' cartoon studio closed its doors.

The long era of theatrical animated cartoons, which stretched back to the turn of the century, back to Émile Cohl, Stuart Blackton, and Winsor McCay, was coming to an end. Not with a bang, not even a whimper, just a click as the lock snapped shut on the Walt Lantz Studio in 1972. The Disney Studio is the only one that never closed.

Pax vobiscum. The Age of Television Animation had begun.

18

Epilogue

The same Philistines who have generously larded our adult television shows with commercial spots for vaginal douches, pile cures, and earnest little men paddling kayaks in toilet bowls laid a heavy hand on the animation medium.

For children's shows the art form has been mutilated into a basket case called "limited animation"! Even more limited is the intelligence level of the plots for these shows. A combination of violence and heavy-handed humor which only proves that a cretin can be taught to type a script. The artists working in these studios have all the creative opportunities of a worker in a paper-bag factory.

All the time I was the head of Famous Studio, the cigar-chewing salesmen pleaded with me to "copy some fuckin' kind of Bugs Bunny or something." But they did not have the power to *force* me to abandon the style of pictures I was creating.

Now the cigar chewers are not pleading, they are commanding. Whether it is a Saturday morning show, a one-minute animated spot or a half-hour special, every step of the process from script to screen is scrutinized and evaluated by people in the networks or advertising agencies.

It is a chilling thought that there are many artists who have worked in the animation profession twenty years or more who have never drawn *one foot* of film that called for their best efforts, nor had *one idea* that did not have to run a gauntlet manned by people who were not their peers.

The frustration, the emotional and spiritual deprivation inherent in these working conditions is enormous. When there is no more rage, when there is a weary acceptance of the situation (which I find in many of my colleagues), it is a sign that the creative urge has been beaten into submission, leaving only the technical expertise. The artist has become a robot, a controllable part of a vast moneymaking machine.

There is no quick panacea for a blight like the Saturday morning children's television programs. The best leverage for change lies with parent and teacher groups, so it seems to me that the unions in New York and Hollywood should be in constant touch with the leaders of these associations.

In addition to artistic deprivation, the networks have compressed the work year into a few months. After that, for most of the Hollywood workers there is idleness and unemployment insurance. The answer might be a planned series of highly experimental animated films made by members of the union on a nonprofit basis. The emphasis should be on unusual subject matter coupled with techniques like sand animation, clay figure stop-motion, paper silhouettes, et cetera. The goal ought to be a group like the Canadian Film Board, which would operate only during the period of unemployment. The income would be used to buy equipment and rent space for more sophisticated productions.

The unions could entice the producers to set high standards in their films by rewarding those studios producing quality films with wage scales lower than the rest of the industry. This is not an impractical idea. For years there was a large difference in the pay for theatrical animation and work on TV commercials. The TV animation groups were paid more because the work was usually transient. Nobody complained because the basic idea was reasonable. So is this suggestion.

When the actors started their guild they allowed extras to become members. It took them only a few years to realize that the two groups were not compatible. The actors pursued a demanding profession, while being an extra took no skill at all. To remedy the situation, they removed the extras from the guild and went on to become one of the most powerful unions in the country. Most important, their goals are based on a shared experience.

I believe that the creative members of our profession have made a similar mistake. Inking, painting, checking, etcetera, are acquired skills . . . skills that can be learned in a few months. This is in sharp contrast to the need for natural talent as an artist and then years of study before one is qualified for a job in the creative area of production. As in the case of the actors and extras, the two groups are not inherently compatible.

The union structure of the animation business is a crazy quilt. The original Hollywood union, the Screen Cartoonists Guild, has probably a dozen members. The dominant union, Local 839, Motion Picture Screen Cartoonists, allows its members to hold cards in both organizations!

Local 841 in New York saddles the creative members with not only a majority group of noncreative people, in addition the union is affiliated with the optical-printer operators. At first the optical workers had joined the cartoonists because they were a small group and needed to make this move because of the insurance benefits. Ironically enough, the cartoonists' membership has diminished because of the lack of work in New York, and the optical membership has increased because of the current fad for special effects. The control of union affairs has shifted to this latter group, and the business agent is an optical man with no experience in the animation field. For obvious reasons non-union animation in New York is on the increase.

Here is a profession with perhaps a little over a thousand people split into three unions. Due to a combination of xenophobia and apathy, the members of these groups have made little or no effort to amalgamate. Personal ambition or lack of vision has kept the leaders of all three unions from taking any steps to combine forces.

For all these reasons unionism in the animation industry has not been the panacea we anticipated. It is true that we now have vacations, sick leave, a bottom under every wage scale, and a pension fund. But the standards of both stories and animation have declined instead of improving. On the West Coast there has been a steady stream of dropouts. Many of the most creative people have left the business. In the East there are more and more two- and three-man non-union studios, the membership of the local has dwindled, and so has the volume of business. The most telling blow is that we are the only creative group in the motion picture profession that does not receive residuals.

If this is the best we can do after forty-odd years of unionism, then it is time for some radical thinking. One answer might be the organization of co-op studios on a national scale. I have been working with a co-op studio in Milan for more than ten years. From my observation I believe that the co-op structure is healthier than the eternal conflict between employer and employees and the power struggles within the union membership. It would be unnecessary to maintain business agents and there would be no more contracts between unions and management. These contracts have been the source of much bitterness, not only between management and unions but within the membership as well.

None of these problems exist when the workers are also the management. Psychologically, co-ops are better because there is then no need to rebel against authority—the authority rests in the hands of workers. Of necessity the staff would have to learn every aspect of the business.

A long time ago, in the 1940s, when I was on the executive board of the Screen Cartoonists Guild, I suggested that we embark on an educational program for the membership. At every meeting we would invite a speaker from the business world: a banker who dealt in motion picture loans, a salesman, an exhibitor, a lawyer involved in motion picture deals. Later I would have suggested talks by advertising agency people, account executives, media buyers, and advertising managers from industry. The idea was hooted off the agenda.

This resistance had its repercussions. Shortly after the war, the motion picture industry was in a slump. When it was time to discuss a new contract with the producers, I suggested that we ask for residuals rather than an increase in pay. The idea was rejected summarily, without discussion, and the union pressed for an increase in pay. We didn't get a dime. It is this blind resistance to education about the business aspects of animation production that has led to our present miserable condition.

The issue of foreign studios supplying the American market is a case in point. Local 839 is up in arms about the idea of Australian, Taiwanese, and other animation studios "taking the bread from our mouths." The historical facts tell a different story: from the earliest beginnings of motion pictures, the American film industry proved to have better distribution methods than our European counterparts. American cartoons, as a result, flooded all the world markets.

During the unsettled period after World War II, when our distribution centers were recovering from utter annihilation, a few countries managed to start animation studios for the first time. Even now they are barely staggering along. For example, there is a group of animators in Milano, Erredia 70, a studio of artists whose talents would challenge the best studio in American animation; yet they will never produce a TV special. Italian television buys Japanese and American animation, dubs an Italian track, and puts it on the air for cheap. Erredia 70 has to be content with making TV commercials. I am sure that the majority of the complainers in the Hollywood unions have never heard of Erredia 70, or many of the other European animation studios that struggle for a meager existence under similar conditions.

When an American film goes out into the world market, it can be estimated that the income from the rest of the world will equal the sum that the picture will generate in the American market. In other words, we, in the U.S.A., take away from our brother animators an amount of money that represents half of our salaries, and leaves them in a distressed condition. Yet since the American unionists are totally ignorant of the problem they pose to foreign studios, there is no guilt, there is only misplaced indignation.

It is time that the animators in America take their place in the international business world, without guilt about beings dogs in the manger. After all, they did it in all economic innocence. But it would be well to have them face the real issues: wage differentials, standards of quality, et al, and then cope with the fact that bread taken from one mouth to put into another is just a manifestation of the workings of the free market, and compete accordingly.

It is a grand old American custom to ask anyone who sports a white beard to make a prognostication based on his vast perspective of the past. I find this role rather fruitless. Who, before his time, could have predicted such inventions as the Hula-Hoop, bubble gum, or plastic flowers. Even when one is dead right, it doesn't pay off in social approval.

For example, in the late 1920s the small group of workers in the animation business in New York gathered in Pirrole's restaurant to attend a testimonial dinner for Winsor McCay, the father of the animated cartoon.

Bootleg whiskey seems to have been the main item on the menu. When Winsor McCay got up to make a speech after dinner it was evident that he was more than a little drunk. Fixing a blurry but baleful eye on the attentive group, he proceeded to castigate us for turning animation, a fascinating and important art form, into shit. That's all we were doing . . . SHIT!

Then he waxed lyrical. Some day, and the time was not far off, animators would be producing feature pictures in color. With that,

McCay sat down heavily. There was a little applause and a lot of derisive laughter. Jesus! Poor old Winsor! Was he pickled!

Without benefit of alcohol I am going to stick my neck out. I predict that, at some future date, animation will attract some of the greatest artists in the world. Their work will appear in museums and art galleries much as paintings are exhibited in our time, except that they will have the added advantages of movement, music, voices, and sound effects.

This incredible revolution in the art world will come about because computerized animation is already making the unwieldy techniques of cel animation as obsolete as the buggy whip. It is difficult to realize that all animators who are presently using cels are primitives. It is difficult to think of an innovator like Walt Disney as a primitive, yet the computer approach to picture making is so superior as to make the most complex cel animation look crude by comparison.

A whole new vista of unlimited varieties of shapes and textures is opening up, plus the ability to animate them with ease. I predict that computerization will provide an enormous stimulus to theatrical and television animation as well.

Winsor McCay produced his animation with one assistant. With modern cel animation techniques the ratio is usually four or five noncreative people to service one animator. A painter averages about twenty-five cels a day, a computer operator can color five hundred images in the same time! Since the color is applied electronically there is no need for pots of paint, brushes, or cels.

The phalanx of paint dispensers, cel polishers, checkers, planners, inkers, and painters, plus their department heads (who all now cost more than half of a production budget) will be phased out except for a very small group who will service the creative staff.

Several years ago I became acquainted with Dr. Alexander Schure, head of the New York Institute of Technology, and his son Louis, who is in charge of the Institute's computer animation center.

Dr. Schure has been an animation buff since he was a child, and his knowledge of the historical aspects of the profession is formidable. Several years ago he won $10,000 on a TV quiz show when he chose animation as his subject.

When he decided to invent computers which would assist in the production of animation, Dr. Schure produced a feature picture, *Tubby*

Dr. Alexander Schure, the pioneer inventor of computerized animation, whose technology has made the first radical change in animation production methods since Earl Hurd invented the cel system more than sixty years ago.

A scene from *Clyde in the Cockpit* by Dick Ludin, a project of New York Institute of Technology's Computer Graphics Lab.

the Tuba, which was made with the conventional cel methodology. This was so he could study the problems of production at firsthand. The results are incredible.

When Louis Schure took me on a tour of his Computer Graphics Lab, he first showed me some scenes from a science-fiction picture, which Lance Williams was designing. Instead of conventional animation drawn on paper, Williams was creating characters mathematically in a computer. He was also moving the creatures mathematically. They were programmed to take into consideration the changes made by a light source, which was also determined by mathematics. Light and shadow, highlights and reflections of great complexity were playing across the surfaces of fantastic creatures. Lance Williams, working with the computer for a few weeks, had done animation which could not have been duplicated by the cel process—not by the best animators at Disney's, nor by Cy Young and his special effects team.

Then I turned to look at another computer screen. Here conventional drawings made by pencil on paper have been transferred to tape and are in the process of being colored. At the base of the screen is a palette of rectangular boxes of colors. An arrowhead appears on the screen and under the guidance of the operator dips into a rectangle and moves up to an area on the drawing. The color appears instantly. The operator repeats this process and in less than a minute the whole character is seen as a finished product. There are no brushes to wipe on paint-stained rags, no dripping paint jars to clean up, no worry about scratches or fingerprints on cels, no tedious camera operations.

Louis led me to another part of the building. Here I watched Paul Xander create a background. Xander, who started out as a classical painter, went on to become one of the top background artists in the Hollywood animation studios. He has now been working with Louis Schure for several years.

First he presses a button and on his computer screen appears a list of brushes from one-inch down to hairline. In addition, there are both charcoal and airbrush possibilities. After selecting a brush size, Xander dips into his row of colors at the bottom of the screen and, using his electronic wand, starts to "paint" a background. After finishing a desert scene in a very short time Xander shows me how he could change from a day to a night shot by merely pressing a button.

The highpoint of my tour was when I was asked to make two pencil drawings of my favorite character, Pluto. I drew him with his head down and his tail drooping. The other pose was Pluto alert, with his head and tail up. The drawings were transferred to tape. When I hit a button the computer swiftly made seven inbetweens. It could have just as easily been seventy. What a historic moment for me when the action was run! I was a link with the primitive past, before sound, color, or tape. I had been permitted to live long enough to see and use the greatest tools for artists that were ever invented. I am convinced that computer animation will produce beautiful works of art—beautiful beyond our most fantastic dreams.

Appendix

While I was writing this book I was very much aware that a writer has a tremendous advantage over the people he is writing about, because for the most part they have no opportunity for rebuttal. Since I have painted Pepe Ruiz in such black colors I decided in 1982 to interview him about his career as a business agent, and give him a chance to defend himself.

The first question I asked him was why he was so antagonistic to the producers. It must be that Ruiz's sunset years have colored his memory with a rosy hue. He stated that all the producers had been his friends. Of course at the negotiating table it was necessary for him to do his job, but other than that he sympathized with us and our problems.

Asked about Joe Rosen's evaluation that the wages were too high and ate up all the profits, Ruiz stated flatly that it was our responsibility to wring more money out of the advertising agencies. While he agreed that we never had the muscle to do it, Pepe insisted that it was his job to get the membership as much money as possible. How we obtained it was our problem.

He added that we went broke because of the nature of the business. When I countered with the fact that the Hollywood studios survived the Eisenhower Depression and we didn't, Pepe repeated that this was the nature of the business. He gave no further explanation.

Why had he not tried to make a national union? Pepe's answer was that Hollywood's wages were lower and the workweek longer, so there was no possibility of amalgamation. He also asserted that the Hollywood labor scene was dominated by communists.

When I reminded him that I had tried many times to start a union art school, Ruiz said that teachers in the West Coast's union's art school were earning a hundred dollars a night. (During all the years that Ruiz was a business agent in New York, every aspect of animation production was taught by the best talent in the Hollywood Local 841 and there was no pay whatsoever.) I had offered to teach for nothing. Pepe said he didn't remember.

At that point the meeting broke off because Ruiz had another appointment.

Filmography

The following list of abbreviations refers to which positions I held during the making of the films.

Animator	An.	Producer	Pr.
Editor	Ed.	Co–Director	CDr.
Layout	Lo.	Co–Writer	CWr.
Writer	Wr.	Co–Layout	CLo.
Director	Dr.		

FLEISCHER STUDIO

1930 *Swing, You Sinners* · · · · · · · · · · · An.
  In the Good Old Summertime · · · · · · · · An.
  The Maine Stein Song · · · · · · CWr., CDr, An.
1931 *Please Go 'Way and Let Me Sleep* · · · · CDr., An.
  Somebody Stole My Gal · · · · · · · CDr., An.
  Alexander's Ragtime Band · · · · · · · CDr., An.
  The Herring Murder Case · · · · · CWr., Cdr., An.
  Minding the Baby · · · · · · · · · CDr., An.
  By the Light of the Silvery Moon · · · · · · Dr., An.
1932 *Show Me the Way to Go Home* · · · · · · Dr., An.
  Crazy Town · · · · · · · · · · · · Dr., An.
  Bamboo Isle · · · · · · · · · · · CDr., An.
  Admission Free · · · · · · · · · · · Dr., An.

IWERKS STUDIO

1932 *The Phoney Express* · · · · · · · · · · · An.
  The Music Lesson · · · · · · · · · · · An.
  The Nurse Maid · · · · · · · · · · · · An.
1933 *Coo-Coo the Magician* · · · · · · · · · · An.
  Funny Face · · · · · · · · · · · · · An.
  Flip's Lunch Room · · · · · · · · · · · An.
  Technocracked · · · · · · · · · · · · An.
  Bulloney · · · · · · · · · · · · · · An.
  A Chinaman's Chance · · · · · · · · · · An.

	Paleface · · · · · · · · · · ·	An.
	Jack and the Bean-Stalk · · · · · · ·	CDr., CLo.
1934	*The Little Red Hen* · · · · · · · ·	CDr., CLo.
	The Brave Tin Soldier · · · · · · ·	CDr., CLo.
	Puss-in-Boots · · · · · · · · · ·	CDr., CLo.
	The Queen of Hearts · · · · · · · ·	CDr., CLo.
	Aladdin and His Wonderful Lamp · · · · ·	CDr., CLo.
	The Valiant Tailor · · · · · · · · ·	CDr., CLo.

VAN BEUREN STUDIO

1935	*The Foxy Terrier* · · · · · · · · · ·	Dr.
	The Merry Kittens · · · · · · · · · ·	Dr.

DISNEY STUDIO

1936	*Orphan's Picnic* · · · · · · · · · ·	An.
	Mother Pluto · · · · · · · · · · ·	An.
1937	*Hawaiian Holiday* · · · · · · · · ·	An.
	Pluto's Quintuplets · · · · · · · · ·	An.
1938	*Snow White and the Seven Dwarfs* · · · · ·	An.
1939	*Society Dog-Show* · · · · · · · · · ·	An.
	Beach Picnic · · · · · · · · · · ·	An.
	The Pointer · · · · · · · · · · ·	An.
	Pinocchio · · · · · · · · · · · ·	An.

FLEISCHER STUDIO

1939	*Gulliver's Travels* · · · · · · · · ·	An.
1940	*Popeye Meets William Tell* · · · · · · ·	Dr.
	A Kick in Time · · · · · · · · · ·	Dr.
	Mr. Bug Goes to Town · · · · · · · ·	Dr.

WARNER BROTHERS

1943	*Inki and the Minah Bird* · · · · · · · ·	An.

WALTER LANTZ STUDIO

1943	*Pass the Biscuits Mirandy* · · · · · · ·	Dr.

	Boogie Woogie Man · · · · · · · · · · ·	Dr.
	Meatless Tuesday · · · · · · · · · · ·	Dr.
1944	*The Greatest Man in Siam* · · · · · · · · ·	Dr.
	The Barber of Seville · · · · · · · · · ·	Dr.
	Jungle Jive · · · · · · · · · · ·	Dr.
	Fish Fry · · · · · · · · · ·	Dr.
	Abou Ben Boogie · · · · · · · · · ·	Dr.
	The Beach Nut · · · · · · · · · · ·	Dr.
	Ski for Two · · · · · · · · · · ·	Dr.
	The Painter and the Pointer · · · · · · · ·	Dr.
1945	*Pied Piper of Basin Street* · · · · · · ·	Dr.
	Chew-Chew Baby · · · · · · · · · · ·	Dr.
	Woody Dines Out · · · · · · · · · · ·	Dr.
	Dippy Diplomat · · · · · · · · · · ·	Dr.
	Loose Nut · · · · · · · · · · ·	Dr.
1946	*Mousie Come Home* · · · · · · · · · ·	Dr.
	The Reckless Driver · · · · · · · · ·	Dr.
	Fairweather Friends · · · · · · · · · · ·	Dr.

SHAMUS CULHANE PRODUCTIONS

1956	*Hemo the Magnificent* (Bell Science) · · · · · ·	Pr.
1957	*The Strange Case of the Cosmic Rays* (Bell Science) ·	Pr.
	Around the World in Eighty Days (titles) · · · · ·	Pr.
1958	*The Unchained Goddess* (Bell Science) · · · · · ·	Pr.
	Showdown at Ulcer Gulch · · · · · · · ·	Pr., Dr.

Between 1947 and 1958 produced over 3,500 TV spots.

HAL SEEGER PRODUCTIONS

1962	*Koko the Clown* TV series · · · · · · · ·	Lo., An.
1964	*Milton the Monster* TV series · · · · · · ·	Lo., An.

STORYBOARD PRODUCTIONS

1965	*The Hat* · · · · · · · · · · · · · ·	An.

FAMOUS STUDIO

1966	*A Balmy Knight* · · · · · · · · · · · ·	Pr., Dr.
	Potions and Notions · · · · · · · · · ·	Pr., Dr.

1967	*The Space Squid*	Pr., Dr.
	Think or Sink	Pr., Dr.
	My Daddy the Astronaut	CWr., Pr., Dr.
	The Trip	Pr., Dr.
	Alter Egotist	Pr., Dr.
	Squaw Path	Pr., Dr.
	The Plumber	Pr., Dr.
	Halt, Who Goes There?	Pr., Dr.
	Robin Hoodwinked	Pr., Dr.
	From Orbit to Obit	Pr., Dr.
	High But Not Dry	Pr., Dr.
	Brother Rat	Pr., Dr.
	Forget Me Nuts	Pr., Dr.
	The Stuck-Up Wolf	Pr., Dr.
	The Stubborn Cowboy	Pr., Dr.
	The Opera Caper	CWr., Pr., Dr.
	Clean Sweep	Pr.
	A Bridge Grows in Brooklyn	Pr.
	The Mighty Thor TV series	Pr.

STEVE KRANTZ PRODUCTIONS

1967	*Rocket Robin Hood* TV series	Pr.

GAMMA FILMS

1970	*The Night the Animals Talked*	Dr.

M.G. FILMS

1972	*Professor Kitzel* TV series	Wr., Lo., Dr., Pr.
1975	*Spirit of '76* TV series	Pr., Ed., Wr.
1976	*Spirit of Independence* TV series	Pr., Wr., Ed.

WESTFALL PROD.

1975	*Noah's Animals* TV special	Pr., Wr., Dr.
1976	*The King of Beasts* TV special	Wr., Dr., Pr.
1977	*Last of the Red-Hot Dragons* TV special	CWr., Dr., An., Lo., Pr.

Bibliography

Adamson, Joe. *Tex Avery: King of Cartoons.* New York: Popular Library, 1975.

Bain and Harris. *Mickey Mouse, Fifty Happy Years.* New York: Harmony Books, 1977.

Barrier, Mike. *Funny World Quarterly.*

Bendazzi, Ginalberto. *Topolino e poi.* Milano: Edizioni il Formichiere.

Blitz, Marcia. *Donald Duck.* New York: Harmony Books, 1979.

Charlot, Jean. *Art from the Mayans to Disney.* Books for Libraries Press.

Culhane, John. *"The Black Hole" Casts the Computer as Movie-maker. The New York Times,* Dec. 16, 1979.

————. *The Old Disney Magic. The New York Times,* Aug. 1, 1976.

————. *Walt Disney's Fantasia.* New York: Harry N. Abrams, 1983.

Edwards, Betty. *Drawing on the Right Side of the Brain.* Los Angeles: J. P. Tarcher, 1979.

Field, Robert D. *The Art of Walt Disney.* New York: The Macmillan Co., 1942.

Finch, Christopher. *The Art of Walt Disney.* New York: Harry N. Abrams, 1973.

Horn, Maurice. *World Encyclopedia of Cartoons.* New York: Chelsea House, 1981.

Hurd, Jud. *Cartoonist Profiles.* New York: Winchester Press.

Lenburg, Jeff. *The Great Cartoon Directors.* Jefferson & London: McFarland.

Maltin, Leonard. *Of Mice and Magic.* New York: McGraw-Hill Book Co., 1980.

May, Rollo. *The Courage to Create.* New York: W. W. Norton, 1975.

Peary, Gerald and Danny. *The American Animated Cartoon.* New York: E. P. Dutton, 1980.

Pudovkin, V. I. *Film Technique and Film Acting.* New York: Grove Press, 1970.

Schickel, Richard. *The Disney Version.* New York: Simon and Schuster, 1968.

Thomas and Johnston. *The Illusion of Life.* New York: Abbeville Press, 1981.

Tobias, Andrew. *Fire and Ice.* New York: Warner Books.

Index

"It took someone of Shamus Culhane's knowledgeable background and experience to write such a wonderful documentary on the animated cartoon profession. Shamus tells in detail how a range of studios got started, how they struggled to succeed, and why some of them failed. It should interest historians of animation, people who love animation, and especially, students who want to make animation a career. (Shamus Culhane) has been a credit to the art of animation."

—Walter Lantz
creator of Woody Woodpecker

"Shamus Culhane has written a brilliant, literate, and very funny remembrance of the Disney 'Golden Years.' Every aficionado of every art will enjoy to the fullest this delightful effort by that charming Irishman Shamus Culhane."

—Art Babbitt
Disney animator

This fascinating insider's history of the animated movie business follows Shamus Culhane's career from errand boy to director of animation and offers a unique education in animation techniques and the creative process.

Shamus joined the business in 1924 at the age of fifteen and spent over fifty years amidst the brightest and the best the animation studios had to offer. During that time, he worked on some of Hollywood's greatest creations: Koko the Clown, Mickey Mouse, Donald Duck, Betty Boop, Popeye, Woody Woodpecker, and the Seven Dwarfs...to name just a few. He has animated Pluto, his favorite character, since 1936, and is considered to be an expert at creating the big-hearted, dim-witted hound's antics. The genius behind the marching "Heigh-Ho" sequence of the Seven Dwarfs is also his—a piece of flawless synchronization and delightful caricature.

In this charming autobiography, Culhane also shares observations about the work and personal idiosyncrasies of illustrious directors and producers, among them Frank Capra, Walt Disney, Max and David Fleischer, and Walter Lantz. He provides clever anecdotes about the work habits of such famous animators as Grim Nalwick, creator of Betty Boop; Norman Ferguson, who developed Pluto; Art Babbitt, the animator of the dancing mushrooms in *Fantasia*; and many more. Best of all, *Talking Animals and Other People* does what no other book of its kind has ever done; it plunges the reader into the vital, chaotic, day-to-day workings of animation studios.

For six decades, the pen of Shamus Culhane has brought scores of fantastic and lovable creatures to life. In this unforgettable memoir, he demonstrates that with words, too, he is a consummate artist, breathing life into the fantastic, lovable (and sometimes not so lovable) geniuses who have created one of the world's most popular art forms.